CULTURES OF LONDON

CULTURES OF LONDON

LEGACIES OF MIGRATION

Edited by Charlotte Grant and Alistair Robinson

BLOOMSBURY ACADEMIC
LONDON • NEW YORK • OXFORD • NEW DELHI • SYDNEY

BLOOMSBURY ACADEMIC
Bloomsbury Publishing Plc
50 Bedford Square, London, WC1B 3DP, UK
1385 Broadway, New York, NY 10018, USA
29 Earlsfort Terrace, Dublin 2, Ireland

BLOOMSBURY, BLOOMSBURY ACADEMIC and the Diana logo are trademarks of Bloomsbury Publishing Plc

First published in Great Britain 2024

Cover design by Gita Govinda Kowlessur
Cover image: *remembering a brave new world*, Tate Britain Winter Commission by Chila Kumari Singh Burman, 14 November 2020–31 January 2021/ Malcolm Park / Alamy Stock Photo © Chila Kumari Singh Burman. All rights reserved, DACS 2023

A catalogue record for this book is available from the British Library.

Library of Congress Cataloging-in-Publication Data

Names: Grant, Charlotte, editor. | Robinson, Alistair (English teacher), editor.
Title: Cultures of London : legacies of migration / edited by Charlotte Grant and Alistair Robinson.
Other titles: Legacies of migration
Description: London ; New York : Bloomsbury Academic, 2024. | Collection of essays by Charlotte Grant and 34 others. | Includes bibliographical references and index.
Identifiers: LCCN 2023030531 (print) | LCCN 2023030532 (ebook) | ISBN 9781350242029 (hb) | ISBN 9781350242012 (pb) | ISBN 9781350242036 (epdf) | ISBN 9781350242043 (ebook)
Subjects: LCSH: Immigrants—England—London—History. | London (England)—Civilization. | Great Britain—Civilization—Foreign influences. | London (England)—Social life and customs.
Classification: LCC DA676.9.A1 C85 2024 (print) | LCC DA676.9.A1 (ebook) | DDC 305.9/0691209421—dc23/eng/20230719
LC record available at https://lccn.loc.gov/2023030531
LC ebook record available at https://lccn.loc.gov/2023030532

ISBN: HB: 978-1-3502-4202-9
       PB: 978-1-3502-4201-2
       ePDF: 978-1-3502-4203-6
       eBook: 978-1-3502-4204-3

Typeset by RefineCatch Limited, Bungay, Suffolk
Printed and bound in Great Britain

To find out more about our authors and books visit www.bloomsbury.com and sign up for our newsletters.

For Londoners everywhere.

CONTENTS

List of Figures   x
Notes on Contributors   xii
Acknowledgments   xvi

Introduction *Charlotte Grant and Alistair Robinson*   1

Central

1   *St Erkenwald* **and the Hidden Histories of St Paul's
    Cathedral** *Alastair Bennett*   19

2   **Ignatius Sancho: Musician, Man of Letters, Grocer** *Markman Ellis*   27

3   **The 'Black-birds' of St. Giles: Rethinking Place and Community
    in Eighteenth-Century London** *Nicole N. Aljoe and Savita Maharaj*   35

4   **Styling the Other: Hazlitt's 'The Indian Jugglers'** *Uttara Natarajan* 41

5   **Begging Places: Poverty, Race and Visibility on Ludgate
    Hill, *c.* 1815** *David Hitchcock*   49

6   **13 Red-Lion Square: The Mendicity Society, 1818–76** *Oskar Cox Jensen* 57

7   **The Chinese Aesthetics of the *Admonitions* Scroll at the British
    Museum** *Kent Su*   63

8   **'A Terrain on its Own': Elizabeth Bowen and Regent's
    Park** *Heather Ingman*   69

Infrastructure: Water

9   **London's Water: City Comedy, Migration and
    Middletons** *Susan J. Wiseman*   79

East

10 **Shakespeare in Shoreditch** *Daniel Swift*   89

11 **19 Princelet Street, Spitalfields: A Case Study in the Architecture
    of Migration and Diversity** *Dan Cruickshank*   95

12 **Hostile Environments: Disinterring a Lascar Barracks in
    Nineteenth-Century Shadwell** *Eliza Cubitt*   103

Contents

13 The Slot-Meter and the East End Avant-Garde *Alex Grafen*   107

Infrastructure: Waste

14 Blockage and Recuperation: Sewer-Hunters in Henry Mayhew's
    London Labour and the London Poor Naomi Hinds   117

South

15 Culture and Horticulture in Lambeth from 'Tradescant's Ark' to
    Vauxhall Gardens *Charlotte Grant*   127

16 The Crystal Palace in Hyde Park, Sydenham and
    St Petersburg *Catherine Brown*   137

17 87 Hackford Road: The London of Vincent van Gogh *Livia Wang*   145

18 Writing London: Hanif Kureishi's *The Buddha of
    Suburbia* Ruvani Ranasinha   155

Infrastructure: Transport I

19 Existing Triply: Race, Space and the London Transport Network,
    1950s–1970s *Rob Waters*   163

West

20 Scotch Hornpipes and African Elephants: The May Fair
    in *c.* 1700 *Alistair Robinson*   173

21 Feathered People in Enlightenment London: Queen of the
    Bluestockings meets Cherokee King *Elizabeth Eger*   181

22 Prince Eugen in Kensington: Anglo-Scandinavian Artistic Networks
    and the Stockholm Exhibition of 1897 *Eva-Charlotta Mebius*   191

23 'What a Relief to be Back in London': The Silences of Lucie Rie
    and Hans Coper *Edmund de Waal*   199

24 Tricksters of the Water: Sam Selvon's West London and the Migrant
    Experience *Peter Maber and Karishma Patel*   205

25 Arabian Nights on the Edgware Road: Hanan
    al-Shaykh's *Only in London* Susie Thomas   217

26 The Grand Prince of Kyiv in Holland Park: The Statue of
    Saint Volodymyr *Sasha Dovzhyk*   223

27 'Is Real Mas Outside': Community, Resistance and Notting Hill
    Carnival *Leighan Renaud*   227

28 'Where the City Dissolves': Suburban Diasporas, Psychosis
and Reparative Writing *Martin Dines*   235

Infrastructure: Transport II

29 A Bus for Everyone: The Role of the London Omnibus in
Enabling Access to the City *Joe Kerr*   245

North

30 Moorgate, Enfield, Edmonton and Hampstead: The Cross-City
Migrations of John Keats *Flora Lisica*   255

31 The Battle for an African Space in London: WASU Hostel and
Aggrey House *William Whitworth*   263

32 Northview: A Snapshot of Multiracial London during the
Second World War *Oliver Ayers*   269

33 Exiles of NW3: The 'Free German League of Culture' in
Upper Park Road *David Anderson*   279

Bibliography   287
Index   293

FIGURES

0.1	Relief sculpture of Mithras (n.d.)	5
0.2	Yoshio Markino, *Earl's Court Station* (1910)	9
0.3	Frank Meisler, *Kindertransport – The Arrival* (2006)	10
0.4	Martin Bloch, 'Bomb Damage, City of London' (1943)	11
0.5	Aleix Barbat, *Bronze Woman* (2008)	13
1.1	Wenceslaus Hollar, *Monument to Saint Erkenwald in Old St Paul's Cathedral* (1656)	21
2.1	Portrait of Ignatius Sancho, frontispiece to *Letters of the Late Ignatius Sancho* (1802)	28
2.2	Ignatius Sancho's Trade Card, 'Sancho's Best Trinidado' (*c.* 1773)	32
4.1	James Green, *The Indian Jugglers* (*c.* 1814)	42
5.1	*Bridge Street, Blackfriars* (1812)	50
5.2	John Thomas Smith, *Charles McGee* (1815)	52
7.1	Gu Kaizhi, *Admonitions of the Instructress to the Court Ladies*	63
12.1	Section of the Vestry map of St-George's-in-the-East (1878) showing New Court off Victoria Street	104
13.1	'Theater Portrait of Sonia Cohen' (n.d.)	109
14.1	'The Sewer Hunter' (1861), printed in Henry Mayhew's *London Labour and the London Poor*	118
15.1	J. Caulfield, *Tradescant House, South Lambeth, London* (1798)	129
15.2	'Royal Vauxhall Gardens' (1848)	133
16.1	*The Crystal Palace at Sydenham* (1855)	139
17.1	87 Hackford Road (2019)	146
17.2	Letter from Vincent van Gogh to Theo van Gogh, Paris, 24 July 1875	152
19.1	Charlie Phillips, 'Man on Westbourne Park Tube Station' (1967)	163
20.1	Charles II Guinea Coin (1663)	174
21.1	Broadside with four woodcuts showing portraits of 'The Four Indian Kings' and the text of their speech to Queen Anne (1710)	183
21.2	*The Three Cherokees, Came Over from the Head of the River Savanna to London* (1762)	187
22.1	Prince Eugen in his studio at Waldemarsudde (1915)	192
23.1	Lucie Rie and Hans Coper, 'Sgraffito Bowl, Manganese Glaze' (*c.* 1950)	201
23.2	David Westwood, 'Lucie Rie in Her Workshop Sitting on a Bench' (n.d.)	202
24.1	BBC Caribbean Service: Caribbean Voices (1952)	206

26.1	Leo Mol, *Statue of Saint Volodymyr* (1988)	223
27.1	Sherween Gonzales, 'The Lajabless and the King Jab' (2021)	228
29.1	Sidney Starr, *The City Atlas* (c. 1888–9)	247
29.2	'Joseph Clough in front of a London General Omnibus Company Bus' (1908)	249
30.1	George Cruikshank, *London going out of Town – or – The March of Bricks and Mortar!* (1829)	257
32.1	'Adelaide Hall and Fela Sowande at the Florida Club' (1940)	272
33.1	Front cover of the pamphlet for the *Allies Inside Germany* exhibition (1942)	282

CONTRIBUTORS

Nicole N. Aljoe is Professor of English and Africana Studies at Northeastern University in Boston. She is the author of *Creole Testimonies: Slave Narratives of The British West Indies, 1709–1838* (2012) and is the co-director of the Early Caribbean Digital Archive.

David Anderson is Leverhulme Early Career Fellow in the Department of Comparative Literature and Culture, Queen Mary University of London. His current research focuses on nostalgia and narrative in contemporary Britain and Germany. His monograph *Landscape and Subjectivity in the Work of Patrick Keiller, W. G. Sebald, and Iain Sinclair* was published in 2020.

Oliver Ayers is Associate Professor in History at Northeastern University London. His research centres on themes of race, urban space and digital historical analysis. His first monograph, *Laboured Protest*, examined Black civil rights activism in the United States during the 1930s and 1940s, and he has also developed the digital projects 'Mapping Black London in World War II' and 'Ignatius Sancho's London'.

Alastair Bennett is a lecturer in Medieval Literature at Royal Holloway, University of London. He is currently working on a monograph about preaching and narrative in William Langland's *Piers Plowman*.

Catherine Brown is Associate Professor of English and Head of the English Faculty at Northeastern University London. Her research is mainly in the fields of D. H. Lawrence studies, Anglo-Russian relations and, more recently, vegan literary studies. She is Vice-President of the Lawrence Society and in 2020 co-edited with Susan Reid *The Edinburgh Companion to D. H. Lawrence and the Arts*.

Oskar Cox Jensen is Senior Research Associate in Politics at the University of East Anglia. He is the author of *Napoleon and British Song, 1797–1822* (2015), *The Ballad-Singer in Georgian and Victorian London* (2021) and *Vagabonds: Life on the Streets of Nineteenth-Century London* (2022); co-editor of *Charles Dibdin and Late Georgian Culture* (2018) and a special forum of the *Journal of British Studies*, 'Music and Politics in Britain' (2021). He is also a novelist and songwriter.

Dan Cruickshank is an architectural historian and television presenter who has written extensively on the history of London. He lives in Spitalfields and his recent books include *Spitalfields: Two Thousand Years of English History in one Neighbourhood* (2016) and *Cruickshank's London: A Portrait of a City in 13 Walks* (2021).

Eliza Cubitt is a researcher and lecturer. She received her doctorate from University College London, and has taught at UCL and at the University of Tübingen, Germany. She is the author of the critical biography *Arthur Morrison and the East End* (2018) and is currently working on a new project on urban wastewaters and marshlands.

Edmund de Waal is an artist who has exhibited in museums around the world. His bestselling memoir, *The Hare with Amber Eyes* (2010), has won many prizes and been translated into twenty-nine languages. *Letters to Camondo*, a haunting sequence of imagined letters to the Count de Camondo, was published in 2021. His work investigates themes of diaspora, memorial and materiality, and engages with ceramics, architecture, music, dance and poetry. De Waal lives in London with his family.

Martin Dines is Associate Professor of English Literature at Kingston University London. His most recent book is *The Literature of Suburban Change: Narrating Spatial Complexity in Metropolitan America* (2020). Other recent publications focus on urban and domestic space in queer post-war British fiction. Dines is the Past President of the Literary London Society.

Sasha Dovzhyk is a special projects curator at the Ukrainian Institute London and has a PhD in English and Comparative Literature from Birkbeck, University of London. She divides her time between London and Ukraine.

Elizabeth Eger is a poet and biographer who lives in Vauxhall. She is Reader Emerita in English at King's College London. Her publications include 'Collecting People: Bluestocking Sociability and the Assembling of Knowledge' in the *Journal of the History of Collections* and, with Lucy Peltz, *Brilliant Women: 18th-Century Bluestockings* (2009).

Markman Ellis is Professor of Eighteenth-Century Studies at Queen Mary University of London. He is the author of *The Politics of Sensibility: Race, Gender and Commerce in the Sentimental Novel* (1996), *The History of Gothic Fiction* (2000) and *The Coffee-House: A Cultural History* (2004); and the co-author of *Empire of Tea* (2015). With Nicole Aljoe and Oliver Ayers he is currently editing Ignatius Sancho's *Letters* for OUP World's Classics.

Alex Grafen is an independent researcher based in London. He has contributed entries to *London's East End: A Short Encyclopedia* and a chapter to *The Edinburgh Companion to Modernism, Myth and Religion*.

Charlotte Grant teaches at Northeastern University London. She has co-edited books on eighteenth-century women's writing and on the representation of domestic interiors, and edited a collection of botanical texts. Grant is currently working on a book about her refugee grandfather, the painter Martin Bloch.

Naomi Hinds is an English PhD candidate at University College London. Her thesis 'Cycles of Waste in Victorian London' explores how the increased concern about bodily waste and its circulatory routes through the city infected the language of nineteenth-century literature.

David Hitchcock is Senior Lecturer in Early Modern History at Canterbury Christ Church University. He is the author of *Vagrancy in English Culture and Society, 1650–*

1750 (2016) and together with Julia McClure he co-edited *The Routledge History of Poverty, 1450–1800* (2020). Hitchcock is Principal Investigator on a project called 'Mapping Values', about people's perceptions of urban space, working with an interdisciplinary team and funding from the British Academy.

Heather Ingman is Visiting Research Fellow in the Centre for Gender and Women's Studies, Trinity College Dublin. Recent publications include *Elizabeth Bowen* (2021), *Strangers to Themselves: Ageing in Irish Writing* (2018), *Irish Women's Fiction from Edgeworth to Enright* (2013), *A History of the Irish Short Story* (2009) and *Twentieth-Century Fiction by Irish Women: Nation and Gender* (2007).

Joe Kerr is a writer, historian and activist. He is also a London bus driver at Tottenham Garage. He has written widely on the history of architecture and on London. Kerr's books include *Autopia: Cars and Culture* (2002), *London from Punk to Blair* (2003) and *Bus Fare: Collected Writings on the London Bus* (2018).

Flora Lisica is Assistant Professor in English at Northeastern University London. She completed her PhD on Romantic literature at the University of Cambridge. Slovenian and Croatian by birth, Lisica lives in South London.

Peter Maber is Associate Professor in English at Northeastern University London. He teaches and researches world literatures in English, focusing in particular on visual cultures, music and the representation of race.

Savita Maharaj recently graduated from Northeastern University in Boston with a BA in English and is now an English doctoral student at Brandeis University.

Eva-Charlotta Mebius is an independent curator and researcher within the Bernadotte Programme at Uppsala University, Sweden. Her interests are interdisciplinary but centre on literature in its broadest definition and art history.

Uttara Natarajan is Reader in English at the Department of English and Creative Writing, Goldsmiths University of London. She has published widely on William Hazlitt, and most recently on the legacy of the Romantic essayists in mid- and late-Victorian literature. Natarajan is Editor-in-Chief of the *Hazlitt Review*.

Karishma Patel is a BBC newsreader and broadcast journalist, currently at BBC Radio 5 Live. She has an MPhil in English Studies from the University of Cambridge, where she focused on critical theory, and a BA from New College of the Humanities. Patel has published BBC investigations across the United Kingdom and India.

Ruvani Ranasinha is Professor of Global Literature at King's College London. She is the author of *Hanif Kureishi: Writers and their Works Series* (2002) and *South Asian Writers in Twentieth-Century Britain: Culture in Translation* (2007), and is the lead editor of *South Asians Shaping the Nation, 1870–1950: A Sourcebook* (2012). Ranasinha's most recent monograph is *Contemporary Diasporic South Asian Women's Fiction: Gender, Narration and Globalisation* (2016).

Leighan Renaud is a UK-based researcher and lecturer. She has published articles in the *Journal of West Indian Literature* and *History Workshop Online*, and has a forthcoming monograph exploring representations of matrifocality in Caribbean literature. Renaud currently works as a lecturer in English at the University of Bristol.

Alistair Robinson is an assistant professor at Northeastern University London. He is the author of *Vagrancy in the Victorian Age: Representing the Wandering Poor in Nineteenth-Century Literature and Culture* (2022). Robinson is the Secretary of the Literary London Society.

Kent Su is a lecturer at Shanghai International Studies University. He did his BA in English Literature and History at the University of British Columbia. He received his MA and PhD degrees from University College London. Su is currently completing a monograph on the philosophical evocation of Chinese landscapes in Ezra Pound's poetry. He is the co-organizer of the London Cantos Reading Group and guest editor of *The Cantos Project*.

Daniel Swift teaches at Northeastern University London and is currently at work on a book about *A Midsummer Night's Dream* and the business of art.

Susie Thomas has written about London literature from Aphra Behn to Hanif Kureishi. Her most recent book is *So We Live: The Novels of Alexander Baron* (2019), which she edited with Andrew Whitehead and Ken Worpole. Thomas was Reviews Editor of the *Literary London Journal* and teaches at the London centres of the University of California, Berkeley and the University of Oregon.

Livia Wang is Creative Director of Van Gogh House, London, and teaches in the Department of Architecture at the University of Cambridge. With a training in architecture, she has completed projects in China with Kengo Kuma and Associates and in Korea as part of the curatorial team for the Seoul Biennale of Architecture and Urbanism. Wang is now based in London, with an interest in building conservation, public art and exhibitions.

Rob Waters teaches modern British history at Queen Mary University of London. He is the author of *Thinking Black: Britain, 1964–1985* (2018).

William Whitworth is an independent researcher. His primary interests lie in digital history and the spatial history of protest movements. Whitworth has published in *Diplomatica: A Journal of Diplomacy and Society*, *Digital Scholarship in the Humanities* and in the *European Review of International Studies*.

Susan J. Wiseman is Professor of Seventeenth-Century Literature at Birkbeck College, University of London. She is the author of *Writing Metamorphosis in the English Renaissance 1550–1700* (2014) and *Conspiracy and Virtue: Women, Writing, and Politics in Seventeenth Century England* (2006).

ACKNOWLEDGEMENTS

Many people have been involved in the creation of this volume. We are grateful to all our contributors for their enthusiasm and commitment to the project, and we would like to thank the team at Bloomsbury, especially Ben Doyle and Laura Cope, for their invaluable assistance. We had a careful and thorough reader from Bloomsbury and we're grateful for their input. We would also like to thank our colleagues at Northeastern University London who have been so supportive of this project, as well as the very many students on the various iterations of the 'Cultures of London' course since it started in 2017. The images in this book have come from a wide variety of sources, and we're particularly grateful to the Rodker family and the Martin Bloch trust, along with Thomas Coulborn & Sons, UCL Library Special Collections, the Van Gogh Museum, and Van Gogh House London, who all waived their fees. We would also like to thank the following institutions and their staff for access to their collections: the British Library, Senate House Library, Victoria and Albert Museum, the British Museum, Museum of London, Prins Eugens Waldemarsudde, the Crafts Study Centre, and the National Gallery of Canada.

Charlotte Grant and Alistair Robinson

INTRODUCTION
Charlotte Grant and Alistair Robinson

Critics and cultural commentators have become increasingly keen to point out that migration, often characterized as a largely post-war phenomenon, has been the capital's cultural narrative from its origins. As Daniel Snowman put it in 2019:

> All migrations bring 'culture' with them, as much of British history testifies: consider, for example, the legacy of the 400-year Roman occupation, the Angles and Saxons, the Normans, the Huguenots, the Irish following the Great Famine, Jews escaping Russian Pogroms in the later nineteenth century and many other migrations since then.[1]

The thirty-three essays in *Cultures of London: Legacies of Migration* express this plurality of culture and affirm the importance of migration in the making of the modern city. They range from the mediaeval to the contemporary and look at buildings and institutions, individuals and communities, objects, visual art, street performances and literary texts. This introduction explains the conception of the volume, its historical moment and its structure. It provides a brief overview of the migrations that have made London, and situates the essays in relation to each other and their historical contexts.

It is not only London's cultures which are diverse; migration is also plural. People, plants, animals and ideologies have all travelled to London, and their journeys have had different forms and qualities. Some people have travelled to settle and create communities; others to sojourn, staying for work or the relative religious and political freedom offered by the city; and others have come as visitors – as ambassadors, as students, as tourists. Some travelled from continental Europe and other parts of the globe, and many came from elsewhere in the British Isles. Examples of these migrations, contoured by sometimes widely different circumstances, are covered in this book, and introduce us to people whose experiences – real, imagined, celebrated, marginalized, criminalized and uncovered – suggest the huge and hugely intriguing diversity of contemporary London and its many histories.

This collection was conceived pre-pandemic, but came together in the two years most impacted by Covid-19, years when Londoners became more focused on their immediate surroundings, noticing, often through navigating the city in unfamiliar ways, the layers of history and culture that make up today's global city. The year 2020 also brought a reassessment of race and history catalysed by the Black Lives Matter movement. This led to an increased self-examination of Britain's colonial past, and new understandings of the legacies of migration set off by the Atlantic slave trade. Whilst our project took on new urgency following the murder of George Floyd in May 2020 and its repercussions worldwide, its timeliness was already evident given the rise of nationalistic and new-right rhetoric in the UK and Europe, with its unashamed scapegoating and vilification of migrant communities.

Migration narratives are everywhere in the news and tug in different directions. On the one hand, migration is a human and political crisis. The incumbent Conservative government in 2023 has caused outrage by its dogged attempts to send asylum seekers to Rwanda. This plan is another manifestation of the Hostile Environment policy designed by Theresa May to reduce immigration levels. The Windrush scandal (surfacing from 2017 onwards) is only one of the most visible manifestations of the inequalities and injustices faced by many first- and second-generation migrants as a result.[2] Pulling in the other direction, the cultural and economic contributions that migrants have made and continue to make to British society are being celebrated, not least through the recognition of the role played by immigrants and their descendants in maintaining the infrastructure of the country – in the National Health Service, in the care sector, in the transport and service industries – which became more starkly visible and politicized though the pandemic.

Typically, the past emerges or is re-examined when the present city is disrupted literally or metaphorically. Physical events, most obviously the Blitz, but also the reconstruction and reimagining of the built environment, including through major infrastructure projects, like the Victoria Embankment or Elizabeth Line, involve digging and uncovering layers of the city's past. The redevelopment of Bankside in 2022 has led to the largest area of Roman mosaic found in London in half a century being uncovered near the Cross Bones graveyard near London Bridge. Metaphorically, it takes a disruption such as the Black Lives Matter movement, which continues to see institutions reassess their colonial past, changing names and decentralizing figures associated with slavery. The Museum of London's Docklands, for example, removed the statue of slave trader Robert Milligan from its plinth in front of the museum.[3] Through disruption and fissures the past emerges and is reseen, redescribed or simply made visible.

History and culture do not stand still. Whilst this book is being written there are other migrations in progress. Mass migration fuelled by conflict and economic hardship has continued to increase globally, and Europe saw a dramatic upheaval following the full-scale invasion of Ukraine by Russia on 24 February 2022. According to the United Nations High Commissioner for Refugees, there were over 11 million border crossings from Ukraine into the EU between late February and mid-August 2022, with over 4 million returning in the same period.[4] Whilst the UK's 2021 census recorded a population of 19,000 Ukrainian-born people living in London, recent estimates suggest over 100,000 have come to the UK since February 2022.[5] This mass movement has added a new poignancy to Sasha Dovzhyk's chapter on the 1988 Statue of Saint Volodymyr. Written before the full-scale invasion, her work highlights an important focal point for London's growing Ukrainian community which is charged with political and cultural meaning.

The essays here are short and focused. They are snapshots that examine the ways in which London's localities – its buildings, parks, streets, districts and boroughs – have been shaped by migration. The result is kaleidoscopic. The collection is not a totalizing, comprehensive overview; instead, it is a bricolage, a contemporary *Wunderkammer* that offers a partial, idiosyncratic and eclectic journey through the city's past as evidenced in the history and culture of a selection of migrants and visitors. In some ways it is an eccentric endeavour, in both meanings of the word: it is somewhat unusual and also decentred, engaging with many canonical figures only peripherally. The essays are written by academics, writers and curators and explore the stories of individuals and wider communities through literature, evidence from the archives, accounts in letters, newspapers, material culture, and in the names and places we still recognize in today's London. Whilst we have aimed at a representative diversity, it is inevitable that many stories both well known and less well known are not represented here. For every essay here there are many others that could have been written, but we hope that what follows will draw attention to the significant input that migrants and visitors have made to London's history and cultural history.

This collection is structured geographically. It starts with a group of essays on Central London and then moves clockwise with sections on East, South, West and North London. Our sense of London's geography is contemporary. In a city like London, geography is not a fixed construct. For centuries, Westminster, Southwark and the City of London were all considered distinct civic entities, while areas like Hackney, Camberwell, Walthamstow and Hampstead, now all identified as 'London', were still villages in the nineteenth century. Our geographical organization emphasizes our focus on the local and reflects our thematic interest in the diversity of London. As Roy Porter wrote at the beginning of *London: A Social History* (1994), 'London is a cluster of communities, great and small, famous and unsung; a city of contrasts, a congregation of diversity. [...] For me the key to London lies in metropolitan heterogeneity, the sense of local habitations and their names.'[6] Porter's belief that localities offer insights into the distinct communities that make up London has been evinced in many more recent publications. It can be detected in micro-histories, like Jerry White's *Mansions of Misery: A Biography of the Marshalsea Debtor's Prison* (2016); in literary works, like Iain Sinclair's *Hackney, That Rose-Red Empire* (2009) and Caleb Femi's *Poor* (2020), whose poems constellate around the North Peckham Estate; and in travelogue-style studies, like Nazneen Khan-Østrem's *London: Immigrant City* (2019) and Ged Pope's *All the Tiny Moments Blazing: A Literary Guide to Suburban London* (2020), both of which are organized by geography.

We have chosen to order the book geographically to emphasize the importance of specific locations, suggesting a kind of forensic interest in the local which, in a city like London, inevitably opens up deep histories of difference and change over time. This structure allows the reader to go out and explore a building or a street with a new perspective, making the city's past navigable – perhaps encouraging the city to be seen as a palimpsest in progress. Between our geographically defined sections sit four essays which explore its infrastructure in different periods, telling different migration stories through the city by looking at the movements of water, sewage and people. The first of these examines early modern water and the development of the New River, still visible today in parts of Islington; the second explores the Victorian sewers and the circulation of waste and capital; the third focuses on race and the London Transport Network; and the fourth describes the development of the London bus as a democratizing force in the city.

* * *

The Romans founded London in the first century AD. Situated on the north bank of the River Thames, London – or Londinium as it was known – was an important centre of trade and administration, connecting foggy, damp Britannia to the rest of the Roman Empire via the ships that sailed in and out of its port. A prosperous city with an estimated population of 26,000 by 120 AD, Londinium cultivated a multi-ethnic society made up of citizens and soldiers from Italy, Greece, Gaul, Spain, North Africa and elsewhere.[7] The city they lived in was enclosed by a wall, parts of which can still be seen beside the Barbican, a place that takes its name from a Middle English word meaning 'an outer fortification or defence to a city'. This walled city was replete with architectural forms imported from the Roman world, including bath houses, an amphitheatre and temples.

One of the most significant Roman excavations of the twentieth century was a Temple of Mithras or *Mithraeum*. Situated near the banks of the River Walbrook, now buried beneath street level, the temple was constructed in the third century and belonged to an Eastern cult from Persia that became popular among soldiers, merchants and imperial officials throughout the empire between the first and fourth centuries.[8] Among several temple artefacts that are now housed in the Museum of London is a relief of Mithras slaying a bull and encircled by the signs of the zodiac (see Figure 0.1). The object is a testament to the migrations of people, materials and ideas that have shaped London from its inception. The depiction of Mithras in his traditional Phrygian cap speaks to the Eastern origin of his cult; the marble on which he is represented travelled from Carrara in Tuscany but was carved by a Briton or Gaul, perhaps in Londinium; and the inscription tells us that 'Ulpius Silvanus, veteran of the second Augustan legion, paid his vow: he was initiated [into the cult] at Orange' (Orange was part of Roman Gaul).[9] The carving is not notably skilful and depicts a commonplace scene, but the story that it tells us about London as a city shaped physically, demographically and ideologically by its place in a global network underlies this volume. It is a story that will surface again and again.

Londinium was abandoned in the fifth century when the Roman Empire began to collapse. It seems that the walled city stood empty; there is little evidence of continued settlement. The Saxons, migrants from mainland Europe, established their own port a kilometre upriver: their London – called Lundenwic – was situated around St Martin-in-the-Fields, which is now in the West End. Although the Saxons eschewed Londinium, at least until 886 when Viking raids prompted them to reoccupy the Roman defences, the city still remained significant. It is telling that when St Paul's Cathedral was founded in 604 it was situated within the walls. This location excited a rumour that it was built on top of a pagan temple.[10] The Middle English poem *St Erkenwald*, which Alastair Bennett discusses in this volume, centres on an encounter between London's patron saint and a pagan judge, whose perfectly preserved remains are disturbed by workmen expanding the cathedral. The city's pagan past was also preserved in other legends. Medieval writers

Figure 0.1 Relief sculpture of Mithras (n.d.). © Museum of London.

frequently claimed that London was founded by Brutus, a descendent of Aeneas and part of the Trojan diaspora. The twelfth-century chronicler Geoffrey of Monmouth recorded that Brutus conquered Britain and then 'came at length to the River Thames, walked up and down its banks and so chose a site suited to his purpose. There then [sic] he built his city and called it Troia Nova [New Troy].'[11] Later in 1500, an unknown Scottish poet hailed London as 'thou lusty Troy Novaunt, / Citie that some tyme cleped was New Troy.'[12]

Whether it was Roman Londinium or Saxon Lundenwic, London was always an important trading settlement. Writing in his *Ecclesiastical History of the English People* in the eighth century, Bede declared that 'the city of London [. . .] is a trading centre for many nations who visit it by land and sea.'[13] It never lost this function. The centuries that followed the Norman Conquest in 1066 witnessed the arrival of European traders and craftsmen: merchants from France and Cologne, weavers from the Low Countries, and Jewish and Italian bankers and moneylenders. The city also attracted migrants from throughout the British Isles, mainly from provincial England but also from Scotland, Ireland and Wales. These people belonged to all classes and all callings, and included some of Britain's greatest writers. William Shakespeare moved to Tudor London from the Midlands: his early days are explored in Daniel Swift's essay. They also included entrepreneurs, like the Welshman Hugh Myddleton, whose New River brought fresh water into London and whose place in early modern culture is examined by Susan J. Wiseman in the first of the four infrastructure essays. Migrants contributed to the vitality of the city and sustained its expansion from a settlement of 200,000 in 1600 to 900,000 in 1800.[14]

By the eighteenth century, London was a port city and national capital increasingly built on the profits of the transatlantic slave trade; it was also the heart of a growing empire, and its imperial position was becoming increasingly evident in some of its newest institutions. The British Museum, for example, was based on Sir Hans Sloane's vast collection of botanical and anatomical specimens, purchased for the nation in 1753. Sloane began his collection while in Jamaica, where he served as personal physician to the colony's governor, and later expanded it by purchasing other collections that were partially funded by his wife, Elizabeth Langley Rose, who owned plantations worked by slave labour.

After the museum opened in 1759, it continued to be a beneficiary of empire. When the German novelist Sophie von la Roche visited in 1786 she entered a room devoted to a collection of objects gathered by Captain James Cook during his Pacific voyages. As she picked her way 'amidst a swarm of foreigners' crowding the exhibition space, she saw 'the pots, weapons and clothes from the South Sea islands just recently discovered [...] crowns, helmets and war-masks, state uniforms and mourning – the former made of tiny shells and feathers, very densely and neatly sewn'.[15] Later treasures obtained through Britain's imperial actions and networks included the Parthenon Marbles, the Benin Bronzes and the Tang Dynasty scroll *Admonitions of the Instructress to the Court Ladies*. This last item became the centrepiece of a 1910 exhibition entitled *Chinese and Japanese Painting AD 500–1900*. The cultural importance of this exhibition and its influence on the American poet Ezra Pound is discussed in Kent Su's essay.

The British Museum was only one manifestation of Britain's growing imperial presence. The goods, animals and people that circulated through the city were also a testament to the reach of the British Empire. At annual fairs, ordinary Londoners saw the empire performed in both theatrical entertainments and the exhibition of exotic elephants, tigers and apes, as Alistair Robinson discusses. Furthermore, visitors from other continents drew the gaze of curious Londoners. Elizabeth Eger describes Elizabeth Montagu's fascination with the 'Cherokee King' who sought an alliance with Britain in 1762, while Uttara Natarajan analyses William Hazlitt's reaction to the juggler and sword-swallower Ramo Samee in his 1819 essay 'The Indian Jugglers'. The growing population of Black Londoners, 10,000 by the end of the eighteenth century, was also a reminder of the pivotal role that London played within the brutal mechanics of empire. Most Black Londoners, as David Olusoga reminds us, 'lived lives of constrained unfreedom as slaves or low-ranking servants'.[16] Others who were not in domestic service were sailors, musicians, performers, prostitutes and beggars.[17] We shall meet some of these men and women in these pages: Nicole N. Aljoe and Savita Maharaj examine the Black community that developed in St Giles, a dilapidated area that became home to many poor migrants in the eighteenth century; and David Hitchcock explores the celebrity of Charles McGee, a well-known beggar in Regency London. In contrast to these marginalized figures, Markman Ellis examines the life of Ignatius Sancho, a composer, businessman and man-of-letters who became the first Black Briton to vote in 1774.

Black Georgians were part of a growing, cosmopolitan population. By 1700 the French were already well established in London, which served as a bolt hole for Protestant Huguenots fleeing France after their civil rights were annulled by the Revocation of the Edict of Nantes in 1685. At the turn of the century, there were already 25,000–50,000 Huguenots, many of them working in the silk weaving industry centred in Spitalfields. In Chapter 11, Dan Cruickshank writes about 19 Princelet Street, a typical Spitalfields house whose early inhabitants were Huguenot weavers. The French also produced luxury goods, working as wig-makers, upholsterers and confectioners, and served in elite households as fencing masters, hairdressers, cooks, valets and footmen. London was also home to German merchants and artisans, and after the succession of George I – the German Elector of Hanover – Britain welcomed German servants, mistresses, artists, actors and composers.[18] In this last category was George Frideric Handel, a long-term resident of London whose music was played throughout the city, including the pleasure gardens at Vauxhall, which Charlotte Grant describes in this volume.

Jews – numbering 15,000 by 1800 – occupied a variety of social positions from wealthy bankers to impoverished pedlars, and the Irish, who made up approximately 3 per cent of the population, worked as plumbers, plasterers, tailors, weavers and hawkers. On the outskirts of London, Romany travellers wintered in Southwark and Norwood, Stoke Newington and Edmonton, selling horses and telling fortunes.[19] When considered alongside the much larger numbers of migrants that came to the city from the English provinces, it is easy to believe that 'around a half of all Londoners and possibly more were born outside the metropolis during much of the eighteenth century', as Jerry White estimates.[20]

In the nineteenth century, London's growth accelerated. In 1800 the capital's population was a little bigger than that of Paris; by 1900 it was two and a half times bigger and home to 6.58 million people. The surge in population was accompanied by extraordinary physical growth. Eighteenth-century London had been a walkable city, five miles from east to west. By the end of the nineteenth century it was more than three times that size, seventeen miles across: in terms of sheer bricks-and-mortar, London remains a largely Victorian city.[21] Such growth was supported by developments in London's transport infrastructure, most iconically the Underground, which opened its first line in 1863, but also the bus network, which from 1829 began opening up London to men and women from a diverse range of classes and backgrounds, as Joe Kerr explains in Chapter 29.

London was not just expanding into green fields; it was absorbing villages that had once provided a rural retreat for city dwellers: Hampstead, Camberwell, Leyton, Brixton, Hackney, Hammersmith and many more were all swallowed up in the city's expansion. London was on the move, troubling the boundary between the country and the city and complicating the city's relationship with nature. This is evident in Flora Lisica's essay, which analyses the interplay of the rural and urban in the life and poetry John Keats, a so-called 'cockney poet' who grew up in leafy Enfield, was educated in central London, and spent much of his short adult life in the emerging suburb of Hampstead.

London's physical expansion and population growth was largely driven by its economic prosperity. Writing in 1840, the French writer and activist Flora Tristan noted that 'London, because of its commerce and its great wealth, attracts large numbers of foreigners, who are almost all engaged in business.'[22] Her observation would only become more apposite. In 1841, London's foreign-born population was 13,000; by the end of the century it was 135,000. These figures exclude London's large Irish population, which grew even larger in the years of the Irish Famine (1845–9), which drove many people to England and its capital. By 1851 there were 109,000 Irish-born Londoners, many of them living in slums in Whitechapel, Leyton, West Ham and St Giles.[23]

London was becoming more accessible, in part due to its booming shipping industry. In 1819, London received 821,000 tons of foreign goods; this increased to 1.9 million tons by 1849 and 9.2 million tons by 1899. Such growth stimulated the expansion of London's docklands: the West India Docks opened in 1802, London Docks in 1806, St Katharine in 1828, Victoria in 1855, Millwall in 1868, Royal Albert in 1880, and the East and West India Docks in 1886.[24] London was visited by sailors from across the British Empire and beyond. Among these were Indian and Chinese sailors, commonly called 'Lascars', who were underpaid, poorly treated and sometimes found themselves stranded on London's streets. Some of these castaways settled in the small but growing Chinese and Indian communities that developed in the waterfront regions of the East End; however, others found themselves effectively interned in the barracks of their employer, the East India Company, as Eliza Cubitt recounts in Chapter 12.

Victorian London's economy expanded due to the city's political and imperial centrality; but although trade was buoyant, the job market was highly competitive and not everyone found regular work. Most industries were seasonal to some extent and depended on a pool of underemployed labour from which they could draw when their services were in demand. For the rest of the year, people had to fend for themselves in whatever way they could. This might involve begging, hawking, wood-chopping, coal-heaving or scavenging in the street.[25] In Naomi Hinds's essay we meet the 'toshers' and 'shoremen' who navigated London's treacherous sewers in search of the salvage that circulated through the subterranean city. These Victorians, living close to deprivation, might well have resorted to the Mendicity Society, a charity that grudgingly doled out food and clothing to the needy from their headquarters in Red-Lion Square, Bloomsbury. Oskar Cox Jensen provides an account of this forbidding organization and its international clientele.

Art – its creation and retail – was one uncertain industry that drew migrants to the city. In 1898, Yoshio Markino 牧野　義雄 arrived in London, working first for the Japanese Navy, then for a tombstone engraver in Norwood, and then as an underemployed artist for illustrated magazines. Markino's foggy London street scenes eventually became fashionable, admired for their unique blend of Japanese and Western styles. His success, however, was preceded by poverty: Markino lived hand-to-mouth in a Brixton boarding house and often starved for want of credit and the threat of mounting debts.[26] Although he described himself as 'London's devoted lover', that love was not always requited.[27] The

Figure 0.2 Yoshio Markino, *Earl's Court Station* (1910). Editor's (Robinson's) collection.

lives of more financially and socially secure artists are explored in this volume. Livia Wang's profile of Vincent van Gogh recalls the formative year that he spent between August 1873 and August 1874 living in Hackford Road, Stockwell and working for the art dealers Goupil & Cie. Through a reading of Van Gogh's letters, Wang recovers his admiration for the city and its suburbs. Meanwhile, Eva-Charlotta Mebius examines London's place in the Anglo-Scandinavian art world. A largely forgotten piece of history, Mebius traces the movements of Prince Eugen of Sweden as he visited London-based artists to secure exhibitors for the 1897 Stockholm Exhibition.

Migrants moved to London for money and for culture, but the British capital also proved a sanctuary for those suffering political and religious persecution in mainland Europe.[28] Their stories surface repeatedly in this volume. In Catherine Brown's essay, which focuses on the influence of the 1851 Crystal Palace on the Russian novelists Nikolai Chernyshevsky and Fyodor Dostoevsky, we are introduced to the agrarian socialist Alexander Herzen, a Russian exile whose Paddington home became a hub of political dissidence. Herzen was one of thousands of migrants who came to nineteenth-century London from the Russian Empire. Most of these were Jews fleeing the pogroms that followed in the wake of Tsar Alexander II's assassination (Jews were blamed for his death). Between 1880 and 1900, London's Jewish population tripled, reaching 140,000 by the end of the century.[29] Many of these refugees settled in the East End and shaped its social, economic and cultural life. Alex Grafen's essay recovers the history of the 'Slot-Meter', a tiny East-End flat that was rented in the 1910s by John Rodker and Sonia Cohen, both the children of Jewish migrants. The flat became the setting for an intellectual and artistic salon that attracted Jewish poets, painters, translators and literary critics living in and around Whitechapel.

Figure 0.3 Frank Meisler, *Kindertransport – The Arrival* (2006). CC-BY-SA-4.0.

More refugees arrived in the twentieth century. In the forecourt of Liverpool Street Station sits Frank Meisler's bronze memorial *Kindertransport – The Arrival* (2006; see Figure 0.3). It is one of five statues by Meisler, each depicting the same group of children, that are located in cities across Europe: London, Hook, Hamburg, Berlin and Gdansk, where Meisler himself boarded the Kindertransport to escape the Nazi regime. The London statue commemorates the arrival of 10,000 Jewish children from continental Europe who passed through Liverpool Street in 1938–9.[30] They were among tens of thousands of refugees who came to London after Hitler's rise to power. These included the potter Lucie Rie who recreated her Viennese apartment in Albion Mews, Bayswater, the place she spent the rest of her life. Her story, and that of her fellow émigré and collaborator Hans Coper, is explored in Edmund de Waal's essay. London also became the home of anti-Nazi institutions: the Warburg Institute relocated from Hamburg in 1933 (it still has premises in Bloomsbury) and the *Freier Deutscher Kulturbund in Großbritannien*, or Free German League of Culture in Great Britain, was established in Upper Park Road, Hampstead in 1939. David Anderson explores this largely forgotten institution and the German refugees that organized its anti-Nazi initiatives.

As the German army rolled over Western Europe in 1940, London became central to the Allied war effort. From 1940 to 1945 it was the home of the Polish, French, Belgian, Dutch and Norwegian governments, and hosted armies from across Europe, the United States and the empire. As American GI Robert Arbib remarked, London 'was not only the throbbing heart of the British Empire, but here too was the capital-in-exile of half a dozen other nations. [...] London was the babel, the Metropolis, the Mecca.'[31] London was a beachhead for the Allied resistance and its political and strategic importance made it a key target for the German Luftwaffe. During the Blitz – September 1940 to May 1941 – nearly 20,000 Londoners were killed.[32] London's endurance, notably captured in Herbert Mason's photograph of St Paul's Cathedral rising above the smoky ruins of the city, became a symbol of defiance at home and abroad. Documentaries like *London Can Take It!* (1940) depicted stoic citizens under fire and were exported to the USA to garner support for the war.[33] But despite narratives of cockney courage, the bombing decimated much of London, as can be seen in the paintings and drawings of refugee artist Martin Bloch (see Figure 0.4). In her wartime story 'Mysterious Kôr' (1945), the Irish modernist Elizabeth Bowen described London as 'like the moon's capital – shallow, cratered, extinct'. This story, set in a 'two-roomed flatlet [...] off the Regent's Park Road', is located near 2 Clarence Terrace, the house in which Bowen lived while serving as an air raid warden.[34] Her attachment to Regent's Park and its recurrence in her writings is explored by Heather Ingman.

It has often been argued that after the Second World War a new, multi-ethnic London emerged due to the mass migration of people from Africa, Asia and the Caribbean. The raw figures support this. In 1951 there were only 4,000 people from the Caribbean in a city of over 8 million; by 1971 there were 170,000. Likewise, there were few Indians and

Figure 0.4 Martin Bloch, 'Bomb Damage, City of London' (1943). © Martin Bloch Trust.

Pakistanis in 1951 but 50,000 a decade later.[35] The sheer weight of numbers, however, disguises the significant presence of Black and Asian intellectuals in the interwar city. 'During this period,' Marc Matera explains, 'the administrative center and capital of the British Empire became a locus of resistance to empire. It served as a meeting point of intellectuals, artists, revolutionaries, and movements for colonial freedom.'[36] This is evident in two of the essays in this collection. William Whitworth provides an account of the West African Student's Union in Camden and the political networks it fostered, and Oliver Ayers explores the multiracial, multinational character of the Northview development, a residential building off Holloway Road. This building was home to several musicians of colour who found a unifying focus in London's emerging jazz scene.

Literature as well as music was altered by first- and second-generation migrants from Asia, Africa, the Caribbean and elsewhere, and this volume contains several essays on authors who have (re)shaped the canon of literary London. Peter Maber and Karishma Patel examine Sam Selvon's famous novel *The Lonely Londoners* (1956) alongside his lesser-known collection of stories *Ways of Sunlight* (1957); Ruvani Ranasinha explores Hanif Kureishi's irreverent masterpiece *The Buddha of Suburbia* (1990); Rob Waters reads the racial politics of London's transport network through the work of E. R. Brathwaite, Barbara Blake Hannah, Linton Kwesi Johnson and Selvon; and Martin Dines analyses the literary treatment of Southall in Bhanu Kapil's *Ban en Banlieue* (2016) and Tim Lott's *The Scent of Dried Roses* (1996). Susie Thomas analyses key locations at the heart of Arab London in Hanan al-Shaykh's novel *Only in London* (2001): Edgware Road, lined with Arab-owned shops, restaurants and cafes, and the London Central Mosque in Regent's Park.

London has been hailed as a successful cosmopolis, free from the ghettoization that has characterized some North American cities, and from the 'guest-worker' culture of continental Europe in which citizenship has been denied to migrant workers.[37] 'The millennia of migration to the capital have ensured that cosmopolitanism has formed a key aspect of London life,' writes Panikos Panayi. 'While ethnic enclaves may have acted as characteristics of migrant settlement since the Norman invasion, so has ethnic intermixing whether through the development of relationships between individuals, especially during the last two centuries, or by the economic and cultural impact of new arrivals.'[38]

However, although London has been called home by many migrant communities over the last 2,000 years, and benefitted culturally, socially and economically from their presence in the city, London and Londoners have also been hostile to them. A few instances must stand for many. In 1290, Edward I expelled the Jews, forcing them from London and other English towns and cities.[39] On 'Evil May Day' 1517, hundreds of apprentices attacked foreigners in the liberty of St Martin-le-Grand, possibly after an anti-alien sermon preached by Dr Beal (or Bell) from St Paul's Cross.[40] In June 1780, London was paralysed by the Gordon Riots which left 285 dead and caused £200,000 worth of property damage. The riots were triggered by an anti-Catholic prejudice which quickly turned into anti-Irish violence in Moorfields and elsewhere.[41] (The Irish were the largest Catholic community in eighteenth-century London.) In May 1915 a week of anti-German rioting broke out after the RMS *Lusitania* was torpedoed: German- and Austrian-owned shops and homes were looted; 257 people were injured.[42] In 1958, 400 working-class white men attacked Black residents in Notting Hill.[43] The rioting, which occurred every night between 29 August and 5 September, prompted activist and journalist Claudia Jones to stage a celebration of Caribbean culture and heritage that became the Notting Hill Carnival. Leighan Renaud discusses the ongoing cultural and political importance of the Carnival in this volume.

Discrimination persists in many forms today. The ongoing process of gentrification, which typically entails the displacement of low-income residents by wealthier individuals, has had a detrimental impact on elderly and working-class Londoners (including migrants) unable to afford the rising cost of rent in their now-desirable boroughs. These movements of the gentrifier and those they displace sit uncomfortably alongside other migrations that are now being celebrated as foundational to the city and its cultures.[44] This is manifest in cultural artefacts, events and institutions. In 2008 the first permanent statue of a Black woman in England was erected in Stockwell Memorial Garden 'In honour and praise of all Caribbean women' (see Figure 0.5). In 2020 the Migration Museum, having transitioned through a series of pop-up exhibitions since 2013, found a home in Lewisham Shopping Centre.[45] And the Ben Uri Gallery, set up in 1915 in Whitechapel to showcase Jewish artists, has, since 2000, embraced a wider remit to include all immigrant artists since 1900.

Major exhibitions by London's art institutions have also increasingly foregrounded questions of migration. Edmund de Waal's travelling installation, *Library of Exile* (2019),

Figure 0.5 Aleix Barbat, *Bronze Woman* (2008). CC BY-SA 2.0.

which explores the idea of language as migration, came to London's British Museum in 2020, and in 2019 the nationwide arts festival 'Insiders Outsiders' celebrated the contribution of refugees from Nazi Europe to British visual culture. Perhaps most spectacularly, Tate Britain's 2020–1 Winter Commission saw Chila Kumari Singh Burman clad Sidney Smith's 1820 neoclassical building in Millbank with a stunning light installation called *Remembering a Brave New World*, which proclaimed 'without us there is no Britain'. Burman's installation opened during the dampened celebration of Diwali in November 2020, a Hindu festival of light in an autumn made dark by the pandemic and a series of lockdowns. Burman recast Britannia, who crowns the Palladian-style façade of the original building, as Kali, Hindu goddess of liberation and power, and, in the foreground created an image of her parents' ice cream van with the motto 'We are Here coz you were there' in orange neon. The essays in this book take on something of Burman's challenge, rendering visible a tiny number of the many ways in which migration and its histories have formed and represent today's London.

Notes

1. Daniel Snowman, 'Introduction', in *Insiders/Outsiders: Refugees from Nazi Europe and their Contribution to British Visual Culture*, ed. Monica Bohm-Duchen (London: Lund Humphries, 2019), 10.

2. For a nuanced discussion of the hostile environment, and anti-immigration politics in the UK more generally, see Maya Goodfellow, *Hostile Environment: How Immigrants Became Scapegoats* (London: Verso, 2019).

3. Many of London's cultural institutions had already begun this process of decolonization, for example the renaming of the Geffrye Museum as the 'Museum of the Home' in late 2019.

4. United Nations High Commissioner for Refugees, 'Operational Data Portal: Ukranian Refugee Situation', https://data.unhcr.org/en/situations/ukraine.

5. UK Government, 'Statistics on Ukranians in the UK', 23 September 2022, https://www.gov.uk/government/statistics/immigration-statistics-year-ending-june-2022/statistics-on-ukrainians-in-the-uk.

6. Roy Porter, *London: A Social History* (London: Penguin, 1994/2000), 13.

7. Richard Hingley, *Londinium: A Biography: Roman London from its Origins to the Fifth Century* (London: Bloomsbury, 2018), 70–1, 88, 235–6.

8. Ibid., 183–4.

9. J. M. C. Toynbee, *The Roman Art Treasures from the Temple of Mithras* (London: London and Middlesex Archaeological Society, 1986), 29–30.

10. Hingley, *Londinium*, 236–40.

11. Geoffrey of Monmouth, *The History of the Kings of Britain*, trans. Lewis Thorpe (London: Penguin, 1966), 74.

12. Anon., 'London, thou art of townes A per se', in *London: A History in Verse*, ed. Mark Ford (London: Belknap Press, 2012), 56–8.

13. Bede, *Ecclesiastical History of the English People*, trans. Leo Sherley-Price and R. E. Latham (London: Penguin, 1990), 107–8.

14. Porter, *London*, 36–7, 54–5, 158–9.

15. Sophie von la Roche, *Sophie in London 1786, being the Diary of Sophie v. la Roche*, trans. Clare Williams (London: Jonathan Cape, 1933), 104, 109.

16. David Olusoga, *Black and British: A Forgotten History* (London: Pan Books, 2017), 111.

17. Ibid., 77–86.

18. See Joanna Marschner, David Bindman and Lisa L. Ford (eds), *Enlightened Princesses: Caroline, Augusta, Charlotte, and the Shaping of the Modern World* (New Haven, CT, and London: Yale Centre for British Art, 2017).

19. Jerry White, *London in the Eighteenth Century: A Great and Monstrous Thing* (London: Bodley Head, 2012), 137–62; David Cressy, *Gypsies: An English History* (Oxford: Oxford University Press, 2018/2020), 120–4.

20. White, *London in the Eighteenth Century*, 90–1.

21. Jerry White, *London in the Nineteenth Century: A Human Awful Wonder of God* (London: Vintage, 2008), 3, 68.

22. Flora Tristan, *Flora Tristan's London Journal 1840: A Survey of London Life in the 1830s*, trans. Dennis Palmer and Giselle Pincetl (London: George Prior Publishers, 1980), 15.

23. White, *London in the Nineteenth Century*, 132–4.

24. Ibid., 130, 182–3.

25. See Gareth Stedman Jones, *Outcast London: A Study in the Relationship Between Classes in Victorian Society*, 2nd rev. edn (London: Verso, 2013), 33–66.

26. For an account of Markino's life in London, see his autobiography, Yoshio Markino, *A Japanese Artist in London* (London: Chatto & Windus, 1910).

27. Yoshio Markino, 'An Essay by the Artist', in *The Colour of London* (London: Chatto & Windus, 1907), xxxix.

28. Panikos Panayi, *Migrant City: A New History of London* (New Haven, CT, and London: Yale University Press, 2022), 179.

29. White, *London in the Nineteenth Century*, 154.

30. Marie-Catherine Allard, 'Modelling Bridges Between Past and Current Issues of Forced Migration: Frank Meisler's Memorial Sculpture *Kindertransport – The Arrival*', *Jewish Historical Studies* 51, no. 1 (2020): 86–104.

31. Quoted in Jerry White, *The Battle of London 1939–45: Endurance, Heroism and Frailty Under Fire* (London: Bodley Head, 2021), 235. Also see, White, *The Battle of London*, 80–1, 233–44; Philip Ziegler, *London at War, 1939–1945* (London: Pimlico, 2002), 213–15.

32. White, *The Battle of London 1939–45*, 140.

33. William Cederwell, *Reading London in Wartime: Blitz, The People, and Propaganda in 1940s Literature* (Abingdon: Routledge, 2019), 1–2.

34. Elizabeth Bowen, 'Mysterious Kôr', in *The Collected Stories of Elizabeth Bowen* (Harmondsworth: Penguin, 1985), 728, 731.

35. Jerry White, *London in the Twentieth Century: A City and Its People* (London: Vintage, 2008), 130–8.

36. Marc Matera, *Black London: The Imperial Metropolis and Decolonization in the Twentieth Century* (Oakland: University of California Press, 2015), 2.

37. Panayi, *Migrant City*, 28–56; White, *London in the Twentieth Century*, 143–4.

38. Panayi, *Migrant City*, 27.

39. Robin R. Mundill, *The King's Jews: Money, Massacre and Exodus in Medieval England* (London: Continuum, 2010), 156–9.

40. Robert O. Bucholz and Joseph P. Ward, *London: A Social and Cultural History, 1550–1750* (Cambridge: Cambridge University Press, 2012), 278.

41. Christopher Hibbert, *King Mob: The Story of Lord George Gordon and the Riots of 1780* (London: Longman, Green, 1959), 70; Tim Hitchcock and Robert Shoemaker, *London Lives: Poverty, Crime and the Making of a Modern City, 1690–1800* (Cambridge: Cambridge University Press, 2015), 343.

42. Jerry White, *Zeppelin Nights: London in the First World War* (London: Vintage, 2015), 76–7.

43. Olusoga, *Black and British*, 509–10.

44. Alberto Duman, 'Dispatches from "the Frontline of Gentrification"', *City* 16, no. 6 (2012): 676–7; Rowland Atkinson, 'The Hidden Costs of Gentrification: Displacement in Central London', *Journal of Housing and the Built Environment* 15, no. 4 (2000): 314, 317.

45. At the time of writing, the Migration Museum announced its forthcoming move to a permanent home in Crutched Friars in the City of London.

CENTRAL

CHAPTER 1

ST ERKENWALD AND THE HIDDEN HISTORIES OF ST PAUL'S CATHEDRAL

Alastair Bennett

The Middle English poem *St Erkenwald*, probably composed in the late fourteenth century, tells the story of a remarkable discovery during building work on St Paul's Cathedral.[1] The poem opens late in the sixth century, shortly after the pagan Saxons, who long ago drove the Christian Britons out of England into Wales, have themselves been converted to Christianity by the missionary saint Augustine. Augustine arrives in London, where he rededicates the pagan temples to Christian saints, including the greatest and most prestigious of all, which he renames St Paul's. The action then moves to the time of Bishop Erkenwald, a little less than a century later. A team of workmen are digging foundations to extend the cathedral when they uncover a mysterious, ornate tomb and, inside it, the body of a man, immaculately dressed and miraculously preserved. Although the man is obviously important, no one can find any record of him in the cathedral's archives, and no one can decipher the ancient lettering on his tomb. Erkenwald is summoned back from Essex to see this marvel and, after spending a night in prayer and performing matins and mass, he goes down into the foundations and commands the body to speak. Miraculously, the dead man answers him. He reveals that, in life, he was a judge in the time of the pagan king Belinus and that although he was widely praised for his scrupulous, impartial judgements, he was condemned to hell when he died because he never had the chance to convert to Christianity. Erkenwald weeps and prays for the judge and, when one of Erkenwald's tears falls onto his face, the judge reveals that he is now baptized, and that his soul has been taken up into heaven.

This is a poem about the way the past persists into the present, and about the way that people in the present engage with the past. It certainly celebrates the capacity of a hegemonic Christian culture to absorb other cultures, and of a hegemonic Christian narrative to absorb other narratives, but it also invites its readers to think about the way that non-Christian people have shaped the values, institutions and architecture of their city, in ways that the historical archive seems to have suppressed or forgotten. *St Erkenwald* is also a poem with a strong sense of place, set in and around the precincts of the cathedral, and it makes an argument for the value of a site-specific history: people and events who are occluded in other narratives become visible again when history is seen from a particular location.

The poem's protagonist, Bishop Erkenwald, had close associations with St Paul's Cathedral, both during his life and after his death.[2] Bede, in his *Ecclesiastical History of the English People*, records that Erkenwald founded the abbeys of Chertsey and Barking, the second of these with his sister Ethelburga, and that he was consecrated bishop of the

East Saxons, with his seat at St Paul's, in 675. After his death, Erkenwald's followers preserved the horse litter that he travelled around in and found that splinters of it performed healing miracles, curing fevers and other illnesses. By the time of the Norman Conquest, he was well established as a saint, with a feast day on 30 April. Erkenwald was buried in St Paul's Cathedral, where his shrine became a focus for religious veneration and his life a focus for literary production. His body survived the fire that destroyed the original building in 1087, and, in 1148, after the cathedral was rebuilt, it was moved to a new shrine east of the high altar. New texts about Erkenwald were composed in this period, encouraging devotion to his cult: a hagiographical life by an anonymous author, and a collection of miracle stories by a cathedral canon called Arcoid. Another new shrine was built for Erkenwald in the early fourteenth century, this time as part of a large-scale project to extend the eastern end of the cathedral that became known as the 'New Work'.[3] This was an ornate and elaborate structure; in 1339, a team of goldsmiths were employed for a whole year to decorate it.[4] Later in the fourteenth century, Robert Braybrooke (bishop of London, 1381–1404) led a new effort to promote the saint, granting a special status to his feast day and ordering new processions in his honour; the Middle English poem *St Erkenwald* might well have been written in connection with this project, supplying the saint with a new miracle story.

The poem *St Erkenwald* alludes to various aspects of Erkenwald's biography. When the judge is discovered beneath the cathedral, for example, Erkenwald has gone to Essex 'an abbay to visite' (l. 108), presumably his own foundation at Barking. Erkenwald's abiding presence in the cathedral has clearly inspired the poet, too. Like Erkenwald himself, the judge in the poem is an ancient figure in an ornate tomb who attracts the attention of the cathedral clergy during periods of building work. At one point, the poet refers to the excavations that uncover the judge's tomb as the 'New Werke' (l. 38), linking them to the fourteenth-century building works that included the construction of Erkenwald's new shrine.

The central story of *St Erkenwald* has no parallels in the earlier accounts of Erkenwald's life, however. Instead, the poet conflates two familiar stories about the salvation of non-Christians that circulated in multiple versions in the Middle Ages.[5] In the first of these, a tomb is discovered beneath an antique city (Thrace or Constantinople) containing the body of a virtuous man from pre-Christian times, with a message that declares his Christian faith. This is a story about the fate of the pagan 'iusti', good people who lived too early in history to become Christians; it offers evidence that the 'iusti' might be granted a secret revelation of Christian faith that would allow them to be saved. In the second story, Pope Gregory hears about the virtues of the emperor Trajan and resolves to pray for him until, finally, he receives divine assurance that the emperor's soul has been lifted out of purgatory and admitted to heaven. This is a story about the power of intercessory prayer: it confirms that prayers for the dead, of the kind that were performed every day in the cathedral's chantries, could be effective even in the most extreme circumstances. The *Erkenwald* poet combines these narratives in an innovative way: he imagines the discovery of a pre-Christian tomb whose occupant has yet to be saved, and an act of prayer that brings the bishop Erkenwald into direct contact with the virtuous pagan he is praying for.

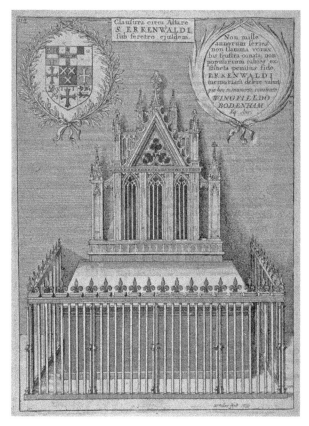

Figure 1.1 Wenceslaus Hollar, *Monument to Saint Erkenwald in Old St Paul's Cathedral* (1656). © Heritage Image Partnership Ltd./Alamy Stock Photo.

The stories that lie behind the narrative of *St Erkenwald* are concerned with exceptional cases, with individuals who test the rules about who can and cannot be saved. The judge in *St Erkenwald* is exceptional, too: he alone insisted on justice at a time when 'Þe folk was felonse and fals and frowarde to reule' ['the people were wicked and false and resistant to rule'] (l. 231). Yet, the judge also stands more generally for those aspects of pre-Christian culture that are worth preserving and celebrating. His virtue lies in his strict adherence to a law that the citizens of London could recognize and respect, even if they did not always obey it. As he explains to Erkenwald, the people buried him like a king because of his commitment to their system of justice: 'For þe honour of myn honesté of highest emprise | Þai coronyd me þe kidde kynge of kene justices' ['To commemorate my integrity of the highest renown, they crowned me the famous king of fearless judges'] (ll. 253–4). Erkenwald's effort on behalf of the judge is, in part, an effort to recuperate this non-Christian justice, and to honour this non-Christian effort at commemoration, at the point when the judge and his tomb, already long-forgotten, are about to be engulfed by a new, Christian structure. The poem shows this pagan law to be incomplete, of course: in order to be saved, this strict advocate of pre-Christian justice will require the intervention of Christian mercy. Yet, it still imagines pagan justice as a recognizable precursor to the law of its own time, a law that requires its proper recognition and acknowledgement.

The poem locates this encounter between Erkenwald and the judge in a narrative of English history that draws on several different sources. The opening account of the pagan Saxons, who drove the Christian Britons into Wales only to be converted in their turn by Augustine, derives from Bede, like the earliest stories of Erkenwald himself. As Ralph Hanna has argued, however, the poem's version of these events is modelled in part on another historical narrative, the foundation of Britain by the Trojan Brutus, that was popularized by Geoffrey of Monmouth in his *History of the Kings of Britain* and rehearsed in other alliterative poems like *Sir Gawain and the Green Knight*: Augustine comes from Rome to convert the English in *St Erkenwald* much as Brutus comes from Troy to establish Britain in Geoffrey and *Sir Gawain*.[6] The poem includes several references to London as 'þe New Troie' (l. 25, and cf. ll. 251, 255), in an allusion to Brutus who named the city 'Troia Nova' when he first established it. When the judge describes his own place in history, he explains that he served during the reign of King Belinus who feuded with his brother Brennius, a story found in Geoffrey rather than in Bede. He also uses an elaborate system of calculations to position his life after the time of Brutus and before the time of Christ:

> After þat Brutus þis burgh had buggid on fyrste,
> Noȝt bot fife hundred ȝere þen aghtene wontyd;
> Before þat kynned ȝour Criste by Cristen acounte,
> A þousand ȝere and þritty mo and ȝet threnen aght,
> I was an heire of anoye in þe New Troie. (ll. 207–11)[7]

> [Not more than five hundred years with eighteen lacking after Brutus first built this city; a thousand years and thirty more, and three times eight more than that, before your Christ was conceived on the Christian account, I was an inheritor of affliction in the New Troy.]

As it weaves these stories together, *St Erkenwald* practices a kind of history that would be familiar to medieval visitors to St Paul's Cathedral. The medieval building contained two large *tabluae* of important historical events that hung near the tomb of John of Gaunt, not far from Erkenwald's shrine: these *tabulae* combined events from universal, national and local histories, drawing material from different sources, and allowed the viewer to calculate the intervals between events, much as the judge does in *St Erkenwald*. Kathryn Kerby-Fulton argues that the *Erkenwald* poet was probably one of the many precariously-employed clerics who staffed St Paul's, serving in its chantries or in the bishop's household. She notes that these clerics would have been very familiar with the *tabulae*, which they used to guide visitors through the history of the cathedral.[8]

St Erkenwald shows how a site-specific history might offer a different view of the past, recognizing the contributions of individuals and cultures who disappear from histories of other kinds. The stories the poet tells are stories about migration, the people who have settled in Britain and shaped its culture: Brutus, with his ties to the antique splendour of Troy, and the Saxons whose pagan temples provide the footprint for later Christian churches. Christianity itself returns to Britain as part of a migration story, as Augustine, like Brutus, comes to settle in Britain, bringing 'þe pure faythe' with him (ll. 12–13). Seen from a single place, history unfolds as the continual movement of people. *St Erkenwald* suggests that the material fabric of the building itself preserves histories besides those that are found in chronicles and texts. When Erkenwald approaches the tomb, the Dean of St Paul's tells him that the clerics have searched for seven days in 'oure librarie' and have consulted 'oure martilage' (the cathedral's burial register), but can find no record of who the dead man is (ll. 154–5). Even so, the tomb itself persists as a monument to the judge's life; the building retains the traces of the people who have passed through it. The fabric of an ancient building, the poem suggests, might bear witness to the contributions of people and cultures who have disappeared from other sources.

The encounter with the pagan judge, and the effort to reconcile him with Christian history, has implications for the way the poem imagines the civic community in its own time. When the tomb is first discovered, the poet describes the citizens of London as they hurry to witness this 'wonder', offering a portrait of the city and its inhabitants:

> Burgeys boghit þerto, bedels and othire,
> And mony a mesters mon of maners dyverse;
> Laddes laften hor werke and lepen þiderwardes,
> Ronnen radly in route with ryngand noyce;
> Þer comen þider of all kynnes so kenely mony
> Þat as all þe worlde were þider walon within a hond-quile. (ll. 59–64)

> [Burgesses arrived there, beadles and others, and many tradesmen's apprentices of different types; lads stopped their work and hurried in that direction, running quickly in a crowd with a resounding noise; so very many people of all kinds arrived there that it was as if all the world had made their way there at a stroke.]

The opening lines of this passage are careful to distinguish men with a special status in London: burgesses, who were freemen of the city; beadles who performed civic offices; and apprentices to the trades and crafts that were regulated by the city guilds. By the end of the passage, however, the poet imagines a crowd that contains people 'of all kynnes' and seems to encompass 'all þe worlde'. Emily Steiner, who compares these lines to a similar street scene in the fourteenth-century poem *Piers Plowman*, notes the perception in both poems that 'a compendious world could be summoned within a London crowd'.[9] The judge himself presents a challenge to this image of the city as a polity that includes and accommodates everyone, however. He demands acknowledgement for the contribution of non-Christians in the city's past, but, through his miraculous appearance in the present, he also poses the question of whether and how medieval Londoners could recognize people of other faiths and cultures as members of their own community.

Late medieval London had a comparatively large population of migrants, drawn from elsewhere in England and from other European countries, but it also saw sporadic outbreaks of violence directed against immigrant communities.[10] The city had relatively few non-Christian inhabitants. The large-scale expulsion of England's Jewish communities in 1290, under an ordinance that remained in place until the seventeenth century, created a situation where only a tiny number of Jews remained, most as converts to Christianity.[11] Hostility to foreign traders in the capital could be expressed in terms that also revealed racial and religious prejudice: in the Good Parliament of 1376, for example, Lombard brokers were maligned as secret Jews and as 'Saracens', the English term for Muslims from North Africa and the Middle East.[12] Read in this context, the encounter with the judge *St Erkenwald* offers a challenge to contemporary readers, asking them to consider the people who are excluded from their own community, to interrogate the hyperbolic claim that their community embraces 'all þe worlde'. The judge himself is absorbed into the hegemonic culture of the Christian city at the poem's conclusion. Even so, as Sarah Salih argues, the poem's 'acknowledgement of London's multiple settlements and synchronic religious plurality can at least be held in suspension with its proclamation of Christian superiority'.[13] As it uncovers the hidden histories of their non-Christian ancestors, the poem asks contemporary Londoners to imagine another version of their city, where they might encounter people of other faiths and cultures as their fellow citizens.

St Erkenwald concludes on an ambivalent note: at the point of his baptism, the body of the judge turns to dust, and the miraculous encounter is over. The poet writes that 'Meche mourning and myrthe was mellyd together' ['Much sorrow and joy was blended together'] (l. 350) when the people departed the cathedral. Before it arrives at this moment of assimilation and dissolution, however, *St Erkenwald* has staged an encounter with the past that produces both challenges and creative opportunities for its contemporary readers. As he restores the judge to his proper place in the historical record, Erkenwald also acknowledges the merits of the non-Christian culture that he represents. As they witness this encounter, meanwhile, the citizens of London begin to imagine their non-Christian ancestors as part of their contemporary community. The poem also invites its readers to consider their built environment in a new way, as a place where hidden histories might come to light. *St Erkenwald* shows how new perspectives on the past can emerge from a site-specific history, that a building like St Paul's might preserve the memory of its inhabitants even when they disappear from the textual archive.

Notes

1. *St Erkenwald* survives in a single manuscript, now British Library MS Harley 2250. The manuscript itself dates from the later fifteenth century (a colophon on fol. 64v notes that the scribe finished copying this part of the book in 1477), but many of the texts it contains were written or revised in the fourteenth century, and *Erkenwald* itself was probably composed

sometime in the late 1390s or early 1400s. In this chapter, I cite *St Erkenwald* from *A Book of Middle English*, ed. John Burrow and Thorlac Turville-Petre, 3rd edn (Oxford: Blackwell, 2005), with my own translations.

2. For an accessible introduction to the life and cult of Erkenwald, see Eamon Duffy, *Royal Books and Holy Bones: Essays in Medieval Christianity* (London: Bloomsbury, 2018), 165–86.

3. Carol Davidson Cragoe, 'Fabric, Tombs and Precinct, 1087–1540', in *Saint Paul's: The Cathedral Church of London 604–2004*, ed. Derek Keene, Arthur Burns and Andrew Saint (New Haven, CT: Yale University Press, 2004), 136–9.

4. Alan Thacker, 'The Cult of Saints and the Liturgy', in *Saint Paul's: The Cathedral Church*, 119–20.

5. For a detailed account of these two traditions and their influence on the poem, see Gordon Whatley, 'Heathens and Saints: *St Erkenwald* in its Legendary Context', *Speculum* 61, no. 2 (1986): 330–63.

6. Ralph Hanna, 'Alliterative Poetry', in *The Cambridge History of Medieval English Literature*, ed. David Wallace (Cambridge: Cambridge University Press, 1999), 506.

7. I have modified Burrow and Turville-Petre's punctuation of these lines.

8. Kathryn Kerby-Fulton, *The Clerical Proletariat and the Resurgence of Medieval English Poetry* (Philadelphia: University of Pennsylvania Press, 2021), 269. See also Michael Van Dussen, 'Tourists and *Tabulae* in Late-Medieval England', in *Truth and Tales: Cultural Mobility and Medieval Media*, ed. Fiona Somerset and Nicholas Watson (Ohio: Ohio State University Press, 2015), 238–54.

9. Emily Steiner, *Reading Piers Plowman* (Cambridge: Cambridge University Press, 2013), 15.

10. Sarah Rees Jones, 'English Towns in the Later Middle Ages: The Rules and Realities of Population Mobility', in *Migrants in Medieval England, c.500–c.1500*, ed. W. Mark Ormrod, Joanna Story and Elizabeth M. Tyler (Oxford: Oxford University Press, 2020), 298–325.

11. W. Mark Ormrod, Bart Lambert and Jonathan Mackman, *Immigrant England, 1300–1550* (Manchester: Manchester University Press, 2019), 3, 183–7.

12. Ibid., 30. On the presence of 'Saracens' in late medieval England, see also 187–92.

13. Sarah Salih, *Imagining the Pagan in Medieval England* (Cambridge: Brewer, 2019), 176.

CHAPTER 2
IGNATIUS SANCHO: MUSICIAN, MAN OF LETTERS, GROCER
Markman Ellis

Ignatius Sancho was a celebrity in eighteenth-century London. Of African descent, he was well known in London as a composer, writer, political commentator and businessman. He was also something of a *bon viveur* whose judgement, as a critic and man of taste, was highly valued. Sancho achieved more in his life than any of his available role models, and what he achieved, he did so on and in his own terms. In a period institutionally hostile to his race, and as a man who constantly suffered from the racism of the English, how did he, almost alone, attain these distinctions? This chapter surveys the evidence of his success in music, writing, politics and business through his own works and their impact on the historical record, considering in turn his achievements in each of these spheres of life, as he allowed it to be represented. At the end of the chapter, the biography of his early life, written by Joseph Jekyll, will be considered. Jekyll fills in the prehistory of Sancho's achievements, but in doing so, invents details and changes their meaning. Jekyll's biography inscribes Sancho in slavery, and turns his life into a slave narrative, a genre that Sancho pointedly eschewed.

Sancho first gained public fame with his popular dance music. He was a gifted performer on the quartet of instruments for which he composed: violin, mandolin, German-flute and harpsichord. In 1767, or thereabouts, Sancho's music was published as sheet music and music books by Richard Duke, one of London's leading violin makers and music publishers.[1] Duke's shop at the Great Turnstile in Holborn was a centre of sociability and intelligence for London's composers and performers. Long before such a term became current, Duke's was a prestigious 'music label'. Sancho's music was the kind that was performed for the *bon ton* at Vauxhall Pleasure Gardens, at assembly rooms and in the private gatherings of his elite patrons and employers. In each of his five published music collections, Sancho signalled the patronage of the polite elite, variously by the dukes of Buccleugh and Montagu, Mrs James Brudenell (the Duke of Montagu's sister-in-law), the Princess Royal and Catherine Anne North, daughter of the first minister, Lord North. The Montagus, like some other aristocratic families, were important patrons of the arts, sustaining not only the composition and performance of concert music, but also its main venues. In 1767, ledgers of the Duke of Montagu's household record a payment of five shillings for 'Musach books by Sancho'.[2] Sancho's first music miscellany was a collection of minuets, a form of music for a social dance by two people in the comparatively slow and stately 3/4 time. Thereafter he published four more collections over the following decade, including songs, further minuets for a quartet, and two collections of cotillions and country dances. The last of these, published in 1779,

Figure 2.1 Portrait of Ignatius Sancho, frontispiece to *Letters of the Late Ignatius Sancho* (1802). © The Trustees of the British Museum.

advertised that it could be purchased from the author 'at his Tea and Snuff-Shop' in Westminster. Sancho was arguably London's first Black dance music celebrity.

Just as Sancho's music was finding a public audience, he made his first impact in writing. In July 1766, he wrote a letter to the novelist Laurence Sterne, pleading with him to address slavery in his writing, for, he observed, few writers have hitherto 'drawn a tear in favour of my miserable black brethren'. Sancho entreated him to 'give half an hours attention to slavery (as it is at this day undergone in the West Indies)'.[3] Sterne was a much-celebrated author, not only for his eccentric novel *The Life and Opinions of Tristram Shandy Gentleman* (nine volumes, 1759–67), which had published its seventh and eighth volume in 1765, but also for *The Sermons of Mr Yorick* (seven volumes, 1760–9). The primary motivation for Sancho's letter was a sympathetic comment on the evils of slavery in the second volume of Sterne's *Sermons*, in which he had commented ' – Consider slavery – what it is, – how bitter a draught, and how many millions have been made to drink of it'.[4] As Sancho says, Sterne's attention to 'that subject, handled in your striking manner, would ease the yoke (perhaps) of many – but if only of one – Gracious God! – what a feast to a benevolent heart!'[5] Sancho's language here firmly allies him with writers of sensibility who urged reform and amelioration of social distress. In reply, Sterne evaded Sancho's request, though in fact the next volume of *Tristram Shandy* (Volume 9) included a disquieting debate between Corporal Trim and Uncle Toby about the inhumane treatment of a 'poor negro girl' encountered working in a shop. Their discussion of their common humanity with this woman underlines Sterne's sentimentally valorized opinion that 'a black wench' should not be used 'worse than a white one'.[6] Sancho's letter to Sterne was private, but Sterne was much taken with it, and copied it into his Letter Book. After Sterne's death in 1768, Sancho's letter was published in *Letters of the Late Rev. Mr. Laurence Sterne* in 1775, edited by his daughter Lydia de Medalle. It was subsequently reprinted in many newspapers and magazines.[7]

Building on his correspondence with Sterne, Sancho gained celebrity as a writer and critic in intellectual and artistic circles in London in the 1770s. He was a close friend of David Garrick, the artist John Hamilton Mortimer, the poet and writer on aesthetics Richard Payne Knight, the painter John Ireland and the sculptor Joseph Nollekens. Sancho was painted by Thomas Gainsborough at one rapid sitting on 29 November 1768 while at Bath, presumably alongside the Montagus, who also had their portraits done at that time. George Cumberland, a young writer making his way in London in 1779, included Sancho among a list of 'Geniuses and Men of Science' he had met over the previous year, in a list that included Sir Joseph Banks, Richard Sheridan, Samuel Johnson and Richard Price. In September 1779, Cumberland wrote to his brother that

> ... a Black Man, Ignatius Sancho, has lately put me into unbounded conceit with myself – he is said to be a great Judge of literary performances (G-d send it may be true.) and has praised my Tale of Cambambo and Journal wh[ich] I read to him, so highly, that I shall like him as long as I live, nothing less than publishing I fear will satisfy him – but what would not one do to oblige so good a kind of Man?[8]

Sancho's opinion was highly regarded, and, as the friend of many in the literary and artistic world in London, he was widely accepted as a judge of aesthetic value in English culture. In the view of the *Monthly Review*, 'Sancho may be styled – what is very uncommon for men of his complexion, *A Man of Letters.*'[9]

Sancho's renown as a writer and critic encouraged his friends to publish a volume of his letters after he died to benefit Sancho's widow and children. They collected over 1,200 subscribers, and made more than £500 for Anne Sancho. The book, in two volumes, was called *The Letters of Ignatius Sancho, an African*. It was published by John Nicholls, printer and bookseller in Red Lion Passage, off Fleet Street.[10] The book comprises 158 letters collected by Sancho's friend, Frances Crewe, herself the addressee of some letters, although some, such as those sent to Soubise in India, may come from copies in Sancho's possession. It is presented as a collection of Sancho's personal correspondence, including private letters addressed to his friends as well as public letters addressed to newspapers. Sancho's *Letters* is exemplary of eighteenth-century epistolary culture, but is also a glimpse into his private life, his networks of friends and acquaintances, and his interests and obsessions. The fact of its publication was a significant event, extending the celebrity he had attained in his lifetime.

Sancho's letters are a stylistic tour-de-force – one of the great displays of eighteenth-century epistolary virtuosity. Sancho's characteristic style has often been described as Shandean, both because his earliest extant letters are those he wrote to Lawrence Sterne, and because he adopts – consciously or unconsciously – a style that imitates or co-opts that of Sterne. This can be observed especially in Sancho's distinctive punctuation, which uses dashes in a variety of lengths to allow a freely flowing stream of ideas and allusions. The consequences are astonishing: dissolving the normal hold of grammar, while liberating creative flashes of brilliance and insight, pushing the paragraph into primacy over the sentence, connecting ideas by a pulsating rhythm. Sancho's prose is comic and satirical, making use of puns and innuendo, but also affecting and sentimental. There is a kind of prescient and experimental modernity to his style, which, like Sterne's, is somewhat out of time.

Sancho's distinctive literary style also has tactical significance in this period. This was a time in which the ability, as well as the right, of Black people to speak, write and, more especially, to publish was refuted or opposed by many. Enlightenment philosophers such as David Hume, Lord Monboddo and Immanuel Kant lined up to describe the very idea of African arts and letters as impossible or even fake. Sancho's tactical coup is that he writes in such an elegant, refined and modern manner, inhabiting a form of discourse associated with high culture and elite urban circles, and with aesthetic modernity. He does not write in the established neoclassical genres associated with formalists such as Alexander Pope, like Phyllis Wheatley. Nor does he write in the prose-fiction forms of Defoe's novels, criminal biography and spiritual biography, influential on Olaudah Equiano and the genre of the slave narrative. Instead, he aligns himself with Sterne and the Shandean *avant garde*: sentimental, comic, epistolary, political.

Sancho's *Letters* provide rich detail of his life and opinions. Readers learn a lot about his health, and that of his family; the movements of his friends and patrons; his interest in food and drink. Many letters touch on his domestic scene, centred on his wife Anne *née* Osborne (1733–1817), whom he had married in 1758 at St Margaret's Church Westminster. Together they had a large family, with nine children that Sancho engagingly referred to as his 'sanchonettas', and a dog called Nutts.[11] Sancho's letters give a lively portrait not only of the quotidian trials and excitements of family life, but also, Sancho's extensive social networks.

Sancho's letters also give evidence of his political opinions. When he first asserted these in the 1760s and 1770s, he did so as a man of African descent and a free citizen of Great Britain. He defended the rights of his fellow Black Britons, and he attacked the legitimacy of the slavery endured by his fellow Africans in the Caribbean. His letters attack the unthinking racism he encountered from ordinary British people, and reflect on the hypocrisy of Britain's supposedly free and Christian civility residing at the heart of the Atlantic slave economy. He was also the first Black British citizen to cast a vote in a British parliamentary election. Reflecting his place of residence, Sancho's electorate was Westminster, which had an unusually broad franchise: to vote one needed to pay 'scot and lot', a law-phrase describing the obligations levied on property owners by the local authorities. As a property owner and a taxpayer in Westminster, Sancho asserted his right to vote in the elections of 1774 and 1780.[12] Although the first stirrings of the anti-slavery movement were already being heard in the 1770s, Sancho wrote before the organized political agitation against the trade in slaves began in the 1780s, such as the 'Sons of Africa' group organized by Ottobah Cugoano and Olaudah Equiano in 1787.[13]

The fourth and final sphere of celebrity Sancho operated in was trade. Sancho capitalized on his celebrity in the last decade of his life by becoming a businessman. In establishing his business he used connections and skills forged while employed as a valet or household manager for the Montagu family – first Duke John (1690–1749), then Duchess Mary (1689–1751) and finally Duke George (1712–90). When he left the family's employment in November 1773, Sancho opened a grocery shop at No. 19, Charles Street, Westminster, close to the Montagu's principal residence in London at Privy Gardens. A contemporary recounted visiting Sancho's shop in 1780:

[A]s we pushed the wicket-door, a little tinkling bell, the usual appendage to such shops, announced its opening: we drank tea with Sancho and his black lady, who was seated, when we entered, in the corner of the shop, chopping sugar, surrounded by her little 'Sanchonets'.[14]

Sancho's shop sold grocery items, including his own brand of tobacco and tea. He wrote to a female friend (Letter XV) that 'the principal thing we aim at' in the grocery trade is to retail 'tea, snuff, and sugar, with the little articles of daily use', such as, he went on, 'soap, starch, and blue, with raisins, figures, &c.'[15] Such consumer goods, especially tobacco, tea and sugar, were products of the empire trade, dependent upon slavery and other forms of unfree labour, – an irony not lost on Sancho. One of his trade cards (see Figure 2.2), for example, advertised his 'best Trinidado', thought to be a kind of tobacco that he branded as being sourced from the Caribbean island of Trinidad. The card depicts a boy dressed in an indigenous Carib costume, sitting with a tobacco pipe and a tankard of beer, beside a puncheon of sugar, while an African boy harvests sugar cane or perhaps tobacco. Exotic commodities and subject races are drawn in zeugmatic embrace: both fictively untroubled by the coercive violence of slavery, and, under the imperial tropes of colonial plenty and leisured labour, freely offering up their exotic harvest to British consumers.

In his life, Sancho achieved celebrity in music, writing, politics and business. Although it was his *Letters* that kept his fame alive over the following decades, the book also reshaped his life and renown. When it was published, it was prefaced by a brief biography – 'Memoirs of the Life' – written by a young English lawyer, Joseph Jekyll, Member of Parliament for Eye in Suffolk. He was a friend of Frances Crewe, but was probably at best only a slight acquaintance of Sancho. As Brycchan Carey has argued, most of what is said in Jekyll's account cannot be corroborated, and indeed, it sometimes conflicts with what Sancho himself said.[16] Jekyll's leaden prose is very much at odds with Sancho's sentimental effusions. Jekyll also imparts a narrative shape to Sancho's life not present in the letters,

Figure 2.2 Ignatius Sancho's Trade Card, 'Sancho's Best Trinidado' (*c.* 1773). © Victoria and Albert Museum, London.

which creates an arc from slavery to freedom, from servant to merchant. While Sancho himself eschewed this emplotment, Jekyll reshaped his life into something that resembled a slave narrative. In doing so, he prepared the way for Sancho's garrulous and sprawling letters to serve as evidence for the nascent anti-slavery movement.

Jekyll's memoirs filled in, or perhaps invented, details of Sancho's early life. Although Sancho himself said he was born in Africa, Jekyll has him born on board a slave ship sailing between Africa and Cartagena, in the Spanish colony of New Grenada, in 1729. He says Sancho's parents died when he was very young: his mother of an illness, his father by suicide so as to escape the 'miseries of slavery'. Brought to Britain while little more than a child, Jekyll says Sancho lived in a household of 'three maiden sisters' in Greenwich. Though they preferred to keep him uneducated, his abilities in reading and writing were noticed by John, Duke of Montagu. The duke, writes Jekyll, 'admired in him a native frankness of manner as yet unbroken by servitude' and so 'indulged his turn for reading with presents of books'.[17] After Duke John's death in 1749, Sancho entered service as a free man in the Montagu family as a butler to the dowager duchess, and later as a valet to George Brudenell, Earl of Cardigan (who married into the Montagus and took their name). Jekyll imposes on Sancho's life some literary commonplaces: after the duke's death, he has Sancho contemplate suicide like his father, and later, having been left an annuity by the duchess, Jekyll suggests he led an indulgent and decadent life, in which he dissipated his fortune on the urban vices of gambling and women. In this period, Jekyll also claims that Sancho pursued a theatrical career, unsuccessfully attempting the parts of Othello and Oroonoko and writing two plays, both unperformed. There is no record of these events. How far Jekyll's account of Sancho's bohemianism can be squared with, in the same decade, his life in the service of the Montagus, and his marriage to Anne, is not clear.

Having entered the historical record in the 1760s, Sancho achieved a remarkable celebrity in London in the 1770s, well before Jekyll penned his memoir. In each sphere of his achievements, as a musician, a writer, a political commentator and a businessman, he reinforced his status as a free and independent citizen.[18] In telling his story, this chapter has relied on Sancho's own productions, as well as the substantial body of research on Sancho, his music, writing and politics, that has emerged in the last three decades. Sancho's own story, understood through his own achievements, eschews the institutionally racist framing given to his life by Jekyll within the emergent abolitionist movement.

Notes

1. Ignatius Sancho, *Minuets, Cotillons & Country Dances for the Violin, Mandolin, German Flute, & Harpsichord Composed by an African Most Humbly Inscribed to his Grace Henry Duke of Buccleugh* (London: Printed for the Author, [*c.* 1767]).

2. Oliver Ayres and Nicole Aljoe, 'Ignatius Sancho's London', New College of the Humanities London and Northeastern University, 2021–2, https://dcrn.northeastern.edu/ignatius-sanchos-london/.

3. Sancho to Sterne, 21 July 1776 [actually 1766], *Letters of the Late Ignatius Sancho: An African*, ed. Vincent Carretta (Peterborough, Ontario: Broadview Editions, 2015), 128–9.

4. Laurence Sterne, 'Sermon X: Job's account of the Shortness and Troubles of Life, considered', in *The Sermons of Laurence Sterne: The Text*, ed. Melvyn New, Florida edn, 9 vols (Gainesville: University Press of Florida, 1996), IV, 99.

5. Sancho, *Letters*, 125–6.

6. Laurence Sterne, *The Life and Opinions of Tristram Shandy, Gentleman: The Text*, ed. Melvyn and Joan New, Florida edn, 9 vols (Gainesville: University Press of Florida, 1978), II, 747–8.

7. Sancho, *Letters,* 333–4.

8. George Cumberland to Richard Cumberland, 17 September 1779, British Library Add MS 36492, f. 204r–v.

9. 'Letters of the Late Ignatius Sancho, An African', *Monthly Review*, December 1783, 492–7.

10. Ignatius Sancho, *Letters of the Late Ignatius Sancho, an African. In Two Volumes. To which are Prefixed, Memoirs of his Life* (London: Printed by J. Nichols, 1782).

11. Mary Ann (1759–1805), Frances Joanna (Fanny) (1761–1815), Thomas Johnson (1761–1805), Ann Alice (1763–6), Elizabeth Bruce (Betsy) (1766–1837), Jonathan William (1768–70), Lydia (1771–76), Catherine Margaret (Kitty) (1773–9) and William Leach Osborne (Billy) (1775–1810). Information on Sancho's children generously shared by Ayres and Aljoe, 'Ignatius Sancho's London'.

12. *A Correct Copy of the Poll, for electing Two Representatives in Parliament, for the City and Liberty of Westminster. Taken Oct. 11, 1774, and the Fifteen following Days* (London: Cox and Biggs, 1774), 15.

13. For the early history of the abolitionist movement, and the contribution of Black writers, see David Turley, *The Culture of English Antislavery, 1780–1860* (London: Routledge, 1991); and Ryan Hanley, *Beyond Slavery and Abolition: Black British Writing, c.1770–1830* (Cambridge: Cambridge University Press, 2018), 31–50, 180–2.

14. John Thomas Smith, *Nollekens and His Times* (1828; repr. London: Turnstile, 1949), 14.

15. Sancho to Mrs H – , 1 November 1773, Sancho, *Letters*, 102–3.

16. Brycchan Carey, '"The Extraordinary Negro": Ignatius Sancho, Joseph Jekyll, and the Problem of Biography', *British Journal for Eighteenth-Century Studies* 26, no. 1 (2003): 1–13.

17. Sancho, *Letters*, 49.

18. Vincent Caretta, 'Select Bibliography', in Sancho, *Letters*, 361–4.

CHAPTER 3
THE 'BLACK-BIRDS' OF ST GILES: RETHINKING PLACE AND COMMUNITY IN EIGHTEENTH-CENTURY LONDON

Nicole N. Aljoe and Savita Maharaj

On the morning of 10 May 1782, Esther Allingham – identified as a 'negro' in the records of the Old Bailey – left the lodgings she rented on Litchfield Street in the St Giles area of London. According to the trial transcript, Allingham had lived on Litchfield Street for 'almost a twelvemonth'. How and when Allingham came to be living in St Giles, we do not know, and nothing in the record suggests that she was an enslaved woman. However, it does seem clear that she was likely engaged in sex work – during the trial, she declared her refusal 'to give up her carcase [sic] [. . .] for nothing'. After leaving St Giles, Allingham made her way south towards Pall Mall in St James's. There she saw a visitor from Portugal, John Baptista, who said he had been at the Orange Coffee-house (likely the Prince Orange Coffee-House near Haymarket and Cockspur) with 'a Black woman with a white gown and white coat on'.[1] Returning west, Allingham re-encountered Baptista, who was now alone. After he propositioned her, Allingham took Baptista to a house in Gloucester Court in Westminster. Subsequently, a loud disagreement ensued, neighbours contacted the police, and Baptista accused Allingham of stealing nine guineas and two half-guineas from him. Allingham was taken into custody and imprisoned to await trial at the Old Bailey on 15 May.

We assume this story would end with Allingham's victimization and further imprisonment. However, instead, the First Middlesex jury, sitting before Judge Mr Baron Perryn, found Allingham 'not guilty'. Her money was returned to her, and Allingham was set free.[2] This brief yet vivid tale of Allingham's legal triumph provides a key example of the complexity and diversity of Black lives in London during the eighteenth century. More specifically, the record of Allingham's trial challenges three key assumptions about Black people and, more specifically, Black women in London during the eighteenth century. First, Allingham's residence in St Giles suggests she might have been a member of the 'St Giles blackbirds' – a supposed eighteenth-century reference to the members of a Black community that lived in St Giles. Though some recent scholarship has called into question the existence of a historically Black community in St Giles in the eighteenth century, archival data and stories such as Allingham's and others suggest that a number of Black people, in fact, did live and work in a likely small, but certainly a kind of Black community.[3] Secondly, the evocative reference to the mysterious Black woman dressed all in white, along with the details of Allingham's movements across London from St Giles to Pall Mall to Gloucester Court, challenges descriptions of the social isolation of the Black community in eighteenth-century London.[4] And finally, the successful outcome of Allingham's trial complicates the rhetoric of isolation often used to suggest the inherent victimization and disempowerment of Black Londoners.[5] Taken together, a close analysis of Allingham's experiences challenges assumptions about the social geographies of London's early Black communities. The narrative of Allingham's encounters and movements across London instead reveals a more nuanced story about eighteenth-century Black people and conceptions of community and place that are neither hidden nor absent from the archives.

*   *   *

St Giles has a history of movement regarding both class and race, especially as London grew. Though incorporated into Camden borough after 1965, St Giles was originally a stand-alone parish situated just north of Westminster. Named after the patron saint of lepers, St Giles housed a leper hospital as early as 1141. Relatedly, the poor also had a long history in the area, and many destitute Irish settled there during the seventeenth and eighteenth centuries. As the city of London grew and more wealthy people moved into Westminster and St James's, St Giles became one of the areas where people who performed domestic services for the upper classes and nobility lived. The St Giles area was also associated with actors and bohemians because of its proximity to the theatres on Drury Lane.[6]

Writing in *Staying Power*, a foundational text on Black British history, Peter Fryer notes:

> There is said to have been a concentration of destitute Black people in the St Giles or Seven Dials district, [...] it was a mass of insanitary hovels where beggars, whores, criminals, and other outcasts congregated. According to one late eighteenth-century source, Black mendicants, conspicuous among London's beggars, were dubbed 'St Giles blackbirds'.[7]

St Giles was also one of several areas in London pejoratively known as a 'rookery' – a term intended to reflect the squalid living conditions in which people seemed to 'roost' on top of one another, like birds. Indeed, it is telling that rooks are a type of black bird. And, as Markman Ellis has pointed out, black birds, at least within the fiction of the era, such as the caged starling in Laurence Sterne's *A Sentimental Journey* (1768) (which comes right before an abolitionist apostrophe) were also metaphorically associated with Black people at the time.[8]

In addition to Fryer, numerous twentieth-century scholars have claimed that a historic Black community existed in the St Giles area in eighteenth-century London.[9] However, more recently, other scholars have argued that there is little explicit demographic documentation of significant numbers of Black people living and working in St Giles to support the existence of such a community. And moreover, 'those who followed [and repeated the detail] without doing any further research [have] created a myth'.[10]

However, dismissing the notion of St Giles as a historical eighteenth-century Black community overlooks the fact that descriptions and definitions of community are often rhetorical moves. Indeed, the term *community* has been deployed throughout society and academic scholarship in a variety of ways.[11] As well, considering the diversity of the Black community at this time – which we know consisted of Black British free citizens, sailors, soldiers, servants, sex workers, enslaved people, free labourers and so on – how would a 'Black community' even be defined at this time? Certainly, it feels presentist and anachronistic to define notions of eighteenth-century Black British community through twentieth-century examples of communities like Brixton and 1960s Notting Hill. Is it possible that the multiple anecdotal and archival references to Black people in the St Giles and Covent Garden area – as well as across the city of London – may instead speak to alternative articulations of community? Indeed, assertions of community amongst Black people in history also offer ways for scholars and Black Britons to claim physical and metaphorical space within British social histories and narratives.

Writing in *Black and British: A Forgotten History*, David Olusoga explains that '[t]here is some evidence that black people living in Georgian London did cooperate and look out for one another, and stronger evidence that they sought out one another's company and came together for social occasions'.[12] The life and letters of Ignatius Sancho, explored by Markman Ellis in this volume, confirm such views of Black British networks of affiliation. Sancho met and married his wife, Anne, a London-born Black woman, and his letters document relationships with several members of Anne's extended family, the Clark-Osbornes (who also lived in London), as well as his relationships with other Black British men such as the dandy Julius Soubise and musician Charles Lincoln.[13] Indeed, as Olusoga notes:

> [B]lack people in seventeenth- and eighteenth-century Britain were what today is called a 'visible minority', they would have been aware of one another and in a position to cooperate potentially. As well as sharing a physical, 'racial' identity they had shared experiences [. . . which] will naturally have drawn them together.[14]

As Olusoga suggests, there are enticing possibilities of affective connections and other alternative manifestations of London's eighteenth-century Black community. One of the most frequently cited is the group of free Africans – possibly including Olaudah Equiano and Ottobah Cugoano – who called themselves the 'Sons of Africa' and were active during the rise of the abolitionist movement in England. Together the 'Sons of Africa' wrote a series of letters advocating abolition and the cessation of the slave trade to the *Morning Chronicle* and *London Advertiser* in 1787, in addition to people like lawyer Granville Sharp and abolitionist MP Sir William Dolben. One of the most striking features of the letters is that they offer a printed representation of an imagined symbolic connection across the community of London's eighteenth-century Black residents – a Black British print public, as it were.[15] Other examples of these networks include the following note that appeared in a London newspaper in 1764:

> Among the sundry fashionable routs or clubs that are held in town, that of the Blacks or Negro servants is not the least. On Wednesday night last, no less than

fifty-seven of them, men and women, supped, drank, and entertained themselves with dancing and music, consisting of violins, French horns, and other instruments, at a public-house in Fleet-street, till four in the morning. No Whites were allowed to be present, for all the performers were Blacks.[16]

The language of the notice suggests that this party was not an isolated event. Olusoga notes that other similar all-Black parties took place at the Yorkshire Stingo, a pub on London's north-western outskirts. Another is documented in the diary of the magistrate John Baker, who served as Solicitor-General to the island of St Kitts. Baker records one evening in the 1760s when he arrived at his London home and discovered that his Black servant, Jack Beef, had 'gone out to a ball of the Blacks'.[17]

In addition to the collaboration amongst the Sons of Africa and other Black networks, German novelist Sophie von la Roche recounts seeing a funeral cortege consisting solely of Black people while on her way to see a play in Sadlers Wells in London in the 1780s.[18] And in his history of London in the eighteenth century, Jerry White notes that in addition to servants, sailors and labourers

> ... some blacks also made a living as performers and exhibits in fairgrounds and public halls. [Including] a black woman rope-dancer in a booth at Bartholomew Fair near Smithfield in East London at the opening of the century, a flexible black man [who] demonstrated his double joints in London in December 1751, and [the exhibition of individuals like ...] Amelia Lewsam, a black albino from Jamaica, in the 1760s and later.[19]

Descriptions of the social movements of Black people in London, and specifically here, Black women, also appeared in *Harris's List of Covent Garden Ladies*. Published between 1757 and 1795, the list operated as an effective marketing tool for the extremely diverse sex industry in London. Listed within are references to at least four women described explicitly as Black, all of whom are described as living in the St Giles and Covent Garden areas: Black Moll at Hedge Lane; Signori Fr-si- at Ludgate Hill, near the King's Bench; Mrs Ends at Williams Cheesemongers, on Church Street in Soho; and finally, Miss W-l-n on Litchfield Street, Soho.[20] One of the most famous Black sex workers in London of the era, Harriot – whose fictionalized story appeared in the TV show *Harlots* (2017–19) – is described in another eighteenth-century guidebook to sex workers, *Nocturnal Revels; Or, the History of King's-Place and Other Modern Nunneries* (1779); she also spent time in Covent Garden, near St Giles. Brought to London from Jamaica by her enslaver, then owner, Harriot turned to sex work after his death. First, she worked in a brothel at King's-Place in Mayfair, then moved to Monmouth Street in Covent Garden for several years. Although this group of sex workers cannot be described as a numerically large or dense community, the fact remains that some Black people did live and work in St Giles.

The myriad references to the Black sex workers, performers, families, the 'all-Black' parties, and the range of other representations in St Giles, as well as in different locations across London, also suggests that Black Londoners might not necessarily have lived and socialized in the same areas.[21] Indeed, denying the possibility of any kind of Black community in St Giles or elsewhere in London seems related to ideologies of exclusion that seek the containment of Black Britishness. Although St Giles might not have been a substantial, permanent or even predominantly Black community like Brixton or Notting Hill in the 1960s, the fact remains that it could have and likely had operated as a kind of community for some Black British people.

This more nuanced portrait of the various movements and locations associated with Black people in London raises the possibility that the stories about the people within that community might also be more varied. A closer examination of the representations of Black people, such as sex workers like Esther Allingham, with whom this chapter began, might contribute to a more subtle understanding of the social geographies of eighteenth-century Black London. Reconsidering the spaces and places where Black people appeared in eighteenth-century London is necessary because it communicates a more complex understanding of the diversity of Black British lives in history that can contribute to more inclusive articulations of British national identities.

* * *

Although recent television shows like *Bridgerton* (2020–) and *Harlots* have been criticized for engaging in 'ahistorical' and 'woke' colour-blind casting in their inclusively diverse articulation of the Regency period, they work to challenge the lack of nuance in the archive in relation to Blackness and Black communities in London and the United Kingdom. Frequently described as 'anachronistic', these representations are castigated for reimagining eighteenth-century Black life outside the usual frames of slavery and abolition. However, these critiques miss an essential component of such casting decisions – we know that prior representations of the era did not reveal its known diversity and complexity. As archival discoveries have challenged our understanding of the locations and lives of women and the working class during this era, they also tell similarly varied stories about the antecedents of today's Black Britons. Although Black people in London in the eighteenth century might have been frequently negatively characterized as living in poverty and disempowered, the reality is that, like all people, they led complex lives.

Notes

1. 'Esther Allingham', *Proceedings of the Old Bailey*, https://www.oldbaileyonline.org/browse. jsp?id=t17820515-27&div=t17820515-27.

2. Ibid.

3. See Kathleen Chater, *Untold Histories: Black People in England and Wales During the Period of the British Slave Trade, 1660–1807* (Manchester: Manchester University Press, 2009), 50.

4. 'Esther Allingham', *Proceedings of the Old Bailey*.

5. Ibid.

6. Chater, *Untold Histories*, 42.

7. Peter Fryer, *Staying Power: The History of Black People in Britain* (London: Pluto Press, 1984), 77.

8. Markman Ellis, *The Politics of Sensibility: Race, Gender and Commerce in the Sentimental Novel* (Cambridge: Cambridge University Press, 1996), 71–9.

9. Gretchen Gerzina, *Black London: Life before Emancipation* (New Brunswick, NJ: Rutgers University Press, 1995), 19; Wylie Sypher, *Guinea's Captive Kings* (Chapel Hill: University of North Carolina Press, 1942), 2; James Walvin *Black Presence: A Documentary History of the Presence of the Negro in England 1555–1860* (London: Orbach & Chambers, 1971), 14.

10. Chater, *Untold Histories*, 50. Chater points out that all references, including that by Fryer and subsequent others, to eighteenth-century Black people in London as 'St Giles' blackbirds' are founded on a letter originally written in French by Carl Wadström, a Swede who had travelled through Europe in 1782, which was reproduced in his *Essay on Colonisation* (1794). She argues that the French word for 'merle' was mistranslated as 'blackbird' – it also means 'rascal' or 'criminal'. And moreover, that this, coupled with the absence of documentary evidence, proves that the idea of a Black community in St Giles is a myth.

11. Ibid., 38.

12. David Olusoga, *Black and British: A Forgotten History* (London: Pan Books, 2017), 99–100.

13. Baptismal Records, St Mary's Church, Whitechapel Parish, London Metropolitan Archives.

14. Olusoga, *Black and British*, 99.

15. Gerzina, *Black London*, 191.

16. *London Chronicle*, 16–18 February 1764.

17. Olusoga, *Black and British,* 100.

18. Sophie von la Roche, *Sophie in London 1786, being the Diary of Sophie v. la Roche*, trans. Clare Williams (London: Jonathan Cape, 1933), 131.

19. Jerry White, *London in the Eighteenth Century: A Great and Monstrous Thing* (London: Bodley Head, 2012), 133.

20. Gerzina, *Black London*, 51; *Harris's List of Covent Garden Ladies; Or, Man of Pleasure's Kalendar for the Year 1793* (London: n.p., 1793), 82; *Harris's List of Covent Garden Ladies; Or, Man of Pleasure's Kalendar for the Year 1773* (London: n.p., 1773), 18; [Anon.], *Nocturnal Revels; Or, the History of King's-Place and Other Modern Nunneries* (London: n.p., 1779), 269.

21. Indeed, more recent archival references that have surfaced due to the increasing digitization of area archives and closer attention to the often-ephemeral references to people of colour, suggest that the story of the St Giles 'black-birds' is a more attenuated one. Working on a recent digital mapping project of eighteenth-century Black London, our team has identified several Black people living in the St Giles/Covent Garden area. Oliver Ayres and Nicole Aljoe, 'Ignatius Sancho's London', New College of the Humanities and Northeastern University, 2021–2, dcrn.northeastern.edu/ignatius-sanchos-london.

CHAPTER 4
STYLING THE OTHER: HAZLITT'S 'THE INDIAN JUGGLERS'
Uttara Natarajan

In 1813, a troupe of jugglers from the Madras Presidency of British India travelled to England, their chief, Ramasamy, having apparently overcome earlier misgivings about making the journey.[1] Their first public performances began in Pall Mall in July of that year, inaugurating the career in Britain, Europe and the United States of 'the most famous Indian magician of the nineteenth century'.[2] He was renamed and surnamed for the purpose, abandoning the south Indian single-name system of nomenclature, as 'Ramo Samee'. The name was to become a byword, synonymous with the feats of sword-swallowing and juggling. In Thackeray's *The Book of Snobs* (1848), for instance, 'the Hereditary Princess of Potztausend-Donnerwetter [...] almost swallow[s] [...her knife], [...] like Ramo Samee, the Indian juggler'.[3] And in an essay of 1854, Dickens describes a young greengrocer, one Slaughter, 'practising Ramo Samee with three potatoes'.[4]

The great urban essayist, William Hazlitt, does not mention the name, but his essay 'The Indian Jugglers' (1819) remains the most eloquent testament by an eyewitness to Ramo Samee's skill.

> Coming forward and seating himself on the ground in his white dress and tightened turban, the chief of the Indian Jugglers begins with tossing up two brass balls, which is what any of us could do, and concludes with keeping up four at the same time, which is what none of us could do to save our lives, nor if we were to take our whole lives to do it in. Is it then a trifling power we see at work, or is it not something next to miraculous? It is the utmost stretch of human ingenuity, which nothing but the bending the faculties of body and mind to it from the tenderest infancy with incessant, ever-anxious application up to manhood, can accomplish or make even a slight approach to. Man, thou art a wonderful animal, and thy ways past finding out! (77–8)[5]

A comparison of this description with another contemporary record, bearing the same title and reviewing Ramo Samee's earliest performances, is illuminating. Here is an extract from a report titled 'The Indian Jugglers' in *The Satirist, or Monthly Meteor* (August 1813):

> The first tricks are performed with cups and balls. These are [...] only remarkable for the superiority of their execution in the hands of this black Juggler. The cups seem enchanted: the balls fly: they increase in number: they diminish: now one,

Figure 4.1 James Green, *The Indian Jugglers* (*c*. 1814) © Thomas Coulborn & Sons. A painting, dated to 1814, by James Green (1771–1834), a watercolour artist of established if modest reputation at the time, is almost certainly of Ramo Samee. Other memorable contemporary portraits include the numerous illustrations that accompanied notices and reviews of his performances, first in Pall Mall and later at the Royal Coburg and elsewhere. Indian jugglers figured regularly as Oriental subjects in English paintings of the nineteenth century.

now two, now three, now none under the cup: and now the serpent, the cobra de capella, usurps the place of a small globule of cork, and winds its snaky folds as if from under the puny vessel. The facility with which this dexterous feat is accomplished, gives life and animation to the sable countenance of the artist [. . .][6]

The tenor of the *Satirist's* comments (playing down the jugglers' abilities, harping on their colour) is markedly divergent from Hazlitt's. Although Hazlitt's 'The Indian Jugglers' was published some years after the *Satirist's* report, its opening reads like a direct riposte. Hazlitt's indignant 'Is it then a trifling power we see at work, or is it not something next to miraculous?' answers the qualification in the *Satirist's* '*only* remarkable' (my emphasis); his inclusion of the jugglers in our common humanity ('Man, thou art a wonderful animal') emphatically counters the epithets of 'black Juggler' and 'sable countenance'. Constructed, certainly, as 'other' to the essayist, his skill an instance of the achievable pinnacle of 'mechanical skill', in contrast to the unachievable perfection of 'art' (82), in Hazlitt's essay, Ramo Samee is categorized on this basis with other renowned London performers: 'Richer, the famous rope-dancer' (79) and 'John Cavanagh, the famous hand fives-player' (86). Notably, the 'other' of the essay is not primarily a racialized other.

I use 'primarily' advisedly. John Whale has rightly pointed out both Hazlitt's failure to name the juggler, denying him individuality in so doing, and his enforcing of cultural difference in his comments on the palpable nature of the juggler's achievements:[7]

> If the Juggler were told that by flinging himself under the wheels of the Jaggernaut, when the idol issues forth on a gaudy day, he would immediately be transported into Paradise, he might believe it, and nobody could disprove it. So the Brahmins may say what they please on that subject, may build up dogmas and mysteries without end, and not be detected: but their ingenious countryman cannot persuade the frequenters of the Olympic Theatre that he performs a number of astonishing feats without actually giving proofs of what he says. (81)

The assertion of the superiority of English rationality to Indian superstition must grate on the present-day reader. But perhaps we should be wary, too, of reacting to one kind of othering by another, when we make Hazlitt's assumption of cultural superiority to the juggler the basis of our assumption of cultural superiority to Hazlitt. At the very least, we might also consider a counter-process, in the extent to which the essay surmounts othering to achieve a form of intersubjectivity.

To begin this consideration, we may fruitfully turn our focus to style. 'The Indian Jugglers' shows convincingly the exemplary fit of the essayistic form to metropolitan content,[8] as an extraordinary urban spectacle finds its consummate expression in the prose that describes it:

> To catch four balls in succession in less than a second of time, and deliver them back so as to return with seeming consciousness to the hand again, to make them revolve round him at certain intervals, like the planets in their spheres, to make them chase one another like sparkles of fire, or shoot up like flowers or meteors, to throw them behind his back and twine them round his neck like ribbons or like serpents, to do what appears an impossibility, and to do it with all the ease, the grace, the carelessness imaginable, to laugh at, to play with the glittering mockeries, to follow them with his eye as if he could fascinate them with its lambent fire, or as if he had only to see that they kept time with the music on the stage – there is something in all this which he who does not admire may be quite sure he never really admired any thing in the whole course of his life. (78)

Valuable in the first place as a record of the performance, Hazlitt's single-sentence description also displays the mimetic capabilities of the essay form, its ability to keep pace with the swift changes and transitions of a sensational West End show. Moreover, and more uniquely to Hazlitt, the sentence encapsulates, like many of his long sentences, the intimate connection between his essayistic style and his moral and philosophical emphases. Characteristic of Hazlitt's essays is the extended compound sentence that gathers amplitude and brilliancy from clause after clause in its progress towards a repeatedly deferred close. In that close, innumerable diverse particulars are at once constituted into a whole, grounded in and revealing the essayist's persona. Each such sentence, indeed, secrets an epistemology, a model of knowledge expressly set out in Hazlitt's philosophical writings. According to this model, our knowledge of things is only possible because of the mind's ability to unify, or to abstract from the infinitesimal particulars that constitute each object of our perception, an intelligible whole. The whole, that is, is both less than the sum of its parts – because it passes over some of those parts – and greater – *because* it is a whole, surmounting the breakdown ad infinitum of each particular detail or characteristic into further particulars. All our perceptions, then, are a symbiosis of the actual (the particular details of the object that we perceive) and the imagined (its wholeness), or synonymously, of real and ideal, object and self. The more detailed our perceptions, the closer they are to what is real, yet also the more creative, attesting to the power of an imagination that is able to combine a myriad of details into a coherent whole. Hazlitt's magnificent compound sentences exemplify this theory of abstraction.[9] The sentence that describes the juggler's performance realizes, in its profuse and vivid detail, the performance for that reader, at the same time that it idealizes it, imparting to it a wholeness and – to use a term from Romantic aesthetics – a sublimity, generated by the essayist's imagination.

The idealizing imagination, entailing the imposition of the self on the object of its perception, has often been described as a colonizing imagination; among numerous other instances, we may conveniently cite Alison Hickey, who 'use[s] the term "imperial" broadly, to refer to a kind of imagination that appropriates, incorporates, assimilates, permeates, infuses difference with unity'.[10] Hazlitt's epistemology, where unity is imposed by the imagining self on the myriad particulars of the other, may surely be said to confirm the epithet. But pulling against the colonizing tendency of imagination in this epistemology is its emphasis on the retention of detail. If the imposition of the self *on* the other is self-centred, an inward-looking activity, the attention by the self *to* the other is outwardly directed; the balance of the two is the condition of knowledge. The greater the detail in the imagination's perception of the other, the more authentic the whole that it creates, yet also the greater its power in generating that whole. Thus detail is the common ground of the real and the imaginary. Precluding the collapse of the other into the self, it is the basis rather of a *relation* between self and other.

Just such a relation is established between the essayist and the juggler in Hazlitt's intensely attentive and, in this case, celebratory rendering of the details of the performance. Its careful and particularizing attention undercuts the anonymizing and generalizing impulse descried by Whale; its celebratory tenor, the antithesis of 'intellectual' and 'mechanical' practices (79) instituted by the essay. In this instance, furthermore, the sentence also deliberately mimics that which it describes, matching, in its perpetual movement, its skilfully deferred conclusion, the balls that the juggler keeps in the air so gracefully and for so long. The outward-looking tendency that already qualifies the epistemological impulse of a colonizing imagination is strengthened as the 'other' becomes – in a version that departs from the more recognizably Orientalist reports of the era – the model for the self.[11] Complicating its own assertion of the superiority of intellectual to manual ability, Hazlitt's essay elicits the resemblance of a skill with balls to a skill in prose. In the mirroring of the visual spectacle by the verbal performance, the juggler becomes the alter ego of the essayist, the act with balls, a metaphor for the act of prose.

This metaphor, suggested at the opening of the essay, is reiterated at its close. That Hazlitt returns at the end of the essay from a sustained exposition of the more arduous demands (and hence pre-eminence) of intellectual effort to a celebration once again of physical dexterity, is telling. His description, reproducing a previously-published obituary, of the legendary fives player, John Cavanagh, an Irish Catholic and also, like Ramo Samee, an immigrant in London, explicitly and repeatedly draws parallels between Cavanagh's physical prowess and the cerebral achievements of his contemporaries, very much to the detriment of the latter:

> His blows were not undecided and ineffectual – lumbering like Mr. Wordsworth's epic poetry, nor wavering like Mr. Coleridge's lyric prose, nor short of the mark like Mr. Brougham's speeches, nor wide of it like Mr. Canning's wit, nor foul like the *Quarterly*, not *let* balls like the *Edinburgh Review*. Cobbett and Junius together would have made a Cavanagh. (87)

The comparisons, by which ball-playing surpasses text, are anticipated by similar comparisons at the start of the essay, where Ramo Samee is the focus: 'The hearing a speech in Parliament, drawled or stammered out by the Honourable Member or the Noble Lord, the ringing the changes on their common-places [...] stirs me not a jot, shakes not my good opinion of myself: but the seeing the Indian Jugglers does. It makes me ashamed of myself' (78–9).

Not the intellectual successes of his contemporaries, but the performances, transformed into metaphor, of two exceptional London players, one in the theatre, the other at sport, provide Hazlitt, himself a keen fives player, with the models to which his own art aspires. The essay begins and ends with the play of balls, the essayist aspiring to make the third in a trio of players. In its arrangement of mutually reflecting mirrors – the juggler, the essayist, Cavanagh – the hierarchy of self and other is destabilized. Yet in the see-saw of merit between intellectual excellence and manual dexterity, Hazlitt's own skill with words shows so far to advantage, that it grants a permanence to the otherwise ephemeral visual experience. Replicated, the astonishing displays of his subjects are retained by the essayist's prose. 'The Indian Jugglers' is all too unconscious of the story, unfolding in and beyond its moment, of Ramo Samee's chequered career and impoverished end. He was to entertain London audiences – in popular venues such as the Royal Coburg (now the Old Vic) and, in the West End, the Adelphi and the Olympic; often also at the more gentrified Vauxhall Gardens – for more than three decades, before he died in August 1850, a pauper at the last, his death announced in *Bell's Life in London*, which undertook, with negligible success, to raise money for his burial in St Pancras Churchyard.[12] Ignorant as it is of the vicissitudes to come, Hazlitt's essay renders his electric effect on his viewers with dazzling immediacy, and as it does so, immediately opens, too, a window, into the spectacular cosmopolitanism of the great city of the Regency era.

Notes

1. The original name is usually assumed to be 'Ramaswamy', but my un-Sanskritized 'Ramasamy' is more in keeping with the very low south Indian caste (*Dombar* or *Dommara*) to which the juggler probably belonged, and which Thurston records as 'a tribe of tumblers, athletes, and mountebanks'. Also, 'They are skilful jugglers, and both men and women are very clever tumblers and tight-rope dancers' – Edgar Thurston (and K. Rangachari), *Castes and Tribes of Southern India*, 7 vols (Madras: Government Press, 1909), II, 185. Thurston adds that 'In the matter of food, they eat all sorts of animals, including pigs, cats, and crows' (ibid., 185–6), which makes nonsense of the notion that Ramasamy was initially reluctant to leave India on caste grounds. The easy assumption of a Sanskritized name, and the ready acceptance from a colonial source of a motivation (unwillingness to cross the ocean or 'black water') applicable only to the higher castes, is an indication of the upper-caste biases that persist in present-day narratives of colonial history.

2. John Zubrzycki, *Jadoowallahs, Jugglers, and Jinns: A Magical History of India* (Delhi: Picador India, 2018), 200. Zubrzycki's book is a lively and informative read, with excellent illustrations; Ramo Samee is the subject of chapter 8, 'Crossing the *Kala Pani*' (192–215).

3. W. M. Thackeray, *The Book of Snobs* (London: Punch Office, 1848), 6. I have used the first edition in the absence of a standard modern edition.

4. Charles Dickens, 'An Unsettled Neighbourhood' (*Household Words*, 11 November 1854), in *Selected Journalism 1850–1870*, ed. David Pascoe (Harmondsworth: Penguin, 1997), 46.

5. All citations of Hazlitt's 'The Indian Jugglers' are from *The Collected Works of William Hazlitt*, ed. P. P. Howe, 21 vols (London and Toronto: J. M. Dent, 1930–4), VIII. Page references to this volume are given in the main body of the text.

6. 'The Indian Jugglers', *The Satirist, or Monthly Meteor*, 1 August 1813, 98.

7. John Whale, 'Indian Jugglers: Hazlitt, Romantic Orientalism, and the Difference of View', in *Romanticism and Colonialism: Writing and Empire, 1780–1830*, ed. Tim Fulford and Peter J. Kitson (Cambridge: Cambridge University Press, 1998), 213, 215–16. Whale's concern is with the way in which the essay exposes the limits of imaginative sympathy, and thus of 'the ethical basis of Romantic aesthetics' (ibid., 207).

8. This fit, of the genre of the essay to the urban subject, has been argued persuasively in recent scholarship, for instance, David Russell's *Tact: Aesthetic Liberalism and the Essay Form in Nineteenth-Century Britain* (Princeton, NJ: Princeton University Press, 2017); see especially Russell's opening chapter on Lamb, 12–40. See also Simon Peter Hull, *The Familiar Essay, Romantic Affect and Metropolitan Culture: The Sweet Security of Streets* (Newcastle upon Tyne: Cambridge Scholars Publishing, 2018).

9. For a fuller account of the way in which Hazlitt's theory of abstraction underwrites his 'familiar style', see Uttara Natarajan, 'The Veil of Familiarity: Romantic Philosophy and the Familiar Essay', *Studies in Romanticism* 42, no. 1 (2003): 35–7.

10. Alison Hickey, *Impure Conceits: Rhetoric and Ideology in Wordsworth's 'Excursion'* (Stanford, CA: Stanford University Press, 1997), 133.

11. A number of scholars have analysed the Orientalist aspects of the representations of Indian jugglers in nineteenth-century Britain. Sarah Dadswell, for instance, offers a useful overview of the changing perceptions from the early nineteenth century to the present day: Sarah Dadswell, 'Jugglers, Fakirs, and *Jaduwallahs*: Indian Magicians and the British Stage', *New Theatre Quarterly* 23, no. 1 (2007): 3–24; see 5–8 for a discussion of Ramo Samee in particular. In an article of the same year, Peter Lamont and Crispin Bates contend that in the nineteenth century, the skills of Indian jugglers contributed to the association of India with magic, in turn central to an English construction of India as a spiritually or mentally advanced Other, evoking elements of awe and admiration notably absent in Said's model: Peter Lamont and Crispin Bates, 'Conjuring Images of India in Nineteenth-Century Britain', *Social History* 32, no. 3 (2007): 308–24.

12. For further details, see Zubrzycki, *Jadoowallahs, Jugglers and Jinns*, especially 205–9.

CHAPTER 5
BEGGING PLACES: POVERTY, RACE AND VISIBILITY ON LUDGATE HILL, *c.* 1815
David Hitchcock

When someone begs, they are asking for more than casual charity. They are asking to be *seen* even just briefly, even just sidelong. Begging asks not for a lingering and considered gaze, but rather for mere acknowledgement: they are here, human, suffering and real. To work at all, begging must be visible, not just in the everyday sense of sight but also socially, so that others may see the person begging be relieved, or spurned, and in turn feel drawn themselves. The relationship between begging, public spaces and urban density accordingly dates to ancient societies; the streets in cities and towns became not just makeshift shelters for the homeless poor at night, but a necessary part of their daytime survival strategies, and streets retain this dual role today. Begging people find begging *places*, they use every aspect of their bodies and surroundings to become as visible as possible, generally without puncturing the ephemeral 'order' of public spaces and people's movements in and through them. Begging also seems to require people to display a map of their misfortunes, often signified visually by ragged clothing or embodied in visible scarring, physical disability or other injury. This mute representation of miseries works to counter the endless distrust that begging people encounter; they represent an ethical quandary for passers-by only solved by either categorically disbelieving all claims to charity, or by stopping and helping. Begging is intrinsically gestural, embodied and spatial: 'by rights', Tim Hitchcock writes, 'beggars were supposed to cringe and supplicate; to hold their bodies in an attitude of submission', but if a more threatening attitude proved successful, beggars would use that too.[1]

How forcefully or often must someone beg to be, or be represented as, a beggar? Do we need to know that someone begged in the past or can we settle for a series of representations of them standing in public in the begging way? Should we lump together poorer and marginalized Londoners working the margins of their urban and charitable landscapes, displaying themselves and their maps of misfortune streetside, as all part of a London that 'begged' for help, whether for casual work or casual charity? Or should we split apart the intrinsically ephemeral economies of makeshift which kept body and soul together in pursuit of more individuated accounts of survival? This chapter takes the first route, and is organized around a person who 'stood' in one place so resolutely that they entered into popular memory, a person shown begging who may not have done, a person who stood 'in the same place longer than many buildings' and so had 'a greater right to appear on a map, than many landmarks'.[2]

Begging *people* make begging places, and the person whose place binds this chapter together is Charles McGee. We first encounter Charles McGee in John Thomas Smith's

Vagabondiana in 1817.[3] Smith informs us that Charles was a one-eyed, elderly Black man from Jamaica who stood at the foot of Ludgate Hill in the late eighteenth and early nineteenth centuries.[4] Charles and other 'famous' beggars of colour like him, whose stoic endurance and resolute emplacement about the city enabled their lives to be interrogated and their likenesses drawn, serve collectively as both cipher and stand-in for an unnamed and unheralded number of homeless people drawn from Britain's imperial peripheries. In Regency London, their presence, difference and visibility marked them both as exotic objects of charity and fascination, and as tattered boundary markers past the limits of urban respectability. Charles stood abutting the Obelisk at the foot of Ludgate Hill, itself apocryphally part of the highest point in the city of London and within shouting distance of St Paul's Cathedral, which towered over the neighbouring coffeehouses, taverns, the nearby Liberty of the Fleet Debtor's Prison, and overshadowed the much humbler parish church of St Martin within Ludgate.

Charles Booth's later 1886–1903 poverty maps of London show Ludgate Hill as a wealthy non-residential area within the city centre, but also show it as well within walking distance of poorer streets in Smithfield (notably near the meat market) and only a short journey from the much poorer neighbourhoods across the Thames in Southwark.[5] Charles McGee's begging place 'opposite the Obelisk' at the 'foot' of the hill suggests he stood at the intersection of Bridge Street and Ludgate Hill (which becomes Ludgate Street and leads to St Pauls), within sight of the 'Albion Insurance Company' prominently housed on one corner of the intersection.

Figure 5.1 *Bridge Street, Blackfriars* (1812). © The Trustees of the British Museum.

The 1812 rendition of Bridge Street (see Figure 5.1) shows us a view that Charles McGee would have taken in on a daily basis; in fact, Tim Hitchcock suggests that McGee has been deliberately whitewashed from this vista. Charles was certainly well known enough to appear in no fewer than eight other prints representing either Bridge Street or race in Regency London.[6] And John Thomas Smith reflects on the astuteness with which McGee chose his begging place, writing that 'Charles is supposed to be worth money. His stand is certainly above all others the most popular, many thousands of persons crossing it in the course of the day.'[7] This begging place on Ludgate Hill also put McGee at the centre of a carceral and judicial geography; Fleet prison loomed behind him, the Old Bailey sessions house was but one street over towards St Pauls, and the Bridewell prison for the poor was a short walk down the street. Layers of sacral, social and commercial meanings crisscrossed Bridge Street square, and we can imagine the useful frames of mind these produced in passers-by, who might contemplate Charles McGee *here* with more sympathy and charity than *elsewhere*.

Charles was himself a distinctive person. A 'Singular' man, as John Thomas Smith describes him. Smith's engraving of him, drawn on 9 October 1815 (see Figure 5.2) shows us a solemn elderly Black man, gazing steadfast but one-eyed out of the picture, and standing slightly hunched but dignified with his shadow cast behind him. Charles holds a battered hat in the begging way in his right hand, and a broom for sweeping streets in his left, signification here of his willingness to perform the work of maintaining the streetscape to further legitimate his presence in it. 'Crossing-sweeper' was already established by 1815 as a prominent street occupation, and contemporaries mused that 'hundreds' of poor Black men might have to have taken to sweeping dust out of the way of well-dressed pedestrians in exchange for a charitable tip.[8] By way of dress, Charles sports a 'smart' frock coat which Smith informs us was presented to him by a pastry chef; ill-fitting castoff pantaloons which are too long for his legs; and ragged shoes from which his toes emerge. His own hair is tied back in a fashionable knot, and seemingly covered with a less fashionable wig. Charles's begging manner works hard to expose him 'decently' to the considerable crowds of the street; he presents himself as respectably ragged, as old but not infirm, as different but not dangerous.

Smith's potted history of Charles works to produce contradictory sentiments in his readers, and he plays with themes of both innocence and cunning. Supposing foremost that Charles was 'worth money', Smith also notes that every Sunday Charles can be found at 'Rowland Hill's meeting-house', marking out his faith as both evangelical and ecumenical and his beggarly status as suspect. This meeting house is likely the 'Surrey Chapel' opened in Blackfriars in 1783.[9] Smith also glosses Charles's blackness, as follows:

Black people, as well as those destitute of sight, seldom fail to excite compassion. Few persons, however humble their situation, can withhold charity from the infant smiling upon features necessarily dead to its supplications.[10]

Here Smith takes liberties, since Charles can quite clearly still see from one eye, and Smith conflates the 'infant smiling' of a blind person with the child-like attributes he

London Published as the Act directs December 31 1815
by John Thomas Smith, N° 4 Chandos Street Covent Garden.

Figure 5.2 John Thomas Smith, *Charles McGee* (1815). © Florilegius/Alamy Stock Photo.

assumes of Black people. It is also instructive that Smith leaves readers with a fairly negative portrait of the Black men that they might encounter on city streets, writing that: 'Black men are extremely cunning, and often witty; they have mostly short names, such as Jumbo, Toby, &c', and he elsewhere writes extensively about another poor Black man named Joseph Johnson or 'Black Joe', who earned a living on the street singing ballads and attracting custom with a model of Nelson's ship perched atop his head.[11] Oskar Cox Jensen suggests that Johnson's studied performance can be read both as sincere patriotism and as 'an exhilaratingly anti-colonial act, creating a non-western space at the centre of a western metropolis'.[12] Charles McGee's more subtle performance might have proven equally destabilizing for contemporaries.

Joseph Johnson's model ship summons for us the spectre of transatlantic empire and the graveyard of enslaved peoples that it haunts. To pass Johnson or McGee on the streets of Regency London was to pass the consequences of 300 years of trading in human lives. And slavery must surely have been on the minds of well-heeled Londoners in 1815, with the trade having been banned only eight years previously; but the institution, and its 'plantation interest', was still very present in British political and cultural life. Michael

Taylor writes that 'when the last slave ship dropped anchor, more than 700,000 people remained in bondage in the British Caribbean. For these men, women, and children, the abolition of the trade made no difference whatsoever to their lives.'[13] We are told that Charles McGee was born in 1744 in 'Ribon, Jamaica', and thus was probably born enslaved, although Smith notes that Charles's father was said to have lived to the unlikely age of 108 and makes no mention of his status as free, unfree or freed. Charles's emancipation (if it happened) was, like Joseph's relative freedom, likely connected to service at sea, and it was probably service at sea which brought Charles to London in the first place.

Being Black and free in Regency England was hardly a blessing. Because parochial settlement could not generally be proven, many Black paupers were denied access to parish relief, leaving mendicity and makeshifts as their only recourse. This situation of racialized access to welfare was understood well enough to feature prominently in the Parliamentary mendicity committee minutes of 1815:

> [Hon. George Rose, question] In the case of Africans, are there any means of taking care of them?
>
> [Michael John Fitzpatrick, Chief Clerk of Guildhall, answer] I know of none; the only way in which we can dispose of them is to fix them on the parish where they fall, as a casualty.[14]

Fitzpatrick also reported to the committee that he was frequently instructed by the Guildhall magistrates to dispense two to three shillings in casual charity to indigent Black people appearing before them, as further evidence of the idiosyncratic ameliorations that legal officials felt compelled to perform when confronted by Black poverty.

We do not know what circumstances carried Charles McGee from Jamaica to London's Ludgate Hill, but we can imagine the social and economic structures, the 'slavery hinterland', which may have kept him there.[15] We also know that by 1815 the United Kingdom had a long history of attempting to export the problems of poverty, whether understood in racialized terms or not.[16] Poor Black veterans of the Seven Years' War and American Revolution, and poor Lascars cast adrift in London after serving on East India Company voyages, had all previously been the subjects of removal campaigns. For instance, the philanthropist and utopian Jonas Hanway became involved in the last years of his life with the disastrous scheme to resettle 'the Black Poor' to Sierra Leone in 1786, as for a brief time did Olaudah Equiano. In 1787, 329 people were eventually sent aboard the *Atlantic* and *Vernon* to the Sierra Leone colony, where they experienced all manner of disasters.[17]

Charles McGee was not shipped to Sierra Leone. He planted himself at the foot of Ludgate Hill and there made a living for himself such as he could. In so doing, McGee's 'singular' presence sweeping the streets for the charity of passers-by entered into local memory and popular culture. He earned a 'begging place' not just by the Obelisk of Ludgate Hill but in the minds and sentiments of his contemporaries. Charles was such a fixture that his apocryphal biography became integral to an 1833 comedic reinterpretation of *Othello*, now subtitled as *The Moor of Fleet Street* and featuring a picaresque Othello in blackface who sweeps the streets near 'Waithman's crossing'.[18] An account of the charitable relationship between McGee and 'Lady Waithman' ends when, upon his death, Charles wills a substantial sum of money to her ostensibly in acknowledgement of her constant charity to him. In the play, Desdemona serenades the begging Othello in a manner reminiscent of *The Beggar's Opera*:

> With his broom so neat he sweeps the street
> From Waithman's door to Ludgate Hill.
> The ladies' hearts he did trepan,
> did my curly-headed African . . .[19]

Though fundamentally placeless, and buried shrouded only in anonymity, the lives of the begging and vagrant poor can cast forth lingering echoes in mind and memory. Their lives and struggles persist in the places they carve out, whether through larger-than-life ramblings and cunning antics enlarged into popular mythology, or through stoic service at one well-chosen urban intersection – a reliable presence on the street calcifying them into a human obelisk as decades pass.[20] London's patchwork of cultures – the city's invisible tissue of place and belonging – was sewn together by more than neighbourhoods and wards, sightlines, markets, lanes and prominent buildings. It was held together too by the places in between: the begging places, where men whose faces and bodies were stories swept out their names over and over in the dust.

Notes

1. Tim Hitchcock, *Down and Out in Eighteenth-century London* (London: Continuum, 2004), 76–7.

2. Tim Hitchcock, 'Place and the Politics of the Past', 29 February 2012, http://historyonics. blogspot.com/search/label/Charles%20McCay.

3. John Thomas Smith, *Vagabondiana: Or, Anecdotes of Mendicant Wanderers Through the Streets of London, with Portraits of the Most Remarkable Drawn from the Life* (London: n.p., 1817), 24–5.

4. I have commented briefly on Charles McGee elsewhere; see 'The Vagrant Poor', in *The Routledge History of Poverty, c.1450–1800*, ed. David Hitchcock and Julia McClure (London: Routledge, 2020), 66.

5. Charles Booth, *Maps Descriptive of London Poverty, 1898–9*, 2nd edn (London: n.p., 1898–9); Plate 7.

6. Tim Hitchcock, 'Place and the Politics of the Past'.

7. Smith, *Vagabondiana*, 24.

8. Mentioned apocryphally in Henry Mayhew's *London Labour and the London Poor* and discussed in Norma Myers, 'Servant, Sailor, Soldier, Tailor, Beggarman: Black Survival in White Society 1780–1830', *Immigrants & Minorities* 12, no. 1 (1993): 67.

9. A. F. Munden, 'Hill, Rowland (1744–1833), Evangelical Preacher', *Oxford Dictionary of National Biography*.

10. Smith, *Vagabondiana*, 25.

11. Joe Johnson is considered in more detail in Oskar Cox Jensen, *The Ballad-Singer in Georgian and Victorian London* (Cambridge: Cambridge University Press, 2021), 176–88. Jensen establishes that the model was not in fact of Nelson's ship, 176.

12. Ibid., 180.

13. Michael Taylor, *The Interest: How the British Establishment Resisted the Abolition of Slavery* (London: Bodley Head, 2020), xv.

14. UK Parliament, *Minutes of the Evidence Taken Before the Committee Appointed by the House of Commons, to Inquire into The State of Mendicity and Vagrancy in the Metropolis and its Neighbourhood* (London: Sherwood, Neely, and Jones, 1815), 17.

15. See Felix Brahm and Eve Rosenhaft (eds), *Slavery Hinterland: Transatlantic Slavery and Continental Europe, 1680–1850* (Woodbridge: Boydell and Brewer, 2016).

16. See Gwenda Morgan and Peter Rushton, *Banishment in the Early Atlantic World* (London: Bloomsbury, 2013), and David Hitchcock, '"Punishment is all the Charity that the Law Affordeth Them": Penal Transportation, Vagrancy, and the Charitable Impulse in the British Atlantic, c.1600–1750', *New Global Studies* 12, no. 2 (2018): 195–215.

17. The National Archives (UK): T 1/643, ff. 135–8 (Feb 1787); digitized as part of an archived exhibition on 'Black Presence', https://www.nationalarchives.gov.uk/pathways/blackhistory/.

18. I am very grateful to Oskar Cox Jensen for this reference and for his notes on the play, which I assuredly would not have otherwise found: Charles Mathews, *Othello, the Moor of Fleet Street*, ed. Manfred Draudt (1833; repr. Tübingen: Francke, 1993), 49.

19. Ibid., 65.

20. Studies of 'rogue culture' show this echo effect quite clearly; see Lena Liapi, *Roguery in Print: Crime and Culture in Early Modern London* (London: Boydell and Brewer, 2019), particularly her introduction; also David Hitchcock, *Vagrancy in English Culture and Society, 1650–1750* (London: Bloomsbury Academic, 2016), chapter 2.

CHAPTER 6
13 RED-LION SQUARE: THE MENDICITY SOCIETY, 1818–76
Oskar Cox Jensen

From the beginning, Red-Lion Square – reputedly the resting place of Oliver Cromwell's body – was built upon class conflict. First, they took the fields. June 1684, and the lawyers of Gray's Inn rose up in inglorious revolution against the 'unscrupulous' developer Nicholas Barbon's workmen, wielding the bricks that were meant to build Red-Lion Square – a new development encroaching on their bucolic back gardens. But Barbon fought the law and Barbon won: the square went up. Next, they took the wilderness. 1737: the garden at the square's centre had become a refuge, an untended oasis for the homeless and the renegades. But the residents – some, by now, lawyers of Gray's Inn themselves – secured a parliamentary levy and the square was beautified. This meant, in the first instance, fortifications: iron railings, watchtowers to the corners, the crenellations of privilege and property. The square was cleansed.[1]

In recompense for – or, seen another way, in subtler evolution of – these aggressive acts of Improvement, the genteel confines of Red-Lion Square soon blossomed with philanthropic foundations. 1769: George Armstrong MD launched his Dispensary for the Infant Poor at No. 7.[2] From the 1830s to the 1850s, Nos 20, 43, 4 and 27 all hosted charitable endeavours.[3] But there was nothing to touch No. 13, the square's largest premises, spreading from the south-south-east entrance halfway down Leigh Street.[4] On 25 March 1818, this imposing edifice opened its doors as the offices of the Society for the Suppression of Mendicity – better known as the Mendicity Society – a pioneering institution that would wage righteous war against London's beggars, in the name of those indigents' own good, for the next 150 years.[5] Still lacking its definitive history, the Society swiftly grew in both fame and infamy, the archetypal organ of patrician private welfare.[6]

Born from the endeavours of natural philosopher and self-appointed social investigator Matthew Martin, begun in 1796, and greatly boosted by the parliamentary committees on mendicity in the immediate aftermath of the Napoleonic Wars, its system was simple.[7] Subscribers were given tickets, which they could dispense to beggars in lieu of cash. Any 'deserving' pauper who presented a ticket at their offices was given bread, soup, perhaps even cheese – in some cases, clothing – and, in later years, a chance of paid labour. Any *un*deserving pauper was given short shrift, and the Society employed a notorious body of 'Officers', up to half a dozen at a time, who roamed the streets in search of sturdy beggars, imposters, public nuisances, on whom they would descend in a body, before dragging these pre-judged miscreants before a magistrate. By the 1850s, some of these officers had even turned detective, exposing fraudulent street beggars who might otherwise have escaped their rough idea of justice. Patronized by royalty, the Society was enormously successful, so far as raising funds was concerned; its Sisyphean task of eliminating mendicity went, unsurprisingly, unfulfilled – while, just as unsurprisingly, it courted a great deal of controversy, receiving regular slatings from radical-leaning papers such as *Lloyd's*, the *Examiner* and the *Morning Chronicle*.[8] In essence, the Society embodied a worldview afflicted by myopia: an inability to see beyond the bugbear of the parasitic mendicant; to perceive its targets as a meaningful, multicultural populace in flux, endlessly remaking the culture of the streets with their voices, musics and stories.

But why settle for this dry resumé, when we can experience it first-hand? Friday, 16 February 1838 finds John James Bezer – a Dissenting cobbler, lately out of work, soon to be a Chartist, husband to an ailing wife, father to an infant child – reduced to psalm-singing on the London streets. All he wants is work. His full account of what follows (published in the *Christian Socialist* and to be taken, of course, with a liberal pinch of salt) is a compelling read, available online.[9] Walking up Holborn, he meets a man who tells him of the Society's general scheme. Specifically, the man is a living, shouting advertisement: 'Give no money to beggars, – food, work, and clothing, are given away to them by applying to the Mendicity Society, Red Lion Square.' Duly informed, Bezer hastens to the profitable begging-ground of Russell Square, where he gets a ticket 'of the third person I asked'. Proceeding to Red-Lion Square, he mounts the imposing steps of No. 13 and knocks at the door 'with joy and boldness'. '"What do you want," said the opener. "Here's a ticket, sir," (showing it for fear he wouldn't believe me) "I want to see the gentlemen inside." "O, go round the corner; that's *your* way," and he slammed the door in my face.'

Naturally, beggars were not supposed to show their face in the square itself. Nevertheless, they did. In 'the late severe winter' of 1829–30, as Edward Pelham Brenton remembered, 'the numbers actually relieved amounted to 27,000 and upwards, and so dense was the crowd in the neighbourhood of Red Lion Square, that the inhabitants loudly, and I think, not unjustly, complained of the nuisance.'[10] In later decades and especially during the Irish Famine, their ranks would swell to double that number, at times threatening to swallow the square whole.[11] But back to Bezer, as he passes

> ... round the corner, and down some dirty steps [...] fully a hundred, of the most emaciated, desolate, yet hardened, brutal-looking creatures, were congregated together in the kitchen, the majority of them munching, like so many dogs, hunks of bread and cheese. I was told to pass on, and then another hundred daguerreotype likenesses of the first hundred met my bewildered gaze, waiting to pass a wooden bar[.]

He spends an hour in line among this 'Devil's crowd', during which he is thoroughly disabused of his hopes:

> I tells you what, old flick, you've been deceived, it[']s all lies, – they only give you a bit of bread and cheese, and you must be up to snuff to get *that*, – not one in

a hundred gets more. Clothing's all my eye. And them as gets work, it's to break stones at six bob a-week – it[']s all lies I tell you.

And so it transpires. Bezer's interview with the board of 'six gentlemen, as people call bears that are dressed well' has to be read in full to be appreciated; it is a tour de force of Dickensian injustice. Even when Bezer gets his 'half-a-pound of bread and a piece of cheese', he is not allowed to take it back to his family, but must eat it on the spot.[12]

'You must, sir,' said the Chairman to me. 'I won't.' 'You must, I tell you, it's the rule, and you must obey it.' 'I don't care about your *rules*, I want to share it with those I love, who are as hungry as I am, and if you are a Devil with no natural feelings, I am not. Get out of the way, beadle,' and out I rushed, like one mad, through the crowd of astonished beggars, right into the street, without one stopping me.

Following Bezer back into the street, we find ourselves reeling between a number of incongruous juxtapositions. A Society whose notion of benevolence rests on prescription, *pro*scription, suspicion. A scheme of supposedly useful, desirable work for 'the better sort' that involves oakum-picking for women, mill-turning for the weak, and stone-breaking for the strong – when the Society's budget of 1876 gives the total annual earnings from oakum-picking as the princely sum of £3 15s, and when the silk workers of Bethnal Green petition against the 'cruel system' of stone-breaking as a cause of eye injuries and disabled hands.[13] A world in which the decorous, well-pointed façades of Red-Lion Square echo to the cries of the hungry multitude, yet in which the Society's benefactors may characterize that same crowd as:

the most degraded outcasts of society [. . .] The mob of reprobates [. . .] boys and young men from sixteen to twenty-two years old, and girls of the most dissolute conduct [. . .] Expression is wanting to describe the infamous language used by these unhappy young girls; and so revolting is their demeanour and that of their male companions, that [. . .] respectable passengers [in the Square] stop their ears to exclude the ribaldry which would defile them.[14]

As is ever the case in this century, in this city, physical congruity can only exacerbate the yawning gulf between the propertied and the dispossessed.

The Society's story, then, is in many respects predictable: the self-appointed regulators of the street poor operated on principles of antagonism and mistrust. In the era before altruism, this might almost pass for welfare.[15] But its annual reports, for all that they (and the avalanche of associated newspaper reports related to their more prominent cases) are eloquent of this stony-hearted system, reveal something more besides. Each report combines a slew of statistics with carefully-curated case studies, pitched at a respectable readership keen to be titillated by, and censorious of, instructive instances of depraved women and unmasked charlatans. As such, they give an invaluable flavour of London's street culture: a shifting picture, more frequent and more specific than the isolated censuses of 1801 and 1851 – which, by their very nature, were ill-suited to pinning down the peripatetic. Above all, they place the comfortable, sober environs of 13 Red-Lion Square at the centre of a truly global system of itinerancy.

This began in 1803 with Matthew Martin's amateur enquiry, finding – from a total of 5,096 cases – that under half hailed from London parishes, and fully a third were Irish.[16] From 1818 (by which date the Irish had overtaken native Londoners) to 1868, the Society recorded French, Germans, Russians, Austrians, Prussians, Spaniards, Portuguese, Italians, Dutch, Swedes, Africans, Asiatics, Americans (all these by 1819), Danes, Gibraltans, Bohemians, Greeks, Maltese, Egyptians and Channel Islanders by 1823, when, feeling the need for greater nuance, it began to count West Indians, Sardinians, Genoese, Algerines, Swiss, Canadians, Sandwich Islanders, South Africans, those 'Born at Sea', South Americans, East Indians, St Helenians, Poles, Arabs, New South Welsh, Norwegians, those from the Isle of Man and Van Diemen's Land, Corfiots, Turks, Tartars, Chinese, Nova Scotians, Ceylonese, Hungarians and New Zealanders – by which point, 1867, the Italians had beaten the Irish to second place. It tallied how many of its non-Europeans were 'Blacks' (117 of 143 in 1819; 58 in both 1820 and 1821), and from which Caribbean islands its West Indians originated. While Central America and India proper were especially perplexing omissions (were they hidden among (South) Americans and Asiatics, and if so, why?), and while we must presume that Belgium, so close at hand, clearly had no beggars, this was otherwise a remarkable collage of the nineteenth-century world, as captured on the London street.

This global influx was revolutionizing the culture of London's streets – its food, its theatre, its social consciousness and, above all, its music. Amidst all the editorializing and sleight of hand of Henry Mayhew's *London Labour and the London Poor* (1860–61) – and in innumerable sources besides – this can be heard loud and clear: a *musica povera*, previously defined by the monophony of the solo ballad-singer, the fiddler or the fife, was swelling into harmony during these decades, thanks to the efforts made by the Society's undesirables to earn their crust. German brass bands, Italian, well, everything, but principally its barrel-organists, Spanish guitarists, Savoyard wind ensembles, the percussionists of the Indian sub-continent and even the artistry of the blackface minstrel troupes – predominantly white Londoners but including the occasional 'genuine' Black musician, inspired by American touring performers, exacting a high price of prejudice for the boon they brought in syncopation, the interplay of bones and banjo, the 2/4 pop song and the earworm chorus – all these amounted to nothing less than a renaissance of London's street culture, augmented by the stand-up routines of the Irish, the dances and acrobatics of the West and East Indies and the first ice-cream, introduced to the streets in 1849 by Swiss entrepreneur Carlo Gatti.[17]

Such sweeping changes were of course brought about not by abstracted historical forces, but by individuals, and we encounter them on almost every page of the Mendicity Society's reports. Not, naturally, as performers, entertainers, anti-slavery campaigners – but as frauds and parasites. In each of their first three reports (1819–21), a 'man of colour' is subjected to righteous violence by their officers: 'W. B.', whose begging-takings are confiscated, which is to say, stolen, by the Society; 'J. W. M.', a fifty-eight-year-old Jamaican, imprisoned and flogged for begging; and 'J. F.', twenty-two, from St Domingo, set upon by four officers at once 'after a most desperate resistance', imprisoned, and flogged twice, with no reason given. In the fourth report, we find 'S. B.', seventeen, a girl from Montego Bay who 'had come over a slave with a lady, but left her on reaching England'. The Society's first impulse, confronted with this newly-manumitted immigrant, was to deport her – a 'send them back to Africa' attitude that, as David Hitchcock discusses in this volume, had been attempted, disastrously, some decades earlier – and it is with indignation that they report that 'when a passage was at length obtained for her, and she was about to be taken on board, she absconded, and has not again been seen'.[18]

While the Society's persecutions were not reserved for Black mendicants, their consistent antagonism on this front is notable, growing to notoriety in later decades when their unprovoked actions against several beggars of colour led to fevered reportage in the national press.[19] Though the Society's conduct was deplored in various left-leaning organs, it was only the Chartist *People's Paper* that placed it in a broader perspective, writing of the ill-treatment of Mahomet Abraham, described as a 'Malay' from Calcutta: 'We cannot but express surprise and indignation at its being considered "criminal" for a blind man, of another colour, clime, and creed, petitioning for the assistance of the philanthropic in that country which has conquered his own, and plundered its inhabitants'.[20]

Two centuries on, there is something of Lear raging at the storm about this taking to task of a defunct institution, enforcing the laws of its time. Yet theirs is a priceless record of London's global street culture, one of precious few places in which we find something of the real diversity of the street poor, of their agency and actions. Red-Lion Square lay, for a time, at the world's centre. Given this unparalleled insight, how depressing it is to encounter these subaltern voices only through a thicket of censure, oppression and petty accusation. At least we have John James Bezer, to stage for us the street's defiance: one voice among thousands that must, in their time, have been raised against these 'gentlemen, as people call bears that are dressed well'.

Notes

1. For an accessible summary, see Ben Johnson, 'Red Lion Square', historic-uk.com/ HistoryMagazine/DestinationsUK/Red-Lion-Square. For a verdict on Barbon, see Roy Porter, *London: A Social History* (1994 repr.; Penguin: London, 2000), 124–5.

2. Peter M. Dunn, 'George Armstrong MD (1719–1789) and his Dispensary for the Infant Poor', *Archives of Disease in Childhood* 87 (2002): F228–31.

3. See UCL Bloomsbury Project, ucl.ac.uk/bloomsbury-project/streets/red_lion_square.htm.

4. The fourth edition of Richard Horwood's *Plan* is the most relevant topographical reference here, best showcased via Matthew Sangster's website *Romantic London*, romanticlondon.org/ the-1819-plan/#19/51.51899/-0.11872.

5. See UCL Bloomsbury Project, ucl.ac.uk/bloomsbury-project/institutions/society_ suppression_mendicity.htm. The date is given in the Society's first annual *Report*, 11 (see note 7).

6. But see M. J. D. Roberts, 'Reshaping the Gift Relationship: The London Mendicity Society and the Suppression of Begging in England, 1818–1869', *International Review of Social History* 36, no. 2 (1991): 201–31.

7. Matthew Martin, *Letter to the Right Hon. Lord Pelham, on the State of Mendicity in the Metropolis* (London: n.p., 1803); *Report from Committee on the State of Mendicity in the Metropolis* (London: n.p., 1815); *Minutes of the Evidence taken before the Committee appointed by the House of Commons to inquire into the state of Mendicity [. . .] to which is added, The Second Report* (London: n.p., 1816); *Annual Reports of the Society Established in London for the Suppression of Mendicity* (London: n.p., 1819–70, 1873, 1876), hereafter *Reports*. See also the Society's *Minutes*, 1818–24, British Library Manuscript Collections Add MS 50136.

8. See, e.g., *The Mendicity Society Unmasked, in a letter to the managers* (London: n.p., 1825).

9. At minorvictorianwriters.org.uk/bezer/b_autobiography.htm, where it forms the final paragraphs of the account. It is also included in David Vincent (ed.), *Testaments of Radicalism: Memoirs of Working Class Politicians 1790–1885* (London: Europa, 1977).

10. Edward Pelham Brenton, *A Letter to the Committee of Management for the Suppression of Mendicity, in Red Lion Square* (London: n.p., 1830), 3.

11. In the winter of 1841, 630 tickets were presented on a single day; in 1847, they recorded 55,721 unregistered cases. *Reports* (1842 and 1848), respectively at 11 and 21–3.

12. *The Practice of the Mendicity Society. By 'One who knows it well'* (London: n.p., 1847), 14. The same source specifies half as much cheese as bread, and a pint of soup: 'The objection of beggars is mostly made to the soup, but this article has over and over again been tested and approved by impartial persons.'

13. *Reports*, vol. 58 (1876), xviii. See also: nationalarchives.gov.uk/education/resources/ workhouse-voices/effects-of-stone-breaking.

14. *The Practice of the Mendicity Society*, 6–9.

15. See Thomas Dixon, *The Invention of Altruism* (Oxford: Oxford University Press, 2008).

16. Martin, *Letter*, 7–8.

17. Besides noting that Mayhew et al.'s opus received a new edition by Dover in 1968, I should mention especially Charlie Taverner, *Street Food: Hawkers and the History of London* (Oxford: Oxford University Press, 2022); Oskar Cox Jensen, *The Ballad-Singer in Georgian and Victorian London* (Cambridge: Cambridge University Press, 2021), esp. chapter 4; Saree Makdisi, *Making England Western: Occidentalism, Race, and Imperial Culture* (Chicago: University of Chicago Press, 2014); John M. Picker, *Victorian Soundscapes* (Oxford: Oxford University Press, 2003); Tom Scriven, 'The Jim Crow Craze in London's Press and Streets, 1836–39', *Journal of Victorian Culture* 19, no. 1 (2014): 93–109; James Winter, *London's Teeming Streets, 1830–1914* (London: Routledge, 1993); Sarah Wise, *The Italian Boy: Murder and Grave-Robbery in 1830s London* (London: Pimlico, 2005); and John E. Zucchi, *The Little Slaves of the Harp: Italian Child Street Musicians in Nineteenth-Century Paris, London, and New York* (Quebec: McGill-Queen's University Press, 1992).

18. *Reports*, vols 1–4 (1819–22), respectively at 41, 32, 27–8, 57.

19. Unlike David Hitchcock's contribution to this volume, which gives due focus to the crossing-sweeper Charles McGee, I cannot begin to do these individuals justice here. But see Oskar Cox Jensen, *Vagabonds: Life on the Streets of Nineteenth-Century London* (London: Duckworth, 2022), especially chapters 3 and 4.

20. Discussed extensively ibid., chapter 4. The case is from 1852. My attention was drawn to the *People's Paper* by Tom Hughes' blog, *Victorian Calendar*.

CHAPTER 7
THE CHINESE AESTHETICS OF THE *ADMONITIONS* SCROLL AT THE BRITISH MUSEUM
Kent Su

In the early years of the twentieth century, London's British Museum was home to the world's most diverse international collection of artefacts. By means of bequests, spoils of war, colonial conflict or commissions, the museum's masterpieces included William Burges's collection of armouries; A. W. Franks's bequests of miscellaneous items; Edward Hawkins's historical medals; bronzes from the West African Kingdom of Benin; the Parthenon Marbles; Assyrian monuments and other relics of the past.[1] One of the British Museum's most significant acquisitions of the period was the so-called *Admonitions of the Instructress to the Court Ladies* scroll. This antique was instrumental in introducing the richness of Chinese art and culture to a British audience.

The *Admonitions of the Instructress to the Court Ladies – Nüshi zhen tu* 女史箴圖 – is a handscroll of narrative paintings first attributed to Jin Dynasty court artist Gu Kaizhi (顧愷之, *c.* 344–406). The original handscroll has, however, been long lost. The current one is an eighth-century facsimile made during the Tang Dynasty and based on Gu Kaizhi's original handscroll. The reason for the creation of this copy is unknown. The

Figure 7.1 Gu Kaizhi, *Admonitions of the Instructress to the Court Ladies*. © The Trustees of the British Museum.

facsimile nonetheless employs a fine linear style of gossamer-like brush strokes resembling the art in Gu Kaizhi's period.

The handscroll is designed to illustrate a long poem composed by the courtier Zhang Hua (張華, *c.* 232–300). The poem shows a court instructress giving didactic rhymed aphorisms to palace women, urging them to follow proper Confucian conduct and etiquette. The overall aim of the poem is to reprimand the overreaching and transgressive behaviours of Empress Consort Jia Nanfeng (賈南風, *c.* 257–300), the wife of the Western Jin emperor Huidi, whose rule spanned 290–306.[2] The empress was known for her cruel, vindictive and manipulative nature, underscored by episodes in which she murdered any potential political rivals. Zhang Hua's 'admonishment' text subtly reflects his opposition to the empress's atrocities and highlights the imperative of moral righteousness.

The handscroll paintings ekphrastically depict nine scenes from the poem. However, there may have been three additional scenes and texts at the beginning of the scroll, which are now missing.[3] The settings of the existing scenes range from the outdoors to the interior quarters of a bedroom. They aim to depict the era's expectation for court and palace ladies to be devout and loyal to the emperor. For example, a scene portrays a court lady named Feng selflessly protecting her husband, the emperor Yuandi of the Han Dynasty, from a black bear that has escaped from a bear-baiting event. In another scene, the emperor rejects the advances of his consort, who has boldly claimed that she is the emperor's favourite. The emperor should always remain impartial and objective. All of the scenes need to be read along with the poetic texts to understand how they correspond with the moral rules and expectations of righteousness placed on the members of the palace.

The handscroll's style exhibits traces of realism and exemplifies the classical tradition of early figure painting. The style aims to transcend the stock depictions of characters that are commonly found in earlier artistic works. The characters in the scenes move with their elegant draperies in a seamless flow, and their subtle facial expressions of grinning, frowning, contemplating or glaring vividly illustrate the characters' individuality. The handscroll aims to 'capture the spirit of depicted figures' and recreate an accurate representation of the daily life expected within the palace.[4]

Since its composition in the Tang Dynasty, the handscroll 'has passed through the hands of many imperial and private collectors, and bears impressions of their seals, and a number of their own paintings and inscriptions on attached lengths of silk and paper'.[5] It also contains four colophons, the two most notable being those that were composed by the Qing Dynasty emperor Qianlong (1711–99). Placing colophons in a painting was a common practice in Ancient China. The colophons may comprise comments written by friends of the artist or the collector; alternatively, they may be written by viewers from later generations. The colophons may comment on the quality of the painting, express the rhapsody of the viewer, give a biographical sketch of the artist, place the painting within an art historical context or engage with the texts of earlier colophons.[6] Qianlong's first colophon records his initial experience of seeing the handscroll after a long summer day in a pavilion, which inspired him to compose an orchid painting to complement the scenery found in the scroll. His second colophon continues his admiration for Gu

Kaizhi's brushstrokes, which have eluded any means of interpretation. Attempting to understand the handscroll would only destroy its inner beauty because it is 'a divine omen from antiquity' (千古法寶).[7] Qianlong felt great delight at having encountered such an artistic work in his lifetime. Following his encounter, he identified the handscroll as the first of the 'Four Beauties' (四 美 具). The other three beauties were paintings from different dynasties: 'XiaoXiang Dream Journey', 'Overview of Shuchuan Victory' and 'Nine Songs'.[8]

Toward the end of the nineteenth century, the Qing Dynasty was in great decline. During the aftermath of the Boxer Rebellion (1899–1900), the facsimile of Gu Kaizhi's painting was acquired by Captain Clarence Johnson (1870–1937), who was stationed at the Summer Palace. The exact nature of his acquisition remains unknown. While he may have received the scroll as a gift from a palace lady, it also may have been war booty.[9] In 1903, Johnson took the handscroll to the British Museum for appraisal, though he himself was more interested in the jade tag that was attached to the scroll. The keeper of the department of Prints and Drawings, Sidney Colvin (1845–1927), and his assistant, Laurence Binyon (1869–1943), immediately recognized the artistic magnificence of the scroll, and the museum purchased it from Johnson for the paltry sum of £25.[10] By the time it had arrived at the museum, the *Admonitions* scroll was already fragile. As reported by Colvin in 1903, its surface was 'much worn and rotted, and bears many traces of ancient repair'.[11] Moving from place to place as it had, the scroll – sensitive to light, humidity, temperature and vibration – needed to be handled with exquisite skill and care.

In 1904, after a yearlong inspection, Binyon published a landmark article for *Burlington Magazine*, documenting the scroll's size, silk material and contents: 'a roll of brown silk, 9¾ in. wide, 11 ft 4½ in. long'.[12] This article effectively introduces the aesthetics of Chinese art to a Western audience. A few years later, when he had gained even greater expertise in the area, Binyon devoted the third chapter of his highly praised book, *Painting in the Far East* (1908), to the handscroll. Binyon successfully authenticates the work to be a copy of Gu Kaizhi's original painting and argues that, though it is merely a facsimile of the original, '[t]he brushwork is confident and spontaneous. The hand that painted it was beyond all dispute the hand of a great master.' Binyon goes on to describe in detail the scenes within the scroll and admires it as 'suave and tender, yet never soft or weak; firm and precise, yet never dry'. Binyon argues that Chinese art has 'that powerful creative instinct and aesthetic perception' superior to many other cultures.[13] Overall, the book makes parallels between the arts of Japan and China in chronological order in an attempt to survey the achievements of East Asian painting, kindle an interest in the art of Asia in the West, and encourage readers to undertake more exhaustive study.

In 1910, Binyon organized the first public display of the *Admonitions* scroll in the exhibition *Chinese and Japanese Painting AD 500–1900* in the White Wing gallery of the Prints and Drawings Department of the British Museum. Binyon published a guide for the public which underscored the significance of such an exhibition. He believed that the British Museum's collections of Chinese art were growing very slowly because of a lack of fine specimens, and cited how, when a similar exhibition took place in 1888, only thirteen out of 237 works in that exhibition were of Chinese origin. Binyon emphasized that the 1910 exhibition would have 108 Chinese artworks, which would give the British public their first opportunity to view such a large collection.[14] Placed first in the catalogue, the extensive explanation of the *Admonitions* scroll recounted the scroll's potential origin, authorship and accretive connoisseurship throughout the dynasties. Such detail and primacy of place in the catalogue acknowledges the artistic significance of the scroll in the historical development of Chinese painting. Binyon describes Gu Kaizhi as 'especially distinguished for the expressiveness and subtlety of his portraits'.[15] Binyon's report succinctly captures the artist's overall style and enables the public to become more culturally aware of China's early engagement with figure painting. When the exhibition commenced, the public's reception was highly positive and the *Evening Mail* reported on it in the following terms: 'English amateurs will soon have an opportunity of realizing to some extent the range and beauty of this [Chinese] art, so long unknown, so unaccountably neglected.'[16] After two years of the scroll being on display, Binyon urged the British public to appreciate the beauty and wonders of Chinese art, calling it 'an epic kind'.[17]

The display of the *Admonitions* scroll in the 1910–12 exhibition further inspired the modernist experiments already being undertaken by the American poet Ezra Pound (1885–1972). Pound, who was born in Hailey, Idaho and grew up in Philadelphia, travelled abroad to Europe and lived much of his life overseas. He stayed in London from 1908 to 1920 and interacted with numerous well-known literary figures including W. B. Yeats and T. S. Eliot. As a migrant figure, he was keen on exploring eclectic, cross-cultural sources from other traditions to advance his own avant-garde poetic agenda. Pound visited the exhibition in 1912, after which he began to frequent the Print Room of the British Museum.[18] His close friendship with Binyon, whom he affectionately called 'BinBin', has been well documented.[19]

Pound's exposure to the philosophical and technical concepts of Chinese art were translated into his poetry. In 1914, he adapted 'Fan-Piece for Her Imperial Lord' from Herbert Giles' *A History of Chinese Literature* (1901) for his edited volume, *Des Imagistes*: 'O fan of white silk, / Clear as the frost on the grass-blade, / You also are laid aside.' Pound excludes Giles' translation and compresses a long poem into a mere three lines. Despite its adaptation from a secondary source, the imagery vividly resembles the scenes from the *Admonitions* scroll. The minimalist brevity of lines metaphorically presents a palace lady as a fan. The reference to 'white' could be suggesting the lady's fair skin, while the word 'silk' might relate to the affluent type of dress only worn in the court. The palace lady's beauty is transitory, disappearing as easily as delicate frost. The second-person pronoun is a direct address to the lady and suggests that she is 'laid aside' by the emperor. Like the scenes in the handscroll, this short poem captures the sense of court lament and expected behaviour of a palace lady in order to gain the favour of the emperor.

In a similar fashion, Pound's 'Jewel Stairs Grievance', which was published in the collection of Chinese poetry entitled *Cathay* (1915), depicts the grandeur of the marble steps in a palace ('jewelled steps') and shows how the dew gradually seeps through the court lady's silk stockings. This shows how long the lady has been waiting outside. She must go indoors when she realizes she is becoming soaked by dew. The poem encapsulates the lament of a palace lady whose long wait for a visit from the emperor behind a 'crystal curtain' is unrewarded. She wistfully watches the moon as it rises overhead. The transitory images evoke a melancholic, elegiac mood. This theme of devotion mimics the tone of obedience and submissiveness found in the handscroll.

Furthermore, the scroll's didactic composition of ethical values and Confucianism in nine different scenes subtly influenced Pound's own obsession with the philosophy. For instance, Pound records in the *China Cantos* how the incompetence of emperors who were unwilling to follow Confucian ethics inevitably resulted in the fall of dynasties. An example is You Wang (周幽王) from the Zhou Dynasty, who had been so infatuated with a particularly favoured concubine, Bao Si (褒姒), that he spared no expense to please her and devoted his attention to her. The result was that he was distracted from the business of governing the country.[20] For Pound, the unethical behaviour of emperors endangered the wellbeing of their empires. This instructional nature asserts the importance of Confucian lessons also inherent in the handscroll.

The *Admonitions* scroll's influence on Pound is manifold. In Chinese artistic tradition, painting and poetry retain a symbiotic relationship and are so subtly interwoven that one wonders whether the poem inspired the painting or vice versa. Guo Xi (郭熙, 1020– 90 CE), an artist from the Song Dynasty, memorably defined the fusion of the two disciplines: 'Poetry is formless painting while painting is poetry of form.'[21] Pound, as an inheritor of Chinese poetry, recreates his own version of the lyrics from the *Admonitions* scroll, showing its importance in initiating an East–West literary dialogue in the twentieth century aided by an object displayed in London's British Museum.

Notes

1. Marjorie Caygill, *The British Museum: 250 Years* (London: British Museum Press, 2003), 5.

2. Michael J. Farmer, 'On the Composition of Zhang Hua's "Nüshi Zhen"', *Early Medieval China* 10, no. 1 (2004): 151–75.

3. Shane McCausland, *First Masterpiece of Chinese Painting: The Admonitions Scroll* (New York: George Braziller, 2003), 37–8.

4. Wen-chien Cheng, 'The Pictorial Portrayal of Women and Didactic Messages in the Han and Six Dynasties', *Nan Nu* 19 (2017): 186.

5. McCausland, *The Admonitions Scroll*, 7.

6. Dawn Delbanco, 'Chinese Handscrolls', Met Museum, http://www.metmuseum.org/toah/hd/chhs/hd_chhs.htm.

7. 'Nüshi zhen tu 女史箴图 (Admonitions of the Instructress to the Court Ladies)', British Museum, https://www.britishmuseum.org/collection/object/A_1903-0408-0-1.

8. Zheng Xinmiao, 'A Review of Identification, Protection and Research of the Qing Imperial Collection of Paintings and Calligraphies', *Journal of Zhejiang University* 45, no. 5 (2015): 55.

9. Richard Curt Kraus, 'The Repatriation of Plundered Chinese Art', *China Quarterly* 199 (2009): 840.

10. Shane McCausland, 'The Admonitions Scroll: Ideals of Etiquette, Art and Empire from Early China', *Orientations* 32, no. 5 (2001): 26–7.

11. British Museum, *Trustees' Reports*, March 1903, 2.

12. Laurence Binyon, 'A Chinese Painting of the Fourth Century', *Burlington Magazine* 4, no. 10 (1904): 39–49.

13. Laurence Binyon, *Painting in the Far East* (London: Edward Arnold, 1908), 39, 42, 50.

14. Laurence Binyon, *Guide to an Exhibition of Chinese and Japanese Paintings in the Print and Drawing Gallery* [of the British Museum] (London: Trustees of the British Museum, 1910), 4–5.

15. Binyon, *Guide*, 11.

16. 'Chinese Painting at the British Museum. A New Acquisition', *Evening Mail*, 9 March 1910, 6.

17. 'Mr. L Binyon on Chinese Art', *Evening Mail*, 24 January 1912, 6.

18. Zhaoming Qian, 'Pound and Chinese Art in the "British Museum Era"', in *Ezra Pound and Poetic Influence*, ed. Helen M. Dennis (Amsterdam and Atlanta: Rodopi, 2000), 111.

19. Woon-Ping Chin Holaday, 'Pound and Binyon: China via the British Museum', *Paideuma* 6 (1977): 27–36; Zhaoming Qian, *The Modernist Response to Chinese Art* (Charlottesville: University of Virginia Press, 2003); Rupert Richard Arrowsmith, *Modernism and the Museum: Asian, African, and Pacific Art and the London Avant Garde* (Oxford: Oxford University Press, 2011)

20. Ezra Pound, *The Cantos* (London: Faber & Faber, 1986), 271.

21. Qian Zhongshu, *Patchwork: Seven Essays on Art and Literature*, trans. Duncan M. Campbell (Leiden: Brill, 2014), 29–78.

CHAPTER 8
'A TERRAIN ON ITS OWN': ELIZABETH BOWEN AND REGENT'S PARK
Heather Ingman

In 1935 Elizabeth Bowen (1899–1973), one of the greatest twentieth-century writers to come out of Ireland, moved into 2 Clarence Terrace overlooking Regent's Park. She was to live there throughout the Second World War, finally moving out in 1952 when her husband, Alan Cameron, took early retirement and they returned to the family estate, Bowen's Court, in County Cork.

In her unfinished autobiography, *Pictures and Conversations* (1975), Bowen highlighted a sense of place as a vital element in her fiction:

> Few people questioning me about my novels, or my short stories, show curiosity as to the places in them [...] Why? Am I not manifestly a writer for whom places loom large? As a reader, it is to the place-element that I react most strongly: for me, what gives fiction verisimilitude is its topography.[1]

Locality mattered to Bowen because she led such a dislocated life. She was born in Ireland but after the age of seven spent the majority of her life travelling between Ireland and England, a country she viewed with the eyes of an outsider. Refugees and the displaced figure prominently in her work.[2] As a member of the colonial class, 'potted at by the Irish and sold out by the British' and regarded with suspicion by both, Bowen pinpointed an 'acceptance of more or less permanent insecurity' as a particularly Anglo-Irish trait.[3] In *Pictures and Conversations*, Bowen defined the sense of difference she felt as a child in England:

> I arrived, young, into a different mythology – in fact, into one totally alien to that of my forefathers, none of whom had resided anywhere but in Ireland for some centuries, and some of whom may never have been in England at all: the Bowens were Welsh. From now on there was to be (as for any immigrant) a cleft between my heredity and my environment, the former remaining, in my case, the more powerful.[4]

At that stage, she explained in 'Coming to London' (1956), London was chiefly known to her through the novels of Charles Dickens and John Galsworthy. Her move in 1935 to the neo-classical residence of Clarence Terrace confirmed her childhood feeling that London was a city out of a book: 'And throughout seventeen years, it did never wholly emerge from art. It was much as I had fancied London would be.'[5]

In a letter to Virginia Woolf, dated 31 July 1935, Bowen described her first sight of the house that was to be her home for the next seventeen years:

> The house we are hoping to take is No. 2 Clarence Terrace, Regents Park. It is about 3½ minutes from Baker St. Station and overlooks the park lake with those coloured-sailed boats and a great many trees. It is a corner house, which is nice, I think, don't you as the windows look different ways. It has high windows and ceilings, and pale-coloured modern parquet floors. The excuse for taking it, and taking it so soon, is that it is a bargain: only just in the market and not very expensive, in fact cheap, because of there being only an eight years lease. The reason to take it is that it is, in a bare plain way, very lovely with green reflections inside from the trees such as I have only seen otherwise in a country house.[6]

Bowen's artistic response to the theatricality of John Nash's nineteenth-century designs for Regent's Park is evident in her essay 'Regent's Park and St John's Wood' (1949), where Bowen, who once confessed that she originally wished to be an architect, traces the historical beginnings of Nash's designs.[7] She details the plans for twenty-six villas, eventually reduced to eight, the construction of the Regency terraces (between 1821 and 1826), the two roads, the Outer and Inner Circles, the four gateways (Hanover, Clarence, York and Gloucester) and, above all, the lake: 'Here, the whole disposition of water and trees round it could not be more lovely [...] I believe London holds no landscape to challenge this.'[8]

Perhaps it was because Bowen saw Regent's Park as 'a terrain on its own', its terraces with 'their theatrical palace-like painted facades' un-English, that she, an outsider in England, felt so at home:

> The impression, on entering by any one of the gates for the first time, is of dreamlike improbability [...] the first thought is, 'Can I be, still, in London?' – for, in this enclave as nowhere else in London, British unostentatiousness drops away, to be succeeded by something stagy, bragging, foreign [...][9]

This theatricality made Clarence Terrace a suitable location for an exile raised in the Anglo-Irish view of life in the Irish Big House as a performance.[10] Life in Clarence Terrace was also something of a social performance as Bowen's home became an important venue for literary gatherings, visited by Virginia Woolf, Rosamond Lehmann, John Buchan, Isaiah Berlin, David Cecil and Cyril Connolly, among others. When, for purposes of their writing, Bowen and Connolly, resident of nearby Sussex Place, jokingly agreed to divide up Regent's Park between them, Queen Mary's rose garden and the boating lake became Bowen territory.[11]

Even before Bowen moved into Clarence Terrace, her fiction revealed her fascination with this part of London. Her fifth novel, *The House in Paris* (1935), published shortly before the move, is partly set in 'one of the tall, cream houses in Chester Terrace, Regent's Park'.[12] The Michaelis' light, airy upper-middle-class home embodies the stability, serenity and decorum of the English liberal tradition which was, the novel implies, about to be challenged by events in 1930s Germany. Despite their domestic settings, Bowen's novels always incorporate references to the wider historical and political context, and in *The House in Paris* she chose a Regent's Park house in order to expose the moral vacuum and anti-Semitism at the heart of upper-middle-class English society. References to the 'theatrical air' of the Nash terraces and the Michaelis drawing room as 'like a stage' reinforce the sense that the way of life represented by the Michaelis family rests on unstable foundations.[13] Bowen's Anglo-Irish background created in her a preternatural awareness of the precarious political structures on which lives are based: having lived through, albeit somewhat remotely, a revolution in her country, she was acutely aware of how private lives can be threatened by public crises. Karen Michaelis' love affair with the rootless foreigner Max Ebhart, a half-French Jew, threatens to blow apart her family's carefully preserved social status.

Regent's Park features in more detail in *The Death of the Heart* (1938), Bowen's first novel published after the move to Clarence Terrace. The crucial opening scene, laying the groundwork for future conflict between Anna Quayne and her husband's half-sister, sixteen-year-old Portia, who has come to live with them, is set on the bridge over the boating lake in Regent's Park on an icy winter's afternoon. The opening paragraph carefully sets the scene:

> That morning's ice, no more than a brittle film, had cracked and was now floating in segments. These tapped together or, parting, left channels of dark water, down which swans in slow indignation swam. The islands stood in frozen woody brown dusk: it was now between three and four in the afternoon. A sort of breath from the clay, from the city outside the park, condensing, made the air unclear; through this, the trees round the lake soared frigidly up. Bronze cold of January bound the sky and the landscape; the sky was shut to the sun – but the swans, the rims of the ice, the pallid withdrawn Regency terraces had an unnatural burnish, as though cold were light.[14]

Anna and her friend, St Quentin, who longs to go indoors, walk round the lake in the deepening dusk, as Anna hastens to give her, prejudiced, account of Portia's upbringing before the 'All Out' whistles sound. Bowen describes how the changing light alters the appearance of Nash's terraces:

> At the far side of the road, dusk set the Regency buildings back at a false distance: against the sky they were colourless silhouettes, insipidly ornate, brittle and cold. The blackness of windows not yet lit or curtained made the houses look hollow inside.[15]

'Hollow' turns out to be an apt description of the interior of 2 Windsor Terrace, Anna and Thomas Quayne's home, which provides the focus of *The Death of the Heart*'s satire on the English upper middle classes. Unlike the Michaelis family, Thomas Quayne is aware that, in a decade which witnessed the growth of the trade union movement and a series of hunger marches, their class is on its way out. He anticipates a working-class revolution: 'The most we can hope is to go on getting away with it till the others get it away from us.'[16] At night, staring at the outside, he is struck by Windsor Terrace as 'empty, stagy, E-shaped, with frigid pillars cut out on black shadow; a façade with no back'.[17]

'Hollow' has a personal as well as a political application to the Quayne household. The stagy, stylish atmosphere of 2 Windsor Terrace, designed by Anna, a failed interior decorator, cannot create a proper family home for Portia. With its segregated living areas – Anna's chilly drawing room, Thomas's fumy downstairs study, Matchett's secret basement, Portia's bedroom – '[t]he rooms were set for strangers' intimacy, or else for exhausted solitary retreat'.[18] In 'The Forgotten Art of Living' (1948), Bowen commented, 'We think out our interiors (spacing, lighting and colour), but then dread to feel them.'[19]

The Canadian diplomat Charles Ritchie, who became Bowen's lover during the Second World War, noted that 2 Windsor Terrace was 'an exact description' of 2 Clarence Terrace, that Thomas Quayne was 'an unsparing portrait' of Alan Cameron, while Anna and Portia were two halves of Bowen herself.[20] This insight seems confirmed by the scene in *The Death of the Heart* where Anna and Portia, walking separately through Regent's Park one early March evening, see the same things but respond to them in different ways, Portia with youthful joy, Anna with dread of further emotional pain:

> At different moments, they both crossed different bridges over the lake, and saw swans folded, dark white ciphers on the white water, in an immortal dream. They both viewed the Cytherean twisting reaches at the ends of the lake, both looked up and saw pigeons cluttering in the transparent trees. They saw crocuses staining the dusk purple or yellow, flames with no power. They heard silence, then horns, cries, an oar on the lake, silence striking again, the thrush fluting so beautifully. Anna kept pausing, then walking quickly past the couples against the railings: walking alone in her elegant black she drew glances; she went to watch the dogs coursing in the empty heart of the park. But Portia almost ran, with her joy in her own charge, like a child bowling a hoop.[21]

For Bowen and Ritchie, both outsiders amongst the English, their first visit to Queen Mary's rose garden, in September 1941, became a defining moment in their thirty-two-year love affair. In his diary entry for 29 September 1941, Ritchie wrote, 'The whole scene, the misty river, the Regency villas with their walled gardens and damp lawns, and the late September afternoon weather blended into a dream of our love.'[22] The affair is portrayed in *The Heat of the Day* (1949), often regarded as Bowen's finest novel, where again the crucial first scene is set in Regent's Park but in a park transformed by war with exhausted, shabby, dislocated Londoners drawn together on the first Sunday of September 1942 to listen to an open air concert: 'at the start of the concert, this tarnished bosky theatre, in which no plays had been acted for some time, held a feeling of sequestration, of emptiness the music had not had time to fill'.[23] The 'great globular roses' in Queen Mary's garden, however, remain 'dazzling'.[24]

The war exacerbated Bowen's divided allegiances as an Irish woman living in London. A novel of espionage and betrayal, *The Heat of the Day* locates political treachery in the heart of an English family, and the Home Counties house where the traitor is nurtured is called Holme Dene, a name reminiscent of The Holme, one of the villas Nash constructed in Regent's Park. Bowen chose to stay in London throughout the war and participate in the war effort, working as an Air Raid Precautions warden patrolling the streets of Marylebone at night as Connie does in *The Heat of the Day*. She also made several trips over to Ireland at the behest of the British Ministry of Information to gather information on the political climate in neutral Ireland. Although her early reports were sympathetic towards Irish neutrality, warning against any attempt to repossess the treaty ports, by 1942 she had become less sympathetic towards Irish isolationism. After her death, when her role in supplying the Ministry of Information in London with reports was revealed, Bowen's behaviour was seen in some quarters as spying.[25]

During the 1940 Blitz, Clarence Terrace was bombed: 'she and Alan were time-bombed out of Clarence Terrace at three minutes' notice, at four o'clock in the morning, and became refugees for a week'.[26] In 'London, 1940', Bowen described their return to Clarence Terrace:

> Just inside the gates an unexploded bomb makes a boil in the tarmac road. Around three sides of the Park, the Regency terraces look like scenery in an empty theatre: in the silence under the shut facades a week's drift of leaves flitters up and down. At nights, at my end of my terrace, I feel as though I were sleeping in one corner of a deserted palace. I had always placed this Park among the most civilized scenes on earth; the Nash pillars look as brittle as sugar – actually, which is wonderful, they have not cracked; though several of the terraces are gutted – blown-in shutters swing loose, ceilings lie on floors and a premature decay-smell comes from the rooms. A pediment has fallen on to a lawn. Illicitly, leading the existence of ghosts, we overlook the locked park.[27]

In such circumstances, it took courage to remain. In a letter, dated January 1941, to Virginia Woolf whose house in Mecklenburgh Square, Bloomsbury had been completely destroyed, Bowen wrote, 'Clarence Terrace is now perfectly empty, except for ourselves in No 2, and one other, a house with a *reputation*, full of rather gaudy, silent young men who come out in the mornings and walk about two and two, like nuns.'[28] Some of this experience found its way into her wartime short stories. 'Oh, Madam …' (1941) is a monologue by a maid to her mistress lamenting the wreckage of her bombed London home which looks out onto an unnamed park. 'The Happy Autumn Fields' (1944) depicts Mary, sole inhabitant of a bombed out, windowless London house that sounds very like 2 Clarence Terrace, whiling away the time between explosions by going through letters the bombs have thrown up.

In July 1944, a series of bomb blasts damaged Clarence Terrace so severely that Bowen and her husband had to decamp for several months while the damage was repaired. Ritchie noted in his diary on 20 July, 'She has at last decided to move out now that all the ceilings are down and all the windows broken and they only escaped being killed by a chance.'[29] Bomb damage to the Regent's Park terraces was so extensive that in 1946 the Gorell Committee was appointed to advise on whether they should be pulled down. Bowen, very concerned, went round to Cyril Connolly's house in Sussex Place to plead with Lord Gorell himself.[30] In 1947, the committee recommended that Nash's terraces be preserved and repaired. Regent's Park played a final role in Bowen's post-war story, 'I Hear You Say So' (1945), where the shadowy figure of an 'obsessed-looking' but now 'aimless' man continues, a week after VE day, to haunt London's parks much as the counter-spy, Harrison, did in *The Heat of the Day*, looking over his shoulder, surveying the crowds, old spy habits remaining though his occupation has gone.[31]

The seventeen years that Bowen lived in Clarence Terrace and published some of her finest work turned Regent's Park into as much of a talisman in her writing as her Irish home, Bowen's Court. Bowen was always, in Sean O'Faoláin's memorable phrase, a 'heart-cloven and split-minded' Anglo-Irish woman, convinced both of the need for attachment and the inevitability of not belonging.[32]

Notes

1. Elizabeth Bowen, *The Mulberry Tree: Writings of Elizabeth Bowen*, ed. Hermione Lee (London: Vintage, 1999), 281–2.

2. See Phyllis Lassner and Paula Derdiger, 'Domestic Gothic, the Global Primitive, and Gender Relations in Elizabeth Bowen's *The Last September* and *The House in Paris*', in *Irish Modernism and the Global Primitive*, ed. Maria McGarrity and Claire Culleton (New York: Palgrave Macmillan, 2009), 195–214.

3. Elizabeth Bowen, *Love's Civil War*, ed. Victoria Glendinning, with Judith Robertson (London: Simon and Schuster, 2008), 54; Elizabeth Bowen, *Selected Irish Writings*, ed. Eibhear Walshe (Cork: Cork University Press, 2011), 234.

4. Bowen, *The Mulberry Tree*, 276.

5. Ibid., 89.

6. Ibid., 211.

7. Elizabeth Bowen, *Listening In: Broadcasts, Speeches, and Interviews by Elizabeth Bowen*, ed. Allan Hepburn (Edinburgh: Edinburgh University Press, 2010), 330.

8. Elizabeth Bowen, 'Regent's Park and St John's Wood', in *People, Places and Things: Essays by Elizabeth Bowen*, ed. Allan Hepburn (Edinburgh: Edinburgh University Press, 2008), 102.

9. Bowen, 'Regent's Park and St John's Wood', 100.

10. Declan Kiberd, *Inventing Ireland: The Literature of the Modern Nation* (London: Vintage, 1996), 364–79.

11. Victoria Glendinning, *Elizabeth Bowen* (New York: Alfred A. Knopf, 1978), 101.

12. Elizabeth Bowen, *The House in Paris* (Harmondsworth: Penguin, 1987), 70.

13. Ibid., 123, 127.

14. Elizabeth Bowen, *The Death of the Heart* (Harmondsworth: Penguin, 1989), 7.

15. Ibid., 12.

16. Ibid., 94.

17. Ibid., 44.

18. Ibid., 42.

19. Bowen, 'The Forgotten Art of Living', in *People, Places, Things*, 395.

20. Bowen, *Love's Civil War*, 25–6.

21. Bowen, *The Death of the Heart*, 124.

22. Bowen, *Love's Civil War*, 24.

23. Elizabeth Bowen, *The Heat of the Day* (London: Vintage, 1998), 7.

24. Ibid., 17.

25. Bowen, *Selected Irish Writings*, 11–13.

26. Glendinning, *Elizabeth Bowen*, 160.

27. Bowen, *The Mulberry Tree*, 24–5.

28. Ibid., 217.

29. Bowen, *Love's Civil War*, 40.

30. Ibid., 87.

31. Elizabeth Bowen, *Collected Stories* (London: Vintage, 1999), 753.

32. Sean O'Faoláin, 'A Reading and Remembrance of Elizabeth Bowen', *London Review of Books*, 4–17 March 1982, 15–16.

INFRASTRUCTURE: WATER

CHAPTER 9
LONDON'S WATER: CITY COMEDY, MIGRATION AND MIDDLETONS
Susan J. Wiseman

What can the seventeenth-century texts about London's water tell us about the cultures of London? Focusing on the decade after 1610, this chapter takes Thomas Middleton's comedy *A Chaste Maid in Cheapside* as its lead. Situating this alongside other literary texts and records, it investigates the economic drivers and textual effects of custom, conflict and migration as illuminated by London's early-seventeenth-century water troubles. The exponential expansion of London was driven by several forms of migration to the capital and this 'constant influx' of people in turn put pressure on London's infrastructure, including water.[1] To excavate how water and waste motivated London's residents and writers, we can start at the end of the decade in question – in 1620.

Thomas Middleton wrote several literary texts concerning water. In 1620, almost ten years after the first performance of *Chaste Maid*, the playwright was commissioned to write a short entertainment of about fifty-five lines which starts to the west of the City when '[a] water-nymph, seeming to rise out of the ground by the conduit head near the Banqueting House', greets the assembled company of the Lord Mayor and aldermen. The occasion is 'the renewing of the worthy and laudable custom of visiting the springs and conduit heads for the sweetness and health of the city', which was 'a visitation long since discontinued'.[2] As they arrive near to the outflow of the river in Whitehall to start their inspection, the nymph greets her visitors:

> Ha! Let me clear mine eyes. Methinks I see
> Comforts approach as if they came to me.
> I am not used to 'em; I ha' been long without.
> How comes the virtue of the time about?
> Has ancient custom yet a friend of weight?
> [...]
> I thought I'd been forsaken, quite forsook,
> For none these seven years, has bestowed a look
> Upon my wat'ry habitation here;
> I mean of power, that ought to see me clear
> For yon fair city's health.[3]

The text was commissioned to celebrate the restoration of the ceremonial annual audit of the City of London's water sources. However, as so often, praise and complaint coincide, and as soon as the nymph spies the approaching group of dignitaries she begins to lament: for 'these seven years' the abrogation of customary inspection has left her neglected – 'quite forsook'. Bluntly, she hasn't clapped eyes on an inspector since she 'beheld the face / Of the last magistrate in power and place'. That 'last' magistrate was Lord Mayor Sir John Swinnerton, and, as she implies, for almost a decade everyone's focus has been elsewhere.

To understand the conduit speech a little better we can return to the year that the nymph's clogged misery begins, which was also probably the same year Middleton's *Chaste Maid* was first performed by Lady Elizabeth's Men. *Chaste Maid* is a 'city comedy', a term used to retrospectively designate a group of plays presenting the City of London as a crucible in which the main issues of the moment can be observed. Some of these plays, like *Chaste Maid*, explore work resources and question the migratory movement of people to the capital. It is difficult to date the play's first performance exactly, but both resources – water – and the lifetime of company – 1611 to 1613/16 – help. Various pieces of evidence, to which this chapter contributes in passing, suggest that 1613 is the most likely year.[4]

Water, and other fluids, flow through the play. It opens in the Cheapside house of a Goldsmith probably on Goldsmith's Row, which by 1613 was both 'a notable centre of trade' and slightly disreputable.[5] In the house are one of the play's central families – the Yellowhammers; a father seeking social advancement, a mother who wasn't a chaste maid, but knows that 'a husband solders up all cracks', and daughter Moll. They are awaiting the arrival of the patriarch Yellowhammer's favoured suitor to his daughter, Sir Walter (Water?) Whorehound, marriage to whom is imagined to hugely raise Moll's social status. There is a Yellowhammer son, Tim, who is to wed an heiress. She is understood by the Yellowhammers to be Sir Walter Whorehound's niece who owns many Welsh mountains, but she is in fact his Welsh mistress whom he brings to London from Wales. Migration is foregrounded; 'whorehound' is a weed. There is much, much more to this plot, but what concerns us here is that, even in the names, we can see a thematic that mixes water, corruption and money.

The play's attentiveness to London's water and waste is emphasized in Act I when Moll's father announces, 'Sir Walter's come. / He was met at Holborn Bridge', and 'in his company / A proper fair young gentlewoman', probably (they imagine) 'his landed neice' (1.1.39–43).[6] Sir Walter, prospective groom, has arrived at the border of the City of London. We imagine him exactly above the Fleet River at Holborn Bridge just west of Ely Place and ready to enter Cheapside – probably passing the colloquially named 'pissing conduit'. He will then proceed to the Yellowhammer house in Goldsmith's Row. Thus, when we first hear of him he is above the River Fleet which rises in Hampstead and flows down to the Thames at Blackfriars, incorporating the long lost Ouldborne Brook as it goes. Known as the 'river of wells', the Fleet had long been honoured as a water source. In drastic deterioration by the early seventeenth century, the Fleet had become an unofficial sewer. Thus, even as he enters, the play pointedly associates Sir Walter with water and waste.

The audience would have been alert to jokes about water. As Julie Sanders notes, it was incredibly important in London's landscape.[7] Water and waste had long been thought to be mired in corruption. In 1544 an Act of Parliament gave the Mayor the first ever powers of compensated compulsory purchase to bring water to the City.[8] Around the same time a water wheel was established in Tower Bridge at the Thames.[9] By the time that John Stow began his *Survey of London* with a celebration of London's advantageous situation and clear waters, the deterioration of the poor Fleet was a matter of scandal. Despite having been 'clensed' at 'diuers times', and 'scowred' as far as the Thames, the river had clogged up. In 1589, money was collected by the 'common Councell' to recleanse but the money was spent, or, as Stow comments, 'the money collected and the Citizens deceiued'. When the 1603 version of Stow's chronicle was published it was 'woorse cloyed' than ever through building over it and 'casting of soylage into the stream'.[10]

Stow's celebration of waters and conduits was also a reminder of their festive status within the City and at its outskirts; as Ann Lancashire writes, medieval records tell of 'elaborate wooden structures' erected at the conduits for royal entries to the City – a clean water supply was valued and the conduits were sites where the City's ability to sustain itself was celebrated and confirmed.[11] The clear implication of the 1603 account of London's 'auncient and present Riuers' is that the Fleet tells a tale of dereliction of civic duty and of danger to London's inhabitants. We meet Sir Walter Whorehound, then, above a clogged stream of waste that was chronicled as evidence of civic corruption.

The Fleet over which Sir Walter rides was so famously dirty that it is the subject of a whole poem by Ben Jonson. 'The Famous Voyage', a comic epic of ordure, was composed around the same time as *Chaste Maid*, after 1612.[12] Written with Jonson's characteristic ambivalent relish for the things of the lower body, this most clogged of journey poems maps the challenge of two men, Sheldon and Heydon, to the heroes of ancient time through an attempted 'voyage' up the Fleet: 'No more let Greece her bolder fables tell / Of Hercules or Theseus going to hell' (ll. 1–2).[13] These two try to force themselves and their boat upstream. Unlike hell, over which many have triumphed, the Fleet was in so deleterious a situation that it defeats his adventurers who 'Calling for Rhadamanthus, that dwelt by' (l. 187), and others, to 'witness' (l. 191) their attempt, abandon the venture. As McRae notes, this poem's river of waste is mixed, evoking a mixed excretory-reproductive feminine bodily passage.[14]

Understanding *Chaste Maid* and 'Famous Voyage' as texts of the water crisis prompts us to look at other textual and archival evidence that suggests Londoners saw stinking waste where living streams should have been. There is an outfall of such material, starting as the new century began. It was evident that a moment was fast approaching when the City would neither be able to rid itself of its dirt and sewage nor provide its citizens with water fresh enough to wash and cook, let alone drink. Two projects from about 1600 show Londoners attempting to solve this crisis. Edward Wright tried to monetize the lack of water towards the east by raising water from Botolph's Wharf. Meanwhile, the landowner and Irish colonist Edmund Colthurst proposed a different solution: to bring water 'from springs in Hertfordshire and Middlesex' to London 'two-thirds of which were to be devoted to scouring the ditches and the remaining one third' to bring water to the houses of Westminster and the City.[15] At this point Colthurst saw the importation of water as addressing the enduring problem of the state of the ditches, with the private piping of water taking a secondary position. At least one of the ditches that Colthurst was planning to cleanse was, of course, the Fleet – so long overdue for a dredge. Significantly, there was Crown rather than City backing and as soon as the enterprise started to make a profit the king was to be paid rent of £20 a year.

Colthurst's plan to bring water via Broxbourne, Wormley, Cheshunt and Edmonton using a new form of canalization that would 'lead' the water to London by gravity eventually led to the construction of the New River. However, well before the project was completed Colthurst seems to have run short of money.[16] On 7 March 1609 he made a new financial proposition to the City: he and his partners would complete the work and take all the profits. The Common Council accepted, but quickly changed their minds. On 28 March they accepted an alternative offer. One Hugh Myddleton took control of the project.

Born in Wales, Hugh Myddleton, or Middleton, was a successful goldsmith and prominent member of the Goldsmith's Company and, like many of them, he also loaned money.[17] When Myddleton acceded to control, Colthurst was kept on and given heritable shares. For all that Myddleton's biographer suggests that this shows some kind of contract, it is also undeniably a demotion. Colthurst now worked as Myddleton's employee. And so, with Myddleton in charge, work on the New River resumed, the sweet water always accompanied by a whiff of unsavoury deals. Many found the private sale of water objectionable.

Texts track the work of 'leading' the river by gravity. It was a huge project to use natural contours to gradually guide the water 45 km along a winding channel to a reservoir in Islington. Work did progress. In March 1613, workers were on the final stretch from Stoke Newington to where the Round Pond was to be constructed. The site was reached on 10 April and, at last, on Michaelmas Day, 29 September, a ceremonial opening took place – involving the Lord Mayor John Swinnerton and the Lord Mayor elect, (alderman) Thomas Myddleton.[18] At this point art was once again needed and the opening was celebrated with a masque written by civic celebrator par excellence, Thomas Middleton. He wrote of the start of flow into the pond: 'At which words the flood-gate opens, the stream let into the cistern, drums and trumpets giving it triumphant welcomes; and for the close of this their honourable entertainment a peal of chambers.'[19]

Just one month later, Hugh Myddleton's brother Thomas became Lord Mayor and the show for his inauguration in autumn 1613, *The Triumphs of Truth*, was one of dramatist Thomas Middleton's most elaborate civic entertainments. So, in 1613 the Myddleton brothers were riding the wave of a potentially profitable business and civic honour. Hugh had water contracts with the City and with King James I. Thomas was Lord Mayor. Water flowed into the great pond and the better-off people of the City paid to make and lay elm pipes to draw it down the hill. Thomas Middleton, the poet, was the official chronicler of these triumphs.

As we have seen, the dramatist Middleton gives us multiple frames through which to see London's water and its waste. He wrote a text on the opening of the New River and he wrote the civic extravaganza for Thomas Myddleton. But, as we have also seen, two further texts – the nymph's discourse on the conduits and *Chaste Maid* – investigate

London's relationships with gold, waste and water and take a distinct view. That *Chaste Maid* might be the dramatist's freest word on the topic is suggested by the fact it was performed at some point after the erection of the New River water supply in 1613 and before the disbanding of the Queen Elizabeth's Men. As must be starting to become clear, *Chaste Maid*'s detailed exploration of the flows of water and waste incorporates acrid satire on the City of London's controversial water debates.

Audiences would have recognized *Chaste Maid*'s reference to the Fleet in Holborn as glancing at the water crisis, and they would also have recognized the figure we left poised above it – Sir Walter Whorehound. When we first meet Sir Walter he is, literally, coming from Wales to London. In London, he has fingers in many pies and has set himself up as the financier of the Allwits' marriage. He has sex with the wife (saving Allwit the labour) and fathers and pays for children; his own fluids are only perversely productive, sliding seven children into the City, none legitimate. Economically, the play presents Sir Walter as a kind of cuckold-making cuckoo.

Most tellingly, perhaps, if we are to situate *Chaste Maid* in relation to London's desperation to clear its rivers and see it as playing on public controversy about private water, the conclusion of two strands of the plot make a new kind of sense – and one that draws together water and civic duty. The comeuppance of Sir Walter Whorehound is tied to the Allwit plot strand. Sir Walter Whorehound, father of Allwit's children, arrives wounded at the house of his 'wittol' or knowing cuckold – but, as by the time he arrives he is wounded in the inheritance even more than in the body and reputation, he now represents not income but incrimination. Sir Walter has his nose rubbed in his new situation:

Sir Walter: Am I denied a chamber? – [To Mistress Allwit] What say you, forsooth?

Wife: Alas, sir, I am one that would have all well
But must obey my husband. – [To Allwit] Prithee, love,
Let the poor gentleman stay, being so wounded:
There's a close chamber at one end of the garret
We never use; let him have that I prithee.

Allwit: We never use? You forget sickness then,
And physic times is't not a place of easement? (5.2.123–9)

The particular plan to stow him in a lavatory room, literally in the faeces, is an instance of natural justice – Sir Walter is to be seen as responsible for the dirty mess of London, both morally and in terms of waste.

Who profited from London's water crisis? As Allwit reminds the audience, in life as in gambling, 'whoe'er games, the box is sure a winner' (5.1.171). Here the 'box', or house, or kitty was owned by was the controller of the water – Myddleton. As *Chaste Maid* and the nymph at the conduit both imply, for a long time Hugh Myddleton's interest in the New River, and his brother's lack of interest in maintaining the conduits, was good for their water business – and there was a bad smell about it. However, this crisis was brought about by the City's dereliction of duty. *Chaste Maid*'s ending in which the Allwits take their money out of the City is paired with the willingness of the goldsmith father to import Whorehound as a son-in-law even after his exposure. It is the failure of the City itself that – Middleton seems to suggest – lets in the privatizing, priapic Welsh migrant who has no investment in the city.

How, then, are water and migration mixed? Sir Walter Whorehound has a watery name, is an aristocrat – and he comes from Wales; he recognizably alludes to Hugh Myddleton. For those in the know, Londoners, *Chaste Maid* satirizes Myddleton's profiteering from water. A part of that satire involves recognition of Whorehound as from a migrant or interstitial family – the Myddletons of Denbighshire.

Chaste Maid's mockery of Welsh speech and of Wales itself as empty of promise might have played well with xenophobic Londoners but masks a rather different and more complex story. Hugh Myddleton was the youngest of nine sons born to Sir Richard Myddleton, MP and governor of Denbigh castle. Sir Richard's sons give us a picture of the ordinariness of migration: one followed him as governor of the castle, one migrated abroad and three – Thomas, Hugh and Robert – migrated to London and to the City.[20] Thomas did excellent business and eventually became Mayor. He gradually moved his interests to London, leaving his Essex manor to his son, Tim. Robert Myddleton migrated wholly to London and took no part in Welsh life. Unlike Sir Walter Whorehound, then, Hugh Myddleton's family were far from landless Welsh gentry in need of City money: they were landowners in Wales. In coming to London as apprentices and entrepreneurs, they followed a familiar pattern. As younger sons from a large family they did need money, of course, and, like so many migrants, they had connections in both places. Once we know who they are, the nature of Middleton's attack on migrants is much clearer. As incomers and not native Londoners they are seen to have no investment in the City and its institutions; their Welsh connections make them further suspect; they prioritize family (as Hugh did Thomas, his brother). The audience of *Chaste Maid* are invited to think that these migrants privatize not merely the water supply, but the very structures of governance that support the City – they lay waste the water, but, more importantly, also the guilds, offices and honours of London. But it could happen because, like the Allwits, the City was soiling its own spaces.

Notes

1. Peter Clark and David Sounden, 'Introduction', in *Migration and Society in Early Modern England*, ed. Peter Clark and David Souden (London: Hutchinson, 1987), 22–3; Jean Howard, *Theater of a City: The Place of London Comedy, 1598–1642* (Philadelphia: University of Pennsylvania Press, 2007), 1–14.

2. Thomas Middleton, *Honourable Entertainments*, ed. Anthony Parr, in *The Collected Works*, ed. Gary Taylor and John Lavignino (Oxford: Oxford University Press, 2007), 14–37.

3. Ibid.

4. Alan Brissenden, 'Introduction', *A Chaste Maid in Cheapside* (London: Ernest Benn, 1968), xiii–xiv.

5. Howard, *Theater of a City*, 137.

6. Thomas Middleton, *A Chaste Maid in Cheapside*, ed. Linda Woodbridge, in *The Collected Works*. Line references are given in the main body of the text.

7. Julie Sanders, *The Cultural Geography of Early Modern Drama* (Cambridge: Cambridge University Press, 2011), 18–22.

8. J. W. Gough, *Sir Hugh Myddleton Entrepreneur and Engineer* (Oxford: Clarendon, 1964), 24.

9. Ibid., 25.

10. John Stow, *A Survey of London*, ed. Charles Lethebridge Kingsford, 2 vols (Oxford: Clarendon Press, 1908) I, 13.

11. Ann Lancashire (ed.), *London Civic Theatre* (Cambridge: Cambridge University Press, 2002), 131.

12. Colin Burrow, 'Introduction', in *The Cambridge Edition of the Works of Ben Jonson*, ed. David Bevington et al., 7 vols (Cambridge: Cambridge University Press, 2012) V, 190, n. 3, 198, n. 194.

13. Ben Jonson, 'On the Famous Voyage', in *London: A History in Verse*, ed. Mark Ford (London: Belknap Press, 2012), 104–9. Line references are given in the main body of the text.

14. Andrew McRae, '"On the Famous Voyage": Ben Jonson and Civic Space', *Early Modern Literary Studies* 3 (1998): 8–31.

15. G. C. Berry, 'Sir Hugh Myddleton and the New River', *Transactions of the Honourable Society of Cymmrodorion* (London: Honourable Society of Cymmrodorion, 1957), 18.

16. Ibid., 29–32.

17. Mark Jenner, 'Myddelton [Middleton], Sir Hugh', *Oxford Dictionary of National Biography*, https://www-oxforddnb-com.

18. Gough, *Sir Hugh Myddleton Entrepreneur and Engineer*, 57.

19. Thomas Middleton, *The Manner of His Lordship's Entertainment*, ed. David M. Bergeron, in *The Collected Works*, 962.

20. See Lloyd Bowen, *Early Modern Wales, c. 1536–c. 1689: Ambiguous Nationhood* (Cardiff: University of Wales Press, 2022).

EAST

CHAPTER 10
SHAKESPEARE IN SHOREDITCH
Daniel Swift

In 1576 the antiquarian John Stow heard of a strange discovery in the north-eastern suburbs of London, so he went to take a look. As he recounted in his *Survey of London*, labourers were digging up the field to the east of the churchyard of St Mary Spittle in order to make bricks to build new houses. There in the clay they had turned up burial urns 'full of Ashes, and burnt bones of men'. These were Roman burial urns, Stow concluded, for some contained copper coins stamped with the names of Roman emperors, and next to them were long-necked pots made of white earthenware. Stow found a crystal vial which he admired and then, pulling the stopper from its neck, tasted the water which was inside. It was fresh, he wrote, like spring water.[1]

Stow was perhaps the greatest antiquarian of London, and his *Survey* is stuffed with the many myths and rumours of the city alongside more reliable historical narrative. This episode sounds so unlikely, and yet it was true. For him, this must have been irresistible. Stow describes the shining, smooth-sided cups he found that day, the jars, the cups, all lying in the earth, and how he could not stop himself from a little grave-robbery. 'I my selfe have reserved amongst diverse of those antiquities there, one Urna, with the Ashes and bones,' he confessed: 'and one pot of white earth very small, not exceeding the quantitie of a wine pint, made in the shape of a Hare, squatted upon her legs, and betweene her eares is the mouth of the pot'. This is an admirable, elegant vision of the past, brought back to view, but elsewhere in the same field were traces of something more brutal. The labourers had found stone coffins, and then the skulls and bones of men who had apparently been buried without coffins, and around the bones were scattered large iron nails, each as wide as a man's finger. Stow records that some of the workmen in the field that day speculated that these iron nails had been driven into the heads of the bodies they found there, but he concludes this to be 'a thing unlikely, for a smaller naile would more aptly serve to so bad a purpose, and a more secret place would lightly be imployed for their buriall'.[2]

The field where Stow marvelled at these treasures was once called Lolesworth and more recently Spitalfields, and it lies on the south-eastern edge of the loosely defined area of London Stow calls in his survey 'Sewerditch' and 'Soresditch' but which we today call Shoreditch. Shoreditch has long been a place where outsiders came to settle. It has equally long been a place about which stories were told: stories of the savage past and the broken, interrupted present. In 2005, Shoreditch was once again being dug up, this time for the extension of the Overground railway, and the Museum of London commissioned an archaeological survey of the area. They found Roman roof tiles and shards of pottery in the gravel pits beneath the old Augustinian priory of St John the Baptist at Holywell, as well as the yellow, green and brown floor tiles, imported from the Netherlands in the fifteenth century, which had once decorated the chapel. Beneath what was in the sixteenth century a grand house called Stratton House, on Shoreditch High Street, there were fragments from a Venetian glass beaker and a bowl in a style known as late Valencian lustreware. These are decorative, expensive items, and unusual. The impression of a showy, aristocratic house is confirmed by another strange find on the site: the bones of birds of prey with tether marks upon them, indicating that these had been kept and used for sport.[3]

The earth beneath Shoreditch is stuffed with exotic foreign objects such as these simply because it is an area across which waves of people have passed, and those people have as often as not been from elsewhere. It is tempting to imagine that worry about foreigners coming in and taking our jobs is a recent and temporary phenomenon, but in the summer of 1593 there were anti-immigrant riots in London. That year, during a debate in the House of Commons, Sir Walter Raleigh warned particularly against the rootless, slippery Dutch. 'The nature of the Dutchman is to fly to no man but for his profit,' he declared, 'and they will obey no man long.'[4] The names and races are different but the worry is the same in our day as it was then.

In the sixteenth century one particular object of fear was what Raleigh calls 'Dutchmen' but who were more specifically Walloons, French-speaking Protestants from the southern Netherlands. There were perhaps 10,000 immigrants in London, of a total population in 1575 of approximately 140,000. Of these, 75 per cent originated from the Netherlands, and they worked dominantly in the textile industry, particularly known for their expertise in weaving and preparing luxury cloths such as silk. English cloth was heavy; the Dutch knew how to make lighter, brighter fabrics. The English economy relied on the manufacture of and trade in cloth, and the chief trading route ran through Antwerp. This collapsed when Antwerp was sacked by the Spanish in 1576, and from 1585, Elizabeth gave military aid to the Dutch. So they were political allies but economic rivals, welcomed for the new skills and weaving technologies they brought in with them and yet double-taxed and strictly limited in laws about what and when they could trade.[5]

Shoreditch was the setting for these debates about immigrants, and work, and what it truly meant to be English. It is the oldest story of all: a nation works out who it is by shutting out those it insists it is not; a city in a time of crisis falls back to building walls and then placing some things, some people, just outside them. And Shoreditch stands just outside the City walls. Immediately to the north of the City wall by Bishopsgate, on the west side of what is now Shoreditch High Street, was a grid of tenements known as 'Petty France', for this was where the French settled, and where, as Stow records, unscrupulous landlords charged high rents. Just to the south was the old priory of Austin Friars, which from 1550 was given as a stranger's church, where European Protestants could worship, and on the wall of this church during the anti-immigrant riots of the summer of 1593 somebody scrawled racist graffiti. 'Conceive it well, for Safe-guard of your Lives,' it threatened: 'Your Goods, your children, and your dearest Wives.'[6]

The clues are tantalizingly few but enough to give a sense of a place defined by its adjacency, by being both too near and yet also so distant, foreign, exotic. In the 1550s, a tenement called the Great House on Shoreditch High Street was known to rent rooms to Spaniards, Italians, Frenchmen and the Dutch. The Bassano family – immigrants from Venice, and celebrated as court musicians – lived on the Kingsland Road. Their most famous member was Emilia, better known as the poet Emilia Lanier, who might have been the dangerous, sexy Dark Lady of Shakespeare's Sonnets and who was baptized in January 1569 at the Church of St Botolphs without Bishopsgate.

The word 'refugee' arrives in the English language with the Huguenots who settled around Shoreditch, fleeing religious persecution in France in the second half of the seventeenth century. Like the earlier Walloons, they too were weavers and they were fleeing religious persecution. We might say that the word 'refugee' is itself a refugee, and we might see this as the history of Shoreditch in miniature. It is a place where things are brought in, and where that which newly arrives changes – even slightly – the existing language.

*　*　*

There's an early biographical rumour, first recorded at about the same time that the word refugee was settling into English, that Shakespeare lived in Shoreditch when he arrived in London in the late 1580s. Perhaps he did; even if he didn't, he certainly should have. East London was where the playwrights lived, and Shakespeare as a new arrival from the Midlands belonged amongst the other immigrants. There is a curious reversal in the meaning of the words 'foreigner' and 'stranger' between Shakespeare's time and ours. In his day, a 'stranger' was one from a foreign country, while a 'foreigner' was somebody from another parish, or an outsider, or simply someone you did not know. When Shakespeare arrived from the Midlands he was a foreigner in London.

The history of London – as Susan J. Wiseman discusses in this volume – is defined by water, but Shoreditch, as the name suggests, is particularly wet. Shoreditch High Street was paved in the 1550s but the lanes around it were muddy; the trees which grew there were those which tended to favour the wet ground, such as willows. Here, on a small plot of land ringed by drainage ditches, a joiner and former actor called James Burbage built in 1576 the first permanent playhouse in England. It was on the site of the old priory of Holywell, and this in turn was named after a muddy well which stood at the source of the Walbrook, one of London's lost rivers. Burbage called the playhouse the Theatre, which appears obvious now but at the time seemed strange and a little pompous. The word 'theatre' was commonly used to refer to illustrated books such as atlases, but it comes from the Latin – and before that the Greek – meaning somewhere that things are shown. Perhaps Burbage liked the grandeur, or the classical flair; or perhaps like Stow he was thinking of London's Roman past. But the name caught on, becoming a synonym for all houses where plays were performed.

Burbage's Theatre was perhaps the perfect product of Shoreditch: a jumble of old and new, an innovation that was itself a recapitulation of past glory and a distinctly English triumph which was itself borrowed from abroad. When Shakespeare arrived in London, it was the most celebrated and most notorious of the playhouses, and while we cannot know Shakespeare's exact movements with any certainty, we do know that by 1594 he was resident playwright at the Theatre, as part of the company called the Lord Chamberlain's Men. At the Theatre, and for the Lord Chamberlain's Men, Shakespeare wrote the cluster of early plays which made him famous. Here, and for James Burbage's son Richard – who was the first and most important Shakespearean actor – Shakespeare wrote *Romeo and Juliet*, *A Midsummer Night's Dream* (both 1595) and *The Merchant of Venice* (1596–7).

In these plays, Shakespeare is working as something like the archetypal immigrant: he is telling stories drawn from foreign sources, making a distinctively English culture from imported pieces and skills. Verona and Venice, or the woods outside Athens: these are the settings of these plays and the places that they dream of even as they were first performed in Shoreditch. *A Midsummer Night's Dream* is the strangest of these plays, and is perhaps best seen as a kind of compendium of foreign things. Greek myth rubs up against Roman poetry; the characters have Latin names, or Greek names, or comically English names. They are called Peter Quince; or Theseus, Duke of Athens; or Oberon, a name borrowed from a French romance and before that from the Old High German for 'elf-king'.

One much-loved character is Nick Bottom, who dreams of wealth and status but ends up with the head of an ass; he is also, we are told in passing, a weaver, and he speaks a phrase in French. This French-speaking weaver on the stage would have echoed immediately with Shakespeare's Shoreditch audience, who met Walloon weavers in the streets, and Shakespeare quietly turns the feared immigrant into an absurd, humane figure. Late in the play, Theseus in an aside conjures up a powerful image of the work of the playwright, whom he calls a poet:

> The poet's eye, in a fine frenzy rolling,
> Doth glance from heaven to earth, from earth to heaven,
> And, as imagination bodies forth
> The forms of things unknown, the poet's pen
> Turns them to shapes, and gives to airy nothing
> A local habitation and a name.

There are plenty of old cliches about poetry as divine madness and these hum beneath the surface of these lines, but Theseus is saying something more particular than this. The imagination of a place sometimes comes before the place, he says, and imagination may invent the place it then comes to find. Even the faintest of things can be given a setting, and can be made real and solid in the world by being placed and named. Shakespeare in Shoreditch invented the theatre at the Theatre, and this was its local habitation and its name.

Notes

1. *A Survey of London by John Stow*, ed. Charles Lethbridge Kingsford, 3 vols (Oxford: Clarendon Press, 1908) I, 168.

2. Ibid., 169–170.

3. Raoul Bull, Simon Davis, Hana Lewis and Christopher Phillpotts, *Holywell Priory and the Development of Shoreditch to c. 1600: Archeology from the London Overground East London Line* (London: Museum of London Archeology, 2011).

4. Simonds d'Ewes, *The Journals of All the Parliaments During the Reign of Queen Elizabeth* (Shannon, Ireland: n.p., 1682), 509.

5. On Dutch immigrants in Elizabethan London, see Nigel Goose and Lien Luu, *Immigrants in Tudor and Early Stuart England* (Brighton: Sussex Academic Press, 2005); Robin Gwynn, *Huguenot Heritage: The History and Contribution of the Huguenots in Britain* (Brighton: Sussex Academic Press, 2001); and Bernard Cottrett, *The Huguenots in England: Immigration and Settlement c.1550–1700* (Cambridge: Cambridge University Press, 1991).

6. Arthur Freeman, 'Marlowe, Kyd, and the Dutch Church Libel', *English Literary Renaissance* 3, no. 1 (1973): 49.

CHAPTER 11
19 PRINCELET STREET, SPITALFIELDS: A CASE STUDY IN THE ARCHITECTURE OF MIGRATION AND DIVERSITY

Dan Cruickshank

Number 19 Princelet Street, Spitalfields is an historic building that is important not for its age, nor for its architecture or origins, but because of what it is now. The building – ancient, worn and fragile – seems to hover between memory and imagination – an authentic and emblematic ruin that is a powerful testament to those who have lived within it, and where history and patterns of occupation are etched deep into the house's fabric. Its histories are diverse, but united by the shared travails faced by different waves of immigrants who – forging new lives in London – have in turns found shelter within the house. It is now, gently and largely unintended, a monument to human endurance and endeavour.

The building history of 19 Princelet Street is unexceptional for Spitalfields. It stands on a small estate, acquired during the second decade of the eighteenth century by two lawyers – Charles Wood and Simon Michell. They laid out a grid of streets between the existing thoroughfares of Brown's Lane (now Hanbury Street) and Brick Lane. Running west off Brick Lane was a shallow court that was extended around 1718 to form Prince (now Princelet) Street to connect to a new north-south street called Wood (now Wilkes) Street. The north side of Princelet Street was divided by the estate into building plots, several of which were leased by a speculating builder named Samuel Worrall. These plots included what was 18 Prince Street – now 19 Princelet Street.

The house was built in 1718–19, as part of a pair with 17 Princelet Street (built by Samuel Phipps in collaboration with Worrall), and were disposed of freehold by Wood and Michell rather than by means of a long building lease (usually ninety-nine years) that was at the time the far more usual manner.[1] Despite this unusual process, the houses are typical of the period: one room wide, two rooms deep and three storeys high above ground, plus a basement kitchen, pantry and scullery. Number 19 would also have had a third floor garret, though probably smaller than the one that can be seen today, which is almost certainly, at least in part, a later eighteenth-century addition. Probably the top floor originally comprised only one small room, located at the rear of the house. The fact that Worrall acquired the freehold of 19 Princelet Street from the Wood Michell estate seems to have obliged him to raise money in 1721–2 by conveying the newly built house to a consortium comprising a 'drugster, a draper and a glover', who were subsequently joined by a 'needleworker'. It seems that it was this consortium that sold the house to the Huguenot master weaver Peter Abraham Ogier.

The Huguenots – French Protestants – had suffered significant religious persecution in their homeland since the late sixteenth century, and from the early 1680s many of these 'refugees' (a word coined at the time) settled in Spitalfields. Here they soon developed the local weaving trade into an enormously valuable silk-weaving industry that produced fabric of the highest quality. Peter Abraham Ogier – born Pierre Abraham in 1690 at Chassais l'Eglise near Sigournais in Bas-Poitou – was one of fourteen children, of whom at least ten lived beyond babyhood. His parents, Pierre and Jeanne Ogier, had chosen to remain in France after the repeal of the Edict of Nantes in 1685 made Protestant worship unlawful; but in around 1697, in trouble for attending Protestant *assemblées* and with her husband recently dead, a heavily pregnant Jeanne decided to flee to England. She brought with her perhaps eight of her children, leaving two sons behind in France.[2]

Jeanne evidently recognized that the silk industry offered the prospects of wealth and security for her family (the Ogiers had not been notable silk weavers or merchants in France) and used some of her money to apprentice Peter Abraham to Samuel Brule, a foreign master. Peter Abraham became a successful master weaver, a freeman of the Weavers' Company in 1716 and a liveryman in 1741.[3] He also became an elder of La Patente de Spitalfields, a church located first in Paternoster Row, within the Fruit and Vegetable Market, and then in Brown's Lane, now Hanbury Street. His success as a weaver is reflected in the fact that in 1745 he was able to offer twenty-eight men to serve the Crown in the face of the threat of the restoration of the Catholic Stuart dynasty – in the shape of Bonnie Prince Charlie – to the throne of Great Britain. Overall, the Ogier dynasty and their six companies were able to volunteer a force of 164 workmen.[4] In 1712, Peter Abraham married a French woman – Esther Dubois (Duboc) – from Normandy at St Dunstan's, Stepney (the parish church that served much of central and east Spitalfields until the creation in 1729 of the parish of Christ Church, Spitalfields), and the couple went on to have twelve children (seven of whom died young). And by the 1740s, if not significantly earlier, Peter Abraham and his family were living at 19 Princelet Street. By 1743 the house was confirmed to be Ogier's residence.[5] So the fabric of the house predates Ogier's occupation – but with one remarkable exception. In the first-floor front room there formerly stood a fine timber-made French-style rococo fire surround of c. 1745– 50, which Ogier must have added in the last years of his life. It shows that his taste in architectural details was, like his taste in silk designs, refined and inspired by French models. The fire surround was stolen in the early 1980s but was later recovered and is now in storage awaiting repair and reinstalment.

The house has, for Spitalfields, an unusually large rear garden (it's one of the distinctive features of the houses on the north side of Princelet Street and the houses on Fournier Street). This would no doubt have contained a 'house of office' set over a cesspit and have served other practical purposes such as a location for fuel and water storage. But it was large enough to have been ornamental as well and, since Huguenots included gardening amongst their many cultural attributes, would probably have been laid out with flowerbeds and plants in tubs set between gravel paths. The plants – including varieties of roses and jasmine – would probably have come from the Shoreditch and Hoxton market gardens of such flower-men and nurserymen as Thomas Fairchild, the author of

The City Gardener (1722). As for the 'house of office', or lavatory, this might well have been disguised as a plant-veiled pavilion, with roses, perhaps, twined around or in front of it. This was not unusual in the eighteenth century, hence the euphemism for going to the lavatory – to 'go pluck a rose' – as explained in verse by Jonathan Swift:

The bashful maid, to hide her blush,
Shall creep no more behind a bush;
Here unobserved, she boldly goes,
As who should say, *to pluck a rose*.[6]

When completed in the mid-1720s, Princelet Street – with its tall houses of regular design and relatively large rear gardens – was one of the best streets in Spitalfields. For a successful master weaver and silk merchant such as Peter Abraham Ogier, it was therefore a suitably prestigious address.

The Land Tax returns of 1743 for Christ Church Middlesex give a very good sense of the community in which Peter Abraham Ogier lived.[7] Peter Abraham's activities as a master weaver were complex and his roles varied. But one thing he would almost certainly not have done, when in his prime as a master, was actually to weave. He was no doubt a skilled weaver and had worked as one in his youth, but as a master he would have been more of an entrepreneurial businessman. He would have acquired raw materials, organized their complex processing, commissioned fabric designs, employed journeymen weavers to make the silk, and overseen its wholesale sale to mercers.

Peter Abraham's business activities must have had a direct influence upon the way he and his family occupied 19 Princelet Street and on the arrangement and appearance of its interior. But weaving almost certainly did not take place there during his occupancy. In the first half of the century the Ogiers would have lived in the house in some style and with a number of servants. Business activities would have been limited to meetings with suppliers, designers, weavers and mercers – presumably in one of the ground-floor rooms (now lost) – that would have served also as a dining parlour and perhaps for the occasional display of the latest products. The small top-floor room, probably at the rear, that existed before the construction of the existing well-lit weaving garret, would presumably have been used for some practical purpose, perhaps as a counting room. The top-floor front room weaving garret, with its long range of windows, is a late eighteenth-century addition. It was probably created in response to the gradual demise of the silk industry, when large houses – once the homes of merchants – were divided to form multi-occupied tenements in mixed use. At this period, around 1800, the weaving garret would have been added, transforming a former roof space into workshop accommodation.

Sadly, there are no records of life in 19 Princelet Street during Peter Abraham's occupation, or indeed detailed records of the daily and domestic lives of any Spitalfields Huguenot families at the time. To attempt a portrait, we have to assemble what physical or documentary evidence survives and speculate. We know the Huguenots made and admired fine silver ornaments, clocks and furniture, and these – combined with their beautiful silks – must have made the interiors of the leading Huguenot families impressive. Their Calvinist principles did not inhibit them in the display of beauty or of riches honestly earned. Surviving wills also suggest that such objects were important and valued. The master weaver Peter Bourdon, of 27 Fournier Street, in his will of 1732 leaves all his 'household goods [and] all my plate' to his wife, who he also confirms in her possession of his 'linen, rings and jewels'. But, more tellingly, he leaves his 'beloved wife Margaret' £3,500 in 'lawful money', with the total value of his bequests being £6,880.[8] The more affluent of these Spitalfields master weavers were rich indeed and, as men who valued property and the display of wealth, and who had made their fortunes through the creation of tasteful beauty, their homes must have been stunning. Archaeological investigation of 19 Princelet Street, and of comparable and contemporary houses in Spitalfields, suggests that their panelled interiors were painted in soft and simple stone colours – either light ochres, pale blue/green greys – or 'drab', and all realized through the mixing of earth pigments such as 'Oxford Ochre' and umber, indigo organic dye, soot (called 'lamp black') or copper carbonates with white lead ground in linseed oil. Strong, dark colours could be achieved with these pigments ('lead' colour for example, olive green, 'wainscot colour' or blue or green verditer). Verditer seems to have been used very rarely in primary rooms in the 1720s, 30s or 40s and was reserved for very occasional use only in kitchens or workshops on plaster as well as timber.[9]

Peter Abraham Ogier died in 1757, and it is not currently known where he and his wife Esther are buried. One way and another, the Ogier family became extraordinarily rich and powerful members of the French merchant community in eighteenth-century London. It was a tightly-knit society that retained its coherence because virtually all marriages and most significant business partnerships were kept within the Huguenot community.[10]

The fate of 19 Princelet Street in the years immediately after Ogier's death remains in many respects uncertain. In the 1770s and 1780s, number 17 was occupied by Samuel Ireland junior, a weaver, and it is around this time, or soon after, that the weaving garret was added to number 19.[11] So it is reasonable to assume that the house was, at least in part, in use during the late eighteenth century as a weaving garret and workshop.

*   *   *

By the time of the 1851 census the once numerous and powerful Ogier family appears to have disappeared from Spitalfields, and number 19 Princelet Street (then still 18 Princes Street) was occupied by two households. One household was headed by John Broadbridge, a thirty-year-old 'Surveyor' who lived with his wife Sarah, aged twenty-nine, born in 'America'. The second household comprised, on the day of the census at least, Elizabeth Carter, aged seventy, the 'House Proprietor' born in East Elm, Essex.[12]

The low density of the occupation of 19 Princelet Street – three people in a house with about ten rooms – was most unusual in mid-nineteenth-century Spitalfields and implies that 19 Princelet Street remained in some form of genteel occupation. More typical was the life being led within nearby 23 Princelet (16 Princes) Street. In stark contrast, this house – built in about 1705 and roughly the same size as 19 – was occupied by five households and contained eighteen people on the day of the census. And the immediate neighbour – 17 Princelet (formerly 19 Princes) Street – was occupied by thirteen people in three households, including the 96-year-old former parish beadle, Thomas Hart.

But all was soon to change for 19 Princelet Street. In 1870 a synagogue named Chevras Nidvath Chen, which was founded by Russian and Polish Jews in 1862 in nearby Fashion Street, relocated to 19 Princelet Street.[13] Given that Eastern European migrant Jews did not start to appear in large numbers in East London until after a wave of Tsarist pogroms got under way in 1881, it's a surprisingly early date for such a place of worship. The house was transformed. The main congregational room of the synagogue (called the United Friends synagogue in the 1871 Post Office Directory) was built upon the garden, and by the 1890s took the form of a double height hall top-lit by roof lanterns and containing galleries supported by cast iron columns. Below the hall, and dug out of the garden, was a large meeting room used primarily by the Friendly Society created in association with the synagogue and intended to support needy members of the congregation. The works also involved the complete remodelling of the ground floor of the 1718–19 house to create a Sabbath school in the front room, with the rear room added to the volume of the synagogue's hall. The first-floor rear room was also added to the volume of the hall, the room's rear wall removed to give easy access to the gallery. Within the room most of the original panelling was left undisturbed. Externally the house was given something of the appearance of an institutional building by covering the ground-floor elevation with stucco and by replacing the two ground-floor windows with a single, large semi-circular arched window adjoining a wide, arched door. The staircase from basement to first floor was also rebuilt in stone, in a robust manner, to serve a greatly increased traffic.

By 1893 the house had become the Princes Street Synagogue and the 1891 census records that the building was – in common with much of the street – far more densely occupied than earlier. By the 1890s, Princelet Street had become a major part of Spitalfields's Russian and Polish Jewish community. It was also one of the area's most crowded and poverty-wracked streets. This is made clear by contemporary documents – the census returns of course, but also the revised edition of the 'Poverty Map', compiled in the late 1890s by the philanthropist and social reformer Charles Booth, and by an 1899 map purporting to trace the pattern of occupation of 'Jewish East London'.

The notebooks compiled by Booth and his secretary George H. Duckworth as they explored Spitalfields with a police guide named Sergeant French survive in the library of the London School of Economics. They record that the group explored 'Fournier Street – late Church Street', which with Spital Square contained the best large early Georgian houses to survive in Spitalfields.[14] Duckworth noted that the houses in Fournier Street were the homes of 'well-to-do Jews' who 'keep servants', and that 'the large Wesleyan chapel at the end of [the] street is now being converted into a synagogue'. The chapel had been built in 1743 to serve as a Huguenot temple and currently houses a mosque. (The 1899 map of 'Jewish East London' suggests that the houses on both sides of Fournier Street were in '95% to 100% Jewish occupation').

Sergeant French stated that – most unusually for the area – there was in Fournier Street only 'one family to each house'. Booth's 'Poverty Map' was organized to record the occupation of London houses within seven colour-coded grades. It was an ad-hoc affair based largely on superficial observation of the inhabitants of houses and streets and on physical condition. Black recorded the 'lowest class', then there was dark blue; light blue; purple; pink; red and finally gold to denote 'Upper Middle and Upper Class' occupants who were 'wealthy'. In the late 1890s, Booth upgraded Fournier Street to 'red rather than pink' as it was depicted on his late 1880s map.

In his 1898–9 re-survey, Booth downgraded the houses on both sides of the east end of Princelet Street (including number 19) to black. The surviving houses on the north side are among the very few structures in London once coded black by Booth that are still standing. A look at the 1891 census suggests why Booth took this action. Number 17 Prince Street (now 21 Princelet Street) – built as a five-storey ten- or eleven-room house between 1705 and 1706 – contained on the day of the census an astonishing forty-eight people, organized as eight family groups. The 1873 Ordnance Survey map shows a large structure in the house's generous rear yard. This could have been in residential use in 1891, but was more likely a workshop or in light industrial use.

Booth describes the occupants of the houses he colour-coded black as the 'Lowest Class. Vicious, semi criminals.' The occupants of 21 Princelet Street might have been the former, but were they also the latter? A look at the trades of some of the occupants suggest that they were not. There was Henry Prollius, a forty-four-year-old cabinet maker born in Germany who lived with his twelve-year-old daughter Elizabeth; Isaac Newman, a thirty-five-year-old 'Hebrew book seller' born in Russia who lived with his Russian wife and eight children; Barnet Cohen, a forty-five-year-old 'Boot finisher from Germany', his Polish wife and three children; William Germantis, a thirty-year-old Polish-born 'Tailor's Presser', his wife, son and five Polish male lodgers – aged eighteen to twenty-five – whose trades were tailors, table makers and a 'skin dresser'; and Philip Swartzh a twenty-year-old tailor from 'Russia Poland', his nineteen-year-old wife and daughter.[15] It is hard to comprehend the manner in which the house was occupied, but it is a distinct possibility that the Germantis family of three were obliged to occupy a single room with five male lodgers. Water would have been supplied to the basement and perhaps to a couple of landings, while the only lavatories – perhaps two – would have been in the backyard.

Number 17 Princes Street, although extreme in its density of occupation, was not the complete exception. Number 18 Princes Street (now number 19 Princelet Street) – which contained the synagogue – was occupied by thirteen people in three family groups in 1891. These people might have been obliged to cram themselves into the building's remaining three or four rooms. One family was formed by Harris Levy, the seventy-seven-year-old synagogue beadle, his wife and cousin, while another of the families comprised the widowed fifty-three-year-old Polish-born Leah Lichenstein and her five grown sons, working as tailors and bootmakers.

Number 19 Princelet Street continued to house a working synagogue and a residential community until the 1960s, when the synagogue gradually ceased to function, as its congregation moved out of Spitalfields. Fading inscriptions painted on the synagogue's gallery fronts testify to the support it once received from eminent Jewish families and, quietly, record its demise. In the 1880s 'N. M. Rothschild & Co.' donated £50, while at roughly the same time Samuel Montagu MP gave £31. 10s. 6d. The last dated donation is from a Mrs R. Cohen on 2 September 1956.

Part of the house remained occupied into the late 1960s but the fabric was decaying and life within the building must have become increasingly desperate as large parts of it fell empty. By the early 1980s the building was abandoned and forlorn in the extreme, but – in a most haunted manner – it retained the long-deserted contents of the synagogue and of some of the homes that had been created within its rooms. At this point the Spitalfields Historic Buildings Trust – a charity formed in 1977 to battle for the fabric, history and community of Spitalfields – felt compelled to take action. For generations, diverse communities have settled and thrived in Spitalfields – and ultimately moved on. This is the story that the Trust believed the building could tell in an inspirational manner, ideally as a museum dedicated to the more creative and positive aspects of migration, and to the trades, products and art and industry of Spitalfields migrants.

The Trust managed to buy the building from the trustees of the synagogue and undertook the most urgent repairs – including stabilizing and repointing the Princelet Street façade. The Trust also undertook, with the Museum of London, the complex business of sorting and cataloguing the interior. It was at this time, in the early 1980s, that the extraordinary story emerged of the enigmatic Jewish scholar David Rodinsky. He had occupied the house's upper floor for nearly forty years, until 1969, in a most reclusive and eccentric manner and seems to have disappeared almost without trace, leaving his home an undisturbed but most informative chaos of newspapers and learned volumes on languages and the Cabbala. The Trust carefully collected and stored Rodinsky's artefacts, which were subsequently photographed, catalogued and described by Rachel Lichtenstein.[16] It is now almost forty years since the project for saving and transforming 19 Princelet Street into a museum and community building was first explored. Such is the complexity of the idea that the scheme remains – as yet – to be fully realized.

Collectively the house retains one of the most evocative historic interiors in London, where little in the way of fittings or displays are needed to tell the building's compelling and emblematic – almost mythic – story of migration and settlement. People who have come to Spitalfields – from far afield and often in desperate circumstances – have found refuge, sustenance and support, have thrived and – in the fullness of time – moved on. This is the story the building tells through its rooms and artefacts. In simple terms, the house is the story – all it requires is the opportunity to speak. It is the star of all the tales latent within its fabric and is a far from mute monument. It tells tales of the lives lived by generations of diverse but ordinary people who – eventually and collectively – have made London a great world city. As such, 19 Princelet Street is an incredibly rare, rich – and very special – survival.

Notes

1. F. H. W. Sheppard (ed.), *Survey of London*, 47 vols (London: London County Council 1957), XXVII, 187.

2. The Ogier genealogy, from Pierre and Jeanne to William born in 1812, is published as figure 8.4 in Theya Molleson, Margaret Cox, A. H. Waldron and D. K. Whitaker, *The Spitalfields Project: The Anthropology: The Middling Sort*, 2 vols (York: Council for British Archaeology, 1993), II, 127.

3. Court Book of the Weavers' Company of London, HSQS XXXIII, 77.

4. 'The Spitalfields Manufacturers and the Young Pretender', Huguenot Society Proceedings 2 (1887–8): 453–6; *London Gazette*, 5 October 1745.

5. Sheppard, *Survey of London*, XXVII, 188.

6. Jonathan Swift, 'A Panegyric on the Dean', in *Jonathan Swift the Complete Poems*, ed. Pat Rogers (London: Penguin, 1983), 436–44 (441).

7. 1743 Land Tax Returns for Christ Church Middlesex. London Metropolitan Archives. MS06008/001-2 [736/8]; Molleson et al., *The Spitalfields Project*.

8. National Archives (UK). PROB.11/649 sig, 5.

9. Dan Cruickshank and Neil Burton, *Life in the Georgian City* (New York: Viking, 1990), 180–9.

10. Molleson et al., *The Spitalfields Project*, 98, 127.

11. Sheppard, *Survey of London,* XXVII, 188.

12. 1851 National Census Returns. National Archives (UK). HO 107 1542, district 12.

13. Sheppard, *Survey of London*, XXVII, 188–9; Rachel Lichtenstein, 'Vision for a Jewish Quarter in East London' (unpublished report, 2019), 7–8.

14. George H. Duckworth's Notebook (1898), Booth/B/351, 124–5, https://booth.lse.ac.uk/notebooks/b351.

15. 1891 National Census Returns. National Archives (UK). RG12/273, district 4.

16. Rachel Lichtenstein and Iain Sinclair, *Rodinsky's Room* (London: Granta, 1999).

CHAPTER 12
HOSTILE ENVIRONMENTS: DISINTERRING A LASCAR BARRACKS IN NINETEENTH-CENTURY SHADWELL
Eliza Cubitt

In 1884, describing his 'Life and Work Among the East End Poor', Reverend Harry Jones of St-George's-in-the-East, a Chaplain-in-Ordinary to Queen Victoria, recalls the accidental disinterring, whilst installing play equipment for Raine's School at Cannon-Street Road, of a Lascar burial ground. Jones's grim discovery of disarticulated remains reminded him that a court had been built nearby as a barracks for the Lascars (sailors from the Indian subcontinent or Southeast Asia) into which they were locked at night, lest they should 'grin and run about the city'.[1] Concomitantly glib, ghoulish and racist, Jones's description reflects the Lascars' treatment in earlier nineteenth-century Britain, during the period when the court was established.

Throughout the nineteenth century, frequent reports of the Lascars' destitution in British ports led to their conflicted perception in British minds. Lascars were imagined as fragile and exploited but also as vagrant and potentially miscreant (if not outrightly subversive). In 1802, the murders of Lascars on board the ship *Union* brought their plight into the press, but their situation remained dire.[2] There were reports that they were left hungry, poorly clothed and underpaid, either stranded in London without wages or forcibly returned to ships on which they were beaten.[3] Lascar sailors recruited in place of British sailors lost in the Napoleonic Wars were, Humberto Garcia has argued, dispossessed and victimized as soon as they were on British soil, existing outside the capitalist system as 'specters'.[4] Viewed as simultaneously delicate and dangerous, they were 'the afflicting, the heart-rending nuisance'.[5] This chapter details how these living spectres were housed, controlled, forgotten and finally recalled through disinterment, within a square mile in the landscape of the nineteenth-century East End.

The great numbers of Lascars destitute in and around nineteenth-century London, as Garcia notes, 'vexed legal definitions of metropolitan citizenship'.[6] Under the terms of the East India Act of 1814, the East India Company (EIC) was ultimately responsible for feeding and housing the Lascars while in England if ship owners failed to provide for them. The EIC subcontracted the care of Lascars to individuals: these were valuable contracts held within close-knit, often nepotistic groups. From 1794 to 1804, one of these subcontractors was John Anthony (1766–1805), an interpreter for the EIC. Anthony's wife, Sarah, was the daughter of another contractor, Abraham Gole, who with his son Abraham Junior (both churchwardens of St-George's-in-the-East) held contracts for housing and feeding Lascars from 1802 and, after the death of their partner, Daniel Osborn of Shadwell, as sole contractors from 1806.[7] The Goles were paid, according to

Michael Fisher, £169,795 between 1803 and 1813. Although currency conversion can be inexact, the National Archives Currency Converter suggests that such a sum had the purchasing power equivalent to £10 million in 2017. Similar family arrangements gave the medical superintendence to William Docker in 1798 and to his brother Hilton after William's death in 1807.[8]

In 1813, a petition by trustees of St George's gathered 192 signatures stating 'the inconvenience, and Nuisances which arise from the Lascars being accommodated in that Neighbourhood and that the Property of the Petitioners has been much deteriorated and reduced in value'.[9] While the trustees' concerns were primarily financial, it must be noted that from May 1813 to May 1814, 122 Asian seamen housed at the Shadwell barracks in Angel Gardens died.[10] An 1814–15 Parliamentary Committee on Lascars and other Asiatic Seamen investigated and found the provisions lacking, but reports of violence by the supervisor were attributed to the *serang* – the Lascar recruiter. These interventions into the Shadwell barracks likely led to the construction by the Goles of the New Court. Near to the previous barracks, the New Court was also proximate to Ratcliff Highway, notorious for the murders of the Marr family in 1811 as well as for petty crime and violence: here, it was supposed that the Lascars would be, as Garcia puts it, 'beyond public view and under stricter supervision'.[11] Despite calls for Lascars to be confined on hulks – prison ships moored in the River Thames and elsewhere – the barrack system continued.[12]

Purpose-built, the New Court barracks was a two-storey building of single rooms without sanitary provision and surrounded by high walls. In her comprehensive 1896 exploration of London's burial grounds, Mrs (Isabella M.) Basil Holmes noted, 'These Lascars used to live in a court near by [sic; near St-George's-in-the-East] and are said to have been locked in at night.'[13] Jones stated that the sailors were 'driven in' at night before being locked in, because they were 'reckoned [. . .] to be dangerous'. Jones's account is

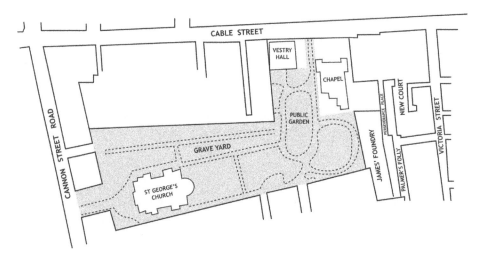

Figure 12.1 Section of the Vestry map of St-George's-in-the-East (1878) showing New Court off Victoria Street.

confirmed in Michael Fisher's *Counterflows to Colonialism*: although the Lascars were free to go where they wished during the day, Gole's men would round up the Lascars at night, locking the gates at 11 pm and opening them at 6 am. Despite the founding of charities – the Society for the Protection of Asiatic Sailors and the Society for the Relief and Instruction of Poor Africans and Asiatics in London – to assist these friendless people, their suffering continued in the barracks.[14]

The flawed system favoured shipowners and captains. The EIC could fine the shipowner for leaving crew behind, but not if the crew refused to return. An 1833 case found thirteen Lascars sleeping on the streets alleging ill-treatment, hunger and beatings on their ship. Mistreatment aboard ship was one reason why some Lascar seamen decided to stay in London. In this instance, their captain wanted them back on board, so would not pay for their lodging at Gole's. The sailors were 'charged with wandering abroad, sleeping in the open air and collecting a mob about them' and eventually they were removed to the ship.[15]

In 1833, the barracks closed, but the court remained.[16] Jones lamented:

> This court now exists. I have tried to get it pulled down and have its site included in our [the church's] Recreation Ground, which it adjoins, but failed. Of course, it ought to be clean swept away, without any pseudo-sentimental thought about its inhabitants [...]'[17]

The 'problem' of Lascars remained tied to the vexed question of to whom the city belonged and who belonged to it.

The Lascars used two non-denominational private burial grounds on Church Lane (called 'Backchurch Lane' from the 1860s onward). A Lascar burial at one of these grounds, known as Cain's Burial Ground (afterward Britton's in 1823), was widely reported in the newspapers as a rite attracting many curious spectators. We can locate the one Jones discovered thanks to Mrs Holmes:

> There was a large burial-ground behind a chapel in Cannon Street Road, E. The building passed to the Rector of St. George's in the East but was afterwards pulled down, and one of Raine's Foundation Schools was subsequently erected on its site. The burial-ground, in which many Lascars were interred, is now in three parts. One is a small playground for the school; the largest is Seaward Brothers' yard for their carts; the third a cooper's yard belonging to Hasted and Sons.[18]

Jones summarized his eerie reminiscence with the offhand speculation that 'the Lascars eventually disappeared, perhaps they all died'. The burial ground had within a score of years become an active part of the city again. The remains Jones discovered were unmarked – he had 'inherited no registers of the dead who lay in that place' – and unremarked.[19] Through British policies and in British interests, Lascar sailors moved across the globe and arrived in our ports. The hostile environment faced by these sailors reveals that exclusion and control are interred in the very fabric of our cities.

Notes

Author's note. Thanks to the Revd Canon M. R. Ainsworth and to Peter Smith.

1. Harry Jones, 'Life and Work Among the East London Poor', *Good Words*, December 1884, 50–4.

2. James W. Frey, 'Getting Away with Murder: The Wrongful Deaths of Lascars Aboard the *Union* in 1802', *International Review of Social History* 59 (2014): 45–68.

3. 'Ill-Treatment of Lascars', *Morning Advertiser*, 29 November 1858, 2; 'Scandalous Treatment of Lascars', *Paisley Herald and Renfrewshire Advertiser*, 24 November 1855, 3; Frey, 'Getting Away with Murder', 45–68.

4. Humberto Garcia, 'The Transports of Lascar Specters: Dispossessed Indian Sailors in Women's Romantic Poetry', *Eighteenth Century* 55, no. 2–3 (2014): 255.

5. Charles Taylor, 'Lascar Seamen', *Literary Panorama*, September 1815, 967–8.

6. Garcia, 'The Transports of Lascar Specters', 264.

7. Information about the nineteenth-century church wardens of St-George's-in-the-East is available at http://www.stgitehistory.org.uk/media/churchwardens.html.

8. Michael Fisher, *Counterflows to Colonialism: Indian Travellers and Settlers in Britain, 1600–1857* (Delhi: Orient Blackswan, 2006), 154.

9. Quoted by Fisher, *Counterflows*, 944.

10. John Seed, 'Maritime Labour and Asian Sailors in Nineteenth-Century Britain', in *Asian Migrants in Europe: Transcultural Connections*, ed. Sylvia Hahn and Stanley Nadel (Göttingen: V&R Unipress, 2014), 43.

11. Garcia, 'The Transports of Lascar Specters', 262.

12. Fisher, *Counterflows*, 171.

13. Mrs Basil [Isabella M.] Holmes, *The London Burial Grounds: Notes on their History from the Earliest Times to the Present Day* (London: T. Fisher Unwin, 1896), 149.

14. Fisher, *Counterflows*, 158–9, 177.

15. 'Alleged Ill-Treatment of a Lascar Crew: Extraordinary Case', *Freeman's Journal*, 15 November 1833, 4.

16. Seed, 'Maritime Labour', 48.

17. In Goad's Insurance Map of 1887, New Court and the neighbouring courts which troubled Jones, Perseverance Place and Palmers' Folly, had been replaced by a Board School. Jones, 'Life and Work', 50–4.

18. Holmes, *The London Burial Grounds*, 149.

19. Jones, 'Life and Work', 50–4.

CHAPTER 13
THE SLOT-METER AND THE EAST END AVANT-GARDE
Alex Grafen

If you were to stand at the corner of Osborn Street and Whitechapel High Street on a winter's evening in 1913, there would be little to catch the eye. From the High Street, you would see a stationer's shut for the night. Turning your gaze upwards, there would be a large sign reading 'W. Straker Ltd' blocking out half the window on the floor above. Look more carefully, however, and you might see some light spilling out above the sign. Listen and you might hear voices.

Enter 1 Osborn Street, climb the stairs and you would find before you a small room: the Slot-Meter. Packed mostly with young men, the room would likely be dense with the smell of bodies, smoke and food. You would hear statements and arguments on recent developments in art, politics, religion and psychology. This talk would go on late into the night. Eventually, people would depart, most going back through the East End streets to wherever their parents lived, some further afield.

How unusual this scene was is hard to say. We know of it because Sonia Cohen, the hostess of this cramped salon, wrote memoirs in which she described how she came to live with the young poet and playwright John Rodker and the meetings they held in their flat. In what follows, I will describe the meetings in more detail before providing some context for their intellectual ferment, and discussing what it would mean to think of these meetings as proof of an East End avant-garde.

Cohen and Rodker rented the flat from the dentist and 'notorious Nihilist' Rosa Nadel.[1] The painter David Bomberg, a friend of Cohen and Rodker, was against their informal marriage. It was he who gave the flat its name when he warned Cohen that she was 'about to live with a long, skinny poet in a slot-meter'.[2] Cohen was not deterred and described how she and Rodker

> [...] were jubilantly self-contained and aloof from the whole world, for our room was isolated from our landlady's apartment and surgery by a flight of stairs that strayed off on its own account. Our furniture we contrived from boxes, which we sandpapered and then covered with blue and scarlet paint. I stitched to the casement cloth that covered our bed, scarlet bands in the key pattern [...] Our bed had no frame, so we were able to call it a 'divan', a word recently borrowed by the furnishing trade from the sumptuous East.[3]

The eclecticism of taste was further exhibited on the walls. A broadside published by the Poetry Bookshop was pinned above the mantelpiece; on it was printed Harold Monro's 'Overheard on a Salt Marsh', a poem that dramatized an exchange between a nymph and a goblin. On the larger walls were figures composed of sharp lines, arranged on white pages: prints based on drawings that the artist Wyndham Lewis had made for plans of an illustrated edition of Shakespeare's *Timon of Athens*. Where Monro's poem bears some resemblance to the early work of Yeats, Lewis's influences are more clearly those of Cubism and Futurism.[4] While the general effect may have been chaotic, it is evidence of a lively engagement with contemporary trends and thus formed a fitting environment for the discussions. In describing her own and her friends' influences around this time, Cohen mentions Walt Whitman, Friedrich Nietzsche, Filippo Marinetti and others.[5] Rodker's poems of the same period show debts to Imagism and French Symbolism.[6]

Cohen's is the sort of role easily elided in histories of literary and artistic movements. As well as the hostess of the Slot-Meter, Cohen was a dancer and model; for a while, she was part of the troupe of the innovative dancer Margaret Morris. She later worked as an actor and as a publishing secretary. In 1937, Cohen authored *The Way to Beauty: A Complete Guide to Personal Loveliness*, a book which gave advice on topics such as diet, make-up and posture. Her interest to critics so far has mostly resided in her recollections of the early years of Bomberg and the poet Isaac Rosenberg, but her significance extends beyond that.[7] Along with Rodker, they were the children of Jewish immigrants to Britain from the Russian Empire. In the Slot-Meter, we can see this second generation of the Jewish East End not simply responding to international cultural developments as they filtered through London, but synthesizing and creatively acting upon it on their own terms.

Some contextualization of their historical moment is useful. The late nineteenth century had seen a dramatic increase in immigration from the Russian Empire, with many of the migrants Jews. They left for various reasons: 'the beginnings of state-managed industrialization, and government restrictions' which undercut Jews' economic independence; demographic growth; and military conscription and increased violence, including pogroms. Even before the Aliens Act of 1905 established a state apparatus to control and deter immigration, various Anglo-Jewish institutions sought to repatriate many of them. They shared wider beliefs about the undesirability of immigration and were wary of the reputational threat posed by Jewish immigrants that were impoverished as well as visibly and audibly foreign.[8] Repatriation was not in every case unwelcome to the migrants, many of whom intended Britain as a station of transmigration on the way to the greater possibilities of the United States. However, not all arrivals were sent on to the States; some were sent back to the Russian Empire; others were sent to South Africa, Canada and Argentina.[9] Those that remained were concentrated in the East End of London. There were important ways in which the Jewish East End formed an autonomous and idiosyncratic unit; at the same time, it was permeated with influences from outside. Anglo-Jewish philanthropy stepped in to support those who remained in Britain. In its efforts to make the immigrant population conform to its standards of religion, employment and etiquette, it struggled against various factions: as well as the anarchist movement, various forms of socialism and Zionism drew adherents.

Figure 13.1 'Theater Portrait of Sonia Cohen' (n.d.). © The Rodker Family.

Initially, at least, Cohen seems to have been fairly isolated from these forces. At a young age, she was sent to the Home and School for Poor Jewish Children in Newington Green by her widowed mother. Missionaries had persuaded Cohen's mother that Sonia's dancing in the street was a sign of future ruin that only their school could avert.[10] The boarding school was run by John Wilkinson, a Methodist missionary who had, from early on in his career, set himself particularly to the conversion of Jews, a task whose 'almost insurmountable difficulties' he considered 'a charm rather than a discouragement'.[11] Cohen records the abuse and anti-Semitism she encountered at Wilkinson's boarding school.[12] It is then perhaps not surprising that she did not embrace Christianity. Lloyd Gartner observes that, despite the best efforts of missionaries like Wilkinson, 'cases of apostasy' among Jewish immigrants were 'nearly infinitesimal'.[13]

While Cohen's early education did not attract her to Christianity, it may have left her more open to political and intellectual trends that rejected religion in general. Visits made to the South Ethical Society, a freethought organization based in Finsbury, were significant for her intellectual development. Cohen initially attended for the concerts and became interested in the lectures and heard Joseph McCabe, a Catholic priest turned campaigner for the freethought movement. She also attended the meetings of the Stepney branch of the Young Socialist League. It is likely that Joseph Leftwich refers to Cohen when he describes a 'Sophie Kahn' addressing the League on 'the obligations of Socialists and particularly of Socialist-Feminists' in July 1911. Leftwich was critical: 'The whole speech was very vague and wandering. She was very self-conscious too and ended each sentence with a smirk.'[14] There is reason, however, to think that Leftwich's objection lay elsewhere than in the style of delivery. The following month, Leftwich and his friend proposed that the League discuss the 'Future of Woman' and then propounded the view that 'suffrage would be a danger to man, inasmuch as it would enforce legal polygamy'; the view, Leftwich wrote, met with less hostility than he had anticipated.[15] It is probably in the meetings organized by Dora Marsden's journal, the *New Freewoman*, attended by Cohen and Rodker, that we can see the best model for the union of politics, science and aesthetics hinted at in the meetings of the Slot-Meter, as well as the belief that the way one lived one's life should be shaped by that union. Cohen not only met the psychoanalyst Barbara Low and the writer Rebecca West; she also met a couple whose attitude to marriage seems to have inspired her decision to live with Rodker.[16]

The above gives us some sense of Cohen and her intellectual development, but a salon is made up of more than one person. Cohen mentions visits to the Slot-Meter by 'vegetarian friends from Hampstead Garden Suburb', a group whom she treats at a slight remove. There were also the 'Whitechapel Boys', a term which Cohen mentions only arose later but which she does not define. While the term has taken on a capacious meaning, extending to many Jewish artists and writers with only a slight connection with Whitechapel, the idea of a coherent group known as the 'Whitechapel Boys' probably owes its origin to careless indexing in Joseph Cohen's 1975 biography of Rosenberg.[17] Sonia Cohen was familiar with the biography, making it a likely source for her use of the term. This in turn means that the other figures she places at the Slot-Meter probably include Bomberg, Rosenberg, Leftwich and the teacher and critic Samuel Weinstein (later known as Stephen Winsten). The painter Mark Gertler, identified as a 'Whitechapel boy' at one point in Cohen's biography, is mentioned separately by Sonia; and William Roberts was apparently a regular attendee. A memoir by the teacher Arnold Harris indicates that he joined the 'avant garde young intellectuals' at least once; he also places the poet Lazarus Aaronson in the flat.[18] Cohen mentions by name Abraham 'Bram' Fineberg, who would go on to emigrate to the Soviet Union and translate many of Lenin's works into English; he emerges in Cohen's account as a considerate man and fond of food. More elusive and sinister is the figure 'T. C.', who was a friend of Rodker's and whom Cohen associated with 'some secret religious order'.[19] Finally, we know of the attendance on at least one occasion by Clara Birnberg, a young Jewish artist.[20] She was unimpressed with what she found: a group squeezed into a room, where they 'discussed or rather "aired" their knowledge of psychology, art and "the movements" in literature'.[21]

In *Modern Life and Modern Subjects*, the scholar Lisa Tickner argues that the years before the First World War saw the growth of 'an embryonic, East End avant-garde'.[22] Tickner finds the main sign for this movement in the 1914 Whitechapel Art Gallery exhibition, specifically, the Jewish Section, which had been curated by Bomberg and the older artist Jacob Epstein. As Tickner acknowledges, the Jewish Section contained paintings that fit neatly into neither the avant-garde nor the East End.[23] The decision to include a Jewish Section was unusual and can perhaps best be understood as part of a self-conscious gesture of continuity from the gallery, which had held an Exhibition of Jewish Arts and Antiquities in 1906. Whatever the motive, it bears some comparison with contemporary efforts to organize cultural activity around Jewishness in London, seen most clearly in the establishment in 1915 of the Ben Uri Art Society by first-generation Jewish immigrants and the less successful Jewish Association of Arts and Sciences.[24]

Definitions of the 'avant-garde' vary, but key features are a combination of aesthetic experiment with opposition to bourgeois society. A belief in the unity of art and life follows from an oppositionality that is political as well as aesthetic. If we were to take 'avant-garde' in a restricted sense, one that focused on a set of stylistic innovations in some form of art, then the Slot-Meter would be of limited interest. It spawned neither a manifesto nor a house style. However, if we work from the more expansive meaning of the term, then the meetings suggest an embryonic East End avant-garde more persuasively than does the Jewish Section, in part because they live up to Tickner's organic metaphor. Disorganized, lively and malodorous, the Slot-Meter shows the avant-garde as a living, breathing thing, taking in and adapting a range of cultural influences. Politics, art and life are interwoven.

If we take evenings at the Slot-Meter as the better instantiation of an East End avant-garde, what features emerge? One of the more striking is that Jewishness assumes less importance than it does in the 1914 exhibition and critical discussions that have focused on it.[25] While a significant proportion of the attendees were Jewish and the children of migrants, ethnicity does not obviously appear as an organizing feature. William Roberts, born in Hackney to non-Jewish parents who came originally from Islington, appears in Cohen's memoirs as a key figure in the constellation. If he is marked out, it is by his behaviour: specifically, his fondness for fish and chips, which he ate 'from newspaper saturated with vinegar'.[26] By contrast, Cohen describes how Mark Gertler visited Osborn Street only once, and suggests that he left because his acceptance into West End society had made him too 'genteel', and he was embarrassed by Roberts's supper.

The distinction regarding Gertler is telling, and we get a further indication of the character of the meetings through comparison with Cohen's evenings with Roberts and Rodker in Bomberg's studio, which appear from Cohen's memoirs to be the closest precedent for those of the Slot-Meter. There, 'prettiness and complacence in Art and Life were condemned to the point of being reviled and spat on: "Down with romanticism and sentimentality!" was the cry.' The approach is distinguished from the 'naughty boy' attitude of Bomberg's fellow Slade students C. R. W. Nevinson and Adrian Allinson, who 'thought they were being suitably anti-romantic by dressing in the clothes of the East End "tough" and then visiting Music Halls for the sole purpose of interrupting the performance. Mere gentlemanly undergraduate high jinks we called this'.[27] We can detect here a belief in a link between aesthetic and social identity, but the ground of that unity is class: it was less significant that Allinson's mother was Jewish than that his father was a doctor. Class, rather than ethnicity, was the guiding social criterion for this grouping, at least by Cohen's measure, something that speaks to the emphasis on class-consciousness in left-wing politics in the East End among their generation, as well as larger trends towards secularization and Anglicization among the immigrants.[28]

A second aspect of the avant-garde emerges from centring the Slot-Meter: the toll that the avant-garde can take and its capacity to reproduce features of the society it seeks to overhaul. Cohen became pregnant with Rodker's child. She did not have money for an abortion from a West End doctor so was treated by a doctor from the East End, and she was ill for a long time afterwards. The 'tender comradeship of the slot meter that asked no questions' does seem to have represented a meaningful system of support at this time.[29] However, Rodker increasingly pursued affairs with other women. In 1915, Cohen gave birth to a child; three years later, Rodker was married to the novelist and occultist Mary Butts.[30]

The Slot-Meter did not survive the onset of the First World War, which scattered, imprisoned or killed many of the attendees who had previously been clustered nearby. Its duration was brief, its achievements uncertain, but the legacies of individual members, in poetry and in art, suggest that its importance was greater than simply that of a vehicle for the ideas of the age. Rather, this small East End flat served as the medium in which those ideas could be developed and reformed. Cohen's generation was not simply absorbed into the British body politic and its culture but, in significant ways, altered their chemistry. Anglicization was no one-way street.

Notes

1. The phrase is from a 1919 report by the Metropolitan Police, quoted in William A. Tyrer, 'The Dentist Chair: Dr. Gessel Schkolnikoff and the Mysteries of Soviet Espionage', *Intelligence and National Security* 34, no. 4 (2019): 597.

2. Sonia Rodker (née Cohen), *The End Has Various Places* (privately published, 2018), 145. Cohen's grandsons, Oliver and Joel Rodker, organized the publication of around thirty copies of this book, which was edited by Cate Chapman. There are copies in the Tower Hamlets Local History Library and Archive, London, and the Harry Ransom Center, Texas.

3. Rodker (née Cohen), *The End Has Various Places*, 144.

4. Background on Monro's poem and its publication can be found in Dominic Hibberd, *Harold Monro: Poet of the New Age* (Basingstoke: Palgrave Macmillan, 2001), 110–11, 138. For an account of the abortive *Timon* project, see Paul Edwards, '*Timon* Rediscovered: The Projected Max Goschen Edition, 1914', *Wyndham Lewis Annual* 11 (2004): 81–3.

5. Rodker (née Cohen), *The End Has Various Places*, 138, 145.

6. John Rodker, *Poems & Adolphe 1920*, ed. Andrew Crozier (Manchester: Carcanet, 1996).

7. See, for example, Jean Moorcroft Wilson, *Isaac Rosenberg: The Making of a Great War Poet: A New Life* (London: Weidenfeld & Nicolson, 2007).

8. David Feldman, *Englishmen and Jews: Social Relations and Political Culture, 1840–1914* (New Haven, CT, and London: Yale University Press, 1994), 148; Lloyd Gartner, *The Jewish Immigrant in England, 1870–1914*, 2nd edn (London: Simon Publications, 1973), 40–1, 306.

9. Gartner, *The Jewish Immigrant in England*, 303–4; Eugene C. Black, *The Social Politics of Anglo-Jewry, 1880–1920* (Oxford: Basil Blackwell, 1988), 300.

10. Rodker (née Cohen), *The End Has Various Places*, 23.

11. Samuel Hinds Wilkinson, *The Life of John Wilkinson, the Jewish Missionary* (London: Morgan & Scott, 1908), 15.

12. Rodker (née Cohen), *The End Has Various Places*, 44.

13. Gartner, *The Jewish Immigrant in England*, 197.

14. Joseph Leftwich, 'Facsimile of Diary', 1911, 1912, Tower Hamlets Local History Library and Archives, entry for 5 July 1911.

15. Ibid., entry for 25 August 1911.

16. Rodker (née Cohen), *The End Has Various Places*, 142–4.

17. For a more detailed account of the development of the term and a proposal that we think instead of a 'Whitechapel Renaissance', see Alex Grafen, 'The Whitechapel Renaissance and Its Legacies: Rosenberg to Rodker', PhD thesis, UCL, 2020.

18. Arnold Harris, 'The Story of Childhood & Other Episodes: Yurbrick (Lithuania) London and Dublin, 1894–1918' (n.p.p: n.p., n.d.), 42. Harris's memoir, written over several years in the 1970s, remains unpublished. My thanks to his granddaughter, Katerina Gould, for allowing me to read it. For more on Harris, see Mark Levene, 'Going against the Grain: Two Jewish Memoirs of War and Anti-War, 1914–18', *Jewish Culture and History* 2, no. 2 (1999).

19. Rodker (née Cohen), *The End Has Various Places*, 151.

20. For more information on Birnberg, later Clare Winsten, see Sarah MacDougall, 'Whitechapel Girl: Clare Winsten and Isaac Rosenberg', in *Whitechapel at War: Isaac Rosenberg and His Circle*, ed. Rachel Dickson and Sarah MacDougall (London: Ben Uri Gallery, 2008).

21. Clare Winsten, 'Memoirs', Whitechapel Gallery Archive.

22. Lisa Tickner, *Modern Life & Modern Subjects: British Art in the Early Twentieth Century* (New Haven, CT: Yale University Press, 2000), 146.

23. Ibid., 155–9.

24. Joseph Leftwich, '"Jewish" London Fifty Years Ago', in *1915–1965: Fifty Years' Achievement in the Arts, Commemorative Volume to Mark the Fiftieth Anniversary of the Foundation of the Ben Uri Art Society* (London: Ben Uri Art Society, 1966). See also David Mazower, 'Lazar Berson and the Origins of the Ben Uri Art Society', in *The Ben Uri Story from Art Society to Museum and the Influence of Anglo-Jewish Artists on the Modern British Movement* (London: Ben Uri Gallery, 2001).

25. Sarah MacDougall, '"Something Is Happening There": Early British Modernism, the Great War and the "Whitechapel Boys"', in *London, Modernism, and 1914*, ed. Michael J. K. Walsh (Cambridge: Cambridge University Press, 2010); Juliet Steyn, 'Inside-out: Assumptions of "English" Modernism in the Whitechapel Art Gallery, London 1914', in *Art Apart: Art Institutions and Ideology Across England and North America*, ed. Marcia Pointon (Manchester: Manchester University Press, 1994); Janet Wolff, *AngloModern: Painting and Modernity in Britain and the United States* (New York; London: Cornell University Press, 2003), 143.

26. Rodker (née Cohen), *The End Has Various Places*, 148.

27. Ibid., 140.

28. Gartner, *The Jewish Immigrant in England*, 268.

29. Rodker (née Cohen), *The End Has Various Places*, 152.

30. The best sources on Rodker's subsequent career are Evi Heinz, 'John Rodker (1894–1955) and Modernist Material Culture: Theatre, Translation, Publishing', PhD thesis, Birkbeck, 2018; and Ian Patterson, 'Cultural Critique and Canon Formation, 1910–1937: A Study in Modernism and Cultural Memory', PhD thesis, King's College, Cambridge, 1996.

INFRASTRUCTURE: WASTE

CHAPTER 14
BLOCKAGE AND RECUPERATION: SEWER-HUNTERS IN HENRY MAYHEW'S *LONDON LABOUR AND THE LONDON POOR*
Naomi Hinds

Henry Mayhew's *London Labour and the London Poor* was a foray into the underbelly of 1840s London. An ambitious if not unwieldy piece of investigative journalism, it sought to survey the lives and landscapes of the city's poorest inhabitants. Comprehensive to a fault, it represented the sprawling urban organism through a bricolage of descriptive tableaus, governmental reports and copious amounts of statistical data, as well as expressive oral accounts of London life drawn from the mouths of the poor. Today we are probably most familiar with *London Labour* as a hefty four-volume collection published between 1851 and 1862, but it was a text which had many forms. Over Mayhew's lifetime, his sprawling project was also a series of articles written for the newspaper the *Morning Chronicle* between 1849 and 1850, a two-penny weekly periodical which ran from late 1850 to early 1852, as well as an assortment of oral performances and theatrical dramatizations.

In *London Labour*, Mayhew cast himself as an explorer into what he termed the 'undiscovered country of the poor', exposing the city's underbelly to the prying eyes of a curious audience.[1] However, *London Labour* did not just consider life on the surface. Its investigative eye penetrated the streets to explore another underworld: the subterranean sewers which functioned as London's intestinal system. These carried more than excrement. Here the residuum of urban life amassed and stagnated. Dirt and ashes swept from the street, broken pottery, dead animals, rotting offal and vegetables, animal dung, blood from abattoirs, rags, scraps of metal, coins, discarded pots and pans and even the bodies of the murdered were said to fester beneath the streets. Gutters and open drains were conducive to the stealthy disposal of any waste that would fit through the grates. Household drains and cesspools too were often used as repositories for miscellaneous kinds of refuse, transporting it out of sight, and seemingly, out of mind. Sewers, according to Mayhew, represented the 'dust-bins and dung-hills of the immediate neighbourhood': an obscene network underwriting the city.[2]

But even in these subterranean spaces, retrieval, recovery and reimagination of forgotten objects was possible, if not necessary for the survival of some of London's workers. Mayhew was fascinated by the lives of sewer-hunters (alternatively known as 'toshers' or 'shoremen') who ventured into the city's depths to scavenge for materials and objects which could be sold for profit. This was dangerous work which required braving gangs of marauding rats, deadly accumulations of carbon monoxide, sudden and powerful rushes of sewerage and the crumbling brickwork of the sewers themselves, as well as apprehension by the police or sewer officials. After filling their bags, the sewer-hunters would carry their findings back to the surface and divide their earnings between all parties.

More than a curiosity in the cast of London's workers, sewer-hunters were enmeshed in the complex processes by which the city absorbed, digested and regurgitated matter. In this respect, they were important economic players. Sabine Schülting makes the case that, 'Wealth in Mayhew's study is dissociated from production and instead linked to circulation.'[3] Examining the sewer-hunter's role in the city's underground spaces reveals how the journeys of waste from the sewer to the river could be subverted for capital gain. Clearing blockages in the sewers, they restored trapped objects to their migratory circuits around London's hectic marketplace.

Choked sewers were a manifestation of an urban body on the brink of catastrophic collapse. With the city imagined as a circulatory organism with blood pumping through its veins and arteries, any congestion – whether it be in sewers, crowded thoroughfares, or cramped residences – was an indication of its disordered functioning. In his damning 1842 report into the sanitary condition of the working classes, the social reformer Edwin Chadwick determined that the accumulation of refuse and filth in streets and homes was

Figure 14.1 'The Sewer Hunter' (1861), printed in Henry Mayhew's *London Labour and the London Poor*. © World History Archive/Alamy Stock Photo.

a direct cause of sickness, death and moral depravity. This judgement emerged out of the then widely accepted miasmatic theory. This dictated that any waste left to stagnate and decompose would release invisible noxious fumes, called miasmas, which would drift through the air, infiltrating even the smallest crack, and infect the bodies of those who inhaled them. Chadwick's proposed solution was an effective method of immediately removing the source of these miasmas: in short, a new sewerage system that would facilitate the rapid and uninterrupted conveyance of waste away from populated urban centres. The monstrous costs that this scheme would incur could theoretically be covered by the sale of sewerage as manure to farmers. He lamented that:

> The quantity is immense which is carried down by the rains in London to the river Thames, serving no other purpose than to pollute its waters. A substance which by its putrefaction generates miasmata may, by artificial means, be rendered totally inoffensive, inodorous, and transportable.[4]

There was a perverse poetry in human excrement being used as a fertilizer. In essence it would complete the cycle between the consumer and producer. The digested remains of consumption, when returned to the soil, could aid the cultivation of more crops to be sold again to the urban population. Beyond being the detritus of urban life, waste's untapped potential energy could be made to serve the economic machine. According to Mayhew, it was akin to 'a precious ore, running in rich veins beneath the surface of our streets'.[5]

But this vision was far from the disorganized sanitary system that Mayhew represented in *London Labour*. It wouldn't be until 1865 that Joseph Bazalgette's unified sewerage system was officially opened. In the 1840s and 1850s, waste was managed by a disjointed network of overflowing cesspools, putrid underground streams, open drains that ran uncovered through busy thoroughfares and the decaying sewers that were the sewer-hunters' harvest ground. By this system's initial design, cesspools, which lay beneath the majority of the city's homes, were the intended destination for all human excrement. Once they had filled up over a period of months, the foul deposits would be carted away by nightmen (so named because they carried out their duties at night), combined with decomposing vegetative matter and road-sweepings to then be sold as manure. Mayhew wrote that 'upwards of three-fourths of the whole was sent in barges into the more distant country parts, having a ready water communication by the Thames or by canal'.[6] This was in grim symmetry with the sewage that would soon corrupt the river's waters. Sewers and drains, on the other hand, were originally intended to only carry away surface rainwater from the streets to the Thames in order to prevent flooding, and until 1815 it was in fact illegal to discharge 'offensive matter' into them.[7]

By the 1840s, not only were many cesspools connected by drains to nearby sewers, but houses built after the 'new mode' drained directly into the sewers and had no cesspools at all.[8] The reason for this shift was partly one of cost and convenience: householders would rather avoid the charges and disruptions associated with having their cesspools emptied by nightmen.[9] But the nightman was also symbolically misaligned with the new vision for sanitation, a vision which prioritized circulation and ease of motion. One particular nightman interviewed by Mayhew recognized his profession's impending obsolescence, reflecting that 'In time the nightmen'll disappear in course they must, there's so many new dodges comes up, always some one of the working classes is a being ruined. If it ain't steam, it's something else as knocks the bread out of their mouths quite as quick.'[10] Unable to compete with the swift incessant motion demanded by a rapidly changing sanitary system, the nightmen, like waste, would be swept away and forgotten. As Mayhew disparagingly wrote, nightmen were 'of the plodding class of labourers'.[11] Just as the cesspool was an obstruction to the free flow and migration of waste, the nightman too was a choke point in the sanitary system, slowing the movement of sewage to a crawl.

The deteriorating sewers of the metropolis were yet another impediment. In *London Labour*, Mayhew quoted a subterranean survey carried out by London's Board of Sewers in their preparation for the planning and construction of a new sewerage system. Concealed beneath streets, buildings and layers of earth, these old sewers were a mystery even to those working towards their reconstruction and could only be accessed by dangerous expeditions into these hidden spaces. The report hardly held back in the vividity of its descriptions. Some sewers, it was reported, were essentially an 'enormous stagnant cesspool', up to five feet thick with the black filth of fermenting waste.[12] In other places, 'putrid matter *like stalactites* descend *three feet in length*'.[13] Beneath Covent Garden the sewers were in such a rotten and decrepit state that to remove the deposit clogging it would 'bring some of them down altogether'.[14] These dangers and obstacles meant that the men sent down into the sewers to survey them were prevented from proceeding in many places, with one man, already stunned by accumulated suffocating gases, 'being dragged out on his back (through two feet of black foetid deposits) in a state of insensibility'.[15]

There were some attempts to dislodge blockages in the sewers. One was 'flushing', which involved creating a dam in the sewers by means of iron gates constructed at intervals. Flushermen, another type of subterranean worker, would open the gates periodically to allow the accumulated water to rush out and wash away deposits of waste. But this only displaced the problem. Only two districts, Holborn and Finsbury, carried out this practice, and flushing could only carry waste so far – often to the sewers of another district or to aggregate around the sewer outlets leading into the Thames.[16] Mayhew made sure to point out that whilst these sewers reduced the movement of waste to a muddy full stop, 'the super-terranean tides of traffic are daily flowing'.[17]

This then was the sewer-hunter's workplace. As they plumbed the depths of the city, they were exploring an uncharted and alien territory which resisted their very presence. Mayhew went to some lengths sketching out their figure, drawing them from the murky underground to be exposed on the page:

These 'Toshers' may be seen, especially on the Surrey side of the Thames, habited in long greasy velveteen coats, furnished with pockets of vast capacity, and their nether limbs encased in dirty canvas trowsers, and any old slops of shoes, that may be fit only for wading through the mud. They carry a bag on their back, and in their hand a pole seven or eight feet long, on one end of which there is a large iron hoe.

The uses of this instrument are various; with it they try the ground wherever it appears unsafe, before venturing on it, and, when assured of its safety, walk forward steadying their footsteps with the staff. Should they, as often happens, even to the most experienced, sink in some quagmire, they immediately throw out the long pole armed with the hoe, which is always held uppermost for this purpose, and with it seizing hold of any object within their reach, are thereby enabled to draw themselves out; without the pole, however, their danger would be greater, for the more they struggled to extricate themselves from such places, the deeper they would sink; and even with it, they might perish, I am told, in some part, if there were nobody at hand to render them assistance.[18]

Sewer-hunters' success and survival were dependent on their ability to nimbly manoeuvre through a hostile and labyrinthine environment. Unlike the subterranean surveyors who struggled in their task of mapping out the sewers, sewer-hunters had committed the twists and turns of the underground passages to memory. Through canny ability and experience they knew how to navigate the obstacles that lay in their way lest they too were to become waste, another decaying body lost in the sewers. For Mayhew, Michelle Allen argues, they embodied a romantic way of life, one which could have been drawn from the thrilling tales of the penny dreadful.[19]

On their travels, equipped with their hoe and lantern, they would search for valuables, sieving the sewage or chipping away at large deposits of waste. Metals, rope and bones: items most likely washed down the sewers from cesspools and house drains were their most common pickings. These were quickly sold when brought above ground, likely to street-buyers who specialized in the purchase of miscellaneous forms of refuse. The migrations of these objects did not stop here. Old metals were in demand by iron-founders, coppersmiths, brass-founders and plumbers; rope could be unravelled and pulverized to form brown paper or oakum, a fibre used in caulking ships; and bones could be sold on to mills who ground them into bonemeal for manure, thus starting the cycle of consumption and excretion again. But if in luck they would come across objects which did not require reconstitution in order to be made useful: ladles, silver-handed cutlery, mugs, drinking cups or even jewellery. These could be sold for a considerable amount to traders who were not deterred by their origins. Such objects, journeying from the dinner table to the sewer, and potentially back, gestured towards the contaminative circulatory relationship which had led to so many deaths in London. It was after all water laced with excrement which was the invisible communicator of cholera.

But it was the crude capital of coins languishing in the sewers, presumably dropped through the grates on the streets above, that fascinated Mayhew most. One sewer-hunter, wistfully remembering his youth in the profession, recalled that, 'I'd put down my arm to my shoulder in the mud and bring up shillings and half-crowns, and lots of coppers, and plenty other things.'[20] These could be found in the bricks at the bottom of the sewers where the mortar had been worn away. The subterranean city, it seemed, was quite literally paved with gold. If such riches could be drawn from the sewers by those who had the nose and perseverance to do so, it was a condemnation of the city's voracious appetite.

Mayhew estimated that £20,000 a year was recovered from the sewers.[21] This was money that would otherwise have remained tantalizingly inaccessible just beneath Londoners' feet. How much more lay undisturbed? Waste was not just redundant matter exhausted of all its usefulness. It was also the excess of the city's inefficient cycles and processes, all that which had been squandered and carelessly discarded. In the sewers where all this congregated and concentrated, even faeces could glint with gold.

Yet despite the sewer-hunters' best efforts, Mayhew reminds us that there are some objects which could not be reclaimed:

> There are in many parts of the sewers holes where the brick-work has been worn away, and in these holes clusters of articles are found, which have been washed into them from time to time, and perhaps been collecting there for years; such pieces of iron, nails, various scraps of metal, coins of every description, all rusted into a mass like a rock, and weighing from a half hundred to two hundred weight altogether. These 'conglomerates' of metal are too heavy for the men to take out of the sewers, so that if unable to break them up, they are compelled to leave them behind; and there are very many such masses, I am informed, lying in the sewers at this moment, of immense weight, and growing larger every day by continual additions.[22]

In this case, if left alone, waste could become a geological feature, the sedimented foundation of London itself. The riches of these immovable and unyielding masses were irrevocably sealed away. One sewer-hunter commented that they could 'stop there I s'pose till the world comes to an end'.[23] Resisting the motion of progress meant to prematurely become a historical artefact forever frozen in time and place. Neither redeemed nor annihilated, they faced an unending purgatory.

If, as Schulting argued, circulation indicated wealth, the sewers theatricalized the dysfunction of the distribution of capital of the city. It was a tragic irony that many Londoners lived in destitution and squalor while riches turned to stone beneath their feet. Even if sewer-hunters and other urban scavengers were able to recuperate some of the value of the spilled excess of the city, it was no means of adequate redress. Physical blockages in the sewers were material evidence of the economic and political blockades which kept wealth concentrated in the pockets of a relative few. Just as waste could coagulate in the cesspool or the sewer, so too were many poor Londoners stuck in place.

Notes

1. Henry Mayhew, *London Labour and the London Poor*, 3 vols (London: George Woodfall and Son, 1851) I, iii.

2. Henry Mayhew, *London Labour and the London Poor*, 4 vols (London: Griffin, Bohn, and Company, 1861) II, 394.

3. Sabine Schülting, *Dirt in Victorian Literature and Culture: Writing Materiality* (London: Routledge, 2016), 21.

4. Edwin Chadwick, *Report on the Sanitary Condition of the Labouring Population of Gt. Britain*, ed. M. W. Flinn (Edinburgh: Edinburgh University Press, 1965), 123.

5. Mayhew, *London Labour*, II, 161.

6. Ibid., 450.

7. Stephen Halliday, *The Great Stink of London: Sir Joseph Bazalgette and the Cleansing of the Victorian Metropolis* (Stroud: Sutton Publishing, 1999), 29.

8. Mayhew, *London Labour*, II, 391.

9. Lee Jackson, *Dirty Old London: The Victorian Fight Against Filth* (New Haven, CT: Yale University Press, 2014), 50.

10. Ibid., 449.

11. Ibid., 137.

12. Ibid., 434.

13. Ibid., 394.

14. Ibid., 395.

15. Ibid., 395.

16. David Sunderland, "'A Monument to Defective Administration'? The London Commissions of Sewers in the Early Nineteenth Century', *Urban History* 26, no. 3 (1999): 360.

17. Mayhew, *London Labour*, II, 394.

18. Ibid., 150–1.

19. Michelle Allen, *Cleansing the City: Sanitary Geographies in Victorian London* (Athens: Ohio University Press, 2008), 32.

20. Mayhew, *London Labour*, II, 153.

21. Ibid., 151–2.

22. Ibid., 152.

23. Ibid., 154.

SOUTH

CHAPTER 15

CULTURE AND HORTICULTURE IN LAMBETH FROM 'TRADESCANT'S ARK' TO VAUXHALL GARDENS

Charlotte Grant

In the early 1990s the Thames Archaeological Survey uncovered London's earliest structure. Tidal erosion caused in part by new building encroaching into the Thames revealed the remains of a previously unseen Bronze Age timber jetty. Six further Metholithic timbers dating from trees growing between 4790 and 4540 BC were subsequently found by the Thames Discovery Programme, providing evidence of the presence of Stone Age hunter gatherers on the river's foreshore near Vauxhall Bridge.[1] Reading the history of the place and street names of today's riverside locations in Lambeth reveals a past where the natural and the urban coexist, where horticulture and culture flourished from the sixteenth to the nineteenth centuries in an area of London which is once again in flux.

The Lakeland poet, William Wordsworth, famously crafted a sublime vision of London in his sonnet 'On Westminster Bridge', describing the city through the lens of Romantic landscape poetry. But his blending of country and city was prompted by what he saw as he looked eastwards to the City and ahead towards the south as he travelled to France early one morning in the summer of 1802:

> This City now doth, like a garment, wear
> The beauty of the morning; silent, bare,
> Ships, towers, domes, theatres, and temples lie
> Open unto the fields, and to the sky.[2]

The fertile south bank of the river had kept its fields, and its agricultural and horticultural associations, longer than many areas to the north, and those associations persist today in place names. The name 'Lambeth' has an agricultural origin which also registers the importance of Lambeth's location by the River Thames: it derives from 'Lambehitha', first recorded in 1062, meaning 'landing place for the lambs'. Dating from the middle of the eighteenth century, John Roque's map of 1746 shows intermittent buildings along the river with a patchwork of farmed land beyond.[3] The map's title – 'A Plan of the Cities of London and Westminster, and Borough of Southwark, with the Contiguous buildings' – suggests the fragmented geography of mid-eighteenth-century London. Westminster Bridge is shown, although it was still under construction; it opened in 1750, the second of London's bridges to be built. 'The New Road' leads from the bridge and crosses 'Lambeth Marsh' towards the wide-open spaces of St George's Fields where rioters would muster in the anti-Catholic Gordon Riots of 1780. It then leads on to Kennington and joins the 'road to Clapham', now the A3 or Clapham Road, following the route of Stane Street, the Roman Road from London to Chichester.

Wordsworth's view heading south from Westminster through Lambeth may have felt rural in 1802, but within less than ten years the City Corporation had obtained an Act of Parliament extinguishing all rights of common over St George's Fields, and by 1813 Horace and James Smith could write:

Saint George's Fields are fields no more;
The trowel supersedes the plough;
Huge inundated swamps of yore,
Are changed to civic villas now.[4]

Two hundred years later, Vauxhall, bordering the Thames in Lambeth, is in the throes of major redevelopment. In 2018 the American Embassy moved from Mayfair's Grosvenor Square to Vauxhall, a focus for a reimagined 'Nine Elms' district, previously an industrial hinterland built on old agricultural land, now a forest of towers variously described as 'mini-Manhattan' or 'Dubai-on-Thames' and funded by money from China, Malaysia and the United Arab Emirates. Where James Smith documented the building of 'civic villas' in 1813, current regeneration in 'The Vauxhall, Nine Elms, Battersea Opportunity Area' includes thousands of flats built to sell to foreign investors. Donald Trump may have refused to open the new Embassy in 2018, referring to Vauxhall as an 'off location', but, as suggested by the Thames Archaeological Survey, Lambeth's riverside has welcomed people, animals, plants and objects from around the world since the Bronze Age.[5] As with the name 'Lambeth', the etymology of 'Vauxhall' tells a story of movement, specifically one of migration: it derives from the first landowner in the area – Sir Falkes de Bréauté, an Anglo-Norman soldier who made his reputation serving King John and then King Henry III and married a widowed heiress, Margaret de Redvers. Her estate in Kennington was renamed Fawkes Hall after him, becoming Falkes' Hall, then 'Fox-hall', as Samuel Pepys referred to it in his diary in 1668, and finally 'Vauxhall'. Vauxhall's riverside location facilitated the movement of people and goods, acting as an intersection between the rural and the urban throughout the seventeenth and into the eighteenth century, and nowhere more so than in London's first publicly accessible museum, 'Tradescant's Ark', and the renowned pleasure gardens, Vauxhall Gardens.

Father and son John Tradescant the Elder (*c.* 1570–1638) and John Tradescant the Younger (1608–62) established their collection of plants and curiosities in Turret House located off the South Lambeth Road and between the streets now named in their memory, Tradescant Road and Walberswick Street. Born around 1570 on the Suffolk coast, John Tradescant the Elder became a gardener for James I's chief minister, Robert Cecil, at Hatfield House in Hertfordshire in 1610. He travelled very widely, visiting France, the Île de Ré and the Low Countries and North Africa on plant-buying missions for Cecil, bringing roses, mulberries and fritillaries back to Cecil's gardens at Hatfield. In 1618 he was part of an unsuccessful diplomatic mission to persuade the Tsar to let

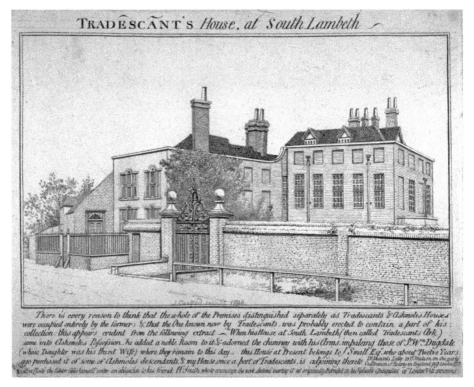

TRADESCANT'S *House, at South Lambeth*

There is every reason to think that the whole of the Premises distinguished separately as Tradescants & Ashmoles Houses were occupied entirely by the former; &, that the One known now by Tradescants, was probably erected to contain a part of his collection: this appears evident from the following extract — When his House at South Lambeth (then called Tradescants Ark) came into Ashmoles Possession, he added a noble Room to it & adorned the chimney with his Arms, impaleing those of S.r W.m Dugdale (whose Daughter was his Third Wife) where they remain to this day... this House at Present belongs to J Small Esq. who about Twelve Years ago purchased it of some of Ashmoles descendants. & my House since a part of Tradescants, is adjoining thereto ...

Figure 15.1 J. Caulfield, *Tradescant House, South Lambeth, London* (1798). © Heritage Image Partnership Ltd/Alamy Stock Photo.

English merchants cross Russia on their way to Persia, but he returned with four types of fir tree, and a Muscovy rose, a new introduction to Britain. His account of the journey is now in the Bodleian Library at Oxford.

John had married Elizabeth Day, the daughter of a vicar from Kent, in Meopham in Kent in 1607 and their son John, born in 1608, was educated at the King's School Canterbury whilst his father worked for Edward, Lord Wotton, whose garden became famous for its melons. The Tradescant family moved to London in 1626 and settled in Lambeth. Like his father, John the Younger was also a gardener and an avid traveller, bringing back around 200 plants from America in 1637, and Turret House became famous for its garden (see Figure 15.1). Whilst the garden contained plants brought from around the world, the house contained a collection of curiosities known as the *Musaeum Tradescantianum* or 'Tradescant's Ark'. By 1634 the collection was so large that it took the visitor a full day to tour. Entrance was charged at 6 pence. A traveller who had returned from India, Peter Mundy, noted that 'a Man might in one date behold and collecte into one place more Curiosities than hee should see if hee spent all his life in Travell'. Mundy saw

... beasts, fowle, fishes, serpents, wormes, (reall, although dead and dryed), pretious stones and other Armes, Coines, shells, fethers etts. Of sundrey Nations, Countries, forme, Coullours [...] Moreover a little garden with divers outlandish herbes and flowers, wereof some that I had not seene elsewhere but in India, being supplied by Noblemen, Gentlemen, Sea Commanders, etts. With such Toyes as they could bringe or procure from other parts.[6]

John Tradescant the Younger compiled a catalogue of the collection with the help of two friends, Dr Thomas Wharton and Elias Ashmole, an Oxford-educated lawyer whom he had met in 1650. Ashmole offered to pay for the publication of *Musaeum Tradescantianum* (published in 1656), which, fatefully, left Tradescant in his debt. In Tradescant's will he agreed to give Ashmole his collection, but only after his wife's death. Following John's death in 1662, Ashmole, who now also has streets in the area named after him (Elias Place, Ashmole Street, Ashmole School and the Ashmole Estate), moved into the house next to Tradescent's widow Hester and claimed the collection after a legal wrangle. Hester was subsequently found drowned. Ashmole added Tradescant's Ark to his own collections, founding the Ashmolean Museum in Oxford which opened in 1683. Highlights from the Tradescant collection remain on display, including Powhatan's mantle (*c.* 1600–38), named after the father of Pocahontas.

Between them through their travels and their plant collecting and cultivating, the Tradescants transformed Britain's botanical landscape. It is hard to be certain how many new plants they brought between them, since the names of different species were fluid until the Swedish botanist Carl Linneus established his system of classification in 1753. Two plant lists survive: a handwritten 'list of plants received by John Tradescant 1629–1633' and a printed list from 1634 entitled '*Plantarum in Horto Iohannem Tradescanti*', which lists over 700 plants. Large numbers of plant introductions have been attributed to them, including the larch from Russia, the horse chestnut from South-Eastern Europe, the lilac from Algeria, Virginia Creepers, Yucca plants, the Swamp Cypress, Pitcher Plant and Tulip Tree from North America and such garden favourites as scented stocks and even poppies which came from France. However, as demonstrated by the Tradescents' biographer, Prudence Leith-Ross, several of the species attributed to them were already in Britain. According to Leith-Ross 'their real achievement lay in cultivating them for all to admire in their botanic garden at South Lambeth and for making many new varieties available as nurseryman's plants.[7] The Tradescants were buried at St Mary's, Lambeth. This former parish church nestled beside the more imposing Lambeth Palace, London home to the Archbishop of Canterbury, and situated across the river from the Palace of Westminster, is now the Garden Museum. The Tradescants' tomb is there, as is a large collection of Tradescantia, including a three-petalled spiderwort from Virginia sent to Tradescant and named after him by Carl Linnaeus as the Tradescantia Virginiana.[8]

Whilst the Tradescants changed the face of British horticulture, and their collection of curiosities became the first publicly accessible museum in London, another Lambeth venue proved hugely influential in the cultural life of London in the following centuries. Vauxhall Gardens was one of the most famous of London's pleasure gardens. Described by John Barrell as 'a cradle of modern painting and architecture, and a music venue vital to the careers of Thomas Arne and George Frideric Handel', the gardens were painted by Canaletto, and described by Pepys, Fanny Burney, Dickens and Thackeray.[9] Vauxhall Gardens embraced local and foreign cultures and in turn its influence stretches from Russia, where train stations are called 'Vokzal', to America, which had a Vauxhall Gardens in Nashville, Tennessee in the 1820s.

Vauxhall was one of several pleasure gardens in London between the seventeenth and nineteenth centuries. Situated a boat ride across the Thames from Millbank, Vauxhall Gardens, or New Spring Gardens, as it was known until 1785, changed in character over its 200-year lifespan from its origins in 1661. Until Vauxhall Bridge was opened in 1816, visitors came by water, travelling across the Thames on one of the many 'wherries' or ferries rowed by the Thames watermen. For example, the Lambeth Horseferry, so called because it could carry a carriage and horses, ran between the Palace of Westminster and the Archbishop of Canterbury's Lambeth Palace and is remembered in the street name 'Horseferry Road'. David Coke and Alan Borg, Vauxhall Gardens' most recent and most comprehensive historians, estimate that around ten million paying visitors visited Vauxhall between 1740 and 1840, its most successful period, describing it as 'the single biggest commercial visitor attraction in the country'.[10]

Vauxhall's origins, as a rural tavern with a seedy reputation, were not auspicious. In 1712, Joseph Addison described Mr Spectator visiting 'The Spring-Gardens at Vauxhall or Fox-hall' with his friend Sir Roger de Coverley. Arriving by water he is initially charmed by the gardens: 'When I considered the Fragrancy of the Walks and Bowers with the Choirs of Birds that sung upon the Trees, and the loose Tribe of People that walked under their Shades, I could not but look upon the place as a kind of *Mahometan* Paradise.' But having been displeased by being accosted by a 'Masque' whom he calls '*a wanton Baggage*', Sir Roger then tells 'the Mistress of the House, who sat at the Bar, That he should be a better Customer to her Garden, if there were more Nightingales, and fewer strumpets'.[11] The gardens' fortunes changed in 1729 when they were bought by Johnathan Tyers, a young tradesman from Bermondsey who set about making them both fashionable and moral. Tyers employed the Swiss empresario John James Heidegger, known for the masquerades he ran in the Haymarket, to help him relaunch the gardens. Their first events were Italian in theme, a 'Ball after the Italian manner at their Carnivals' in spring 1731, followed a year later by a Ridotto (a form of public entertainment involving music, dancing and frequently masquerade), both of which were open to a wide cross section of society.[12] The anonymous poem *Spring Gardens* describes an oyster girl, a barber's apprentice, a lawyer, an army captain, a doctor and a number of prostitutes among the visitors.[13] The official opening, also in the form of a Ridotto, took place in the presence of Frederick, Prince of Wales, in June 1732, with a more select crowd ensured by the much higher entrance fee of a guinea.

In 1735, Tyers built a new octagonal bandstand or 'Orchestra' and introduced a shilling entrance fee. He employed up-and-coming British artist William Hogarth to design the entrance tickets, and, over time, reinvented the gardens as London's premiere place of polite culture. One of Tyers' key commissions was a sculpture of George Frederic Handel by the London-based Huguenot sculptor Louis Francois Roubiliac, which was unveiled in 1738. Born in Germany, Handel himself had arrived in London from Hamburg and Italy in 1712 to become one of the most prominent figures in England's music scene, and his compositions became a mainstay of Vauxhall's music. Despite the 'Ridottos' of the early years, Tyers was keen to promote English music (Handel 'counted' as English) as opposed to the Italian music popular in London's theatres and operas. Thomas Arne became Tyers' in-house composer and Director of Music from 1745. In 1749, Vauxhall hosted the rehearsal for Handel's *Music for the Royal Fireworks* in front of an audience of thousands, Tyers securing the coup by offering to supply oil lamps for the main performance in Green Park. Lighting was a speciality in Vauxhall: at a given signal, lamplighters lit specially laid cotton-wool fuses which illuminated thousands of oil lamps simultaneously to the delight of visitors.[14]

The visual culture on display was eclectic and international: it combined an English sentimental vision with a Rococo style developed from French Baroque, and drew on Chinese and other influences. Francis Hayman, an associate of Hogarth's from the St Martin's Lane Academy, was employed to paint morally suggestive scenes, many of them taken from English literature, as backdrops to the series of small enclaves designed as supper boxes where visitors would sit and dine al fresco, watching and being watched by other visitors. The scenes chosen from Shakespeare – the wrestling scene from *As You Like It* – or from Samuel Richardson's hit sentimental novel of 1740, *Pamela*, were designed to entertain, but also to suggest how passion – be it love or lust or anger – might lead to disaster: a salutary lesson for a garden which had a reputation for dissolution to put behind it. Visitors were treated to spectaculars like a representation of the Falls of Tivoli with backdrops designed by the great theatre artist James De Loutherbourg, and the supper boxes were punctuated with 'Chinese Pavillions'.

Following Tyers' death in 1767, Vauxhall Gardens was run by his heirs until 1792. In the early nineteenth century its appeal was kept alive by firework displays and by the presence of the French Balloon empresario André-Jacques Garnerin, who led balloon flights at Vauxhall from 1802 onwards. For four years from 1816, the French tight-rope walker and ropedancer Marguerite Antoinette Lalanne (1786–1866), known as Madame Saqui, was the main attraction.[15] A poster for Vauxhall Gardens in 1848 (see Figure 15.2) suggests that the entertainment provided during the Victorian period continued to be both eclectic and international. It advertises a 'Grand View of Constantinople' and other attractions including 'Van Amburg! With Lions, tigers etc.' and 'Boz's Juba as Lucy Long'. 'Juba' was an African-American dancer and performer, usually identified as William Henry Lane, who was born around 1825 in Providence, Rhode Island, and died in London in 1852. Lane was a key figure in the development of tap dance, a hybrid dance form combining elements of African-American dance (including the Juba dance which was performed by enslaved African Americans on the plantations of the American South and which gave Lane his name) and Irish and English clog dancing.[16] His billing as 'Boz's Juba' refers to the story that Dickens saw him perform during his 1842 American tour. Describing a dance in the Five Points district of New York where poor Irish and African-American families lived side by side, Dickens pronounced him 'the greatest dancer known [...] spinning about on his toes and heels like nothing but the man's fingers on

Figure 15.2 'Royal Vauxhall Gardens' (1848). © British Library.

the tambourine'.[17] In England, 'Master Juba' sang and danced as part of a blackface minstrelsy troupe, C. W. Pell's Ethiopian Serenaders, and, as advertised on this poster, performed in drag as 'Lucy Long'.

Despite this wide variety of entertainment on offer during the Victorian period, the gardens were already in decline by the 1830s, as Dickens suggests in 'Vauxhall-Gardens by Day' in *Sketches by Boz* (1836). The disappointment Dickens depicts is not just that the viewers see the gardens in the harsh light of day when they were designed to be seen in splendid lamplight, but that what remains is an empty shell bereft of magic:

> We paid our shilling at the gate, and then we saw, for the first time, that the entrance, if there had ever been any magic about it at all, was now decidedly disenchanted, being, in fact, nothing more nor less than a combination of very roughly-painted boards and saw-dust. We glanced at the orchestra and supper-room as we hurried past – we just recognised them, and that was all. We bent our steps to the firework-ground; there, at least, we should not be disappointed. We reached it, and stood rooted to the spot with mortification and astonishment. *That* the Moorish tower – that wooden shed with a door in the centre, and daubs of crimson and yellow all round, like a gigantic watch-case![18]

Vauxhall Gardens closed permanently in 1859. Tyers is still remembered in local place names: Tyers Street, now home to Vauxhall City Farm, Jonathan Street and Tyers Terrace. The land was sold and used for housing but then returned to a public park in the post-war period and was recently renamed 'Vauxhall Pleasure Gardens'.

Today, Vauxhall is known as home to one of London's largest Portuguese communities (approximately 30,000–35,000 Portuguese-speakers reside in the borough of Lambeth)[19] and as a centre for LGBTQ+ nightlife. The Royal Vauxhall Tavern, built on land once belonging to Vauxhall Gardens, and home to drag artists since the Second World War, was Grade II listed for its historic and cultural significance by Historic England in 2015. Less well known is that Vauxhall was the first London home of Claudia Jones, founder of Britain's first Black newspaper and the Notting Hill Carnival. Jones was living in the nostalgically named Meadow Road SW8 in 1958 when she founded *The West Indian Gazette* and when she imagined what was first described as 'Claudia's Caribbean Carnival' in response to the Notting Hill race riots of 1958. Reading the place names and histories of Vauxhall, like so many areas of London, gives a dynamic and layered sense of the past. And whilst Vauxhall's present is increasingly overshadowed by steel, concrete and glass, its past tells of generations of diverse people and plants, culture and horticulture mapped around and beneath the city's streets and gardens.

Notes

1. N. Cohen, J. Cotton and G. Milne, 'London's Top Secret', *London Archaeologist* 12 (2010–11): 287–9; Nathalie Cohen and Eliott Wragg, *The River's Tale: Archaeology on the Thames Foreshore in Greater London* (London: MOLA, 2017).

2. William Wordsworth, 'Composed upon Westminster Bridge, September 3, 1802'.

3. John Roque produced his first map of London in 1746 with the engraver John Pine (1690–1756). Roque was himself a migrant of Huguenot descent who later also lived in Dublin. Pine was a friend and collaborator of Hogarth's who had provided the frontispiece for Daniel Defoe's *Robinson Crusoe*.

4. Horace Smith and James Smith, *Horace in London: Consisting of Imitations of the First Two Books of the Odes of Horace* (London: John Miller, 1813), 153.

5. 'Trump hits out at "lousy location" of US embassy in London', *Guardian*, 29 April 2018, https://www.theguardian.com/us-news/2018/apr/29/trump-hits-out-at-lousy-location-of-us-embassy-in-london.

6. *The Travels of Peter Mundy*, cited in Prudence Leith-Ross, *The John Tradescants, Gardeners to the Rose and Lily Queen* (London: Peter Owen Publishers, 2005), 15, 154.

7. Leith-Ross, *The John Tradescants*, 195.

8. 'History of the Garden Museum', https://gardenmuseum.org.uk/the-museum/history/.

9. John Barrell, *Times Literary Supplement*, 27 January 2012, 3.

10. David Coke and Alan Borg, *Vauxhall Gardens: A History* (New Haven, CT, and London: Yale University Press, 2011), 2.

11. Joseph Addison, *The Spectator*, 20 May 1712, in *The Spectator*, ed. Donald F. Bond, 5 vols (Oxford: Oxford University Press, 1965) III, 436, 438–9.

12. Coke and Borg, *Vauxhall Gardens*, 43.

13. *Gentleman's Magazine*, June 1732, 820.

14. Coke and Borg, *Vauxhall Gardens*, 202–5.

15. Ibid., 275–80.

16. Marshall and Jean Stearns, *Jazz Dance: The Story of American Vernacular Dance* (New York: Macmillan, 1968), 44; Lynne Fauley Emery, *Black Dance from 1619 to Today* (London: Dance Books, 1988), 185–90.

17. Charles Dickens, *American Notes for General Circulation*, ed. Patricia Ingham (London: Penguin, 2000), 101–2.

18. Charles Dickens, 'Vauxhall-Gardens By Day' [*Morning Chronicle*, 26 October 1836], in *Sketches by Boz*, ed. Paul Schlicke and David Hewitt (Oxford: Oxford University Press, 2020), 461.

19. Maria-Joao Melo Nogueira, David Porteous and Sandra Guerreiro, 'The Portuguese-Speaking Community in Lambeth: A Scoping Study', *Middlesex University Research Repository* (2015).

CHAPTER 16
THE CRYSTAL PALACE IN HYDE PARK, SYDENHAM AND ST PETERSBURG
Catherine Brown

In Russia's post-revolutionary future – as imagined by the heroine of an 1863 novel by Nikolai Chernyshevsky – the masses would live in crystal palaces. Later that same year one of Fyodor Dostoevsky's most famous protagonists argued that a crystal palace was no fit dwelling for a free person.

To understand why this intra-Russian dispute between a rationalist materialist feminist revolutionary and an Orthodox peasant-orientated anti-revolutionary Slavophile played out around the image of a building constructed in London twelve years earlier, we need first to revisit the circumstances of its creation. The 1851 Great Exhibition, the world's first 'world fair', showcased 17,000 exhibitors including 384 from Russia.[1] The visitors were similarly international:

> In the crowds there were [. . .] flags of all peoples [. . .] the French Tricolore and the Dutch lion, the British unicorn and Irish harp, the two-headed eagle of Austria, the black eagle of Prussia, and the white eagle of Russia. All these banners, which until now had only been found on the battlefield, are now flying together peacefully in the industrial basilica. Under the arches of this building, people were speaking in every dialect, as in the time of Babel.[2]

Such was the enthusiastic May 1851 report in *Современник* (the *Contemporary*), which reported regularly on the exhibition. It was particularly enthusiastic about the exhibition's building, which was 'so remarkable that we would like to offer some pleasure to our readers by presenting them with a view of its facade, which we await hourly from London'.[3] The English soubriquet soon coined for Joseph Paxton's building was as early as May 1851 translated into Russian as *кристальная палата* ('crystal chamber', presumably because 'palata' sounds closer to 'palace' than the direct translation *дворец*, 'dvorets'); by July the *Contemporary* was imitating the English version by using initial capitals.[4]

The *Contemporary* was not the only Russian journal to report on the exhibition, but, given its radicalism, it was unsurprising that its coverage was positive. That journal represented the Westernizing trend in Russian society, which looked to Europe as a model to be emulated, and which (especially in the post-Napoleonic anti-French reaction) held England in particular to be the epitome of liberalism, technocracy and modernity. Westernizers were also, as the *Contemporary*'s coverage suggests, liable to understand the Crystal Palace in similar terms to its English admirers – as a manifestation of enlightenment, healthiness (it was well lit and ventilated), egalitarianism (its transparency contrasted with French autocratic architecture) and celebration of both natural history and industry (the two in combination creating a narrative of evolution).[5] By such English and Russians as embraced this conception, Russia was by contrast seen as undeveloped and autocratic. The Russian exhibits may have underlined this: chiefly raw materials on the one hand, and such malachite ornaments as were commissioned by the aristocracy on the other.[6] From this perspective it would have seemed just that the host nation (empire included) gave itself pride of place in the exhibition, occupying half the display space and taking half the gold medals for best products; Russia was awarded 1 per cent.[7]

Russian visitors would have been less enthusiastic about the xenophobic fears voiced by many English opponents of the exhibition, concerned by the large number of foreigners drawn to London by the event and the fact that they included radicals taking refuge in the wake of the failed 1848 European revolutions.[8] Nonetheless, radicals had good reason to be drawn to England, which was markedly tolerant of political refugees. Moreover, the tensions between the British and Russian governments in the build-up to the Crimean War gave the British a motivation to tolerate Russian dissidents specifically. Thus it was that the agrarian socialist Alexander Herzen came to London the year after the exhibition, escaping the Second Empire that had just been established in France, and having previously left Russia where he had spent five years in Siberian exile. The following year he opened the Free Russian Press, which produced several Russian-language journals (most famously the *Bell*) that argued for reforms such as the emancipation of the serfs. Herzen turned London into a hub of dissident cultural activity, just as German refugees would during the Second World War, as David Anderson explores in this volume. Herzen's journals evaded tsarist censorship by being smuggled into Russia, where they became widely influential. From that point onwards, Herzen's London home became a focal point for Russian political activists – often visiting him either in order to remonstrate with him from a position of greater radicalism or from one of greater conservatism.

In June 1859 one such visitor in the former category was the thirty-one-year-old Nikolai Chernyshevsky, a theorist of rationalist utilitarian socialism with Russian characteristics. In July 1854 he had demonstrated his enthusiasm for the Crystal Palace by writing a glowing review (based on others' accounts) of its reopening in the suburb of Sydenham: 'everything demonstrates that the new Crystal Palace in Sydenham is something unusually magnificent, elegant, and dazzling'.[9] The reason for his visit to Herzen was that the latter had criticized his generation of radicals for over-reliance on abstractions and an extremism that played into the hands of reactionaries. Both failed to convince the other, and the dispute continued in the pages of the *Bell* and the *Contemporary*, of which Chernyshevsky had in 1853 become the editor.[10]

It is not certain that Chernyshevsky visited the Palace in 1859, but, given his enthusiasm for the building as demonstrated both before and after his London visit, it is highly likely. He returned to a Russia in which pressure was building on Alexander II to

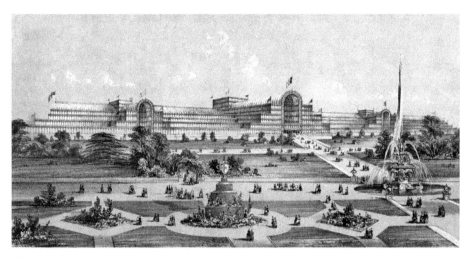

Figure 16.1 *The Crystal Palace at Sydenham* (1855). © Lordprice Collection/Alamy Stock Photo.

emancipate the serfs. After he did so in 1861 the new climate of reform and relaxed censorship encouraged further radicalism, and in St Petersburg in 1862 there were a series of student protests and suspicious fires.[11] It was in this context that Chernyshevsky was on 7 July (wrongly) arrested for connections to a revolutionary organization, and imprisoned in the Peter and Paul Fortress pending his trial.[12]

It was there – having convinced his guards to give him pen and paper with the promise that he would only write fiction – that he wrote his only novel and most famous work, *What is to be Done?* It inverted the depiction of the younger generation of 'nihilists' in Turgenev's *Fathers and Sons* of earlier that year by positively representing four young radicals. Its heroine, the lower-middle-class Vera Pavlovna, escapes from an oppressive family and sets up successful sewing cooperatives and communes before training as a doctor. Her ideological emancipation is marked and helped by four dreams hosted by a female spirit. In the first she is shown a young woman of fluctuating nationality ('First she's English, then French; now she's German, then Polish; she becomes Russian, English again') being liberated from 'a damp, dark cellar' into a beautiful field. Later the novel's readers are similarly enjoined to ideologically 'Come up out of your godforsaken underworld [...] Come out into the light of day, where life is good.'[13] In the fourth and most famous dream, Vera sees the future. In a rural paradise,

> There stands a building, a large, enormous structure [...] What style of architecture? There's nothing at all like it now. No, there is one building that hints at it – the palace at Sydenham: cast iron and crystal, crystal and cast iron.

'Crystal palace' is translated *хрустальный дворец*, the noun now directly translating 'palace', and the adjective *хрустальный* connoting the heavenly and sublime (in contrast to the *Contemporary*'s *кристальный*, which connotes cold, crystalline form). In the building, over a thousand people are dining with place settings made of aluminium and crystal. It is a worker's cooperative where 'What everyone can afford together is provided free; but a charge is made for any special item or whim.' Vera is then shown the Russian far South, where the former desert has been irrigated and covered by 'enormous buildings stand[ing] three or four versts apart [...] the same sort of enormous crystal building'. Here the population live during the cold months. Everyone is elegantly dressed; the dining hall (with room for 9,000) is lit by electric light, and sound-proofed rooms lead off it where couples may retire to have sex. Nobody is forced to live communally; those who wish live 'just as you now live in those Petersburgs, Parises, and Londons of yours'; but 99 per cent of the people choose to do so. The guide ends Vera's dream by enjoining her to 'Strive toward it [this future], work for it, bring it nearer, transfer into the present as much as you can from it.'[14]

The idea of communal living in large buildings was pioneered by the utopian socialist Charles Fourier, an important influence on both Chernyshevsky and Herzen; he called such institutions *phalanstères*. The journalist Henry Mayhew may have been influenced by his conception in his 1851 novel *1851; Or, the Adventures of Mr. and Mrs. Sandboys and Family who came up to London to 'enjoy themselves,' and to see the Great Exhibition*. The eponymous family is invited to stay in a 'Monster Lodging House which was to afford accommodation for one thousand persons from the country'. In response, Sandboys asks 'whether it was probable that he, who had passed his whole life in a village [...] would, in his fifty-fifth year, consent to take up his abode with a thousand people under one roof, with [...] policemen to watch him all night, and a surgeon to examine him in the morning!'.[15] He is, however, focused on getting a ticket to the Crystal Palace, which he sees as a haven of rationality even if one of imperfect accessibility (the tickets initially cost £1; only a month later were they reduced to a shilling on certain days, which still excluded the poorest).[16] Chernyshevsky, therefore, combined the vision of a phalanstery with the architecture of the Crystal Palace; universal accessibility with modern luxuries; and the roles of education-provision and pleasure-provision that were less perfectly combined at Sydenham.

What is to be Done?, exfiltrated from prison, was published in the *Contemporary* in 1863. By this time Chernyshevsky had been tried, put through a mock execution and sentenced to fourteen years' hard labour and lifelong exile in Siberia. He wrote little more.[17]

* * *

A few months before his arrest, Chernyshevsky had been visited by Dostoevsky, himself only three years returned from a decade's exile in Siberia after his own trial, and mock execution, for seditious activities. But Dostoevsky was now at the beginning of a trajectory towards a more conservative, Slavophile (anti-Westernizing) position. He saw Chernyshevsky as dangerously siding with the forces causing disturbances in St Petersburg in 1862, and wished to remonstrate with him. Like Herzen, he failed to change Chernyshevsky's mind.[18]

Not long thereafter, shortly before Chernyshevsky's arrest, Dostoevsky decided to finally inspect Europe, which had been the object of veneration in the Fourierist circles of his radical 1840s youth. As he parodically put it, 'After all, literally almost everything we can show which may be called progress, science, art, citizenship, humanity, everything, everything stems from there, from that land of holy miracles. The whole of our life, from earliest childhood, is shaped by the European mould.'[19]

So, Dostoevsky spent two and a half months of 1862 in Europe, including eight days in London where he visited Herzen at his Paddington home.[20] In the previous year, Herzen had been visited by Tolstoy, the revolutionary Bakunin (having escaped Siberian exile by travelling eastwards round the world), and Turgenev. Herzen and Dostoevsky soon discovered that they were both troubled by Chernyshevsky's generation of 'nihilists', and that they both believed that the future of Russia lay in a system based on the peasant commune (albeit Herzen's conception was atheist and Dostoevsky's Orthodox).

It is not known whether Dostoevsky visited the Crystal Palace at Sydenham, but he certainly visited the World Fair which was held between May and November 1862 in a new building (later partially rebuilt as the Alexandra Palace) in South Kensington. This exhibition sought to outdo that of 1851, and the intervening imitative fairs such as Paris 1855, on every criterion – thus enacting the spirit of competition that it praised, and proving its own hypothesis of progress.[21] There were twice the number of exhibitors as in Hyde Park and the building was much larger; its two domes were the world's largest made of glass.

Back in Russia, Dostoevsky wrote a rumination on his tour, *Winter Notes on Summer Impressions*, published in 1863. In it he described London in a chapter entitled 'Baal', adumbrating the idea that England worshipped a monstrous individualist spirit with complete frankness:[22]

> The immense town, for ever bustling by night and by day, [...] the magnificent squares and marks, the town's terrifying districts, such as Whitechapel with its half-naked, savage and hungry population, the City with its millions and worldwide trade, the Crystal Palace, the World Exhibition [...][23]

He uses the term *кристальный дворец*, using the adjective which connotes crystalline clarity. The two last terms in the paragraph above suggest that he is not conflating them, but his response to both is aligned:

> The Exhibition is indeed amazing [...] And you feel nervous [...] Can this, you think, in fact be the final accomplishment of an ideal state of things? [...] You look at those hundreds of thousands, at those millions of people obediently trooping into this place from all parts of the earth [...] It is a biblical sight, something to do with Babylon [...] You feel that a rich and ancient tradition of denial and protest is needed in order not to yield [...] if you had seen how proud the mighty spirit is which created that colossal décor and how convinced it is of its victory and its triumph, you would have shuddered at its pride, its obstinacy, its blindness.[24]

Three years later, in *Crime and Punishment*, Dostoevsky would make the connection between London's poverty and its famous palace by ironically naming a seedy

St Petersburg pub *Хрустальный дворец* (using the more ethereal adjective).[25] These views have much in common with Herzen's, and it is highly likely that Dostoevsky's conversations with Herzen coloured his view of a city where he spent only eight days and could not speak the language.

In the following year (1864), Dostoevsky published *Notes from Underground*. The fact that the nameless underground man intentionally inhabits a spiritual underground recalls and inverts the message of *What is to be Done?*, which is to draw its readers out of their mental cellars, whereas *Notes from Underground* drags the reader into that of the narrator. The extent to which he is intended to be an unreliable narrator is the subject of intense debate. It seems relevant that the narrator's brief statement of yearning for Christian faith was edited out by the censor, leaving only the hint: 'I know myself [...] that it isn't really the underground that's better, but something different [...] that I long for, but I'll never be able to find!'[26] What is clear, however, is that the novel is a deliberate attack on *What is to be Done*? of the previous year. When the narrator asks, 'Oh, tell me who was first to announce [...] that man does nasty things simply because he doesn't know his own true interest' (15), the answer is, as his readers would have known, Chernyshevsky. He continues parodically:

> [N]ew economic relations will be established, all ready-made, also calculated with mathematical precision [...] Then the crystal palace will be built. [...] Of course, there's no way to guarantee [...] that it won't be, for instance, terribly boring. (18)

Dostoevsky's critique of Chernyshevsky's utopianism has a considerable overlap with Aldous Huxley's Savage's objections to the Brave New World:

> Man needs only one thing – his own *independent* desire, whatever that independence might cost and wherever it might lead [...] there is one case, only one, when a man may intentionally, consciously desire even something harmful to himself [...] namely: in order *to have the right* to desire something even very stupid and not be bound by an obligation to desire only what's smart. (19, 21)

Life in the *хрустальный дворец* is therefore oppressive:

> [S]uffering is not permitted in vaudevilles, that I know. It's also inconceivable in the crystal palace [...] Yet, I'm convinced that man will never renounce real suffering [...] perhaps I'm so afraid of this building precisely because it's made of crystal and it's indestructible, and because it won't be possible to stick one's tongue out even furtively. (25)

The doubly repressed (by the narrator and the censor) Christian sentiment of the novel may also have been offended by the irreverent ecclesiastical aspect of the Crystal Palace, with its nave and transepts, three times the size of St Paul's, and by the same token vastly bigger and lighter than any Orthodox church.

In 1870 Herzen died; two years later Dostoevsky depicted him as the inadvertent intellectual father of the nihilists in the character of Verkhovensky in *The Demons* (Verkhovensky is appalled to discover the evolution of his own ideas in a novel called *What is to be Done?*). Chernyshevsky, meanwhile, was a model for the eponymous demons of the younger generation. That year Chernyshevsky finished his penal servitude, but had another seventeen years of Siberian exile still ahead of him. Two years later the reforming Tsar Alexander II visited the Crystal Palace at Sydenham, implicitly affirming its importance – albeit conflicted – in the Russian imagination. In 1881, the month after Dostoevsky had died, Alexander was assassinated by populists, as Dostoevsky's novels had implicitly predicted.

What is to be Done? inspired many revolutionaries through the decades of reaction that followed (Lenin foremost amongst them), and the novel became canonical reading in the Soviet period, when it was far more read than any of Dostoevsky's works. Vladimir Tatlin's famous 1919–20 crystalline design for the tower of the Third International was arguably the Soviet version of the Crystal Palace. But it was never built, and by the time that the Sydenham palace had burned down in 1936, Soviet architecture had moved away from sheet glass and towards the Stalinist baroque, arguably in reflection of Bolshevism's departures from its founding idealism. Back in London, the Millennium Dome beat the reconstruction of the Crystal Palace as a proposal to celebrate the millennium, presumably due to a rejection of the latter's associations with empire and a desire to be similarly forward-looking. Indeed, the Millennium Dome was its modern British equivalent: like its forebear, gigantic, panoptical, nationally self-celebratory, and self-consciously progressive – yet with scant celebration of cosmopolitanism, and with nothing like the same effect on the world. The fact that the Millennium Dome has had a fraction of the Crystal Palace's international attention, let alone its impact on international political debate (a latter-day Dostoevsky would dislike the Dome's ethos, but is unlikely ever to have heard of it), fits with Britain's reduced status and (since Brexit) its reduced openness, and appeal, to the world.

Notes

Author's note. I would like to acknowledge the support and advice given to me in researching this chapter by Sean Mitchell, a London Blue Badge Guide specialising in the history of Russian expatriates in London.

1. Sarah J. Young, 'Russian Perspectives on the Great Exhibition (6)', *Russian Literature, History and Culture*, 28 July 2011, https://sarahjyoung.com/site/2011/07/28/russian-perspectives-on-the-great-exhibition-6/. The four blog posts by Young referenced in this article are based around transcriptions, and Young's own translations, of articles about the Great Exhibition published in the *Contemporary*.

2. Sarah J. Young, 'The Opening of the Great Exhibition: A View from Russia', *Russian Literature, History and Culture*, 29 May 2011, https://sarahjyoung.com/site/2011/05/29/the-opening-of-the-great-exhibition-a-view-from-russia/.

3. Young, 'Russian Perspectives on the Great Exhibition (6)'.

4. Young, 'The Opening of the Great Exhibition'; Sarah J. Young, 'Russian Perspectives on the Great Exhibition (2)', *Russian Literature, History and Culture*, 9 June 2011, https://sarahjyoung.com/site/2011/06/09/russian-perspectives-on-the-great-exhibition-2/.

5. Philip Landon, 'Great Exhibitions: Representations of the Crystal Palace in Mayhew, Dickens, and Dostoevsky', *Nineteenth-Century Contexts* 20, no. 1 (1997): 27–31.

6. Sarah J. Young, 'Chaucer, Chernyshevsky and the Crystal Palace', *Russian Literature, History and Culture*, 15 July 2011, https://sarahjyoung.com/site/2011/07/15/chaucer-chernyshevsky-crystal-palace/.

7. Landon, 'Great Exhibitions', 29.

8. Ibid., 28.

9. Michael R. Katz, '"But This Building: What on Earth Is It?"', *New England Review* 23, no. 1 (2002): 69.

10. Aileen M. Kelly, *The Discovery of Chance: The Life and Thought of Alexander Herzen* (Cambridge, MA: Harvard University Press, 2016), 486.

11. Michael R. Katz and William G. Wagner, 'Introduction', in Nikolai Chernyshevsky, *What is to be Done?*, trans. Michael R. Katz (London: Cornell University Press, 1989), 6–7.

12. Katz and Wagner, 'Introduction', 14.

13. Nikolai Chernyshevsky, *What is to be Done?*, trans. Michael R. Katz (London: Cornell University Press, 1989), 129–30, 313.

14. Ibid., 370–2, 375–9.

15. Henry Mayhew, *1851; Or, the Adventures of Mr. and Mrs. Sandboys and Family who came up to London to 'enjoy themselves,' and to see the Great Exhibition* (London: David Bogue, 1851), 17.

16. Landon, 'Great Exhibitions', 49.

17. Katz and Wagner, 'Introduction', 14.

18. Joseph Frank, *Dostoevsky: The Stir of Liberation, 1860–1865* (Princeton, NJ: Princeton University Press, 1986), 151.

19. Fyodor Dostoevsky, *Winter Notes on Summer Impressions*, trans. Kyril FitzLyon (Richmond, VA: Alma Books, 2016), 13.

20. Dostoevsky, *Winter Notes*, 3, 9; Frank, *Dostoevsky*, 188.

21. Britt Salvesen, '"The Most Magnificent, Useful, and Interesting Souvenir": Representations of the International Exhibition of 1862', *Visual Resources* 13, no. 1 (1997): 1–2.

22. Dostoevsky, *Winter Notes*, 48–9, 58.

23. Ibid., 49–50.

24. Ibid., 50–1.

25. Fyodor Dostoevsky, *Crime and Punishment*, trans. David McDuff (London: Penguin, 2003), 191.

26. Fyodor Dostoevsky, *Notes from Underground*, 4th edn, trans. Michael R. Katz (New York: Norton, 2001), 27, 95–6. Future references will be made to this edition in the main body of the text.

CHAPTER 17

87 HACKFORD ROAD: THE LONDON OF VINCENT VAN GOGH

Livia Wang

I crossed Westminster Bridge every morning and evening and know what it looks like when the sun's setting behind Westminster Abbey and the Houses of Parliament, and what it's like early in the morning, and in the winter with snow and fog.

When I saw this painting I felt how much I love London.

Vincent van Gogh to Theo van Gogh, Paris, 24 July 1875[1]

Vincent van Gogh (1853–90) arrived in London in May 1873 as an eager twenty-year-old, training to be an art dealer. From August 1873 to August 1874, he lived in a boarding house at 87 Hackford Road in Stockwell, South London. The time he spent living here was described by his sister-in-law and biographer Jo van Gogh-Bonger as 'the happiest year of his life'.[2] Now a museum and artists' residency, the end-of-terrace house has been Grade II listed and features a Greater London Council blue plaque stating that 'Van Gogh, Painter, Lived Here'.

Throughout this period Vincent wrote regular letters, to his younger brother Theo and his sister Anna and their parents, as well as to a number of friends. These letters reveal a broad range of Vincent's experiences, from expressive observations on nature and the details of his commute, to reporting on the art and literature the city offered. Through his correspondence we catch glimpses of Victorian London from the perspective of the young man.

Vincent wrote lyrically of the changing seasons: 'There are lilacs and hawthorns and laburnums etc. blossoming in all the gardens, and the chestnut trees are magnificent. If one truly loves nature one finds beauty everywhere.'[3] Paying close attention to colour and texture, the letters are full of descriptive vignettes that paint London as a richly planted city, despite the construction taking place.[4] London was also a city of slums, child labour and poverty, deprivation Vincent witnessed both in person and through contemporary novels, paintings and illustrated newspapers – media that he consumed with a 'violent passion'.[5]

It was only six years later, in 1880, that Van Gogh would make the decision to become an artist. This chapter looks at his formative experiences as a young Dutch migrant in London, in the years before he became a painter, placing him within the wider context of nineteenth-century London and its population, infrastructure and visual cultures.

* * *

Figure 17.1 87 Hackford Road. Photograph by Thomas Parsons. © Van Gogh House London 2019.

Aged sixteen, Vincent had moved from his childhood home in Zundert, a rural town in the south of the Netherlands, to The Hague, taking up a position as the youngest employee of Goupil & Co., art dealers. Van Gogh's uncle, also named Vincent van Gogh, was a partner in the company and helped secure a position for his nephew.[6] With headquarters in Paris, the firm had further locations in Berlin, Brussels, London and New York, building an international reputation for dealing in contemporary paintings and reproductions. After nearly four years as a junior apprentice, Vincent was transferred, with a 'splendid testimonial', to the firm's new branch in London.[7]

Located at 17 Southampton Street in Covent Garden, Goupil's London office dealt primarily in the distribution of wholesale prints made for the growing middle-class market. Functioning as a warehouse, the office lacked a showroom and was not open to the public. As a clerk, Vincent's work consisted of administrative tasks, with little chance to see paintings first-hand.

Vincent's first London address is unknown. He reported to his parents that he had found a suburban boarding house run by two landladies who each kept a parrot.[8] These lodgings were shared with three Germans who played music in the evenings and took him on outings, though he bemoaned that 'those gentlemen spend a great deal of money and I shan't go out with them anymore.'[9]

Determined not to be a tourist, Vincent's initial correspondence reveals an interest in city life: 'I haven't yet been to the Crystal Palace and the Tower, nor to Tussaud's; I'm not at all in a hurry to go and see everything. For the time being I have enough with the museums, parks, etc., which attract me more.' He took a particular liking to Rotton Row in Hyde Park which he described as '[o]ne of the nicest things I've seen here.'[10] Eager to dress the part, he wrote home requesting money for a top hat claiming that 'you cannot be in London without one.'[11]

A keen walker, the letters mention trips to the southern reaches of Dulwich and a six-hour journey to Box Hill in Surrey.[12] Exploring London's newly growing suburbs, he imagines his own future as a commuter: 'The countryside here is so beautiful; many people who have their business in L. live in some village or other outside L. and come to the city every day by train. Perhaps I'll soon be doing that as well, if I can find a cheap room somewhere.'[13]

Finding this 'cheap room' was imperative. The cost of living was high, and Vincent admitted to his family that 'Life here is very expensive. I pay 18 shillings a week for my lodgings, not including the washing, and then I still have to eat in town.'[14] Goupil's paid Vincent a salary of £90 a year, the equivalent of 1,090 Guilders, and nearly twice as much as he had earned in The Hague. Although this was in line with other junior clerks in the city, his parents worried for him, noting that he still had 'to live frugally owing to the great hardship there; the boarding-house and his midday meal cost him 890 guilders a year', more than three-quarters of his income.[15]

* * *

After three months of searching, Van Gogh finally settled at 87 Hackford Road, the home of Sarah Ursula Loyer. Known by her middle name, Ursula was widowed and ran a school and boarding house with the help of her nineteen-year-old daughter Eugenie, both commonly accepted means for a widowed woman to make a living. Vincent clearly felt at ease at the Loyers', writing after six months, 'Things are going well for me here, I have a wonderful home and it's a great pleasure for me to observe London and the English way of life and the English themselves.'[16] He sowed 'sweet peas, poppies and mignonette' in the small garden and observed the fashion for making scrapbooks.[17]

Part of a terrace of four buildings named Jazer Terrace, the house is consistent with late Georgian housing seen across London: a modest three-storeyed brick-and-timber construction faced in white stucco with a valley roof, sash windows and a small garden.[18] Built in 1826, on the boundary of historic Stockwell and Lambeth Wick estates, Jazer Terrace was part of some of the earliest development in the area, initiated by the construction of Vauxhall Bridge (1816) and subsequent laying-out of Camberwell New Road.[19] The area remained semi-rural as market-garden and pasture until the 1840s when construction began in earnest.[20] Hackford Road (originally named St Ann's Road) was formed as a collection of cottages and villas, which were in turn demolished in the late 1870s to make way for Victorian red-brick terraces.[21]

Arriving in the 1870s, Vincent experienced Stockwell in a transitory phase. House building was still taking place up until the 1900s in response to the opening of new suburban bridges (Lambeth in 1862 and Albert and Wandsworth bridges in 1873) and the opening of the City and South London Railway (the forerunner of the Northern Line) in 1890.[22] Land along Brixton and Camberwell New Roads had been leased in piecemeal plots to local speculative builders, operating on a small scale. The result was small clusters of ten or fewer houses being built at a time, forming an 'untidy and haphazard appearance' which still characterizes the area to this day in contrast to the uniformity found in areas like Bloomsbury where large landowners oversaw development.[23]

Built for 'clerks, shopkeepers, skilled artisans and the rank and file of the commercial world',[24] the Loyer family reflected the 'fairly comfortable' middle-class population that lived here throughout the nineteenth century, from the 1820s to when the Booth poverty map was extend to include Stockwell in 1891.[25] Ursula and Eugenie Loyer are recorded in the census at Hackford Road in the years 1871, 1881 and 1891, growing from a household of five to ten after Eugenie married and had five children. The mother and daughter took on two to three lodgers at a time, who ranged in income and social standing. These included children who attended their school as boarders; clerks on an income similar to Vincent; and dressmakers, including Ursula's sister Mary Wilson. The house could easily have felt crowded.[26]

The ground floor features a front parlour where the schoolroom would have been, a back parlour where (in the absence of a range) meals were cooked, connected by a narrow hallway to the small garden where a lean-to scullery was built, with an accompanying privy. The first and second floors are made up of two rooms at each level, the larger rooms with two windows facing the street, whilst the smaller have one window looking out across the neighbouring gardens. Ursula and Eugenie may have shared the master room on the first floor, with the remaining three bedrooms let out.

It is likely that Vincent was able to afford the second-floor room to himself, a space that could comfortably house a single bed, a writing desk and chair, a washstand and dressing table, with clothes hung on hooks either side of the chimney breast. He cryptically described what his room was not like: 'I now have a room, as I've long been wishing, without sloping beams and without blue wallpaper with a green border.'[27] His windows looked out north across the newly built villas and terraces, towards Vauxhall and Westminster.

*   *   *

I enjoy the walk from home to the office and in the evening from the office back home. It takes about three-quarters of an hour [. . .] It's wonderful to be finished so early here; we close at 6 o'clock and yet we work none the less because of it.

Vincent van Gogh to Theo van Gogh, London, Thursday, 30 April 1874[28]

From Hackford Road, van Gogh was able to establish a consistent routine. Walking to and from work each day, he would cross the river at Westminster Bridge, and stop to sketch: 'How often I would stand on the Thames Embankment and draw as I made my way home from Southampton Street in the evening.'[29] His free time was spent reading, drawing and looking at art. The letters are dotted with references to books, paintings, exhibitions and museums, plotting a still-navigable map of London's galleries and institutions: the British Museum, Christie's, the Royal Academy of Arts, the National Gallery, the Wallace Collection, the South Kensington Museum (now the Victoria and Albert Museum) and Dulwich Picture Gallery.

Through the artists he encountered at Goupil's, and his exploration of London's rich cultural offerings, Van Gogh developed a language and a sharpened eye for art and literature. Initially sceptical of English paintings, finding them 'with few exceptions, very disagreeable and feeble', he soon began to identify the painters he admired:[30] John Everett Millais and George Henry Boughton for the figures they depicted; Constable, Reynolds, Gainsborough and Turner for their landscapes.

An avid reader, Van Gogh made direct comparisons between these painters and the writers he encountered. Paintings such as Millais' *Chill October* (1870) and Constable's *Valley Farm* (1835) resonated with Vincent for their depictions of autumn, which he saw mirrored in Keats' 1819 poem 'To Autumn', noting the poet as being a 'favourite of the painters here'.[31] Urging Theo to read George Eliot's *Adam Bede* (1859), he declared the 'whitewashed huts with green, moss-covered roofs' as of being 'by [Georges] Michel', and in John Bunyan's *A Pilgrim's Progress* (1678) Van Gogh identified a favourite painter, George Henry Boughton, along with 'something of M. Maris or of Millet', seeing in these works 'a reality more real than reality'.[32] This representation of 'reality' was a contemporary concern, central to the writers Vincent was reading. From George Eliot and Charlotte Brontë to Thomas Carlyle and Charles Dickens, they explored to varying degrees the lives of ordinary people under the impact of industry, migration and social reform.

*   *   *

More than 10 years ago I used to go every week to the display case of the printer of The Graphic and [The Illustrated] London News in London to see the weekly publications. The impressions I gained there on the spot were so strong that the drawings have remained clear and bright in my mind, despite everything that has since gone through my head.

Vincent van Gogh to Anthon van Rappard, The Hague, Sunday,
4 February 1883[33]

The text, image and politics of nineteenth-century London came together in a particular form, the illustrated newspaper. The *Illustrated London News* and the *Graphic* were the leading publications in this field, printing monochrome illustrations with black ink that were known colloquially as 'Black and Whites'.

Founded by Herbert Ingram in 1842, the *Illustrated London News* was the world's first illustrated newspaper. At the height of its success in the 1860s it reached a weekly circulation of over 300,000.[34] Prior to the advent of the *Illustrated London News*, images were only published on exceptional occasions. As a newsvendor, Ingram had noticed much higher sales of these illustrated issues. Making use of new technology, Ingram employed draughtsmen and engravers to draw from photographs and illustrate news articles. The speed at which these engravings could be produced meant not only that there could be more images, but that these images could be marketed as a source of objective, 'truthful' information, representing events 'as they transpire'.[35]

In 1869, William Luson Thomas set up the *Graphic* in left-wing opposition to the conservative *Illustrated London News*. A wood engraver by trade, Thomas distinguished the *Graphic*'s production process by commissioning artists rather than draughtsmen and encouraging them to choose their own subjects. With this agency, artists of the *Graphic* drew from life and their experience, rather than in the drafting room.[36] Depicting individuals, their body language and facial expressions, these illustrations presented an 'embodied objectivity' that set the *Graphic* apart from the *Illustrated London News*.[37]

The overriding focus of these illustrations was poverty. With the Poor Law Amendment Act (1834) and subsequent Metropolitan Houseless Poor Act (1864), poverty was institutionalized in the workhouse, police stations and prisons.[38] This architecture was captured in *London, a Pilgrimage* (1872) by journalist Blanchard Jerrold and illustrator Gustave Doré, with 180 engravings and a series of texts portraying the extremes of city life to a sensational degree. From soup kitchens and opium dens to the auctions and balls of the wealthy, Doré's Londoners are drawn in the context of oppressive crowds and a densely hatched urban infrastructure.

Van Gogh admired these engravings and their illustrators, both for the issues they conveyed and their use of light and shade: 'I wonder whether the London sketches [...] wouldn't be a little less compelling and full of character if painted than they are in the rough Black and White.'[39] The Black and Whites were 'accessible, exchangeable, comparable' and Van Gogh identified a tension between these journalistic, mass-produced images and the tradition of history painting.[40]

In the summer of 1874, Vincent visited the Royal Academy Summer exhibition where he would likely have seen both Frank Holl's *Deserted – A Foundling* (1874) and Luke Fildes' *Applicants for Admission to a Casual Ward* (1874), existing engravings translated into paint by their illustrators.[41] Holl and Fildes were illustrators at the *Graphic* and although their paintings were not critically successful, they set the wheels in motion for an emergent social realism. *Applicants for Admission to a Casual Ward* was a reworking of Fildes' original engraving 'Houseless and Hungry' (1869). Published in the first issue of the *Graphic*, the image had caught the attention of Millais, who in turn showed it to Dickens. Dickens went on to commission Fildes to illustrate what would be his last (unfinished) novel, *The Mystery of Edwin Drood* (1870).

*   *   *

My whole life is aimed at making the things from everyday life that Dickens describes and these artists draw.

Vincent van Gogh to Anthon van Rappard, The Hague, 19 September 1882[42]

In the early 1880s, when living in The Hague, Vincent would bargain with booksellers for editions he could afford, amassing an impressive collection of 'at least a thousand prints, English (mainly SWAIN'S), American, French [...]'.[43] He pored over these prints in his studio, writing about them frequently to his brother Theo and friend Anthon van Rappard. One letter to Van Rappard mentions the *Graphic* no fewer than eight times, urging him to pay a visit.[44] Having made the decision to become an artist, it is Dickensian subject matter that Van Gogh returned to, finding purpose in drawing run-down cityscapes and portraits of the destitute, 'types one comes across on the street'.[45] He prepared portfolios of his own drawings of laundry lines, peasants, miners and the impoverished, captioned in English with the idea that he might return to London and find work as an illustrator himself.

Although Vincent did not fulfil this ambition, the influence of the Black and Whites can be seen in the dark shadows and embodied perspective of *The Potato Eaters* (1885) and very directly in the composition of *Prisoners Exercising* (1890), a reinterpretation of Doré's *Newgate Prison Exercise Yard* (1872). Van Gogh's paintings *Van Gogh's Chair* (1888) and *Gaugin's Chair* (1888) make reference to Luke Fildes' *The Empty Chair* (1870), an engraving published on the occasion of Dickens' death. Vincent relayed the story of the drawing in a letter to Theo: 'Luke Fildes [...] comes into his room on the day of [Dickens'] death – sees his empty chair standing there, and so it was that one of the old Nos. of The Graphic had that striking drawing.' Vincent prized his copy.[46]

*　*　*

I have a rich life here, 'having nothing, yet possessing all things'. Sometimes I start to believe that I'm gradually beginning to turn into a true cosmopolitan, meaning not a Dutchman, Englishman or Frenchman, but simply a man.

Vincent van Gogh to Caroline van Stockum-Haanebeek, London, Monday,
9 February 1874

Through Van Gogh's letters written from Hackford Road, the reader experiences Victorian London from the perspective of a culturally engaged young clerk. Not yet the outsider he would later be regarded as, these early letters speak in the voice of someone growing into the role of a worldly 'cosmopolitan'. Applying this first-person narrative to the context of the industrializing city gives a voice to key moments of Victorian progress, of suburbia, infrastructure and social reform.

London was also where Van Gogh received an early art education. Moving between novels, paintings and print, he encountered questions around objectivity, realism and the communicative potential of images that left a deep impression on him. Growing into his critical voice, Van Gogh found a number of heroes amongst British writers and artists. Long after he left Britain, he would go on to refer to 'Dickens and Eliot and Currer Bell [Charlotte Brontë]' being 'as powerful as, say, a drawing by Herkomer or Fildes or Israëls'.[47]

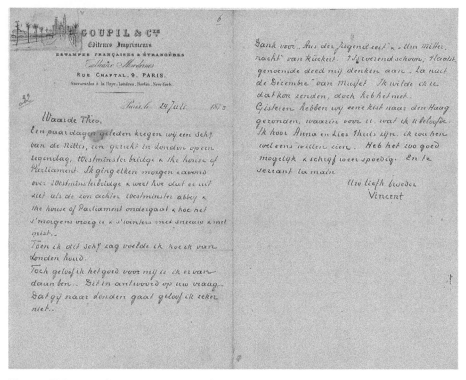

Figure 17.2 Letter from Vincent van Gogh to Theo van Gogh, Paris, 24 July 1875. © Van Gogh Museum.

Vincent's time in Hackford Road came to an end in August 1874. It is believed that he had proposed to Eugenie but was rejected; she was already secretly engaged to a previous lodger.[48] On 10 August, Vincent wrote an abrupt note at the end of a letter to Theo: 'We're going to move and will live in a house completely overgrown with ivy; we'll write to you again soon from there.'[49] By the end of 1874, Vincent was transferred, dejected, to Paris, before being eventually let go from Goupil's in the spring 1876. Without direction, he returned to the UK as a teacher, first in Kent, then Isleworth, west London. It was here that he found new direction as a preacher, eventually leaving Britain for the last time in December 1876.

Notes

1. Leo Jansen, Hans Luijten and Nienke Bakker (eds), *Vincent van Gogh – The Letters* (Amsterdam and The Hague: Van Gogh Museum and Huygens ING, 2009), 39.

2. Vincent van Gogh, *The Complete Letters of Vincent Van Gogh*, 3 vols (London: Thames and Hudson, 1978), I, xxiv.

3. Vincent to Theo van Gogh, April 1874, *The Letters*, 22.

4. Carol Jacobi, *Van Gogh and Britain: The Ey Exhibition* (London: Tate, 2019), 36; Jerry White, *London in the Nineteenth Century: A Human Awful Wonder of God* (London: Jonathan Cape, 2007), 37–67.

5. Vincent to Theo, June 1880, *The Letters*, 15.

6. Martin Bailey, *Young Vincent: The Story of Van Gogh's Years in England* (London: W. H. Allen, 1990), 22.

7. Van Gogh, *The Complete Letters*, I, xxiv.

8. Ibid.

9. Vincent to Theo, June 1873, *The Letters*, 9.

10. Vincent to Willem van Stockum and Caroline van Stockum-Haanebeek, August 1873, *The Letters*, 10–12.

11. Bailey, *Young Vincent*, 21.

12. Jansen, Luijten and Bakker, *Vincent van Gogh – The Letters*, 9, 12, 27.

13. Vincent to Willem and Caroline, August 1873, *The Letters*, 12.

14. Vincent to Theo, June 1873, *The Letters*, 9.

15. Theodorus van Gogh to Theo, July 1873, *The Letters*, 15.

16. Vincent to Theo, January 1874, *The Letters*, 17.

17. Vincent to Willem and Caroline, October 1873, *The Letters*, 14.

18. Charles Booth, 'Maps Descriptive of London Poverty, 1898–9', https://booth.lse.ac.uk/map/14/-0.1174/51.5064/100/0. Census of England and Wales, 1861, London, Lambeth, Stockwell, 87 Hackford Road; National Archives of the UK, reference series RG 9/361.

19. C. and J. Greenwood, 'Map of London, Made from an Actual Survey in the Years 1824, 1825, & 1826' (1830), https://id.lib.harvard.edu/curiosity/scanned-maps/44-990102029440203941.

20. White, *London in the Nineteenth Century*, 83.

21. George Philip, 'Philip's New Plan of London, 1873', https://id.lib.harvard.edu/curiosity/scanned-maps/44-990102025370203941.

22. White, *London in the Nineteenth Century*, 83; F. H. W. Sheppard (ed.), *Survey of London*, 47 vols (London: London County Council, 1956), XXVI, 1–17, www.british-history.ac.uk/survey-london/vol26.

23. Sheppard, *Survey of London*, XXVI, 108–22.

24. Ibid.

25. Booth, 'Maps Descriptive of London Poverty, 1898–9'.

26. Census of England and Wales, 1871, London, Lambeth, Stockwell, 87 Hackford Road; National Archives of the UK, reference series RG 10/678; Census of England and Wales, 1881, London, Lambeth, Stockwell, 87 Hackford Road; National Archives of the UK, reference series RG 11/610; Census of England and Wales, 1891, London, Lambeth, Stockwell, 87 Hackford Road; National Archives of the UK, reference series RG 12/404.

27. Vincent to Theo, September 1873, *The Letters*, 13.

28. Vincent to Theo, April 1874, *The Letters*, 22.

29. Vincent to Theo, October 1883, *The Letters*, 394.

30. Vincent to Theo, September 1873, *The Letters*, 13.

31. Vincent to Willem and Caroline, August 1873, *The Letters*, 12.

32. Vincent to Theo, March 1875, *The Letters*, 30; Vincent to Theo, June 1880, *The Letters*, 155.

33. Vincent to Anthon van Rappard, February 1883, *The Letters*, 155.

34. Christopher Hibbert, *The Illustrated London News' Social History of Victorian Britain* (London: Book Club Associates, 1976), 14.

35. Andrea Korda, *Printing and Painting the News in Victorian London: The Graphic and Social Realism 1869–1891* (London: Routledge, 2018), 19.

36. Ibid., 120.

37. Ibid., 2, 61.

38. Ibid., 10.

39. Vincent to Anthon, February 1883, *The Letters*, 307.

40. Jacobi, *Van Gogh and Britain*, 51; Korda, *Printing and Painting the News in Victorian London*, 12.

41. Bailey, *Young Vincent*, 24.

42. Jansen, Luijten and Bakker, *Vincent van Gogh – The Letters*, 267.

43. Vincent to Theo, June 1882, *The Letters*, 234.

44. Vincent to Anthon, February 1883, *The Letters*, 307.

45. Vincent to Anthon, September 1882, *The Letters*, 268.

46. Vincent to Theo, December 1882, *The Letters*, 293.

47. Vincent to Anthon, May 1882, *The Letters*, 232.

48. Van Gogh, *The Complete Letters*, I, XXIV.

49. Vincent to Theo, August 1874, *The Letters*, 28.

CHAPTER 18
WRITING LONDON: HANIF KUREISHI'S
THE BUDDHA OF SUBURBIA
Ruvani Ranasinha

Born to a white British mother and Indian father in South London in 1954, Hanif Kureishi became one of the most significant, provocative, versatile and popular British writers of his generation. For four decades, as novelist, screenwriter, playwright and essayist, his vivid evocations of marginalized subjects have redefined images of British identity and explored the social contradictions of a wealthy, lively cosmopolitan capital beset with a concentration of turmoil and poverty.

Almost all Kureishi's work is set in and around London, which he has called his 'playground'.[1] The writer's early films challenged traditional images of London. Envisaged as a riposte to a British culture mostly concerned with the historic experience of white Britons and Raj revisionism, *My Beautiful Laundrette* (1985) and *Sammy and Rosie Get Laid* (1987) foreground the contemporary experience of minority Londoners as well as the urban decay, drugs, violence, unemployment and homelessness of Thatcherite Britain. Set in a derelict part of South London – '*beautiful in its own falling-down way*' – *My Beautiful Laundrette* revolves around the unlikely romance between lower middle-class mixed-race Omar and his old school friend Johnny, a white working-class, former skinhead and National Front sympathizer now adrift, homeless and broke, as they embark upon renovating a dilapidated South London launderette gifted to Omar by his wealthy, entrepreneurial paternal uncle Nasser.[2] (The launderette set was located in a row of shops – between a dry cleaners and accountants – in Wilcox Road, Lambeth. Papa and Omar's flat perilously close to the railway lines overlooking the London Stainless Steel Exhaust Centre was filmed in Battersea.) Having initially envisioned their film as a sequel to *The Godfather*, Kureishi and director Stephen Frears opted for an ironic, light comedy instead. The gangster elements remain as an expression of the city: alienation, random violence, mobs and gangs in South London. Kureishi and Frears move from London's Pakistanis to the broader canvas of inner-city racial tensions and a more diverse cross section of South Londoners in their second film, *Sammy and Rosie Get Laid* (1987). British-educated father Rafi Rahman visits the capital from the subcontinent after a thirty-year absence. The urbane, engaging former politician is shocked to find his beloved, beleaguered London amid an incendiary urban riot. When Rafi offers his son money to move anywhere else 'not twinned with Beirut', the film cuts to a Woody Allen-esque *homage* to London scenes. '*Now we see a number of London scenes that* SAMMY *and* ROSIE *like*', including visits to bookshops, Thames riverside walks along the Hammersmith tow-path, the Royal Court Theatre and the Institute of Contemporary Arts.[3]

Kureishi's semi-autobiographical debut *The Buddha of Suburbia* (1990) is the novel for which he is best known. It is a comic analysis of cultural moments of the 1970s mediated through mixed-race teen narrator Karim's expanding consciousness and coming of age, as he leaves his suburban home for theatrical and sexual adventures in London and subsequently New York. The novel's famed, pithy opening proclaims its repudiation of outdated, narrow notions of 'Britishness'. It attests to its concerns with fluid post-imperial identities and the interplay between race, place and nation. The son of Haroon and Margaret announces, 'My name is Karim Amir, and I am an Englishman born and bred, almost. I am often considered to be a funny kind of Englishman, a new breed as it were, having emerged from two old histories. But I don't care – Englishman I am (though not proud of it), from the South London suburbs and going somewhere.'[4] With these words, *The Buddha of Suburbia* became and remains a seminal text in bringing race, class and sexuality to the forefront. Kureishi himself would position himself as a Londoner rather than a Brit.

Kureishi represents London as a city of self-reinvention and self-discovery, where divisions of race and class are reflected in the geography of the city and its suburbs. Kureishi's cartography of hybridized, post-colonial London is central to his politics and purpose: his sustained exposure of its underbelly, dereliction and violence as well as his celebration of its freedoms and energizing creativity. How does *The Buddha of Suburbia* contribute to and reshape our understanding of London as a diasporic city in the twenty-first century? What does it mean to write London? London is as much a creation of the imagination as of bricks and mortar; and how we understand London is closely connected to how we represent it. Stimulated by Dickens and Thackeray's depictions of the nineteenth-century metropolis as exerting incessant pressure on its inhabitants, Kureishi portrays a London defined by both limitless possibilities and amorphous squalor. His narratives echo many of the tropes ubiquitous to Victorian fictionalizations of London: the obscure city of *flâneurs*, crime and riots, illicit and excessive pleasures, pretence and vulgarity, 'quality' and taste, aggressive capitalism and poverty, and endless variety in people and things.

One of the novel's central concerns is London's transformation both demographically and imaginatively as a consequence of Britain's imperial legacy. Kureishi's forerunners, such as writer Sam Selvon, whose work is discussed by Peter Maber and Karishma Patel in this volume, explored the voyage to, and represented the establishment of minority communities in, the old imperial centre. The story of arrival is not British-born Kureishi's experience, but is instead traced in the novel through the perspective of Karim's father, Haroon, who arrived in Britain from India in 1950, much like Kureishi's own father. Haroon and his childhood friend and fellow migrant Anwar have left more comfortable, privileged lives back home to which they were expected to return. The story traces the downward mobility of Anwar's wife, nicknamed Princess Jeeta, who after her marriage finds herself living in a dirty one-bedroom flat in Brixton and later running a corner shop. Through the eyes of its first-generation migrant protagonist, the novel demythologizes the colonial metropolis in a deft reversal of the colonial gaze. On arrival in the freezing shock of the Old Kent Road, Haroon is

[a]mazed and heartened by the sight of the British in England [...] Dad had never seen the English in poverty, as roadsweepers, dustmen, shopkeepers and barmen. He'd never seen an Englishman stuffing bread into his mouth with his fingers, and no one had told him that the English didn't wash regularly because the water was so cold [...] And when Dad tried to discuss Byron in local pubs no one warned him that not every Englishman could read or that they didn't necessarily want tutoring by an Indian on the poetry of a pervert and a madman. (24–5)

Critic Sukhdev Sandu contrasts V. S. Naipaul's reverential attitude to London and his poignant desire to 'find the centre' and its supposed stability and assurances with Kureishi, who revels in London's 'disruptions and upheavals' and its fluidity and possibilities.[5] In this, Kureishi's work further contrasts with anglophile Indian writer Nirad Chaudhuri's search for 'Timeless England' years before him.

Rather than the voyage from the colonial periphery to the imperial centre, Karim and his peers negotiate a differently classed trajectory from the provincial margins of suburban tedium to the centrality of cultural capital. Karim, like his creator, grows up in the suburb of Bromley: a small town on the outskirts of Southeast London, where the urban sprawl reaches into the Kent countryside. Though only nine and a half miles by train from central London, Bromley, to Karim, seems light years away from the cultural capital – 'a carnival of consumerism' where 'it was said that when people drowned they saw not their lives but their double glazing flashing before them' (23). The novel satirizes the materialism of Karim's white aunt Jean and her husband Ted, who 'measured people only in terms of power and money' (34), and is equally critical of Anwar and Jeeta's insularity and parsimony: 'They knew nothing of the outside world' and for whom 'the idea of enjoyment [...] had passed by' (51).

The early chapters mercilessly lampoon white suburbia's parochialism and crude racism. In Chapter 3, Karim is confronted by the furiously racist father of his white girlfriend Helen. When Helen's father rudely ejects Karim from their posh Chislehurst home, he tells Karim, Helen 'doesn't go out with wogs. We're with Enoch' (40).[6] Further humiliation follows when Karim is trapped in Helen's walled garden with the gate locked and mounted by Helen's father's insistently amorous Great Dane. Karim's extended white family's condescension towards Haroon – 'we never had no objections to him marrying Margaret, though some people didn't like her marrying a coloured' (44) – is also noted. There's a mapping of social and urban geography as Ted and Karim take a train to a football match through the suburbs into London. This, Karim tells us,

[w]as the journey Dad made every day to work, bringing keema and roti and pea-curry wrapped in greasy paper in his briefcase. Before crossing the river we passed over the [at the time] slums of Herne Hill and Brixton, places so compelling and unlike anything I was used to seeing that I jumped up, jammed down the window and gazed out at the rows of disintegrating Victorian houses. The gardens were full of rusting junk and sodden overcoats; lines of washing criss-crossed over the debris. Ted explained to me, 'That's where the niggers live. Them blacks.' (43)

The opening chapter is a microcosm of the novel's cartography of social status and gradations of culture through the different neighbourhoods Karim inhabits as he navigates his way around Britain's class system. The first pages are an intensely comic imagining of charismatic father-figure Haroon's transformation from civil servant and commuter into yoga teacher and Eastern mystic. One evening Haroon hurries home from his tedious job unusually intent on practising yoga. Set against a background of suburban uniformity, the spectacle of Haroon stripped to his vest and pants performing a yogic headstand in the front room prompts his retiring English wife Margaret to complain, 'All the front of you's sticking out like that so everyone can see!' She yells at her teenage son to 'at least pull the curtains' (4). Father, 'handsome in a black polo neck sweater, black imitation-leather jacket, and grey Marks and Spencer cords', and son 'in turquoise flared trousers; a blue and white flower-patterned see-through shirt; blue suede boots with Cuban heels, and a scarlet Indian waistcoat with gold stitching around the edges' leave their respectable lower-middle-class neighbourhood for Eva's larger home with its patterned armchairs and glass-topped tables in wealthier 'tree-lined' Beckenham (6, 8). To Karim's surprise, and to the distaste of a few of Eva's 'terribly white' suburban guests, it turns out 'the brown Indian' has been invited to lecture on Buddhism and demonstrate yoga.

The novel charts a hero who follows the author's own trajectory from the stifling suburbs to London's theatre-land where 'the city so bright, fast and brilliant made you vertiginous with possibility' (126). Like the protagonists of countless other nineteenth- and twentieth-century British novels, Kureishi's characters escape to London in order to reinvent themselves. Like the titular protagonist in Keith Waterhouse's *Billy Liar* (1959), who seeks to escape his working-class Yorkshire background, Karim and the ambitious Eva (who becomes his father's girlfriend) seek to assimilate into the middle class and scour off their 'suburban stigma' (134). Their aspirations are embodied in Karim's wealthy actress girlfriend Eleanor, who 'always did whatever occurred to her, which was, admittedly, not difficult for someone in her position, coming from a background where the risk of failure was minimal; in fact you had to work hard to fail in her world' (187). Like the titular character of Henry Fielding's *Tom Jones* (1749), Karim is awestruck by the cultural capital inherited by Eleanor's crowd. For these, 'hard words and sophisticated ideas were in the air they breathed from birth, and this language was the currency that bought you the best of what the world could offer. But for us it could only ever be a second language, consciously acquired' (178). And just as Estella's condescension in Dickens' *Great Expectations* (1860–1) makes Pip ashamed of his rough hands for the first time ('I had never thought of being ashamed of my hands before, but I began to consider them a very indifferent pair'), so Eleanor makes Karim feel self-conscious about his working-class accent: his 'cute [...] street voice [...] different to my voice of course'.[7] Karim resolves to lose the accent he, like Pip, had not hitherto known he possessed: 'whatever it was, it would go. I would speak like her. It wasn't difficult. I'd left my world; I had to, to get on' (178). Mirroring Pip's trajectory in Dickens' novel, Karim makes a circular journey and moves towards an acceptance of his culturally hybrid origins towards the novel's close: 'But I did feel, looking at these strange creatures now – the

Indians – that in some way these were my people, and that I'd spent my life denying or avoiding that fact' (212).

The novel is also influenced by Salman Rushdie and Homi Bhabha's fictional and theoretical insights in their respective *The Satanic Verses* (1989) and *The Location of Culture* (1990) in its emphasis on London as a global city where identities constantly change; where hybrid combinations help create the 'new', while authentic traditions or any claims to 'Western' superiority are destabilized. Kureishi too extols a hybrid London whose multicultural possibilities arise from its diverse, chaotic mix of races and sexualities. At the same time, however, Kureishi's novel is no idyllic portrait of easy multicultural mixing, nor is it a nostalgic celebration of 1970s London. Rather, it documents the climate of fear created by Enoch Powell's racist hate-mongering in the late 1960s in the context of the Commonwealth Immigrants Acts (1962 and 1968), which further reduce the rights of Commonwealth citizens to migrate to Britain; the escalation of vicious racist attacks; and the National Front's violent marches. The novel's most urgent passages provide a compelling picture of rise of the National Front and 'Paki-bashing', by tracing its impact on Anwar and Jeeta's daughter Jamila, Karim's best friend and sometimes lover who lives with her family in Penge:

> The area in which Jamila lived was closer to London than our suburbs, and far poorer. It was full of neo-fascist groups, thugs who had their own pubs and clubs and shops. On Saturdays they'd be out in the High Street selling their newspapers and pamphlets. They also operated outside the schools and colleges and football grounds, like Millwall and Crystal Palace. At night they roamed the streets, beating Asians and shoving shit and burning rags through their letter-boxes. Frequently the mean, white, hating faces had public meetings and the Union Jacks were paraded through the streets, protected by the police. There was no evidence that these people would go away – no evidence that their power would diminish rather than increase. The lives of Anwar and Jeeta and Jamila were pervaded by the fear of violence [...] Jeeta kept buckets of water around her bed in case the shop was firebombed in the night. Many of Jamila's attitudes were inspired by the possibility that a white group might kill one of us one day. (56)

The novel traces the emerging anti-fascist politics uniting Londoners of all backgrounds against racism.

Unlike Rushdie, who seeks to recreate the 1950s and 1960s Bombay of his childhood, Kureishi is drawn to London's transience. And he has a special talent for capturing its changes. His subsequent short story 'That Was Then' (1999) evokes the flavour of wrecked pubs in a Notting Hill on the cusp of gentrification in the early 1990s before their transformation into gastropubs:

> Natasha and Nick [...] both liked [...] the rougher places [of London] that resembled a Colin McInnes novel. Nick had come to know wealthy and well-known people; he was invited for cocktails and launches, lunches and charity

dinners, but it was too prim to be his everyday world. He started to meet Natasha at two o'clock in a big deserted pub in Notting Hill. They'd eat, have their first drinks, talk about everything and nod at the old Rastas who still seemed permanently installed in these pubs. They would buy drugs from young dealers from nearby estates and hear their plans for robberies. Notting Hill was wealthy and the houses magnificent, but it had yet to become aware of it. The pubs were still neglected, with damp carpets and dusty oak bars covered in cigarette burns, about to be turned into shiny places crammed with people who looked as though they appeared on television, though they only worked on it.[8]

Kureishi's second novel, *The Black Album* (1995), powerfully describes urban poverty and decay as a crucible for white racism and Islamic fundamentalism that spiked during the economic recession of the early 1990s. As ever, the imagined city, fuelled by literary and filmic versions, clashes with its realities: 'before Shahid came to the city, sat in the Kent countryside dreaming of how rough and mixed London would be, his brother Chili had loaned him *Mean Streets* and *Taxi Driver* as preparation. But they were eventful films which hadn't steadied him for such mundane poverty' and the sight of derelict lives amongst building sites and skips.[9] Kureishi would continue to map the capital's social contradictions and turmoil and the increasing divide between rich and poor Londoners in his subsequent writings.

Notes

1. Colin McCabe, 'Interview: Hanif Kureishi on London', *Critical Quarterly* 41, no. 3 (1999). For a fuller discussion of these and related issues in Kureishi, see Ruvani Ranasinha, *South Asian Writers in Twentieth-Century Britain: Culture in Translation* (Oxford: Oxford University Press, 2007).

2. Hanif Kureishi, *My Beautiful Laundrette and Other Writings* (London: Faber, 1996), 13.

3. Hanif Kureishi, *Sammy and Rosie Get Laid* (London: Faber, 1988), 32

4. Hanif Kureishi, *The Buddha of Suburbia* (London: Faber, 1990), 3. Hereafter, pagination from this edition is included in the main body of the chapter.

5. Sukhdev Sandhu, *London Calling: How Black and Asian Writers Imagine a City* (London: HarperPerennial, 2004), 268–9.

6. The shadow Defence Secretary and Tory MP stirred racial bigotries and sparked an escalation of vicious racist attacks against Black and Asian citizens with his populist, racially incendiary 'Rivers of Blood' speech against immigration on 20 April 1968 that inflamed the nation.

7. Charles Dickens, *Great Expectations*, ed. Charlotte Mitchell (London: Penguin, 2003), 60.

8. Hanif Kureishi, 'That Was Then', in *Collected Stories* (London: Faber, 2010), 263.

9. Hanif Kureishi, *The Black Album* (New York: Simon & Schuster, 1996), 11.

INFRASTRUCTURE: TRANSPORT I

CHAPTER 19
EXISTING TRIPLY: RACE, SPACE AND THE LONDON TRANSPORT NETWORK, 1950s–1970s
Rob Waters

The photograph below (Figure 19.1) was taken in the summer of 1967 by the Jamaican-born photographer Charlie Phillips, at Westbourne Park underground station in West London. Westbourne Park is the next station from Ladbroke Grove on the Circle Line. As Phillips recounted when speaking about the photograph some three and a half decades later, young Black Londoners used to get off at Westbourne Park to walk down Portobello Road, and to visit All Saints Road – 'our front line'. 'So,' as Phillips recalled, 'Westbourne Park station you walk down, Ladbroke Grove station you walk up, Notting Hill Gate, you walk across, to get to the front line.'[1]

Notting Hill, as is well known, developed into one of the centres of Black settlement in London from the early 1950s, as West Indian migrants settled in those cramped bedsits and rooming houses that dominate the literature of the 'Windrush' generation.[2] By the

Figure 19.1 Charlie Phillips, 'Man on Westbourne Park Tube Station' (1967). © Charlie Phillips/ www.nickyakehurst.com.

late 1960s, as the rise of Black Power and soul culture took hold in British cities, Notting Hill became a centre of Black politics, and also – because this was a politics which always placed Black visibility close to its core – it became a centre of Black style. As Phillips says of the man he photographed at Westbourne Park underground, 'I don't know his political background, but this [...] was just iconic *exposure* [...] A lot of people [were] wearing black. Black was the thing to wear at the time.'

London's topography was racialized in the post-Second World War era more than at any other time. Notting Hill and Brixton overtook the East End and docklands as the centres of Black settlement in the city. As they did so, they became identified as Black city spaces – 'frontlines', defined by displays of Black visibility, by Black style and by institutions of what were increasingly understood as markers of distinctively 'Black' lifestyles – barbers, record shops, dancehalls and shebeens, youth clubs, political headquarters, supplementary schools and bookshops.

This chapter concentrates on experiences of using the transport network as it worked to connect, and often to disconnect, the increasingly racialized topography of the city: its 'black' and 'white' spaces. With the entrenchment of the racialization of city spaces in the second half of the twentieth century, using the transport meant entering into new, less predictable and more fraught social and spatial relationships. I aim to provide a snapshot of some of the meanings and experiences of the transport network for Black Londoners between the 1950s and the 1970s, as it offered them an opportunity to lay claim to the city, but also as it marked them as interlopers in that city. When London was increasingly lived through a racialized topography, the transport network, moving between racialized spaces, became a site in which the possibilities and limits of belonging in a multicultural city were determined.

The London transport network was a site of racialization, a space in which people *became* racialized subjects. It produced new affective relations, and new ontologies, enforcing a racialized materiality of the body. The title for this chapter – 'Existing Triply' – is borrowed from the Martinican writer Frantz Fanon. The phrase is from the pivotal chapter in *Black Skins, White Masks*, Fanon's famous 1952 work on lived experiences of race, in which he describes his experiences of racialization, living as a Black man in Lyon.

Fanon argues that consciousness of the body, in the lived experience of blackness, is always a 'third person consciousness', 'woven', as he famously wrote, 'out of a thousand details, anecdotes, stories'.[3] But this lived experience is not only about consciousness, but also about one's lived, spatialized materiality. The situation that defines Fanon's experience of racialization, in the scene that opens that chapter, is train travel:

> In the train it was no longer a question of being aware of my body in the third person, but in a triple person. In the train I was given not one but two, three places. [...] It was not that I was finding febrile coordinates in the world. I existed triply: I occupied space.[4]

Here we can see how racialization works in material, and not simply psychological, terms; how it organizes the material relations of the body. This experience of 'existing triply', described by Fanon on a French train, appears also in accounts of Black Londoners navigating the city's transport network.

In the Guyanese writer E. R. Brathwaite's autobiographical novel *To Sir, With Love* (1959), based on his experiences teaching in the East End of London in the early 1950s, the narrator finds himself, like Fanon, taking up space:

> As the bus moved slowly on, a bright-eyed little boy in school cap and blazer paused momentarily beside the vacant seat and then quickly moved a little way on in courteous deference to a slim, smartly dressed woman who followed behind. As I looked up she smiled her thanks to him and was preparing to sit when her eyes met mine. Surprise flickered briefly on her face as she straightened up and moved forward to stand in the narrow aisle beside the boy, who looked up at her with a puzzled expression.
>
> The conductor approached [...] and [...] casually remarked as he took her fare:
> 'Empty seat beside you, lady'.
> She received her ticket and murmured 'Thank you', but gave no sign that she had heard him.
> 'Seat for you here, lady'.
> The conductor indicated the vacant place with a turn of his head and moved on to examine the boy's school pass and exchange a word with the youngster. On his way back he paused to look at the woman, who returned his gaze with the cool effrontery of a patrician.
> 'No standing on the bus, lady'.
> The conductor's voice was deliberately louder, with an angry rasp to it [...] The slim woman remained standing, cool, remote, undismayed by the conductor's threatening attitude or the pointedly hostile glances directed at her [...] My quick anger at the woman's undisguised prejudice was surprisingly tinctured by a certain admiration for her fearless, superior attitude [...] She looked the conductor straight in the eye and around her mouth I could discern the muscular twitchings of a suppressed smile. I guessed she was secretly enjoying herself.[5]

Barbara Blake Hannah, who came to London from Kingston in the early 1960s, remembers the transport network as a similarly charged environment, in which decisions between the bus and the tube were balanced between the possibilities each offered for avoiding a flinching touch:

> I preferred to take the Tube than ride on the bus. Why? Because taking the Tube meant that I could often buy a ticket from a machine, or if not, from a winder where the seller didn't have to touch me to hand over the ticket. Then again, on the Tube I could find a seat by myself on the long benches which were divided by arm rests. That way no one would have to touch me when they sat down, not because I did not want to be touched (which, of course, I didn't)

but because I was told and could observe that the White people did not want to be touched by blacks.[6]

But if tubes might have had greater potential for negotiating personal space as a way of maintaining the integrity of the body, buses beat tubes for avoiding the unwanted stare:

The buses not only had the advantage of a view of this interesting, bustling city, but best of all, on the buses I didn't have to avoid the eyes of the passengers opposite, standing upright jammed against me. In the Tube I learned how to avoid looking at people and how to concentrate instead on some interesting matter, or in the subconscious world of one's thoughts.[7]

As the historian Simeon Koole has demonstrated, since the 1920s the development of the London transport network, particularly the tube, had 'heightened worry over the loss of personal space as an increasingly diverse mix of passengers were thrown together and forced to develop new strategies of indifference'.[8] As Koole insists, the concept and practice of personal space – and, of course, its 'lived experience' – was crystallized 'in and through the transformation of bodily transactions that informed and were informed by physical transformations of the tube'.[9] The architecture of the tube forced passengers into new proximities with strangers, breaching established social relations of class, gender and now race, and producing a concept of their 'personal space' through that encounter.[10] As Fanon's, Brathwaite's or Blake Hannah's accounts reveal, if the cramped economy of modern transport networks produced personal space, then taking the transport became a particularly charged experience for those whose belonging in the city's spaces was most hotly contested: it was here that race was lived at a higher intensity. Through the production of the racialized politics of personal space, bodies could be made to *feel* out of place and the city's racialized topography could be enforced.

The transport network, then, might be a site at which urban belonging was most contested for Black Londoners. And yet, time and again, the transport network figures in Black British writing of the 1950s and 1960s as offering a means of laying claim to the city, of asserting urban belonging.

In the Trinidadian writer Sam Selvon's 1956 novel, *The Lonely Londoners*, mastering the transport network serves as a symbol that one has truly 'arrived' in London.[11] Certainly, mastering the transport network was a hard job. In Lord Kitchener's 1950 calypso 'The Underground Train', the protagonist finds himself increasingly frustrated at the maze of escalators and intersecting train lines, which send him endlessly forward and backward in a disorientating swirl as he tries to navigate his way from Piccadilly to Lancaster Gate.[12] But while it was a difficult job, mastering the transport, as Blake Hannah remembers, offered a way of recognizing how the 'key centres and neighbourhoods' could be 'linked up with one another'. A city often experienced as fractured, anonymous and hostile could come to be known.[13]

Knowing and *claiming* the city mattered. Selvon's novels and short stories are famous both for their representation of the creolization of the capital's working-class neighbourhoods (places like Notting Hill and Brixton) and for their depiction of West Indian migrants laying claim to and inhabiting the city's central sites. The characters in *The Lonely Londoners* long, as the narrator writes, 'to have said: "I walked on Waterloo Bridge", "I rendezvoused at Charing Cross", "Piccadilly Circus is my playground"'.[14] Asserting urban belonging here worked on two levels at once: it required both the transformation of the city's neighbourhoods – Notting Hill, Brixton, the East End – and the claim to belonging in those most centred sites of London's iconic landscape. Mastering the transport network held a double promise, both offering a means to connect up the centres of West Indian settlement with the centres of London and standing as a symbolic institution close to the heart of London's civic identity itself.

The duality of the transport network in Selvon's novels, or Kitchener's calypso, however, also reveals the difficulty of that dream of inhabiting the city in the way that Selvon's characters desire. When the reggae poet Linton Kwesi Johnson turned to the theme of the transport network in his famous rewriting of the experiences of the 'Windrush' generation of migrant workers for his 1980 poem 'Inglan is a Bitch', this underground world offered not a means of connecting up and claiming the city above ground, but a distancing from that city:

wen mi jus come to Landan toun
mi use to work pan di andahgroun
but workin pan di andhagroun
yu dont get fi know your way aroun.[15]

Far from rendezvousing in Charing Cross or playing in Piccadilly Circus, Johnson's narrator ends up working in a factory in Brockley.

* * *

London's topography was racialized in the post-war era more than at any other time, as the city's districts, streets and homes became identified as 'black' or 'white' spaces.[16] Part of the story here – though certainly only part – is the consolidation of particular neighbourhoods as home territory, as 'black' neighbourhoods. When Linton Kwesi Johnson strolled through Brixton for a BBC documentary in 1979, he insisted that 'living and growing up in Brixton, you don't get all that distant from Jamaica, because Brixton has a lot of the feel of Kingston [. . .] the market, the record shops, the general vibes of Kingston'.[17]

And yet, as these claims for belonging were made upon particular spaces within the city, claims for belonging to the city as a totality also became increasingly fraught. In the mid-1970s, the politics of the 'mugging crisis' dominated media discussions of Black immigration and multiculturalism in Britain, driving and driven by a consolidation of heavy policing against young Black men and women in British cities. As police responded to and in turn fuelled public fears of the folk-devil figure of the young Black mugger, policing strategies effectively worked to remove young Black men and women from city centres, and to police their movement about the city.

The politics of mugging is well known, following Stuart Hall's contemporary exploration of the phenomenon in *Policing the Crisis* (1978). However, it is important to emphasize that this was a spatial politics, which developed through a fear of cities as racialized spaces, and it was consolidated by the material processes through which city spaces became racialized. As the Guyanese barrister Rudy Narayan, speaking at the height of 'sus' policing in the late 1970s, argued, anti-'mugging' and 'sus' policing was used to effectively clear Black people – and particularly Black youth – from the city centre. 'The mere presence of a black youth,' Narayan said, 'unless he be an absolutely well-tailored and obviously affluent person, in the presence of a city centre, is an incitement to a police officer to ensure his absence from that centre if necessary by prosecution.'[18] This, Narayan noted, was particularly prevalent in the area around Oxford Street and Piccadilly.

A study of police arrests in these areas, to which Narayan was contributing, repeatedly found them taking place at bus stops where police descended on young Black men and women, arresting them and warning them not to return to the West End. Again, Linton Kwesi Johnson was quick to pick up on this situation, with the bus stop becoming the key site in his famous anti-sus poem 'Sonny's Lettah':

mi an Jim stan-up
waitin pan a bus
nat cauzin no fus
wen all af a sudden
a police van pull-up.[19]

The locations at which the mugging panic and its policing took place are important. The freedom of movement of Black people – particularly young men and women – was being policed here.

In London, the first 'Anti-Mugging Squad', serving as the prototype for others to follow, was formed from the Transport Police Special Squad.[20] This squad patrolled underground platforms and tube trains. When questioned about their tactics at the trial of two Rhodesian students from Oxford University arrested on the underground in April 1973, the officer in charge of the squad admitted that his team were on the lookout for 'coloured young men' on the Northern Line.[21] It was on bus stops and tube stations that the policing of mugging was focused.

*   *   *

London was a place to be claimed by the 'Windrush' generation and their descendants: 'London is the place for me', as Lord Kitchener put it in his famous calypso of the same name, composed upon the *Windrush* itself.[22] The promise of laying claim to the city was part of the romance of migration – '[W]here you really want to live,' wrote Stuart Hall, 'is right on Eros Statue in Piccadilly Circus.'[23] And claim-making upon the city did happen. Brixton, Notting Hill and other, smaller neighbourhoods across the city became increasingly assertive Black localities, home territories. These may, as Charlie Phillips remembered as he thought about the London of his man at Westbourne Park underground station, have been lived often, and often proudly, as the 'frontlines' in a conflict-ridden city; but they were also sites of community and peace – backyards, too.[24] And yet, as the possibility of laying claim to the city through these strongholds and community spaces developed, the possibility of laying claim to the city as a whole appeared to recede.

The transport network was a site in which questions of civic identity and urban belonging in London were played out, where one could mark oneself as having 'arrived' in the city, and as knowing and being at home in the city. But it was also a site where claims to urban belonging might be contested. In those accounts of riding the transport with which I opened this chapter, we see how a body's materiality was drawn attention to through racialized social interactions – as Fanon puts it so directly, 'I occupied space.' Here, the pointed negotiation of proximity worked as a process for racialization, and as I've suggested, this was liable to be more intensely experienced on the transport network. In the 1970s, the bus and tube network became a frontline in the police assault on those young Black men and women whom they tried to erase from the city's central sites – from Oxford Street or from Piccadilly Circus. We don't know where Charlie Phillips's Londoner was going, but we know that as he moved down from the 'frontline' of Notting Hill's All Saint's Road to the underground platform at Westbourne Park, he was entering a racially charged environment in which, for all the bravado clearly on display, his claims for urban belonging might easily be put to the test.

Notes

1. Charlie Phillips, interviewed by Kelly Foster, 14 August 2013, Black Cultural Archives, ORAL/3/3.
2. See James Procter, *Dwelling Places: Postwar Black British Writing* (Manchester: Manchester University Press, 2003); Chiara Briganti and Kathy Mezei, (eds), *Living with Strangers: Bedsits and Boarding Houses in Modern English Life, Literature and Film* (London: Routledge, 2020).
3. Frantz Fanon, *Black Skin, White Masks* (London: Pluto Press, 2008), 83–4.
4. Ibid., 84.
5. E. R. Brathwaite, *To Sir, With Love* (London: Vintage, 2005), 9–10.
6. Barbara Blake Hannah, *Growing Out: A Biography* (London: Hansib, 2010), 39–40.
7. Ibid., 50–1.
8. Simeon Koole, 'How We Came to Mind the Gap: Time, Tactility, and the Tube', *Twentieth Century British History* 27, no. 4 (2016): 526–7.
9. Ibid., 527.
10. On modern transport and new social relations in British cities, see James Vernon, *Distant Strangers: How Britain Became Modern* (Berkeley: University of California Press, 2014), 35–7. Specifically for the underground, see Danielle K. Dodson, 'Minding the Gap: Uncovering the Underground's Role in the Formation of Modern London, 1855–1945', PhD dissertation, University of Kentucky, 2016.
11. See, for example, Sam Selvon, *The Lonely Londoners* (London: Penguin, 2006), 80–3.

12. Lord Kitchener, 'The Underground Train', Shellac 10" (Parlophone, 1950).

13. Blake Hannah, *Growing Out*, 50.

14. Selvon, *Lonely Londoners*, 137.

15. Linton Kwesi Johnson, 'Inglan is a Bitch', in *Selected Poems* (London: Penguin, 2006), 76.

16. Stephen Brooke has written on this in the 1980s, though the politics he traces here has a genesis from the late 1960s. See Stephen Brooke, 'Space, Emotions and the Everyday: The Affective Ecology of 1980s London', *Twentieth Century British History* 28, no. 1 (2017): 110–42. See also Rob Waters, 'Respectability and Race between the Suburb and the City: An Argument about the Making of "Inner City" London', *Urban History* 50, no. 2 (2021): 214–31.

17. *Dread, Beat and Blood*, dir. Franco Rosso (BBC, 1979).

18. Narayan speaking in *Breaking Point: The Sus Law and Black Youth*, dir. Menelik Shabazz (ATV, 1978).

19. Linton Kwesi Johnson, 'Sonny's Lettah (Anti-Sus Poem)', in *Selected Poems*, 59.

20. Stuart Hall, Chas Critcher, Tony Jefferson, John Clarke and Brian Roberts, *Policing the Crisis: Mugging, The State, and Law and Order* (London: Macmillan, 1978), 40.

21. Ibid., 43–4.

22. Lord Kitchener, 'London is the Place for Me', Shellac 10" (Melodisc, 1952).

23. Stuart Hall, 'The Local and the Global: Globalization and Ethnicity', in *Culture, Globalization and the Third World System: Contemporary Conditions for the Representation of Identity*, ed. A. D. King (Basingstoke: Macmillan, 1991), 24.

24. See Ferdinand Dennis, *Behind the Frontlines: A Journey into Afro-Britain* (London: Gollancz, 1988); Stuart Hall, 'Frontlines and Backyards: The Terms of Change', in *Black British Culture and Society: A Text Reader*, ed. Kwesi Owusu (London: Routledge, 2000), 135–8.

WEST

CHAPTER 20
SCOTCH HORNPIPES AND AFRICAN ELEPHANTS: THE MAY FAIR IN *c.* 1700
Alistair Robinson

Summertime was fair-time in eighteenth-century London. Between May and September, fairs took place across the city, each one lasting about a fortnight, and providing Londoners with opportunities for pleasure and profit. Bartholomew Fair was the oldest and most famous of these and took place every August in West Smithfield, close to Newgate prison and the Old Bailey. It was accompanied by smaller fairs in Clerkenwell and Tottenham Court Road (also held in August) and was followed by Southwark Fair, which filled Borough High Street in the first weeks of September. But the beginning of the fair season, and the focus of this chapter, was May Fair. Running for sixteen days from the first of May, it was situated near the south-east corner of Hyde Park in the City of Westminster.[1] By mid-century this area had acquired the enduring name of Mayfair, as well as a reputation for being 'the Residence of many of the first Gentry'; but in 1700 the streets and squares of this exclusive district were not yet built and it was known by an older, more prosaic name: Brookfield.[2]

Although May Fair was established as an annual market when it was founded in 1688, it soon discarded its utilitarian function and became a popular resort of entertainment, one that relied heavily on migrant labour. The satirist Ned Ward (who had recently arrived from the Midlands) attested to this in *The London Spy* (1698–1700), a rollicking account of low-life London. When the Spy visited the May Fair, he reported seeing a 'Theatre [that] Entertain'd the Publick with the Wonderful Activity of Indian Rope-Dancers' cheek-by-jowl with a series of 'Scandalous Boosing Kens', or drinking tents, one of which held 'a parcel of Scotch Pedlars and their Moggies [female partners], Dancing a Highlanders Jig to a Horn-Pipe'. Meanwhile, in another tent, 'the Cheshire-Booth', he saw 'a Gentlemans Man [who] was playing more Tricks with his Heels in a Cheshire-Round, than ever were shewn'.[3] The Indian ropedancers and Scotch pedlars reveal that immigrants and itinerants were key economic participants in the fair; but the 'Boosing Kens' also gesture towards a much larger migrant community. The 'Cheshire-Booth' in particular, a tent dedicated to a popular but distinctly provincial dance, suggests that many of the fairgoers were not from London. This is certain. Not only did the fair attract people from the surrounding counties, but a large number of Londoners were not born in the metropolis: between 1700 and 1750 approximately 8,000 migrants arrived in the capital each year from Scotland, Wales, Ireland, Continental Europe and provincial England.[4]

For some fairgoers the sound of a Scotch hornpipe, or the sight of a country dance, might have been flavoured with savoury thoughts of home; but their desire for the familiar must have been tempered by the prospect of encountering the exotic. London's fairs contributed to a popular understanding of Britain's commercial and military empire, and the people, animals and objects that it touched.[5] From the late seventeenth century, imported animals from India and Africa formed regular exhibits, becoming so frequent that Ward's Spy resisted describing 'a couple of Tygers' at May Fair because they had 'grown so common'.[6] Yet not everyone shared this indifference and beast shows proved an enduring attraction. In 1660 the diarist John Evelyn saw 'Monkeys and Apes dance' at Southwark Fair. Forty years later, in the anonymous poem 'A Trip to the Devil's Summer-house' (1704), the speaker describes a similar scene when he encounters an ape-handler touting for trade at May Fair: 'He Cuts you a Caper three Foot from the Ground, / And Dances expertly the whole Cheshire round', the showman boasts.[7]

England's imperial trade networks furnished the fairs with beasts, but imperialism itself also proved an attractive ideology. The actor and entrepreneur William Pinkethman, whose lavish theatrical booth was often cited as a May Fair landmark, capitalized upon this. In 1704 he delivered 'an Epilogue upon an Elephant between Nine and Ten Foot high, arriv'd from Guinea, led upon the Stage by six Blacks'.[8] As this advertisement makes plain, Pinkethman's show was not just an animal exhibit; he was also showcasing the promises of empire: power, wealth, dominion. The staging of the epilogue was supposed to be awe inspiring with Pinkethman elevated far above the crowd, riding an animal whose strength must have been palpable within the confines of the booth; but this scene, and the way it was marketed, was also loaded with imperial symbolism. 'Guinea' was the

Figure 20.1 Charles II Guinea Coin (1663). © The Trustees of the British Museum.

English name for a 2,000-mile-long stretch of West African coastline that was associated with expensive commodities. Gold imported from this area was coined into 'guineas', which were stamped with the symbol of the Royal African Company, an elephant. Pinkethman's mount may therefore have had an auriferous air for contemporary audiences. But even if it didn't evoke the chink of gold coins, its tusks would have prompted thoughts of ivory, an import used in the luxury goods trade. The epilogue would also have evoked one of England's most profitable industries: the slave trade.[9] Most people sold into slavery were shipped from Africa to the Caribbean to work on plantations, but some were brought to London where they were often employed as footmen or pageboys, conspicuous posts where they served as status symbols for merchants and aristocrats.[10] Not all Black people were enslaved in the eighteenth-century metropolis, and the essays in this volume by Markman Ellis, Nicole N. Aljoe and Savita Maharaj, and David Hitchcock reveal the diverse occupations and social positions they held; but the 'six Blacks' in Pinkethman's epilogue – tellingly arranged in positions of servitude – were evidently supposed to evoke the opulent life of the slaveholder while also contributing to the exotic atmosphere of the show.

The presence of outsiders added spice to the fairs' entertainments, and made them appear more varied, mysterious and exciting. Ethnicity and nationality were often used as marketing tools by fairground impresarios and were remarked upon by contemporaries.[11] An advert from 1701, printed in the *Flying Post*, promised that troops of European ropedancers, 'the most Famous Companies as ever were in England', would be present at the next May Fair; in 1704 another newspaper publicized 'the best Rope-Dancers, Vaulters and Tumblers in Europe'; and the following year 'The High German Performer', a man without arms who did 'Things with his Feet that no Body can do with Hands', appeared in 'the Booth joyning to Mr. Penkethmans [sic]'.[12] Meanwhile, Ward's Spy surveyed Bartholomew Fair. Entering a rope-dancing booth, he reported 'the great satisfaction of the Spectators' when they saw a Black woman perform with 'much Art and Agility', and their mirth when an Irish woman 'waddled along the Rope, like a Goose over a Barn Threshold'. These women were followed by a German acrobat whose ethnicity was clearly important to the show's promoters: 'they stile her in their Bill' as 'the German Maid'.[13]

The emphasis that advertisements placed on origins reveals that the promise of seeing 'foreign' bodies was an enticing prospect for audiences. It added a frisson of danger and 'the threat of the unknown', as Anne Wohlcke argues.[14] However, this obscures the fact that many of these performers may well have been Londoners, permanently residing within the city. The temporary and peripheral nature of fairs suggests that their constituents – their actors, acrobats, pedlars and so on – dispersed when they were dismantled. This would have been true for itinerant hawkers and performers who travelled throughout the country; however, the longevity of London's fair season from May to September provided locals with a series of ready markets to sell their wares and services. We will never know whether the elephant's attendants in Pinkethman's show accompanied it from West Africa as the advertisement implies, but it seems just as likely that they were among the thousands of Black Londoners who lived in the metropolis.[15]

Most were employed in domestic service, but many made livings as musicians and performers who would have profited during fair-time. The Germans also had a strong presence in the late seventeenth and early eighteenth centuries, as did the Irish, who accounted for around 3 per cent of London's population.[16] While the otherness of foreigners was emphasized on playbills and titivated in the press, they were only as unknown as the many other migrants who had settled in a city of strangers.

Migrants were everywhere at the May Fair, helping to create and consume its carnival culture; but they also contributed to its reputation for disorder and promiscuity. Since 1688 and the departure of King James II, social reformers had been trying to improve the morals of Londoners by prosecuting them for a range of vices including sabbath-breaking, drunkenness, swearing and prostitution. Unable to afford the luxury of privacy, the poor were convicted more often than the rich, and were particularly vulnerable at fairs, which offered a variety of ad hoc pleasures.[17] Bartholomew Fair was renowned for the improvised brothels and gambling-booths that mushroomed in its nearby cloisters, and May Fair was often portrayed as a place of unbridled lust. As the anonymous author of *Reasons for Suppressing the Yearly-Fair in Brook-field, Westminster* (1709) put it:

> Such abominable Acts of Lewdness have been openly committed in these Fields, before the Noon-day Sun, as may not be so much as mention'd in Tenderness to Christian Modesty: And even the Offenders themselves have been found to shift the Habits of their Sex, to give the Reins to their base Inclinations with greater Freedom.[18]

Coy yet provocative, this accusation expresses common concerns about the unruly passions that fairs gave rise to. Like theatres, streets and other public places, fairs hosted a thriving sex trade, and literary descriptions of May Fair often included what Ward called a 'Throng of Beggarly, Sluttish Strumpets'.[19] This was another element of metropolitan culture that migrants were engaged in, as Aljoe and Maharaj note elsewhere in this volume. Jerry White estimates that migrants accounted for at least half of London's 3,000 to 7,000 female sex workers.[20] May Fair was considered an auspicious time for these women. Commencing on the first of May, the fair was part of the broad weave of May Day celebrations that took place across the country and that were associated with youth, mischief and lust. It was for these reasons that May Fair was understood to be an especially 'licentious Fair'.[21]

In *Reasons for Suppressing the Yearly-Fair in Brook-field* this promiscuity finds its clearest expression in the defiance of gender norms: fairgoers changing 'the Habits of their Sex, to give the Reins to their base Inclinations'. This oblique charge of transvestism could refer to the 'exotic' ropedancers that we have already encountered: women regularly swapped their petticoats for breeches in order to perform, and the exchange could prove titillating.[22] In *Bartholomew Fair: An Heroi-Comical Poem* (1717), for example, the speaker describes how 'airy Females in short Breeches [. . .] bewitch th' amorous Standers by' with 'A well-shap'd Leg, and a round handsome Thigh'.[23] Too, it might refer to 'mollies', a contemporary slur for cross-dressing men who were strongly associated with same-sex love and prostitution. Unlike the ropedancers, these men were not particularly connected with fairs, but they did become the subject of several vicious and sensational works in the early eighteenth century. These included John Dunton's *The He-Strumpets* (1707) and a satire by the ubiquitous Ward – he incorporated a 'Gang of Sodomitical Wretches [. . .] who call themselves Mollies' into his *Complete and Humorous Account of the Remarkable Clubs and Societies in the Cities of London and Westminster* (1709).[24] Readers of *Reasons for Suppressing the Yearly-Fair in Brook-field* may well have known these contemporary texts and found clues to the nature of those 'abominable Acts' in their pages.

The licentiousness and perhaps queerness of May Fair prompted a series of efforts to suppress it. In 1702, reformers employed parish constables to arrest 'several Lewd Women in May Fair, in order to bring them to Justice'.[25] Later, in the winter of 1708–9, the Justices of the Peace for Middlesex and Westminster published three petitions condemning May Fair as a 'Nursery of Vice and Debauchery'.[26] Queen Anne, undoubtedly aware of the fair's noxious proximity to St James's Palace, her royal residence, responded by issuing a proclamation in April 1709 forbidding the construction of booths 'for any Plays, Shows, Gaming, Musick-Meetings, or other Disorderly Assemblies', and commanding her 'Subjects not to Resort to the said Fair for any such Unlawful Purposes'.[27]

It is difficult to know how effective this ban on fairground entertainments was. In general, London's fairs were extremely resilient, readily defying the orders that magistrates and monarchs issued to curtail them.[28] However, in this case there is some evidence of success. On 26 May 1709 a facetious article appeared in Joseph Addison and Richard Steele's periodical, the *Tatler* (1709–11), which recorded the 'downfall of May-fair': 'That fair is now broke,' it declared, 'but it is allowed still to sell animals there. Therefore, if any lady or gentleman have occasion for a tame elephant, let them enquire of Mr. Pinkethman, who has one to dispose of at a reasonable rate.'[29] Later, William Stow observed in his directory, *Remarks on London* (1722), that May Fair 'hath been put down for some years'.[30] However, perhaps the most compelling evidence is the silence of the newspaper archive: after 1709 the advertisements for plays, entertainments and beast shows ceased to be printed. This absence does not mean that the fun stopped entirely; but it does suggest that the fair, at least for a time, became a more sedate affair.[31]

The advertisements resumed in the 1740s, after Sir Nathaniel Curzon was granted a licence by King George II to hold a market on the site of Brookfield. By then the fair had a different setting. The development of the Grosvenor Estate, the most ambitious building project in eighteenth-century London, had been underway since 1720, and had swallowed parts of the old fairground.[32] But the mutable, fleeting, adaptable fair acclimatized to these new surroundings. J. Carter, a correspondent of the *Gentleman's Magazine* (1736–1833), recalled that the first floor of the market-house was 'used as a Theatre at fair-time' and that 'mountebanks, fire-eaters, ass-racing, sausage-tables, dice ditto, up-and-downs, merry-go-rounds, bull-baiting, grinning for a hat, running for a shift, hasty-pudding eaters, eel divers, and an infinite variety of other similar pastimes' took place in the streets.[33] Writing in 1816, he was remembering the fair in its final years. In 1764 the Earl of Coventry, opposed to such raucous displays of plebeian frivolity, successfully lobbied for its abolition.[34] Its name, long habituated to the palace and the drawing room, and now polished smooth by the tongues of lackeys and aristocrats, was the only remnant to survive.

Notes

1. Anne Wohlcke, *The 'Perpetual Fair': Gender, Disorder, and Urban Amusement in Eighteenth-Century London* (Manchester: Manchester University Press, 2014), 19–48.

2. Daniel Defoe, *A Tour Thro' the Whole Island of Great Britain*, 6th edn, 4 vols (London: n.p., 1761), II, 103. This observation was not in the first edition, nor was it made by Defoe, who had been dead for thirty years; it belongs to an anonymous editor.

3. Ned Ward, *The London Spy Compleat, in Eighteen Parts*, 4th edn (London: n.p., 1709), 172–3.

4. Jerry White, *London in the Eighteenth Century: A Great and Monstrous Thing* (London: Bodley Head, 2012), 90–1.

5. Wohlcke, *The 'Perpetual Fair'*, 189–97.

6. Ward, *The London Spy*, 175; see also Hannah Velten, *Beastly London: A History of Animals in the City* (London: Reaktion, 2013), 120, 148.

7. Printed as 'A Trip to the D – – – l's Summer-house', the blanks have been filled for ease of reading. Evelyn quoted in Velton, *Beastly London*, 120; 'A Trip to the D – – – l's Summer-house; or, a Journey to the Wells: with the Old Preaching Quaker's, Sermon to the London-mobb' (London: n.p., 1704[?]), 1.

8. *Daily Courant*, 28 April 1704, 2.

9. P. E. H. Hair and Robin Law, 'The English in Western Africa to 1700', in *The Origins of Empire: British Overseas Enterprise to the Close of the Seventeenth Century*, ed. Nicholas Canny (Oxford: Oxford University Press, 1998), 241, 256–7.

10. David Olusoga, *Black and British: A Forgotten History* (London: Pan Books, 2017), 86–91; White, *London in the Eighteenth Century*, 127.

11. Wohlcke, *The 'Perpetual Fair'*, 38–40.

12. *Flying Post*, 24 April 1701, 3; *Daily Courant*, 28 April 1704, 2; *Flying Post*, 3 May 1705, 2.

13. Ward, *The London Spy*, 241–3.

14. Wohlcke, *The 'Perpetual Fair'*, 40.

15. Between 5,000 and 10,000 Black people lived in eighteenth-century London. White, *London in the Eighteenth Century*, 127.

16. White, *London in the Eighteenth Century*, 127–33, 142–3, 157.

17. Tim Hitchcock and Robert Shoemaker, *London Lives: Poverty, Crime and the Making of a Modern City, 1690–1800* (Cambridge: Cambridge University Press, 2015), 34–42.

18. *Reasons for Suppressing the Yearly Fair in Brook-field, Westminster; Commonly Called May-fair* (London: n.p., 1709), 6.

19. Ward, *The London Spy*, 173. See also 'A Trip to the D – – – l's Summer-house', 4, and 'The Humours of May Fair', *Universal Magazine of Knowledge and Pleasure*, May 1760, 265.

20. White, *London in the Eighteenth Century*, 346–8.

21. Paul Griffiths, *Youth and Authority: Formative Experiences in England, 1560–1640* (Oxford: Clarendon Press, 1996), 145–6; *Reasons for Suppressing the Yearly Fair in Brook-field*, 5.

22. See, Wohlcke, *The 'Perpetual Fair'*, 40–1.

23. *Bartholomew Fair: An Heroi-Comical Poem* (London: n.p., 1717), 14.

24. Peter Ackroyd, *Queer City: Gay London from the Romans to the Present Day* (New York: Abrams Press, 2018), 109–12.

25. *Post Man and the Historical Account*, 16 May 1702, 3.

26. Quoted in *Reasons for Suppressing the Yearly Fair in Brook-field*, 38.

27. 'By the Queen, A Proclamation' (London: n.p., 1709).

28. Wohlcke, *The 'Perpetual Fair'*, 109–14.

29. Joseph Addison and Richard Steele, *The Tatler, with Illustrations and Notes, Historical, Biographical, and Critical*, 6 vols (London: n.p., 1786), I, 217–18.

30. William Stow, *Remarks on London* (London: n.p., 1722), 51.

31. See Sybil Rosenfeld, *The Theatre of the London Fairs in the Eighteenth Century* (Cambridge: Cambridge University Press, 1960), 112–13.

32. Rosenfeld, *The Theatre of the London* Fairs, 113; White, *London in the Eighteenth Century*, 29–30.

33. J. Carter, 'May Fair', *Gentleman's Magazine*, March 1816, 228.

34. Wohlcke, *The 'Perpetual Fair'*, 110.

CHAPTER 21

FEATHERED PEOPLE IN ENLIGHTENMENT LONDON: QUEEN OF THE BLUESTOCKINGS MEETS CHEROKEE KING

Elizabeth Eger

Alexander Pope's poem *Windsor Forest*, first published in 1713, celebrated the signing of the Treaty of Utrecht, which ended the War of the Spanish Succession and aimed to ensure the balance of power in Europe. The treaty followed the *asiento* agreement, a contract which granted Britain exclusive right to supply the Spanish colonies with African slaves for the next thirty years.[1] Towards the poem's conclusion, Pope described the expansion of Britain's empire in a triumphalist vision of the River Thames, a tributary that connected the people of Britain to those around the world, in an audacious metaphor of cultural enrichment:

> The Time shall come, when free as Seas or Wind,
> Unbounded Thames shall flow for all Man-kind,
> Whole Nations enter with each swelling Tyde,
> And Seas but join the Regions they divide;
> Earth's distant Ends our Glory shall behold,
> And the new World launch forth to seek the Old.
> Then Ships of uncouth form shall stem the Tyde,
> And Feather'd people crowd my wealthy Side,
> And naked Youths and painted Chiefs admire
> Our speech, our colour, and our strange Attire!
> Oh stretch thy Reign, fair Peace! from Shore to Shore,
> Till Conquest cease, and Slavery be no more:
> Till the freed Indians in their native Groves
> Reap their own Fruits, and woo their Sable Loves,
> Peru once more a Race of Kings behold,
> And other Mexicos be roof'd with Gold.[2]

Pope's utopian vision of a bounteous, balmy river of peace appears confident in culture's power to erase discord. His glance to a future in which there is no slavery is intended to be rousing. He not only connects the local to the global but inverts the power relationship between the colonizer and the colonized. He imagines a moment in which his own culture has become a curiosity to be admired by 'feather'd people' who remark on the speech, colour and costume of London's inhabitants. Pope's poem may seem overblown and ambiguously imperialistic to today's reader, but it reminds us, very powerfully, of just how global a city he lived and worked in and invites us to compare London with other cities around the world. The burgeoning of trade and migration to Britain in the previous century meant that by 1700 London was the largest city in Europe and a refuge, being Protestant, in particular for Dutch, German and Swedish immigrants as well as home to several thousand labourers from West Africa and the Caribbean.[3]

Pope's poem highlights the historically precarious nature of empires, which both rise and fall, a theme that had classical and Miltonic roots and remained a powerful topos in later poems, including Anna Barbauld's *Eighteen Hundred and Eleven* (1812).[4] In her stark jeremiad, Barbauld imagines a future moment when the curious traveller will contemplate London's faded glories:

> The mighty city, which by every road,
> In floods of people poured itself abroad;
> Ungirt by walls, irregularly great,
> No jealous drawbridge, and no closing gate;
> Whose jealous merchants (such the state that commerce brings)
> Sent forth their mandates to dependant kings;
> Streets, where the turban'd Moslem, bearded Jew,
> And woolly Afric, met the brown Hindu;
> Where through each vein spontaneous plenty flowed
> Where wealth enjoyed and Charity bestowed.
> Pensive and thoughtful shall the Wanderers greet
> Each splendid square, and still, untrodden street;
> Or of some crumbling turret, mined by time
> The broken stairs with perilous steps shall climb,
> Thence stretch their view the wide horizon round,
> By scattered hamlets trace its ancient bound,
> And, choked no more with fleets, fair Thames survey
> Through reeds and sedge pursue his idle way.[5]

In this extraordinary image, Barbauld depicts her city, London, as the multicultural hub of empire from which people 'flood' the city and beyond with the benefits of trade. However, this cannot last for ever. The Thames, once crowded with fleets of ships, will return to nature: reeds and sedge. While both Pope and Barbauld might be characterized as poets who were writing within a national tradition, their work shares an awareness of culture's role in defining nations more broadly across the globe, acknowledging the inherently competitive nature of national sentiment at this time as well as the historical relativity of any notion of cultural supremacy.[6] In both poems, the London at the heart of the British Empire is depicted as resplendent yet precarious, fertile and yet potentially doomed to failure.

Looking back to the eighteenth century from the twenty-first, one might assume Pope's allusion, in 1713, to 'feather'd people' to be based solely upon travellers' tales and reports from American colonies. However, he was highly likely to have been aware of a recent political visit. The first Native American group to travel to London on political business was a band of four chiefs from the Iroquois tribe, who arrived in 1710 to petition Queen Anne for more financial support for an expedition against New France (or Quebec, as it is now known).[7] The visit was greeted by Londoners with much curiosity and enthusiasm. On one occasion, a performance of Macbeth at the Queen's theatre in Haymarket had to be interrupted to make space for the chiefs to be seated, in full view of the audience, on stage.[8] Queen Anne was receptive to their diplomatic mission and held them in great esteem. News of the delegation reached a more popular audience through the circulation of a broadside ballad (see Figure 21.1), intended to assert and make binding the alliance between the English and Iroquois, who desired to join forces against the French. The broadside is accompanied by a full copy of the speech that was made by the delegation and which makes their mission clear. The political purpose of the visit was achieved and Queen Anne was persuaded to send a fleet of over sixty ships to join

Figure 21.1 Broadside with four woodcuts showing portraits of 'The Four Indian Kings' and the text of their speech to Queen Anne (1710). © The Trustees of the British Museum.

183

a colonial Iroquois force to attack New France. However, the journey ended in disaster when a combination of poor leadership and storms sank ten ships.[9]

The editor of the *Spectator*, Joseph Addison, used the story of the four chiefs to embark on a dissection of British customs, writing accounts of the four men's observations upon their hosts: 'The men [of England] are very cunning and ingenious [. . .] but so very idle, as to be carried up and down the streets in little covered rooms [...] Their dress is likewise very barbarous.' Addison is primarily making fun of his peers but at the same time imparting a moral message of cultural relativism that remained powerful throughout the century and sparked a number of accounts of Britain's cultural degeneracy as witnessed by an innocent outsider.

*   *   *

Half a century later, the *London Evening Post* for 19–22 June 1762 reported that the King of the Cherokee Indians, accompanied by two Chiefs, had reached Salisbury, having landed at Plymouth from Virginia. The men were described as being '[w]ell made men, near six feet high, dressed in their own country fashion, with only a shirt, trowsers, and mantle round them; their faces are painted of a copper colour, and their head adorned with shells, feathers, ear-rings, and other trifling ornaments'. They were depicted in cheap prints, caricatures and plays, and even modelled in wax by Mrs Salmon for her waxwork museum in Fleet Street (a precursor to Madame Tussaud's). James Boswell recorded his visit to see the 'famous waxworks' in his diary for July 1763 and deemed the exhibition 'excellent of its kind'.[10]

Among those who had a chance to see the Cherokee King in person was Elizabeth Montagu, called 'Queen of the Bluestockings' by Samuel Johnson, and celebrated in her time as a woman who advanced the intellectual status of her sex. Her strategic employment of patronage, conversation and correspondence helped launch and support the careers of several writers, of both sexes. The assemblies she held in her Mayfair homes, first at Hill Street and later in Portman Square, became famous as new spaces for the life of the mind.[11] Montagu's house in Portman Square was built with the money she had made from her coal mines in Newcastle. When she became a widow in 1775, she inherited a substantial fortune, which she invested in various philanthropic projects. Montagu held an annual May-day breakfast for London's chimney sweeps on the front lawn of her home, thus advertising her virtue. Her salon was something of a cultural hub in late eighteenth-century London and was a famous destination for visitors to London from the provinces and further afield.

Montagu described her visit to see the King of the Cherokee Indians in a letter to William Pulteney, Lord Bath:

> In the morning yesterday I went with a party to see the Cherokee King. His complexion is of a bright copper colour, his lids & ears are painted of a brick dust red, his cheeks & chin of a dark blue & he is painted blue between the eye brows, he wears one lock of hair very long in the Chinese fashion, the rest cut short, his throat is painted of the same colour as his ears.

Montagu has clearly been extremely attentive to the visual aspect of her new acquaintance, picking up on every detail of his posture, facial expression and his clothes. She draws on a mixture of classical, European and Oriental references to describe his appearance:

> He is remarkably strong built, & he steps like Homer's Neptune, he would measure the globe at three strides. The general cast of his physiognomy is not amiss, nor is he so different in features from an English man as our near neighbour, the French. On his breast he had an ornament of silver fasten'd by some wampam, he had silver bracelets on his arms, but these silver ornaments were made here. He wears the chinese boot, as we see them in the pictures.[12]

Montagu detects a curious hybridity of elements that make up the Cherokee's identity, suggesting that his appearance draws upon a wide spectrum of influences and acquired objects: his bracelets, for example, 'were made here'.

Montagu chose to decorate the interior of her salon with a hybrid mixture of classical and Oriental decoration at Hill Street and later created a vast, original wall of feather work in her Great Room at Portman Square.[13] As well as being a thing of great beauty, it reflected the extent of her global networks and connections, including gifts from friends and contacts from London to Barbados, Tahiti to China. It is tempting to think that the Cherokee, with their 'feathers, shells and ear-rings', were part of the inspiration. Montagu's original form of tapestry was considered remarkable in its time and provoked a number of literary descriptions. The young poet William Cowper wrote a poem in 1788 for the *Gentleman's Magazine*, 'On Mrs Montagu's Feather Hangings':

> The Birds put off their every hue,
> To deck a room for Montagu.
> The peacock sends his heav'nly dyes,
> His Rainbows and his Starry eyes;
> The Pheasant, plumes which round enfold
> His mantling neck with downy gold;
> The cock his arch'd tail's azure show;
> And river-blanch'd the Swan his snow.
> All tribes of Indian name
> That glossy shine or vivid flame,
> Where rises and where sets the day,
> What'er they boast of rich and gay,
> Contribute to the gorgeous plan,
> Proud to advance it all they can.

Montagu House, in all its feathery glory, became famous for its grand literary assemblies and a destination for any aspiring writer finding their feet in the capital, quill in hand and with an eye to the future.[14] Cowper's poem might be construed as a vivid satire upon metropolitan culture, in which writers and artists jostled and vied for

Montagu's attention in order to secure a place in her orbit, but is in fact a thinly veiled request for protection and patronage for himself. He describes Montagu's home as a shelter from the fray:

> There, Genius, Learning, Fancy, Wit,
> Their ruffled plumage, calm, refit
> (For stormy troubles loudest roar
> Around their flight who highest soar)
> And in her eye, and by her aid
> Shine safe, without a fear to fade.
> She thus maintains divided sway
> With yon bright Regent of the day,
> The Plume and Poet both we know
> Their lustre to his influence owe,
> and she the work of Phoebus aiding,
> Both Poet Saves and Plume from Fading.

As her literary networks flourished and expanded, Montagu continued to seek out different literatures and people. She wrote to her sister in 1790 to tell her about a 'little assembly' she planned at her house that evening: 'it will be composed of Persons of so many different Nations, that if each should speak his Mother Tongue, it would resemble the company at the building the Tower of Babel'.[15]

As far as we know, the Cherokee delegation did not make it to Montagu's salon, but they had been drawn into the privileged world in which she was so influential. And they won their place there not through their impressive appearance but because of their political importance in a global perspective. As with the 1710 delegation that seems to have inspired Pope, the delegation of 1762 was primarily diplomatic in purpose. Again, it was rivalry with France that provided the incentive for the British to treat the Cherokee in a 'civilized' manner. The *Royal Magazine* reported what was at stake:

> In short, there is sufficient reason to think that this visit of the Indians will be of very great consequence to the British colonies in America, as at their return they will not fail to inform their nation of all they have seen in England, and extol the kind of treatment they have received in this country; by which means false ideas they have conceived of the English nation, by the unjust and artful representations of the French, will be effectually obliterated, and exchanged for others more conformable to truth and justice.[16]

Something of their social and political status is captured in the portrait engraved by graphic artist George Bickham (see Figure 21.2), which showed a group of figures at ease with each other and projecting a sense of individuality (very different from the depiction of the Iroquois delegation fifty years earlier). Bickham's figures are standing in a less formal position, gesturing to each other and smiling. The artist has tried to create

Figure 21.2 *The Three Cherokees, Came Over from the Head of the River Savanna to London* (1762). © The Trustees of the British Museum.

a sense of conversation, and the Cherokees certainly seem lively in comparison to the murky and mysterious European figure, lurking in the shadows at the far left of the image.[17] The inscription beneath the plate provides a key to the identities of each figure and includes a strange figure in profile at the edge of the picture: 'Their Interpreter, who was poisoned.' This aspect of the Cherokees' identity – the inaccessibility of their language – arguably increased the curiosity of many spectators. From the start there was much anxiety about how they should be treated, especially since their interpreter had been lost en route, 'which obliges them to make their wants and desires known as well as they can by dumb signs.'[18] Among those intrigued by the untranslatability of the Cherokee King's speech was the Queen of the Bluestockings. In her letter to William Pulteney, Lord Bath, she had told him of her visit to see the Chief, whose complexion was 'of a bright copper colour.'[19] As her description moved from the visual to the aural, her sense of his identity became more complicated, more intimate and more sympathetic: 'The most extraordinary circumstances in these savages is that their language is sweet & not gutteral, & it seems he laugh'd heartily at the speech of an Irish man.' Montagu seems to be placing the 'sweet' language of the Cherokees above the more 'gutteral' speech of the Irish, and, above all, she longed for dialogue in the face of inevitable silence:

I wish their interpreter was arrived, for one should be glad to hear their observations on what they see here. All civilized people have prejudices in favour of their national customs, & therefore do not judge with candour those of other countrys but here we should hear the voice of nature.[20]

Montagu's vision blurred the distinction between type and individual, noble savage and political ambassador. Her encounter remains ambiguous, hovering between fascination with the Cherokee's otherness – the voice of 'nature' – and a wish to learn from 'observation' and 'judgement'.

Later in 1762, a few months after the Cherokee delegation had returned to America, Montagu began her voyage into what was for her the uncharted territory of literary criticism, by beginning work on her *Essay on Shakespeare*, first published in 1769. In another letter to Lord Bath, she referred to her lack of an interpreter to guide and shape her thoughts so that she could communicate with others:

There are certain genius's that seem to be sent into the World as interpreters, they explain, express, unfold, what is absolutely unintelligible in itself to ordinary Understandings. With one of these inspired persons I had lately the happiness to travel about in a post chaise, but I am now in the state of the Cherokee Kings, who have lost their interpreter; like them I go about to divert my eyes, but wish for the Assistance of him who could inform my mind.[21]

In the relatively intimate form of the literary letter, Montagu thus anticipated the far more explicit, and more public, cultural relativism of Barbauld's *Eighteen Hundred and Eleven*.

While Montagu could easily divert herself by using her eyes to see around her, and responded to the Cherokee King and his Chiefs as part of a rich tapestry of London's social diversions, she was also aware of another strand of untapped experience lying beneath the surface of the Cherokee's painted mask. Like others, she was fascinated by these 'feather'd people', and much of her encounter remains shaped by the political significance of their mission. But here, we also catch a glimpse of a possible meeting of minds. The Queen of the Bluestockings seems not only to identify with the 'King' of the Cherokee Indians, but ponders the possibility that were she able to have a conversation with him, she might learn something about herself.

Notes

1. On the history of slavery, see Peter Linebaugh and Marcus Rediker, *The Many-Headed Hydra: Slaves, Commoners, and the Hidden History of the Revolutionary Atlantic* (London: Verso, 2000).

2. Alexander Pope, *Windsor Forest*, in *The Poems of Alexander Pope*, ed. John Butt (London: Routledge, 1996), ll. 397–412.

3. See James Delbourgo, *Collecting the World, The Life and Curiosity of Hans Sloane* (London: Allen Lane, 2017), 21.

4. See Edward Gibbon, *The History of the Decline and Fall of the Roman Empire*, 6 vols (London: Strahan and Cadell, 1776–89).

5. Anna Barbauld, *Eighteen Hundred and Eleven* (London: Joseph Johnson, 1812), ll. 160–175.

6. See Suvir Kaul, *Poems of Nation, Anthems of Empire: English Verse in the Long Eighteenth Century* (Charlottesville: University Press of Virginia, 2000).

7. See Stephanie Pratt, 'The Four Indian Kings', in *Between Worlds, Voyages to Britain, 1700–1850*, ed. Jocelyn Hackforth-Jones (London: National Portrait Gallery Publications, 2007), 22–35. See also Coll Thrush, Kate Shanley and Ned Blackhawks (eds), *Indigenous London: Native Travellers at The Heart of Empire* (London: Yale University Press, 2016).

8. Pratt, 'The Four Indian Kings', 26.

9. Richard Aquila, *The Iroquois Restoration: Iroquois Diplomacy on the Colonial Frontier, 1701–1754* (Detroit: Wayne State University Press, 1983), 88–90.

10. *Boswell's London Journal, 1762–63*, ed. Gordon Turnbull (London: Penguin Classics, 2010), 257.

11. Her home was dubbed a 'lyceum' or 'academy' by her friends. For a more extended discussion of the bluestocking salon, see Elizabeth Eger, 'Luxury, Industry and Charity: Bluestocking Culture Displayed', in *Luxury in the Eighteenth Century: Debates, Desires and Delectable Goods*, ed. Maxine Berg and Elizabeth Eger (Basingstoke: Palgrave Macmillan, 2002), 190–204.

12. MO 4529 Montagu, Elizabeth (Robinson) to William Pulteney, Earl of Bath, July, London, Huntington Library. See also Blunt, *Mrs Montagu*, I, 26.

13. David L. Porter, 'Monstrous Beauty: Eighteenth-Century Fashion and the Aesthetics of the Chinese Taste', *Eighteenth-Century Studies* 35, no. 3 (2002): 395–412.

14. For further discussion of Montagu's contribution to women's intellectual life, see Elizabeth Eger, '"The noblest commerce of mankind": conversation and community in the Bluestocking circle', in *Women, Gender and Enlightenment: A Comparative History*, ed. Barbara Taylor and Sarah Knott (Basingstoke: Palgrave, 2005), 288–305.

15. MO 6198 January 14, 1790, London Elizabeth Montagu to Sarah Scott, Huntington Library.

16. Cited by Troy O. Bickham, *Savages within the Empire: Representations of American Indians in Eighteenth-Century Britain* (Oxford: Oxford University Press, 2005), 30.

17. See Stephanie Pratt, 'Reynolds "King of the Cherokees" and Other Mistaken Identities in the Portraiture of Native American Delegations 1720–1762', *Oxford Art Journal* 21, no. 2 (1998): 133–50. Pratt argues that attempts to depict the Cherokee chiefs were characterized by an inevitable tension between the urge to record the discovery of a new type of people in an ethnological spirit and an attempt to convey a sense of individual character.

18. *London Evening Post*, 19 June.

19. MO 4529 Montagu, Elizabeth (Robinson) to William Pulteney, Earl of Bath, July, London. See also Blunt, *Mrs Montagu*, I, 26.

20. Ibid.

21. MO 4534, 10 August, Sandleford. Montagu, Elizabeth (Robinson) to William Pulteney, Earl of Bath, A.L.S. Copy, 4p. 4to. 1762.

CHAPTER 22
PRINCE EUGEN IN KENSINGTON: ANGLO-SCANDINAVIAN ARTISTIC NETWORKS AND THE STOCKHOLM EXHIBITION OF 1897
Eva-Charlotta Mebius

From the naturalist Carl von Linné (1707–78), to the mystic Emanuel Swedenborg (1688–1772), to the architect Sir William Chambers (1723–96) and the Victorian photographer Oscar Rejlander (1813–75), the Swedish influence in London has been wide-ranging and has left an enduring legacy – and yet a history of these contributions has yet to be written.[1] In the eighteenth and nineteenth centuries Swedish artists in particular were drawn to set up studios in the capital: Joshua Reynolds' student Carl Frederik von Breda in St James's Street, the landscape painter Elias Martin in Soho, the watercolourist Egron Lundgren in Kensington, and the painter Anna Nordgren in Bolton Studios, Chelsea, to name but a few. This chapter discusses a less familiar instance of cultural and artistic exchange between London and Sweden in the late nineteenth century, and in so doing draws attention to a rather unique view of the mechanics of patronage in 1890s artistic London.

In the spring of 1896, the landscape painter Prince Eugen of Sweden, the youngest son of King Oscar II and Queen Sophia, travelled to London as chair of the Art Committee to visit the London studios of British artists and convince them to contribute their work to the upcoming Stockholm Exhibition of 1897. The reputation of British art was on the rise in Sweden in the 1890s. A newspaper article from 1891 identified the third Paris World's Fair in 1878 as the moment when English art had come of age on the Continent. In Sweden, the Pre-Raphaelites were seen as particularly intriguing and original.[2] With an eye on France, the writer noted how the French artist Jean-Charles Cazin had taken inspiration from the English. Moreover, Swedish artists had begun to do the same. In the nineteenth century, the watercolourist Egron Lundgren had been one of the first to set up a studio in London in 1851, eventually settling near Holland Park at Upper Phillimore Gardens, Kensington, a favourite haunt of painters such as Frank Dillon and Henry Tanworth Wells RA. Lundgren's London career had been helped by Queen Victoria taking an instant liking to his work, and they appear to have got on well. 'You cannot even imagine how charming the Queen is,' Egron wrote to his brother Mildhog in April 1851.[3] Lundgren was eventually elected as a Member of the Society of Painters in Water Colours in the late 1860s. Other important painters of the period, like Anders Zorn, found in Lundgren 'a signpost [sic] which directed him on his path' and led him to similarly hire a studio on Brook Street, Mayfair, in the 1880s.[4] It was during this time that Zorn was taught etching by another Swedish expatriate, Axel Herman Hägg/Haig (1835–1921).

By the time the planning for the Stockholm Exhibition began in 1895, the art of the British School had become increasingly familiar. Lectures by the author Viktor Rydberg, articles and books by the writer Gustaf F. Steffen, and articles by Helen Zimmern in the magazine *Ord & Bild* helped popularize British art.[5] London correspondents such as Leopold Katscher also played a part in introducing the Swedish public to some of the household names of British art in the late nineteenth century.[6] Regular reviews of major annual exhibitions in London at the Royal Academy, New Gallery and Grosvenor Gallery appeared in Swedish newspapers throughout the 1880s and 1890s, in which British artists were continually praised.[7] The illustrated arts magazine the *Studio* and Erik G. Folcker's (1858–1926) pioneering shop Sub Rosa (a small but highly influential shop in Stockholm selling English furnishings, decorative arts and prints between 1892 and 1895) were other ventures that prompted the introduction of British aesthetics.[8] And so, for the Stockholm Exhibition, it seemed vital to have a strong selection of British art on display, which partly explains Prince Eugen's extended stay in London.

The trip became a formative experience for the landscape painter, who wrote several letters about his journey to his mother Queen Sophia. Prince Eugen's correspondence was stimulated by his mother's decidedly Anglophone interests. Having grown up in an English-speaking home in the Duchy of Nassau, Queen Sophia showed a deep interest in British and American culture throughout her life. Her interest in the work of Florence Nightingale, which she witnessed first-hand in London in 1881 at St Thomas' Hospital,

Figure 22.1 Prince Eugen in his studio at Waldemarsudde (1915). © Prins Eugens Waldemarsudde.

had a profound impact on her and led to the founding of a new hospital and a training school for nurses in Stockholm: Sophiahemmet. Fluent in English herself, it was also of particular importance to Queen Sophia that her sons learnt the English language. She engaged the writer Augustus Hare as a travelling companion for her eldest son, later King Gustaf V.[9] There was also a family connection. Sophia's mother, Princess Pauline of Württemberg (1810–56), was the granddaughter of Frederick I of Württemberg and his first wife, Duchess Augusta of Brunswick-Wolfenbüttel (daughter of King George III's sister Princess Augusta of Great Britain and sister of Queen Caroline). Because of her parents' turbulent marriage, Sophia's mother Pauline and her sister, Princess Charlotte of Württemberg (later Grand Duchess Elena Pavlovna), were mostly raised by their grandfather's second wife, Charlotte, Princess Royal (the daughter of King George III).[10] Sophia's interest in the Anglosphere, which she shared with her husband King Oscar II, was also reflected in her book collection in the Bernadotte Library, where fiction written in English dominated the collection.[11] Her notebooks and private diaries in the Bernadotte Archive, often written in English, also show her familiarity with the English language, and there remains much to say about her many trips to England.

Hence, as Eugen arrived in London in late April with his travelling companions Carl Anton Ossbahr of the Royal Armoury and Baron Rolf Cederström, he promptly wrote to his mother. The trip included a visit to the village of Widdington, where Eugen stayed with his friend the painter Sir George Clausen RA and his wife Agnes Mary Webster, and day trips to Windsor and Cambridge. But the main attraction was London and the studios the prince visited there. As he explained to Queen Sophia, 'Today I begin my campaign and visits to the painters, most of whom are in London so it should not take too long.'[12] Kensington was his first stop, where he visited Edward Burne-Jones at The Grange, the painter's house in West Kensington, and John Everett Millais at 2 Palace Gate. The latter, along with his wife Effie Gray, were described as 'frail' but 'most gracious' and they had promised Eugen any painting he desired.[13] Burne-Jones, on the other hand, was a 'darling old man with the most beautiful voice'. Prince Eugen reverently described the painter's 'quiet life' at The Grange, solely dedicated to 'reflecting on his work and his poetry'.[14]

A day trip to Hampton Court and Richmond followed where he met up with his friends, the artist couple Ferdinand and Anna Boberg. Eugen wrote to his mother that England reminded him of Italy and described having dinner on a terrace in Richmond as the lights of London began to 'glimmer' in the distance before the group of merry friends caught the last train back. He was utterly 'charmed' by England. 'The English are immensely appealing to me,' he wrote.[15] Eugen explained that the day had been a welcome break from the hectic schedule of studio visits in Kensington where he had been particularly taken with G. F. Watts of the Holland Park Circle.[16] 'Sir G. F. Watts is probably the most interesting person that I have met,' he wrote.[17] Their friendship had been helped by a letter of introduction from George Clausen, who had explained to Watts that Prince Eugen was a painter himself. Eugen thought this had done much good, and Clausen continued to be of 'great service to him' in introducing him to London's art world.[18] Clausen brought Eugen to a gathering of the Art Workers' Guild. Later, Eugen was invited to G. F. and Mary Watts' home outside London, Limnerslease, and enjoyed a Royal View of the Summer Exhibition of the Royal Academy. However, it was G. F. and Mary Watts who impressed him the most.[19]

The General Art and Industrial Exposition of Stockholm opened on 15 May 1897. The *Official Guide* noted the 'many fine English pictures' that were shown in the room of the Art Hall dedicated to British and American art.[20] The English, Welsh, Irish and Scottish artists represented were William Morris' apprentice Frank Brangwyn, Briton Rivière, Burne-Jones, George Clausen, Walter Crane, Henry Davis, Stanhope Forbes, Hubert von Herkomer, Sir John Lavery, Sir Frederic Leighton, Sir James D. Linton, William Quiller Orchardson, James Paterson, J. J. Shannon, William Stott of Oldham, John M. Swan, J. W. Waterhouse and G. F. Watts.[21]

Overall, it was the British-American section that was the most intriguing according to most Swedish reviews.[22] Prince Eugen's personal favourite, G. F. Watts, or 'Old Man Watts' as he called him, was particularly well received by important Swedish critics such as Georg Nordensvan and Edvard Alkman.[23] His reception may have contributed to Watts' election as a Foreign Member of the Royal Swedish Academy of Fine Arts on 1 December 1897.[24] While the painter John Ludvig Kindborg had been more critical of Watts' 'unnatural' blue in his review, Tor Hedberg in *Svenska Dagbladet* commended Watts' 'beautiful' portraits of Lady Somers (1860) and 'especially the blue' of Violet Lindsay and its 'dreamlike' mood.[25] Besides his portraits, it was *Paolo and Francesca* (1872–5) that gripped the imagination of visitors to the Art Hall.[26]

While the Stockholm Exhibition served to further acquaint the Swedish public with British artists, Eugen's trip marked the beginning of a mutual interest in Swedish art in Britain. An article on Prince Eugen was published in 1904 in the *Pall Mall Magazine*, and the landscape painter would come to exhibit his work several times both in London and elsewhere alongside other prominent Swedish artists of the period.[27] In April 1911, the Swedish minister Count Wrangel opened the Brighton Exhibition of Swedish Art. The paintings of Prince Eugen, among which were one of his most famous compositions, *The Cloud* (1896), were introduced as one of the highlights of the exhibition.[28] Later, in January 1924, the Swedish Art Exhibition opened at the Royal Academy. It had been arranged in collaboration with the Anglo-Swedish Society, founded after the First World War. In the *Observer* it was noted that the 400 paintings, drawings and sculptures on view at Burlington House constituted the 'largest and most important' exhibition that had 'ever been arranged by Swedish artists outside their own country'.[29] The critic P. G. Konody particularly appreciated the work of Anders Zorn, Carl Larsson, Eugene Jansson, Prince Eugen and Gustaf Fjaestad, as well as the sculptors Christian Eriksson and Carl Eldh. Konody welcomed the exhibition that served as a guide to the 'terra incognita' that was Swedish art.[30] The *Times* wrote that 'Sweden is fortunate in Prince Eugen, as any country would be in the possession of a wealthy and eager patron who was also himself so good an artist that the reputation of his paintings owes nothing to his rank.'[31]

In 1931, an exposition of Swedish Industrial Arts and Crafts followed the successful art exhibition of 1924. It was held at Dorland House and opened by Prince Eugen. At the opening, Major-General Sir Harold Wernher, chairman of the British Executive Committee and later President of the Anglo-Swedish Society, took the opportunity to also extend his sincere thanks to Eugen's nephew, the Crown Prince Gustaf Adolf, later King Gustaf VI Adolf, who had taken a keen interest in the organization of the exhibition. Wernher was sure that it would come to fulfil 'the object' of the Anglo-Swedish Society 'to bring about a better understanding between Sweden and England'. Prince Eugen echoed this sentiment in his speech, in which he stated that he hoped exhibitions such as this one would not only tend 'to further progress, as they were apt to create a spirit of emulation between artists, designers, and manufacturers for the purpose of making life more agreeable, useful, and harmonious', but that 'it might also strengthen the bonds of friendship between Great Britain and Sweden'.[32] After all, he was speaking from personal experience. Eugen's experience of the culture of London and the subsequent success of British art at the Stockholm Exhibition of 1897 constitutes a perfect example of how such exhibitions could serve to foster artistic dialogue and international collaboration.

Notes

Author's note. Research for this chapter was generously supported by a Research Support Grant from the Paul Mellon Centre and a Research Grant from Berit Wallenbergs Stiftelse. I would also like to thank His Majesty Carl XVI Gustaf for allowing me access to the Bernadotte Archive, and Hans Henrik Brummer, Karin Sidén, and Palace Librarian Arvid Jakobsson for their invaluable advice and generous encouragement during the process of preparing this chapter.

1. Gunnar Pettersson, *London: en berättelse om en stad* (Stockholm: Natur & Kultur, 2018).

2. N. Pr., 'En egendomlig art af engelskt måleri', *Sydsvenska Dagbladet*, 30 December 1891. All translations from the Swedish are my own.

3. Egron Lundgren, 'Till Mildhog Lundgren – London 26 April 1851', in *Egron Lundgren: Reseskildringar, anteckningar och bref*, ed. Georg Nordensvan (Stockholm: Albert Bonniers Förlag, 1905), 207. Queen Victoria and Prince Albert employed Lundgren as a painter from 1854. In 1859, he accompanied the Queen as an artist in residence at Balmoral.

4. Erik Wettegren, 'The Art of Anders Zorn', *Fine Arts Journal*, March 1914, 133. See also M. G. van Rensselaer, 'A Swedish Etcher. (Anders Zorn.)', *Century Illustrated Magazine*, August 1893, 582.

5. See Gustaf F. Steffen, *Från det moderna England* (Stockholm: Albert Bonnier, 1893).

6. Leopold Katscher, 'Från London', *Göteborgs Handels- och Sjöfarts-Tidning*, 17 May 1882, 1.

7. 'Romantiken i den engelska konsten 1890', *Sydsvenska Dagbladet*, 22 May 1890, 1–2.

8. See Karin Sidén, 'Prins Eugen, Prerafaelitisk Konst och Arts and Crafts: En svensk kontext', in *Edward Burne-Jones: Prerafaeliterna & Norden*, ed. Alison Smith et al. (Stockholm: Prins Eugens Waldemarsudde, 2019), 95–124; Elisabeth Stavenow-Hidemark, *Sub Rosa: När skönheten kom från England* (Stockholm: Nordiska museets förlag, 1991). For more on the exhibition's significance for Anglo-Scandinavian cultural exchange, see also Knut Ljøgodt, 'Det jordiska paradiset: Edward Burne-Jones, prerafaeliterna, och Norden', in *Edward Burne-Jones: Prerafaeliterna & Norden*, ed. Alison Smith et al. (Stockholm: Prins Eugens Waldemarsudde, 2019), 61–94, and Elizabeth Doe Stone's illuminating essay 'American Art at the Stockholm Exhibition 1897', *Konsthistorisk tidskrift* (2020): 1–18.

9. See Augustus Hare, *The Story of My Life*, 6 vols (London: George Allen, 1900), V.

10. See Marina Soroka and Charles A. Ruud, *Becoming a Romanov: Grand Duchess Elena of Russia and her World (1807–1873)* (London & New York: Routledge, 2016).

11. Britt Dahlström, *Drottningarnas Böcker* (Stockholm: Carlsson Bokförlag, 2006).

12. Prince Eugen, 'Brev', n.d. (1896), Archive of Prins Eugens Waldemarsudde, 1–6, 3. Translations are my own.

13. Ibid., 5–6.

14. Ibid., 6.

15. Prince Eugen, 'Brev, 29 April' (1896), Archive of Prins Eugens Waldemarsudde, 1–8, 1.

16. For more on the artist colony of Holland Park, see Caroline Dakers, *The Holland Park Circle: Artists and Victorian Society* (New Haven, CT: Yale University Press, 1999).

17. Prince Eugen, 'Brev, 29 April', 3.

18. Ibid., 4.

19. Eva-Charlotta Mebius, 'A Visit to Limnerslease: the Wattses and Prince Eugen of Sweden', *Watts Magazine* (Winter, 2020): 20–1.

20. Thore Blanche, *Official Guide to Stockholm and the Great Art and Industrial Exhibition of 1897*, trans. George W. Lithman (Stockholm: Samson & Wallin), 65.

21. C. A. Ossbahr, 'Konstafdelningen', in *Allmänna Konst- och Industri-Utställningen i Stockholm 1897*, ed. Ludvig Looström (Stockholm: Wahlström & Widstrand, 1899), 305–35.

22. See, for example, the landscape painter John Ludvig Kindborg's review written under the pseudonym Rosina: 'Bland prerafaeliter och andra berömdheter', *Hvad Nytt från Stockholm?*, 25 September 1897.

23. See Georg Nordensvan, 'Konstutställningen i Stockholm', *Göteborgs Handels- och Sjöfarts-Tidning*, 24 May 1897, 1; 'Konstutställningen. England och Amerika', *Aftonbladet*, 15 July 1897; Edvard Alkman, 'Konstutställningen. George Frederick Watts', *Dagens Nyheter*, 22 June 1897.

24. Mebius, 'A Visit to Limnerslease', 20. Hubert von Herkomer and W. Quiller Orchardson were also elected.

25. Kindborg, 'Bland prerafaeliter och andra berömdheter', Tor Hedberg, 'Från Konsthallen', *Svenska Dagbladet*, 11 July 1897, 2. See also, Edvard Alkman's review 'Konstutställningen. George Frederick Watts', *Göteborgs-Posten*, 28 July 1897, 1.

26. See, for example, 'Intryck från Konsthallen', *Nya Wermlands-Tidningen*, 16 November 1897, 2.

27. Georg Bröchner, 'A Royal Painter and His Friends', *Pall Mall Magazine*, [October] 1904, 210–18. See also the writings of the extraordinary art critic, novelist and biographer Haldane MacFall, who was one of the first to praise Swedish artists, such as the landscape painter Anna Boberg, in the eighth volume of his *A History of Painting* (London and Edinburgh: T. C. and E. C. Jack, 1911).

28. K. P. N., 'Prince Eugen of Sweden – An Artist Prince', *Sphere*, 29 April 1911, 112. For more on Eugen's international exhibitions, see Hans Henrik Brummer's monumental *Prins Eugen: Minnet av ett landskap* (Stockholm: Norstedts, 1998).

29. 'Swedish Art in London: Some Features of the Exhibition', *Observer*, 13 January 1924, 15.

30. P. G. Konody, 'Art and Artists: Swedish Art at Burlington House', *Observer*, 20 January 1924, 8. See also 'Swedish Art at Its Best Modern Period: A Notable Exhibition at the Royal Academy', *Graphic*, 19 January 1924, 79, and Frank Rutter, 'Swedish Art in London', *Sunday Times*, 13 January 1924, 16.

31. 'Swedish Art. Exhibition at the Royal Academy. Prince Eugen as Painter', *The Times*, 14 January 1924, 17. Interest in Prince Eugen continued through the twentieth century. His etchings were shown at a display of Northern Graphic Art at the V&A in 1938, and a posthumous exhibition of fifty paintings in gouache opened at Wildenstein's, 147 New Bond Street, in 1958.

32. 'Swedish Industrial Art. Exhibition Opened by Prince Eugen', *The Times*, 18 March 1931, 9. Gustaf VI Adolf had a particularly close connection to the UK. His first wife, Princess Margaret of Connaught, also a painter of landscapes, was the granddaughter of Queen Victoria. After her tragic death in 1920, he remarried three years later. His second marriage was to Lady Louise Mountbatten, who became Queen of Sweden in 1950.

CHAPTER 23

'WHAT A RELIEF TO BE BACK IN LONDON': THE SILENCES OF LUCIE RIE AND HANS COPER

Edmund de Waal

Even in old age the potter Lucie Rie (1902–95), slight, immaculate in white, could be dauntingly rude. I wanted to write 'direct', but realized that this doesn't capture her ability to speak in a way stripped back from social niceties. Years later I realize that it was a habit, shared by other Viennese émigrés, of getting to the point. She answers a writer's request, 'I do not want to be in your book. I like to make pots – but I do not like to talk about them. I would answer your questions today but they would be wrong tomorrow.' She tells students at Camberwell College that their work is hopeless and to try teapots 'for discipline'. There was a divide between émigrés: those who never mentioned Vienna and those who couldn't stop, artists who explain their lives and those who are silent. She fell into the latter category with some force.

Lucie Rie and Hans Coper (1920–81) were émigrés and they were urban potters. 'What a relief to be back in London,' said Coper. 'I am an asphalt plant.'[1] They were silent.

Lucie Rie, famously, never wrote about her work. Hans Coper's short and beautiful statement of 1969 (a 'predynastic Egyptian pot, roughly egg-shaped, the size of my hand') he later regretted having published.[2] Shortly before he died, he burned the manuscript of his writings. So there is a hermetic silence surrounding both potters. No letters to magazines, articles puffing their own or others' work, no 'Life in the Day of' or 'Towards a Standard'. None of the public interventions that characterize the texture of the English craft world – the joinings, resignations, committees, associations, protests. The serious, private kernel remains unbroken. Being much written about and filmed is not the same as a single magisterial intervention: their silence accretes seriousness around them. Their not joining in is a form of silence too.

When considering their lives in London, I kept thinking of *getting to the point* as their essential trajectory. Born in an apartment off the Ringstrasse into affluent assimilated Jewish culture, Lucie Rie's life was one strong iteration after another of independent thinking. Through her training as a potter in Vienna to her exile in London, and to her creation of a style of making that had no counterpoint to the earthy functionalism of British pottery, she projected a force-field of separation from the expectations of those around her.

Vienna could be toxic for a young woman in the arts. There were comments by Adolf Loos about 'Frauleins who regard handicrafts as something one can earn pin money or while away one's spare time until one can walk up the aisle'.[3] They were 'daughters of senior civil servants'.[4] The Wiener Werkstatte was renamed the 'Wiener

Weiberkunstgewerbe', the Viennese Vixen Crafts Association. In Joseph Roth's *The Imperial Tomb* (1938), a novel set between the wars, the hero returns to discover news of his estranged wife. He guesses from the demeanour of his mother that his wife has become something dreadful, like a 'dancer': 'My mother shook her head gravely and said, almost mournfully, "No a craftswomen. Do you know what that is? She designs, or rather carves, in fact – crazy necklaces and rings, modern things, you know, all corners, and clasps of fir."'[5]

Lucie Rie learnt to make pots in Vienna in the 1920s. She studied at the Arts and Design School with the great designer Josef Hoffmann, a man who had a strong sense of how handmade objects could work in settings of luxurious simplicity. Hoffmann's vision of all the arts and crafts working together depended on wealthy and informed patronage, something that Lucie Rie benefitted from in her early career. Her austere pots – mainly dishes and bowls – were glazed to give a rugged and pitted surface, the perfect kinds of pot to sit on a sideboard in a light-filled Modernist apartment. You can imagine them, a trio of vessels perhaps, with an abstract painting behind them and some good Bauhaus furniture in the foreground.

These early pots, modern things, were made with an extremely limited palette of colours: beige, white, grey and black on a few variants of beaker or bowl. It is possible to read them as parallel to the use her mentor, the architect and designer Josef Hoffmann, made of the square across his practice – as a syntactical device, a way of allowing disparate elements to sit alongside each other. It allowed Rie to make coherent groups of work in a way that the baroque, effusively garlanded effusions of her peers could not.

Lucie Rie's early tribulations of trying to separate her life from that of her mother, who lived in the neighbouring street, were almost comically played out. You marry: you are given a room in the apartment. You are given a family apartment nearby, but instructed to keep a family maid. The maid leaves. You begin your working life as a potter: your mother handles the orders, another maid picks up pots from the workshop. But Lucie Rie, a fiercely determined woman, was successful from the start, winning gold medals in exhibitions and biennales across Europe. She commissioned an elegant apartment from a young Viennese architect, Ernst Plischke, in which to live in Vienna and – crucially – in which to show her work. It was made with walnut cupboards, versatile shelves that could be rearranged and dismantled. Most poignantly, Rie brought her apartment into exile with her in 1938, re-erecting the shelves and tables and cupboards in the mews house in Bayswater in which she was to spend the rest of her life. Her workshop – with its potters' wheels, electric kilns, buckets of glaze and the endless plaster moulds for the ceramic buttons which she made to keep herself going during the war – was downstairs. It was in this high-ceilinged studio that she took on other émigré artists as assistants, including the young Hans Coper, who she took on in 1946. Upstairs was a bit of *moderne* Vienna: careful arrangements of her pots to show to collectors over coffee and cake.

Lucie Rie's London was full of architects, writers and artists, many of them from similar urbane middle-European backgrounds. This meant that her pots belonged to a distinctly contemporary world where pots took their place alongside other arts and

Figure 23.1 Lucie Rie and Hans Coper, 'Sgraffito Bowl, Manganese Glaze' (*c.* 1950). © Estate of Lucie Rie. Image kindly provided by the Crafts Study Centre, University for the Creative Arts.

within a modern lifestyle. There was no sense of pottery being a lesser art. You can see this self-confidence, this lack of grandstanding, when you look at the pots that she and Coper jointly made in the 1950s.

Unlike the potter Bernard Leach, whose studio in St Ives produced a huge range of green-and-brown Standard Ware, pots to fill every possible domestic need from casserole, soupbowl, honey pot to egg-baker, the pots from Rie's Bayswater studio were carefully chosen for a modern life. Rie and Coper didn't try to make everything. Their coffee pots and cups, with their dense matt black-and-white glazes, reveal an undemonstrative, urbane and controlled tension. Each pot is careful. Pick up a teacup and look underneath. There is the fine white line of the unglazed porcelain, the glaze stopping in a perfectly controlled way. And then there is a radiating series of very fine lines scratched through one glaze to another below, framing the joint seals LR and HC. All this work for the base of a cup. You could buy these beautifully considered sets in Heals in London or Bonniers in New York. They were perfect for wedding presents for a design-conscious young couple. They were reassuringly expensive.

By not having what Leach sententiously labelled a local taproot (something he said that American potters didn't possess), the émigrés' deracinated condition makes them susceptible to heterodox influences and trends. Growing spindly and etiolated by not belonging to a place or tradition, however recently invented, but living as an exile the maker is, de facto, self-conscious. And to call someone self-conscious is a very English anathema in the crafts world.

In the absence of their words, we have the photographs. There are a few published photographs of Hans Coper's various studios, many more of Lucie Rie's studio and flat at Albion Mews. In a photograph of Hans Coper at Digswell, in the late 1950s, he sits in his studio in front of a desk heaped with plans and books. A ladder leans behind him. A long line of 'poppy head' pots sit on a suspended shelf, many containing grasses. An open door behind him leads to his living quarters: a table can be seen, possibly a bed. The image is one of great austerity in making and in living; both so closely linked. The walls of his house remained in their original unpainted state while he lived there; his possessions were equally exiguous. This quality of minimalism needs a definite sensibility: to value objects or surfaces so highly that their habitual accumulation is thwarted. He is recorded as having said that he lived very simply so that the bailiffs would have to leave with nothing, but his aestheticism is more self-willed even than that. The inventory – one table, one chair, one bed, one coffee pot – is also the concrete poetry of the clarity of objects. This is the *via negativa* of the maker, less and less is more and more. His discards were legendary.

In the photographs of Lucie Rie's studio and flat at Albion Mews, the smallness of it all strikes one at first. It is on an impossible scale: everything is fiercely concentrated. The

Figure 23.2 David Westwood, 'Lucie Rie in Her Workshop Sitting on a Bench' (n.d.). © Estate of Lucie Rie. Image kindly provided by the Crafts Study Centre, University for the Creative Arts.

shelves stretch up high on the studio walls with button moulds and finished pots. There are stacks of sgraffito coffee cups and saucers, bowls, coffee pots, vases. And then in the flat above there is the wall of fitted shelving.

These images of Rie and Coper's spaces show their ease with architecture as a discipline. Architectural collaboration was part of this identity. Architects and engineers were amongst their earliest collectors and patrons, Ove Arup being one of them. Coper designed the extension to his own final house so exactly because 'basic' architecture was so important to him.[6] During what he called his 'architectural period' at Digswell, he designed wall sculptures and acoustic tiles, for cladding walls, as well as a washbasin: not accoutrements but the hardware of buildings. His candleholders designed for Coventry Cathedral in 1962 were made in response to Basil Spence's challenge for something 'in scale with the huge concrete altar. Obviously an ordinary design would look puny. This is the pitfall.'[7] They were seven feet tall and constructed of multiple thrown sections threaded together on metal rods. Coper engineered them as much as crafted them: in their construction they took to lathes and the apparatus of a factory rather than to a studio. Rie's outward self-confidence reveals the particularity of a Viennese centre of gravity: the Vienna where architects were part of a movement, not a movement apart. These affiliations may explain how Rie and Coper simply (almost disingenuously) failed to notice the great lacuna in the post-war English craft world – the gap of understanding between makers and architects.

It also goes someway to explain the 'relief' they both felt to be in London. For to be an émigré in London was to disappear, not to stand out. In not writing about their art of ceramics they revealed no accent, no unfortunate trace of the past. They could make themselves, remake their studios, trace the lines of desire into the base of a coffee cup.

Notes

1. Tony Birks, *Hans Coper* (London: William Collins, 1983), 55.

2. John Houston (ed.), *Craft Classics Since the 1940s: An Anthology of Belief and Comment* (London: Crafts Council, 1988), 99.

3. Jane Kallir, *Viennese Design and the Wiener Kerstätte* (London: Thames & Hudson, 1986), 108.

4. Gabriele Fahr-Becker, *Wiener Werkstätte* (Cologne: Taschen, 1995), 148.

5. Quoted in Kallir, *Viennese Design and the Wiener Kerstätte*, 110.

6. Birks, *Hans Coper*, 68–9.

7. Quoted in David Whiting, 'Coper at Coventry: Hans Coper and the Coventry Cathedral Candlesticks', *Studio Pottery*, April/May 1996, 19.

CHAPTER 24

TRICKSTERS OF THE WATER: SAM SELVON'S WEST LONDON AND THE MIGRANT EXPERIENCE

Peter Maber and Karishma Patel

Sam Selvon moved from Trinidad to London in 1950. He would become known as one of the first and defining novelists of the Windrush generation, telling in pioneeringly creolized voices of the struggles, yet spirited survival of the West Indian arrivals. Ambivalence characterizes Selvon's assessment of his time in London, as it does the mindsets and trajectories of many of his characters: 'It was always a struggle to survive in London, not only because of my non-whiteness, but money,' he would reflect; yet 'I got out of London what I had hoped for. Let me put it that way. Walking the streets of London and looking at the landscape [. . .].'[1] Selvon's protagonists likewise wander across London, but it is the 'little worlds' of Notting Hill and Bayswater ('the Gate' and 'the Water'), where so many of the Windrush generation settled, with which he is most strongly associated and where so many of 'the boys' of his London stories and of his 1956 novel *The Lonely Londoners* live, in the cramped bedsits into which decaying Victorian townhouses were converted.[2]

Like Bar 20 and Fred in his story 'Basement Lullaby' (1957), Selvon first took a damp basement bedsit in Bayswater. He wrote *The Lonely Londoners* over six months 'sat in a friend's house in Ladbroke Grove', but Moses Aloetta, the central character who holds the narrative together, is again based in a lower room in Bayswater, symbolically hoping to rise to an upper floor.[3] Selvon's experiences of living in London for the first time, without any security, gave him first-hand knowledge of the wider struggles faced by the Windrush generation. Successes and setbacks went hand in hand: he might have been awarded a Guggenheim Fellowship that took him to America in 1955, but back in Bayswater he was cleaning bars in small hotels.[4] When his novel *Turn Again Tiger* was published in 1958 with some publicity, he was recognized 'swabbing out the shithouse' at a club in Paddington. Selvon discovered that 'my life in London taught me about people from the Caribbean, and it was here that I found my identity'.[5] That paradox is at the heart of Selvon's representations of the migrant experience. The identities which emerge are characterized by their in-betweenness, formed by gains and losses, discoveries and confusions, progress and retrogression.

Selvon was born in Trinidad in 1923. His parents were themselves migrants, English and Hindi-speaking Christian Indians who had moved to the island from Madras; his maternal grandfather was Scottish.[6] Selvon grew up in the city of San Fernando, thinking of himself as part of a generation 'who grew up Westernized [. . .] who are Creolized as it were'.[7] Leaving school at fifteen, he worked as a wireless operator during the Second

World War for the Royal Naval Reserve, and began writing to pass the long periods of inactivity. After the war, he worked as a journalist for the *Trinidad Guardian* in Port of Spain, and began to publish sketches of island life. He was working on his first novel, *A Brighter Sun*, while crossing the Atlantic in 1950. Although set entirely in Trinidad, the coming-of-age narrative demonstrates the development of Selvon's international consciousness. The protagonist, Tiger, is initiated into the workings of the empire by his friend Boysie, on a first visit to Port of Spain. He asks Boysie:

> 'When I used to work in the canefield, and help make sugar, it went to England too?'
>
> 'Yes, man.'
>
> 'You think the people who eating sugar over there does think about we who making it here?'
>
> 'You does tink bout who make de shoes yuh wearing?'[8]

But, like Tiger, Selvon precisely *does* think about such questions as where products, and people, and culture more broadly, originate, where they end up and what they become.

So Selvon moved to London with such questions in mind, in search of new experiences and hoping to advance his writing career in the UK, together with a host of other

Figure 24.1 Pauline Clothilde Henriques and Sam Selvon. BBC Caribbean Service: Caribbean Voices (1952). © BBC.

Caribbean writers all seeking a wider audience and publishing success in the 'Mother Country'. He joined many, including V. S. Naipaul and George Lamming, in broadcasting on *Caribbean Voices*, the BBC radio programme which gave a platform to Caribbean writers. Meanwhile he completed work on *A Brighter Sun* between the Bayswater basement and an office in the Indian Embassy, where he worked for a spell as a clerk. Like Tiger, Selvon seemed always caught between worlds; it was a struggle to be accepted at the embassy: 'how could I be an "Indian" if I did not come from India[?]'.[9]

Selvon's 1957 volume of stories, *Ways of Sunlight*, charts some of the changes which were taking place to Selvon the writer: the stories represent first Trinidad and then London, in sections with those names, composed mainly in those locations, and demonstrating stylistic and thematic developments. Ambivalence was always one of Selvon's greatest narrative tricks: the opening 'Trinidad' story, 'Johnson and the Cascadura', begins, 'There's a native legend in Trinidad which says that those who eat the cascadura will end their days in the island no matter where they wander.'[10] It sounds like straightforwardly detached narrative commentary, but the story is ultimately undecided about what laws are in operation: 'some people have their own beliefs and others other'. Meanwhile, in the opening 'London' story, 'Calypso in London', we hear, 'Mangohead come from St Vincent, and if you don't know where that is that is your hard luck. But I will give you a clue – he uses to work on a arrowroot plantation. Now I suppose you want to know what arrowroot is, eh?' (*Sunlight*, 125).[11] Rather than pretend to orient the reader, the creolized narrative voice is abrupt, irreverent, rhythmically complex and multilayered. Such a new voice, which is typical of the London stories, demonstrates how it was writing in, of and to London that Selvon's already accomplished verbal dexterity would fully flourish. In moving to, and writing of, London, Selvon imports and heightens his narrative ambivalences, keeping alive multiple possibilities and tantalizing his readers with what is given, transformed and withheld. The origins of such multiplicities can be traced back to distinctly Caribbean forms, chiefly the trickster tale and the calypso – forms whose own origins are complex and uncertain, and whose impulses can be contradictory. Imported to London, these forms, like Selvon's characters, persist through both adaptation and resistance, becoming expressive of the London migrant experience; and they are figured too, we suggest here, in the particular forms that Selvon's creolized language takes.

A tension between being given your bearings and being denied them is a hallmark of Selvon's London writing. While the London narrators often assume ignorance of the Caribbean on the part of the reader, and may not be willing to help, familiarity with London is usually taken for granted; but the familiar can turn strange, and our expectations are continually being performed and adjusted. 'Down by Ladbroke Grove,' the narrator begins in 'Obeah in the Grove', 'and I don't mean the posh part near to Holland Park, but when you start to go west: the more west you go, the more worse things get – it have a certain street, and a certain house, and in front the house have a plane tree, and one day if you pass there and you look up in the plane tree, you will see a green bottle dangling on a piece of twine, and a big bone stick up between two branch' (*Sunlight*, 167). We are led from the named to the unnamed, to a scene or scenario that sits somewhere between the specific and the general, just as Selvon's characters sit somewhere between individuals and types, just as his stories themselves sit somewhere between the real and the emblematic.

The reader who encounters this story in *Ways of Sunlight* has already had an initiation into obeah and the practice of perfecting spells by hanging enchanted objects in trees in the Trinidad story 'The Mango Tree'. Ma Procop is an outsider figure, seen as an eccentric in her village. She uses the identity cast upon her to protect her fine mango tree by hanging bones and bottles from its branches: her trick doesn't lie in sorcery, but in creating the illusion of magic to ward off potential thieves. But another superstition ends up having still more ambivalent agency in this story: a boy and a girl climb the mango tree in spite of the semblance of obeah, and in spite of another belief, that, as the boy puts it, 'if girls climb fruit trees, the fruit will be sour' (*Sunlight*, 99). Some of the fruit *does* end up being sour, but, in the absence of any guarantees, we are left to wonder whether the curse has come true, and how to interpret the story as a whole.

If the mango tree is symbolic of Ma Procop, surviving in spite of adversities (even if the struggle has turned her sour), then the London plane tree of 'Obeah in the Grove' might have a symbolic connection with the story's West Indian protagonists. London plane trees are a hybrid species and a product of migration. Formed from *platanus orientalis*, the oriental plane, and *planatnus occidentalis*, the American sycamore, their hybridity makes them stronger, able to withstand the harsh London climate. The story sees 'the boys' – Buttards, Fiji, Winky and Algernon – move into a tenement house whose white owners welcome them with open arms and charge them hardly any rent; but of course it's too good to be true, and it's a racist ruse on the part of the owners to use 'the boys' to scare away existing tenants so they can sell the house, which is in a bad way. 'The boys'' trickery, in contrast to Ma Procop's, lies in their *belief* in obeah: before leaving, they hang the bottles and bones, on which Fiji has performed spells. The house becomes unsellable, all but collapsing, and further misfortunes for the owners follow. This time the narrator does take a stance, declaring 'that house have the vengeance of Moko on it' (*Sunlight*, 174), and dismissing our questions, but not obeah itself: 'Now you and me ain't going to argue about obeah. I have other things to do.' But, with the house already having been in a bad state, the story has precisely been set up to cause us to ask questions. Like the plane tree, and like the West Indian characters themselves, the story exists somewhere in between absolutes. At the same time, it demonstrates the possibility of reversals: Trinidadian English and Trinidadian beliefs appear to become stronger in London than they were in Selvon's Trinidad; characters go from being disempowered, taken advantage of, to achieving at least the perception of power.

The protagonists of this story, like so many of Selvon's male Caribbean characters, are trickster figures, whose origins lie in the particular incarnations of trickster tales that arrived on the islands through the slave trade. The Atlantic crossings of the Middle Passage brought anthropomorphic tales to the New World from West Africa, and it was tales of the Akan figure Anansi the spider that took particular hold in the Caribbean. In common with other tricksters from cultures across the world, Anansi is able to use his resourcefulness to outwit those in a more powerful position; the stories therefore have particular resonance in the context of slavery. Yet tricksters can also exhibit moral ambivalence, and Anansi sometimes uses his powers of trickery unfairly, which can necessitate the moral resolution of the stories lying in Anansi himself ultimately being tricked. Tricksters are thus agents of change, who, in Esther Priyadharshini's terms, 'jolt the world out of established or habitual modes of being'; but the results of those disruptions might not straightforwardly bring change for the greater good.[12]

Carnivals are often dominated by a trickster spirit. In Trinidad, the modern carnival evolved from its colonial origins to become a festival for the dispossessed, the opportunity to speak back to the colonizers. After emancipation in 1834, the Canboulay, an imitation of the colonial Mardi Gras, named after the French *cannes brulées*, became the dominant version of carnival, and was marked by contests including stick fighting and the singing of kaisos: call-and-response songs with syncopated rhythms, which again have their roots in West Africa. Canboulay turned the world on its head, suspending, if only for its duration, the colonial orders. In the twentieth century, the contests became musical. The kaiso evolved into the calypso, songs with upbeat rhythms and melodies, which can reflect the bravado but belie the struggle articulated in the lyrics. Calypsonians would compete to become the Calypso King (or Calypso Monarch today), displaying their wit and bite – *picong* – often by taking on topical themes in a satirical vein. In the spirit of reversals of the hierarchies, calypsonians typically give themselves mock-noble or mock-heroic names like The Mighty Destroyer and Growling Tiger. From the start, Selvon cast himself as a calypsonian, publishing his early sketches in Trinidad under calypsonian aliases such as Big Buffer and Ack-Ack (referring to the noise of anti-aircraft gunfire, and capturing the spirit of attack that can characterize political calypsos). He takes his cue from the calypsonian's dexterity in his wit, satire, reversals, distinctive language use and syncopated rhythms. Like the calypso, Selvon's writing is bittersweet: he can 'laugh kiff-kiff' (*Londoners*, 138) and at the same time give bite.

'Calypso in London' brings the traditions of the trickster and the calypso together. While 'Obeah in the Grove' reflects on the challenge of finding housing, this story begins with two further common difficulties encountered by the Windrush generation on arriving in London: finding profitable work and coping with the climate. Mangohead, the protagonist, is another trickster figure, who at the story's start finds that he can no longer continue with his job as a road worker: 'One frosty morning while he was digging, he lift up a spadeful of dirt to throw up on the bank, and when he throw his hands over his shoulder, as if his hands cramp and couldn't come back' (*Sunlight*, 125–6). Knowing that his friend Hotboy is a keen calypsonian, he tries to distract him with a calypso so good he will agree without thinking to lending Mangohead money he has no hope of getting back. Mangohead's first attempt draws on his personal experience:

It had a time in this country
When everybody happy excepting me
I can't get a work no matter how I try
It look as if hard times riding me high.

But Hotboy is unimpressed: 'Lord old man, you can't think of anything new? You think we still in Trinidad? This is London, man, this is London. The people want calypso on topical subject' (*Sunlight*, 127–8). Once again, Caribbean forms seem to become heightened in Selvon's London. So, in order to give his calypso more bite, 'Mango, as if he get an inspiration, start to extemporize on Nasser and Eden and how he will give them the dope – the best thing is to pass the ships round the Cape of Good Hope' (*Sunlight*, 129). It's a telling contemporary reference: in riffing on the Suez Crisis of 1956, Selvon is calling attention to a pivotal moment in the turning of the fortunes of the British Empire, giving precise political contexts to his many symbolic reversals.

The story can be read as both a calypso and a trickster tale. There's the literal calypso Mangohead and Hotboy go on to finish together. There's the way their calypso takes on and aims to better calypsos back in Trinidad, which recalls the spirit of the carnival competitions. There's the way Mangohead tricks Hotboy; and once again a complication of the initial trick: at the end we hear from the narrator that Hotboy has told Mangohead 'that he sell the calypso. But up to now I can't hear it playing or singing anywhere' (has Hotboy ended up quids in or not?) (*Sunlight*, 131). Then there's the way the story functions as a kind of calypso in inculpating Britain both at home and in its place in the wider world. Finally, the story plays its own kind of trick on Britain by intervening in the representation of London and in the representation of the English language.

In Selvon's best-known London work, *The Lonely Londoners*, published in 1956 and whose composition overlaps with some of the stories of *Ways of Sunlight*, in-betweenness operates at both local and structural levels. Although labelled a novel, the work seems as much a collection of interlinked vignettes, which follow the fortunes of a cast of West Indian characters trying to 'get on' in London but often struggling to 'get by' (*Londoners*, 88). Selvon is clearly influenced by his experience of the short story form, developing his folkloric style, his gift for sketches with improvisatory qualities, and his seamless movements between instance and generality and between the real and the typic. The longer form allows for more sustained exploration of the trickster and carnival tropes of opposition and reversal, and of the states of liminality and feelings of ambivalence with which they are associated.

With a wider cast of characters, Selvon is able to explore different strategies for responding to the city. Moses, from Trinidad, has been in London for ten years; like his biblical namesake, he is a leader (although, uncertain of the future, including his own, he is limited as a prophet). He holds 'the boys' together, and in the process holds the book together. At Harris' St Pancras Hall fete, prototype for the 1959 Caribbean Carnival that would inspire the Notting Hill Carnival (discussed elsewhere in this volume by Leighan Renaud), a clue to Moses' character is revealed when he becomes an informal 'master of ceremonies with the boys, giving them all the latest lowdown and ballad as they coast a drink' (*Londoners*, 114). Moses is continually there for support and advice, absorbing their stresses, although it also takes its toll. They gather in his Bayswater room on Sunday mornings for their own version of a Sunday service, 'coming together for a oldtalk', keeping alive their West Indian identities and finding relief from the fragmented loneliness of city life (*Londoners*, 138).

The degree to which the characters hold onto their pasts, and bring them to bear on their London experiences, varies. There are those who attempt as complete an assimilation as possible: Bart, for example, who uses his 'light skin' to try to pass as 'a Latin-American' (*Londoners*, 61); and Harris, who 'like to play ladeda, and he like English customs and thing' so that 'when he dress, you think is some Englishman going to work' (*Londoners*, 111). Such satirical caricatures are underpinned with serious sociological critique of the limitations and racism motivating such responses: Bart is 'frighten for the lash' (*Londoners*, 61), while Harris' performance is always incomplete: 'Only thing, Harris face black' (*Londoners*, 111). At the other end of the spectrum, and in a spirit of resistance, there is Tanty, who refuses to adapt her behaviour, rather insisting that London itself adapts; so she installs a Caribbean system of credit in the backstreet grocers by sheer force of insistence: 'Where I come from you take what you want and you pay every Friday' (*Londoners*, 79). Names are an indicator of reseeing and remaking the city. When Henry Oliver, himself newly renamed by Moses as Sir Galahad, first hears he will lodge in Bayswater, island life is on his mind: 'Is a bay? It have water?' (*Londoners*, 35). Similarly, Tanty makes sense of, and fears, London buses in relation to her experience of the sea in Jamaica: 'I feel as if they would capsize' (*Londoners*, 82). The initiated make the city their own through abbreviation, speaking of the Grove, the Gate, the Water, the Arch and the Circus; but only, as Moses tells Galahad, after 'you living in the city for at least two years' (*Londoners*, 35). Pushing renaming further still, Big City, always deferential to big city life, refuses to accept his habit of confusing names, so that we end up with 'Nottingham Gate' and 'Gloucestershire Road' (*Londoners*, 95). Perhaps Galahad's 'miracle of metabolism' (*Londoners*, 123), his inability to feel the cold in the winter when everyone else is suffering (and its reversal: that he starts to feel cold in the summer) functions as an allegory of resistance, of not adapting to the new surroundings.

Galahad nonetheless undergoes transitions and transformations from his arrival at the start of the novel, fresh off the SS *Hildebrand* and meeting Moses at Waterloo station. His first strategy is to 'play boldface' (*Londoners*, 39), but he ends up getting lost on Queensway and 'a feeling of loneliness and fright come on him all of a sudden' (*Londoners*, 41), resulting in a kind of identity crisis: 'a feeling come over him as if he lost everything he have' (*Londoners*, 42). Thereafter he is always divided between his feelings of awe for London's fame – admiration for the 'big romance' of being able to say 'I was in Oxford Street' – and at the same time his acute sense of London's problems, chiefly its racial injustice. The odds are against the new arrivals; this is a London that 'divide up in little worlds' (*Londoners*, 74) and whose inhabitants are unable to see 'how other people does affect their lives' (*Londoners*, 76). In Praed Street a notice appears reading 'Keep the Water White' (*Londoners*, 89); such division can be reversed only in Big City's fantasy of striking it rich: 'I would put a notice on all the boards: "Keep the Water Coloured, No Rooms For Whites"' (*Londoners*, 97). The divided city leads to divided identities. Galahad becomes inured to discrimination; in a variation of Frantz Fanon's 'Look, a Negro!' revelation in *Black Skin, White Masks*, Galahad kindly addresses a small child who has singled him out with 'Mummy, look at that black man!', only to face, in a more complex performance still, the mother's embarrassment 'with so many white people around' (*Londoners*, 87). As in

Fanon, such episodes lead to reification: Galahad comes to think of 'the colour Black' as a distinct person that 'causing botheration in the place' (*Londoners*, 88). The racialized self has become fully divided.

Sir Galahad is of course a calypsonian moniker, alluding to the Arthurian romances. A prominent calypsonian at the time, who brought calypso to the United States, was called Sir Lancelot; Selvon would doubtless have been aware of his work, especially since he visited the US just prior to writing *The Lonely Londoners*. In the legends, Galahad is Lancelot's illegitimate son, and he's one of the knights who manages to reach the Holy Grail. In this context, the male protagonists of *The Lonely Londoners* become a version of the Arthurian knights in their quests for their own versions of the Grail: food – at times a quest for survival – but also in their quests to fulfil their sexual appetites. In their episodic adventures, these latter-day knights, tricksters of the Water and of the Gate, reinvent both the romance form and the picaresque novel.

When 'the vengeance of Moko', as in 'Obeah in the Grove', falls this time upon 'the boys' one winter, Galahad and Cap grotesquely literalize the animal traditions of the trickster tale in order to get by. Selvon delights in combining the allegorical form with London specificity: Galahad snatches a pigeon near an entrance to Kensington Gardens, 'as soon as you cross over the zebra, a little way down from Queensway' (*Londoners*, 124) (such an area, with the 'iron railing there, so you can't get right up to the birds', still exists, at the entrance opposite the Queensway crossing). A little further west, Cap ensnares seagulls from his 'top room in Dawson Place, near the Gate' (*Londoners*, 134). While such tricks can be read as quests for survival, 'the boys'' empowerment also takes the form of sexual conquest, which generates some of the ugliest scenes in the novel. Moses, Selvon acknowledges in interview, is a 'very strange, ambivalent figure'; 'he's almost an Anansi spider character'.[13] The trickster's ambivalence perhaps explains how Moses can both be a moral compass to 'the boys', yet play cruel tricks on women, and trick Lewis into thinking Agnes is having an affair, leading him to abuse her. It can be difficult to find many ways out of the novel's sustained patriarchal focalization, although awareness of the ambivalence of the trickster figure and the patriarchal nature of the calypso (and that of the European courtly) tradition with which Selvon is working provides potential distancing.

A vital aspect of Selvon's success is his command of the language form in which he writes. He said that he spent two of the six months it took to complete *The Lonely Londoners* working on its language, drafting firstly a series of 'wonderful anecdotes' with 'most of the dialogues in dialect', but found 'I could not really move' with the main narrative 'in straight English'.[14] Yet once he started using his distinctive form 'of Caribbean language' for the whole, the composition 'just shot along'.[15] Although Selvon had employed creolized English in the narrative sections of earlier works, especially in the short stories, he suggested he was not 'quite conscious of it' until working on *The Lonely Londoners*. The language deepens the connection between the disparate characters; it facilitates the representation of West Indians as what Selvon referred to as a 'third race', a concept which he felt also allowed him to give voice to Caribbean characters who are Black as well as Indian.[16]

Again, we find in-betweenness emblemized in this creolized language: it is adapted to facilitate wide readership. As Selvon explained, 'I really try and keep the essence, the music of the dialect'; 'I don't do any phonetic spelling, and I try to avoid some words or phrases which I feel would be very difficult for an audience outside of the Caribbean to follow' (115). But there is also something strange in employing such vernacular-orthography at all: to write a version of an entirely spoken language is a paradox and unique challenge.

Both the concept and the specific linguistic feature of hiatus create further bonds between the language and the characters. For the characters are in hiatus between the Caribbean and London, flats and jobs, women and commitments; types of English. Hiatus is an experience they have to accommodate at every turn, and which involves remarkable adaptations of language and culture. Hiatus is broadly understood as a 'break in continuity' but it has a precise definition when it comes to language. Phonologically, hiatus is having two adjacent vowels in different syllables, as in 'a apple'. Reading that aloud is uncomfortable, so languages have evolved to restrict hiatus with consonants – 'an apple' – or by changing the sounds of vowels when they are next to each other, like 'cooperate'. Another example is 'the ear', which is said as one word, because the vowels turn into a diphthong – two vowels in one. This is all for prosodic purposes: to make the language flow. Adapting to or accommodating an uncomfortable state of hiatus, then, is not only a core theme of the novel – migrant limbo – but lies in the language itself. The reader is also left in the dislocation between the letters on the page and the true sound of this musical language.

In *The Lonely Londoners*, we see what appears to be untreated hiatus everywhere: when 'the boys' come together for 'a oldtalk', for example. How would you pronounce that? What we fail to see on the page is that hiatus in Trinidadian English is usually tackled with glottaling. To glottal is to use a glottal stop, 'a form of plosive in which the closure is made by bringing the vocal folds together', between the two vowels – almost a catch in the throat which acts like a consonant.[17] Here, the sound would have the same function as an 'n', as with the glottal in 'A&E'. Creolized forms of English use adjacent vowels more often, but they adapt the vowel sounds in innovative ways. Speaking fluidly with Caribbean oral rhythms is the priority. Glottaling is the usual choice but is hard to express on the page in the prose form. An arguably accurate written version of Trinidadian English would have to use phonetic alphabets and markings. For example, the phonetic transcription of 'a old' in Trinidadian English is 'ɑʔ ɔl', where 'ʔ' is the glottal stop in the International Phonetic Alphabet. The glottal stop could also be transcribed with an apostrophe, so Selvon might have written 'a'ole talk', but it is still unclear how to pronounce the vowels there.

Language for a migrant is survival – is quick communication, adapted to accommodate the experience of being between cultures. The migrant story is a succession of hiatuses dealt with creatively and quickly, and this is reflected in the vernacular, where hiatus in language is creatively dealt with, using sounds that have no corresponding letters or marks for the page in standardized written English. The reading experience would be very different with a diacritical alphabet – more clinical, less accessible, but a text made to be read aloud. As it stands, the Standard English speaker cannot pronounce the many adjacent vowels because Selvon does not provide a roadmap for pronunciation, but the text is readable on the page. This suggests to the reader that they cannot truly engage with the migrant experience. The reader is an outsider pressing their ear to the door, trying to hear and mouth the intimate sounds between friends together in a foreign land.

The Lonely Londoners moves – in spite of many digressions, its own migrations – from winter to summer; that summer fully flourishes in an extended passage set for the most part in Hyde Park, phrased in a single sentence. The grammar collapses; boundaries and conventions are made soft and malleable. No commas or periods separate the words, let alone markings around hiatuses: 'summer does really be hearts like if you start to live again you coast a lime by the Serpentine and go for a row on the river or you go bathing by the Lido though the water never warm no matter how hot the sun is' (*Londoners*, 106). The passage might be read as an interlude in Selvon's attempt to fit any 'standard' conventions around grammar or novels. Like a Russian nesting doll, this is a hiatus within a hiatus, drawing attention to the idea of a 'hiatal' or in-between state. The passage functions as a kind of quasi-Shakespearean green space in which greater freedom, greater subversion is possible, including from European literary precedents; once again we are in the tradition of the Trinidadian calypso, performing freedom by taking on and outwitting colonial precedents.

The passage is a celebration of the awakening of the natural world, and of being reminded 'what it like to see blue skies like back home' (*Londoners*, 102), but more than just a counterpart to the brutal winter and to cramped bedsit living, this summer in the park is the site of far more transgressive reversals, of the 'big thrills' on offer (*Londoners*, 107). Trees now 'have clothes on' (*Londoners*, 102), but 'girls throw away heavy winter coat' (*Londoners*, 101). By night 'the world turn upside down' (*Londoners*, 109) and Hyde Park's history as Henry VIII's deer park becomes reinvented as a contemporary 'happy hunting ground' (*Londoners*, 107). For this extended sentence is also a release from the pent-up city: 'everybody look like they frustrated in the big city the sex life gone wild' (*Londoners*, 109).

The sexual freedoms of the park provide a kind of levelling: 'it ain't have no discrimination when it come to that in the park in the summer' (*Londoners*, 104); high and low unite in sex, but this is first and foremost a patriarchal alliance, bringing together 'all sorts of fellars from all walks of life'. Both sex workers (who prove good at 'business' (*Londoners*, 104)) and 'the boys' (who are seen to collude in the fetishization of people of colour (*Londoners*, 108)) appear to be able to benefit from the discriminatory practices at work; perhaps that can be read as an attempt to pull in different directions, to blur the question of who is hunting whom, although it is far from finding a way out, including from the celebratory tone.

'That is life that is London' this hiatal section sings (*Londoners*, 109), but it ends with a contrast between Galahad, appreciating the 'sweetness of summer', and Moses 'who frighten as the years go by wondering what it is all about' (*Londoners*, 110). Increasingly it is Moses who is brought into focus, and the speed of oscillation between feelings of euphoria and of despair intensifies, as we enter his mind. Should he save up and try to return home or not? Feelings of paralysis come upon Moses when he senses he is 'getting no place' (*Londoners*, 98), that it is 'like he unable to move his body' (*Londoners*, 141). While Selvon uses the winter to emblemize stagnation, he also uses the transition from winter to summer to represent the push and pull of this debate about going or staying: 'I will wait until after the summer, the summer does really be hearts' (*Londoners*, 141). When Moses comes closest to being a prophet, looking beneath the surface of things as he looks into the Thames in the novel's final scene, he is speaking also of the artistry of the novel and its own wanderings: 'Under the kiff-kiff laughter, behind the ballad and the episode, the what-happening, the summer-is-hearts, he could see a great aimlessness, a great restless, swaying movement that leaving you standing in the same spot' (*Londoners*, 141). And when we hear that he has learnt of the literary success of 'all kinds of fellars writing books', we sense that perhaps Moses is in fact the implied author of *this* novel (*Londoners*, 142). Though Selvon's own in-betweenness has notable differences, it intersects with that of Moses: Selvon would describe living in London as living 'in two worlds. Hanging about with Moses and the boys, and at the same time hustling to earn something with my writing.'[18]

States of in-betweenness are everywhere in Selvon's writing of London. They can result in frustration, loss and alienation; they might also hold sources of strength in their potential to bring about new forms of identity. London has, after all, been the constant site of such reinvention through the power of cultures colliding. Selvon ultimately demands of his reader the ability to navigate multiplicities, which in their potential for disorientation create textual experiences to mirror those of the migrants. And if we can't keep up with it all, if the ultimate trick is on us? 'Well that is your hard luck.'[19]

Notes

1. See Sam Selvon, 'Finding West Indian Identity in London', *Kunapipi* 9, no. 3 (1987): 37; and John Thieme and Alexandra Dutti, '"Oldtalk": Two Interviews with Sam Selvon', in *Something Rich and Strange: Selected Essays on Sam Selvon*, ed. Martin Zehnder (Leeds: Peepal Tree, 2003), 75.
2. See Sam Selvon, *The Lonely Londoners* (Harlow: Longman, 2005), 74. Future references to this text will be given in parentheses in the main body of the text.
3. Selvon, 'Finding West Indian Identity in London', 37.
4. Ibid., 36–7.
5. Ibid.
6. See 'Sam Selvon: Interview with Reed Dasenbrock and Feroza Jussawalla', in *Tiger's Triumph: Celebrating Sam Selvon*, ed. Susheila Nasta and Anna Rutherford (Hebden Bridge: Dangaroo Press, 1995), 122–3.
7. Ibid., 120.
8. Sam Selvon, *A Brighter Sun* (Harlow: Longman, 1996), 88.
9. Selvon, 'Finding West Indian Identity in London', 36.
10. Sam Selvon, *Ways of Sunlight* (Harlow: Longman, 1981), 11. Future references to this volume will be given in parentheses in the main body of the text. This story was originally published

in 1948. For a bibliographic chronology by Susheila Nasta, see Sam Selvon, *Foreday Morning: Selected Prose 1946–86*, ed. Kenneth Ramchand and Susheila Nasta (London: Longman, 1989), 226–48.

11. Originally composed in 1952 as 'Calypsonian' and set in Trinidad; the London setting is added for the 1957 version.

12. Esther Priyadharshini, 'Thinking with Trickster: Sporadic Illuminations for Educational Research', *Cambridge Journal of Education* 42, no. 4 (2012): 547–61.

13. 'Sam Selvon: Interview with Reed Dasenbrock and Feroza Jussawalla', 117.

14. Michael Fabre, 'Samuel Selvon: Interviews and Conversations', in *Critical Perspectives on Sam Selvon*, ed. Susheila Nasta (Washington, DC: Three Continents Press, 1988), 66.

15. Thieme and Dutti, '"Oldtalk"', 74.

16. 'Sam Selvon: Interview with Reed Dasenbrock and Feroza Jussawalla', 116, 119.

17. Arthur Hughes, Peter Trudgill and Dominic Watt, *English Accents and Dialects* (New York: Routledge, 2013), 43.

18. Selvon, 'Finding West Indian Identity in London', 37.

19. Selvon, 'Working the Transport', *Ways of Sunlight*, 132.

CHAPTER 25
ARABIAN NIGHTS ON THE EDGWARE ROAD: HANAN AL-SHAYKH'S *ONLY IN LONDON*
Susie Thomas

In the prologue to Hanan al-Shaykh's *Only in London* (2001), four strangers are thrown together on a bumpy flight from Dubai to Heathrow; the novel tracks their developing relationship to each other and to London in the 1990s. Samir, a gay transvestite from Lebanon, who has never been to England before, can scarcely believe his eyes when he sees shisha cafes lining the Edgware Road: 'It's incredible! Mazraa Street [in Beirut] has moved to London!'[1] He is befriended by Amira, a Moroccan sex worker, who plies her trade around the corner in the Dorchester Hotel. Lamis, who was unwillingly married off aged seventeen after her family fled Saddam Hussein's Iraq in 1982, is trying to make a new life as a divorcée: after years of living as an expat, she is determined to make London her home. She panics when she loses her British passport on the plane and when an Englishman returns it to her she feels as if he 'had given her back her life' (2). He is Nicholas, a dealer in Arabic *objets d'art*, who divides his time between Oman and London: he, too, is unsettled and looking for a framework for his life.

This chapter traces the characters' trajectories in London, focusing on three key settings – Leighton House Museum, the Edgware Road and the Regent's Park Mosque – in order to show how the novel locates Arab culture at the heart of the metropolis and its history even though the Arab characters are recent arrivals, eking out an often precarious living.[2] In the process it explores how *Only in London* affirms the possibility of crossing cultural boundaries and creating new identities in the city.

*   *   *

Frederic Leighton (1830–96) remains an enigmatic figure: he lived alone, guarding his privacy, but became one of the most famous British artists of the Victorian age. He was made President of the Royal Academy of Arts in 1878 and a life peer shortly before his death. He spent much of his peripatetic childhood on the continent with his wealthy family and studied art in Florence, Paris and Rome. After settling in London, he began planning a studio-house in Holland Park in 1865, which was designed by his friend, the architect George Aitchison. Financed by sales of his work, the house was extended over the next thirty years. Conceived as a temple to art, which could hold soirées and exhibitions, its synthesis of styles is most dramatically on display in the Arab Hall (1877–81), which was based on La Zisa, a twelfth-century Arab-Norman palace in Palermo. In the centre is a pool beneath a dome, and the walls are decorated with historic Islamic tiles (some taken from mosques) sourced in Iznik, Damascus and Persia. Leighton began collecting Arab *objets d'art* during his travels in the Ottoman Empire in the early 1870s;

more tiles were shipped to London by his friend, the explorer and diplomat Richard Burton. William De Morgan, Walter Crane and Randolph Caldecott – Leighton's fellow proponents of the Aesthetic Movement – were involved in the decoration of the opulent interior.[3] Perhaps surprisingly, the museum has not addressed the issue of cultural appropriation, which has become a source of debate for other historic houses and collections, but Leighton House, and Richard Burton's translation of *One Thousand and One Nights* (1885), could be seen as prime examples of the European plunder and misrepresentation of the East that Edward Said analysed in *Orientalism* (1978).

When Lamis attends a promenade performance for Lord Leighton's centenary (1996) in *Only in London*, the house becomes a stage, not for a pageant about Leighton, but for Lamis's construction of her own hybrid Arab-British identity. As she makes her way through the building on her own, 'an actor cloaked from head to toe in a white abaya' flings 'open the doors to a vista from *One Thousand and One Nights*': 'Turquoise domes overhead, brilliant tiles depicting birds drinking from fountains, borders of white and black and grey mosaics, Victorian columns holding aloft Qur'anic verses painted in blue' (61).

Transported back to her childhood in Najaf, Lamis feels an affinity with the *mise-en-scène* that Leighton created and claims it as her own: 'I know what those silent artefacts would like to say. I know their history and what they've seen' (61–2). She is particularly drawn to the wooden lattices which cover the windows at the top of the Arab Hall: 'she could envisage women who were desperate to become pregnant, to see their husbands return, or to be cured of illness; women whose features were blurred behind the circles and squares of the carved screens' (61–2). When Lamis walks through the house a second time with Nicholas, the Englishman she met on the plane, the reader is alerted to the possibility that what he sees in her is the beauty and allure of the Orient. He is an expert in Islamic art at Sotheby's, whose fleeting encounters with Arab women in the Gulf states had left him feeling that they were out of bounds to him, while she has been longing to meet an Englishman to have 'a way in' to English society (16). When they kiss under the turquoise domes, it seems as if they are performing roles in a romantic fantasy of East meets West, but as their relationship develops over the course of the novel, al-Shaykh shows how characters do not have to remain prisoners of their culturally conditioned misconceptions of each other.

Like the artefacts in Leighton House, the stories in *The Arabian Nights* have a variety of sources and a complex history: once disdained in the Arab world as lewd and vulgar and fantastical – and lapped up in French and English translations for similar reasons – they have recently been hailed as the book which 'changed the world on a scale unrivalled by any other literary text'.[4] Marina Warner, drawing on another concept from Edward Said, has argued:

> *The Arabian Nights* is a pre-eminent example of the travelling text, an extraordinary case of cross-fertilisation, retelling, grafting and borrowing, imitation and dissemination back and forth between Persia, India, Iraq, Turkey, Egypt and Europe over several centuries.[5]

The framing device of Scheherazade spinning her tales to save her life has been of particular significance for women writers. Orientalists tended to reduce her to a slave girl with a gift of the gab, and al-Shaykh initially resented the clichéd way Western publishers marketed her as 'the new Scheherazade', when she wanted to be the new Simone de Beauvoir. But al-Shaykh later reclaimed her as 'the first feminist'; and produced her own reimagining of *One Thousand and One Nights* in 2011.[6]

* * *

A kind of colonization-in-reverse took place in West London in the 1960s as Egyptians and Iraqis made the Edgware Road their home; during the civil war in Lebanon, the area became known as Little Beirut.[7] Many Arabs in London are refugees from foreign occupation and repressive regimes and by the 1990s, when the novel is set, some 150 Arabic papers and magazines were based in the city.[8] Born in 1945, al-Shaykh was one of the intellectuals and journalists who came to London in the 1980s, but she found that the character of an Arab academic, with which she began the novel, died on the page; it was Amira and Samir, whose stories she heard on the grapevine, who came to life.[9]

The interconnecting tales in *Only in London* mix the factual with the fantastical: every locality is precisely identified, from Ranoush Juice and Maroush on Edgware Road to Claridge's, where Amira impersonates a princess and allows a visiting Gulf Arab to seduce her. The thought that he had 'fucked royalty' transforms the hotel into a scene from *One Thousand and One Nights*: 'he was Clever Hassan [...] who had reached the jewel in the dragon's mouth and snatched it from the flames' (147). Samir's adventures with the monkey, Cappuccino, which he smuggles into the country stuffed with diamonds, becomes another folk tale which Samir later uses to entertain customers in the 'Arab haunts' in West London (270). But al-Shaykh is also drawing on the trope of the city as a stage for reinvention, which has been a staple of London literature from the story of Dick Whittington, to Dickens and Hanif Kureishi. As in many London novels, whether the protagonist comes from the country, like Nicholas, or from another country, al-Shaykh's characters see the city as a place of possibility.

For Samir, who had to hide his homosexuality first from his mother and then his wife and children, London is an erotic fantasy: he imagined 'he'd see rows of English boys undulating like golden ears of wheat' (88). But Samir finds it harder to get laid than he imagined: he thinks a card in a phone box is advertising a brothel but on arrival discovers it is an HIV clinic. When his wife and children follow him to London he is forced into ever more comic and humiliating encounters in locked bathrooms (246). The fantasy begins to fade and he finds himself longing for a young man who works in a restaurant on the Edgware Road, who 'cut tomatoes into flower shapes that unfolded at his touch, the same colour as his cheeks' (237). After he persuades his family to return to the Emirates, he remains with Amira. However precarious his existence, 'London was freedom. It was your right to do anything, any time' (149).

Amira, who left a poverty-stricken village in Morocco only to go from one maid's job to another in freezing London, makes a good living from sex once she discovers that tourists from the Gulf find the veil a more erotic provocation than 'a bewildering array of tightly clad arses' (75). Some of her clients even cry as they beg for her services: 'How could she lose [. . .] if sex was over that fast, and was that ordinary, like a seed popping in your face?' (170). She refuses to feel ashamed, even though her mother thinks the money Amira sends home is polluted, until her impersonation of a princess is discovered by a real prince. Outraged that Amira has been passing herself off as a member of his family, he arranges for her to be beaten up by his hireling. As the man aims blows at every part of her body, she thinks, 'He was her father, brothers, cousins, any number of men from home beating her up' (254). It is a humiliating punishment because she knows the prince had done it because she was 'a whore' (255). She consoles herself that at least 'she wasn't an Englishwoman on her way to the police station, after being caught in a squad car's lights trying to pick up a john' (257).

At first glance, Lamis's story seems to confirm Geoffrey Nash's argument that Western publishers want novels that conform to Orientalist stereotypes of Arab women as victims. According to Nash, the cross-cultural sexual encounters introduced by Ahdaf Soueif in *In The Eye of the Sun* (1992) and found in *Only in London* are 'romantic updates of Spivak's celebrated nostrum of white men saving brown women from brown men'.[10] But al-Shaykh undermines the victim/saviour stereotypes. There is no Muslim male tyrant in Lamis's story: her mother pressured her into marrying because the family was poor and desperate; her gentle father was too weak to make a stand against the marriage. Her wealthy husband is not a sexual predator: he struggles to consummate the marriage and is 'never seized with any powerful emotion without suffering from severe flatulence' (234). He pays the bills on Lamis's flat off the Edgware Road until she finds her feet, and places no restrictions on her access to her son.

The white Englishman, Nicholas, who initially has all kinds of Orientalist preconceptions about Arab women, gradually falls in love with Lamis, but runs away when she refuses to marry or even move in with him. Eventually he cracks and sends Lamis a letter from Oman explaining his disappearance: 'I convinced myself I was just another Englishman to you' and that all she wanted was a holiday romance (272). The kiss he gave her in Leighton House may have liberated Lamis, but he gradually realizes that the English are riddled with taboos about sex (161). Nicholas's absence from the novel allows al-Shaykh to show Lamis establishing herself in London rather than being given back her life by the Englishman. She votes in the election, which makes her feel that 'she belonged' (262). She enrols in college and gets a job in a flower shop so that she will not be financially dependent on her ex-husband. Once she is good and ready, she flies to Oman to bring Nicholas back to London.

Although Lamis begins the novel determined to renounce everything Arab – food, dress, even her mother tongue – so that she can assimilate, as she sits on the plane she can hardly believe that she had ever considered 'doing away with her heritage' (275). Losing Arabic would mean ceasing to breathe. In this she is like Hanan al-Shaykh, who writes in Arabic, despite having moved to London in the 1980s: 'My language. If I lose it, *chalas*, finish. No Hanan, no writing.' She collaborates closely with her translator, Catherine Cobham, but never 'bends' the text in order to explain British references to an Arab reader or vice versa.[11]

*   *   *

The plan for a Central London Mosque and Cultural Centre was first proposed in the early 1900s, but it took seventy years to get sponsorship and planning approval. British governments blocked the proposal until 1940, when the War Cabinet donated a site in Regent's Park as a goodwill gesture to the millions of Muslims in the empire: the BBC trumpeted the gift most loudly in Egypt, Iraq and Palestine. The architect Sir Frederick Gibberd fused Modernist and Islamic design and the mosque eventually opened its doors in 1977, funded by donations from across the Arab world.[12] With its golden dome and 44-metre-high minaret, it is a landmark of British and Arab cooperation, however uneasy or unequal. In *Only in London*, it is the place where Amira looks for answers at a time of crisis towards the end of the novel, just as Lamis searches for acceptance in Leighton House at the beginning.

All four characters have religious backgrounds: Amira, Samir and Lamis are from Muslim families, while Nicholas's father is a vicar in the Church of England with missionary tendencies (78). None of them is devout but when Amira's best friend, Nahid, is dying of cancer she decides to become a 'proper Muslim'. After spending the night with a punter who refused to pay and finding herself dead drunk banging the empty bottle against the bathroom wall, she tells Amira: 'I felt the Prophet's hand (peace be upon him) leading me [...] and protecting me' (206). Nahid's death in exile is a poignant event: the veiled sisters from the Regent's Park Mosque try to stop her old friends from the days of her *jahiliyyya* (ignorance) from visiting her sickbed, but they refuse to leave. Amira, with characteristic generosity, offers to pay for the body to be flown back to Egypt, but Nahid's own mother does not want her. Amira makes one more visit to Regent's Park Mosque, on the night she is beaten up, telling the attendant she is looking for her mother's body (257). She starts crying hysterically because there is nothing there for her: like Nahid, she has no family that will acknowledge her and, unlike Nahid, no religious belief to console her. On leaving the mosque, Amira has difficulty hailing a cab because she is wearing a veil, and one of the drivers even spits at her: '"Fuck you," she said in English' (258).

The celebration of the city in *Only in London* owes something to millennial optimism: the British capital is no longer the imperium, which must be resisted; and the novel takes place before the war on terror, which rendered Muslims suspect. Earlier classics of Arab literature, such as Tayeb Salih's *Season of Migration to the North* (1966; translation 1969) and Waguih Ghali's *Beer in the Snooker Club* (1964), while very different from each other, are both examples of writing back to the centre. For Salih, a cross-cultural love affair in London is as doomed as Othello and Desdemona's proved to be; it can only end in murder. Meanwhile, Ghali's protagonist, Ram, has a whale of a time in West London: gambling on the Edgware Road and denouncing the British Empire in the pub, while adoring women beg him to be their lover. In *Beer in the Snooker Club* the dream of London is shattered by the invasion of Suez, and Ram is deported after hitting a policeman on the head at a demo in Trafalgar Square. Leila Aboulela's *Minaret* (2005) and Robin Yassin-Kassab's *The Road from Damascus* (2008), contemporary fictions of the diasporic experience, are both post-9/11 novels in which the protagonists struggle to establish a Muslim identity. For Sami, in *The Road from Damascus*, the Edgware Road is where white students at SOAS go on anthropological expeditions, and he finally suspends his disbelief in Islam at the Brick Lane Mosque: 'Formerly synagogue. Formerly Methodist Chapel. Formerly Huguenot church.'[13] Aboulela's heroine Anjwa, lost and lonely, looks up and sees 'the minaret of Regent's Park mosque visible among the trees. I have never seen it so early in the morning in this vulnerable light. London is at its most beautiful in autumn.'[14] Unlike Amira, Anjwa finds genuine peace and a sense of belonging there. *Vive la différence*. In the end, it is both the bonds and the differences between people in the metropolis that al-Shaykh celebrates in *Only in London*: the cross-cultural love of Lamis and Nicholas; and the chosen family that Amira and Samir create together as they tell their stories of the Princess and Cappuccino.

Notes

1. Hanan al-Shaykh, *Only in London* (London: Bloomsbury, 2002), 23. Subsequent page references are cited in the text.

2. For more on the characters' economic struggle, see Susan Alice Fischer, 'Women Writers, Global Migration, and the City: Joan Riley's *Waiting in the Twilight* and Hanan Al-Shaykh's *Only in London*', *Tulsa Studies in Women's Literature* 23, no. 1 (2004): 107–20.

3. Robin Simon (ed.), *Lord Leighton (1830–1896) and Leighton House: A Centenary Celebration* (London: Apollo Magazine, 1996).

4. Saree Makdisi and Felicity Nussbaum (eds), *The Arabian Nights in Historical Context: Between East and West* (Oxford: Oxford University Press, 2008), 1.

5. Marina Warner, 'Travelling Text', *London Review of Books* 30, no. 24 (2008), https://www.lrb.co.uk/the-paper/v30/n24/marina-warner/travelling-text.

6. Hanan al-Shaykh, 'Scheherazade: From Storytelling "Slave" to "First Feminist"', *NPR*, 9 June 2013, https://www.npr.org/2013/06/09/189539866/scheherazade-from-storytelling-slave-to-first-feminist.

7. The major histories of London say little about the Arab presence in the city. Ramy M. K. Aly's *Becoming Arab in London: Performativity and the Undoing of Identity* (London: Pluto Press, 2015) is the first ethnographic study. See also Nazneed Khan-Østrem's section on Arab London in *London: Immigrant City*, trans. Alison McCullogh (London: Robinson, 2021).

8. Jerry White, *London in the Twentieth Century: A City and Its People* (London: Bodley Head, 2016), 140.

9. Christiane Schlote, 'An Interview with Hanan al-Shaykh', *Literary London: Interdisciplinary Studies in the Representation of London* 1, no. 2 (2003), http://www.literarylondon.org/london-journal/september2003/schlote.html.

10. Geoffrey Nash, 'Arab Voices in Western Writing: The Politics of the Arab Novel in English and the Anglophone Arab Novel', *Commonwealth Essays and Studies* 39, no. 2 (2017): 10.

11. Schlote, 'An Interview with Hanan al-Shaykh'.

12. A. L. Tibawi, 'History of the London Central Mosque and the Islamic Cultural Centre 1910–1980', *Die Welt Des Islams* 21, no. 1 (1981): 193–208.

13. Robin Yassin-Kassab, *The Road from Damascus* (London: Penguin, 2008), 329.

14. Leila Abo.leila, *Minaret* (London: Bloomsbury, 2005), 1.

CHAPTER 26
THE GRAND PRINCE OF KYIV IN HOLLAND PARK: THE STATUE OF SAINT VOLODYMYR
Sasha Dovzhyk

In one of the smartest areas of West London, where Holland Park Avenue, lined with Victorian terraces and elegant plane trees, meets Holland Park, stands the bronze statue of a man in antiquated attire, with an impressive moustache, a cross in one hand, a shield in the other. As a stern bishop towering above pleasure-seeking laity, he appears ready to act as the Lord's emissary on earth. You would not know he was a Viking. The very Viking, in fact, who brought the Viking Age to an end in late-tenth-century Kyivan Rus, converted the Slavs to Christianity in 988 and built an enduring state from Kyiv that lasted until the Mongol invasion in the thirteenth century. Erected in London in 1988, the monument commemorates the millennial anniversary of the 'Christianisation of Ukraine-Rus' by Saint Volodymyr, or Prince Volodymyr the Great.

Figure 26.1 Leo Mol, 'Statue of Saint Volodymyr' (1988). Photograph courtesy of Sasha Dovzhyk.

One of the most important documents of Slav history, a manuscript known as the *Chronicle of Nestor* or *The Tale of Bygone Years*, presents the baptism of the pagan Rus land as a consequence of Volodymyr's 'picking and choosing' between Islam, Judaism and Roman as well as Byzantine styles of Christianity. Volodymyr's eventual choice of the religion of Constantinople, as the historian Serhii Plokhy clarifies, brought with it the bonus of marrying into an imperial family, 'which promptly elevated the status of his house and realm'.[1] The legendary Kyivan chronicler, however, would have us believe that the choice was primarily an aesthetic one:

> Then we went to the Greeks, and they led us to [the place where] they serve their God. And we knew not whether we were in heaven or on earth. For on earth there is no such splendour or beauty, and we are unable to describe it. We only know that God dwells there among men, and that their service is better than [those] of all other lands. For we cannot forget that beauty.[2]

One cannot help but wish that Leo Mol, the Canadian sculptor of Ukrainian origin and author of the Holland Park monument, had drawn inspiration for his statue from the Kyiv chronicler's beauty-struck, albeit imaginary, account. Instead of Byzantian splendour, Mol's monument bears traces of the stifling 'realist' style which prevailed in the Soviet Union, where the sculptor studied in the late 1930s. We can also detect traces of the dominant official art style of Nazi Germany to which he fled at the start of Second World War, before eventually emigrating to Canada in 1949.[3] Commissioned by the so called 'old' Ukrainian diaspora, 'the community of post-World War Two immigrants and their descendants', the monument's stylistic orientation is towards respectability and tradition.[4]

However, the artistic characteristics of Saint Volodymyr's statue can hardly explain the fact that online tourist reviews of the site range from 'interesting religious and military sculpture' to statements like 'fake history'. What is at stake here is the symbolic significance of Prince Volodymyr as a historical and mythical figure to modern Ukraine and Russia, two Eastern European nations that, alongside Belarus, trace their origins to the Kyivan Rus. Sadly, the polarity of this monument's online reviews reflects the context of the ongoing war that Russia launched against Ukraine in 2014, supporting the onslaught of its troops with revised historical narratives as part of hybrid warfare.

The contested status of Volodymyr and his realm is epitomized by the fact that an 18-metre-tall monument to the Prince of Kyiv was built in the centre of Moscow in 2015. The Prince's namesake, Russian President Vladimir Putin, was present at the opening ceremony where he spoke about the medieval ruler as 'a gatherer and protector of the Russian lands'. The Russian annexation of Crimea merely a year earlier constitutes only the most recent attempt to 'gather' the lands to the west of Moscow into an entity evoking the medieval state of Kyivan Rus.

As Plokhy shows in *Lost Kingdom*, Russian rulers were preoccupied with 'the claim for the Kyivan inheritance' since the second half of the fifteenth century, when an independent Russian state began to take shape. The first one among these rulers was Ivan III of

Muscovy, the polity that formed in the fourteenth century in the north-east of the territories ruled by the Golden Horde. Almost five centuries after Volodymyr, having opposed the suzerainty of the Mongol khans, Ivan III sought to extend his power to other principalities of Mongol Rus. When attempting to subordinate the powerful city-republic of Novgorod, Muscovite envoys referred to the Kyivan inheritance in their address: 'From antiquity, you [...] have been my patrimony, from our grandfathers and our ancestors, from Grand Prince Volodymyr [...] who baptized the Rus' land.' The assertion of the Kyivan root of his princely line became ideologically indispensable for the separation of Muscovy from the Mongol heritage and its reframing as a successor to Byzantium.[5]

The idea of 'gathering Rus lands' persisted in Moscow's imperialist discourse throughout the early modern and modern eras. Yet Russian rule over the western territories of the former medieval state, that is, the western regions of modern Ukraine, lasted for only forty-six years between the end of the Second World War and the collapse of the Soviet Union. Perceived as the 'mother of all Russian cities', independent Kyiv presented a challenge for the founding myth of the contemporary Russian state. Russian statesmen addressed the issue in 2014 by annexing Crimea, the alleged site of Prince Volodymyr's baptism, and then by invading Ukraine in an attempt to expand what the Kremlin's propagandists dub the 'Russian World'.[6] Echoes of this neo-imperialist campaign resonate in online reviews of Leo Mol's Holland Park bronze.

Today, the monument to Saint Volodymyr is a crucial meeting point for the Ukrainian community in London. There are no official statistics regarding the number of Ukrainians in the United Kingdom, and the estimates provided by the community organizations' leaders vary between 30,000 and 100,000 people. Ukrainians as well as diaspora organizations are mostly concentrated in London.[7] For discerning eyes, the map of the area surrounding the statue of Saint Volodymyr is peppered with designated Ukrainian spaces which include the embassy, the Association of Ukrainians in Great Britain, the Ukrainian Institute London, a cultural club, and a community Saturday school. The nearly 3-metre-high monument provides a fitting background for official photo shoots, processions of richly attired priests, and political demonstrations. On quieter days, one can spot wreaths for the victims of the current war being placed at the granite pedestal by local Ukrainians.

*　*　*

A year after this piece was written, on 12 July 2021, Vladimir Putin authored an essay entitled 'On the Historical Unity of Russians and Ukrainians'. Its 'essential idea', as Timothy Snyder explains, is 'that Russia has the right to Ukraine because of things that happened a thousand years ago in Kyiv'.[8] According to Putin, the affinity of Russians and Ukrainians is determined by the shared heritage of the Kyivan Rus and by Saint Volodymyr's mythical choice of Christian faith. This myth has served as an ideological basis for Russia's full-scale invasion of Ukraine on 24 February 2022. At the time of writing, Ukrainians have been disputing this weaponized vision of history with arms for nearly eight months of the all-out war and for more than eight years of Russia's undeclared military aggression.

Notes

1. Serhii Plokhy, *The Gates of Europe: A History of Ukraine* (London: Allen Lane, 2016), 34.

2. Sean Griffin, *The Liturgical Past in Byzantium and Early Rus* (Cambridge: Cambridge University Press, 2019), 139.

3. D. V. Stepovyk, 'Molodozhanyn Leonid Grygorovych', in *Entsyklopediia istorii Ukrainy*, ed. V. A. Smolii (Kyiv: Naukova dumka, 2010), http://www.history.org.ua/?termin=Molodozhanyn_L.

4. Iryna Lapshyna, 'Do Diasporas Matter? The Growing Role of the Ukrainian Diaspora in the UK and Poland in the Development of the Homeland in Times of War', *Central and Eastern European Migration Review* 8, no. 1 (2019): 53.

5. Serhii Plokhy, *Lost Kingdom: A History of Russian Nationalism from Ivan the Great to Vladimir Putin* (London: Allen Lane, 2017).

6. Plokhy, *The Gates of Europe*, 350.

7. Lapshyna, 'Do Diasporas Matter?', 56.

8. Timothy Snyder, 'Putin's Case for Invading Ukraine Rests on Phony Grievances and Ancient Myths', *Washington Post*, 28 January 2022.

CHAPTER 27
'IS REAL MAS OUTSIDE': COMMUNITY, RESISTANCE AND NOTTING HILL CARNIVAL
Leighan Renaud

The summer of 2020 saw something unprecedented happen. In light of the Covid-19 pandemic, and the understanding that large gatherings were simply unsafe, Caribbean carnivals worldwide were cancelled. From Grenada to St Lucia, Rotterdam to Notting Hill, revellers and masqueraders dealt with their disappointment at the cancelled celebrations. But the year 2020 was unprecedented for other reasons. In light of the murder of George Floyd in Minnesota, people around the world became increasingly aware of the fact that, whilst Covid-19 was killing people of colour at disproportionate rates, institutionalized and systemic racism was still a bigger threat to Black lives.

In May 2020, Instagram user ras_714 posted a picture of a Minnesota protester dressed in black and holding a pig's head. The caption to this post read:

> Jab Jab inna Minnesota. I said it earlier this month, Republican rituals keep in the month of May. More Fire. More Oil in the Lamp. Burn baby burn. A rastaman once said 'now that the fire is out of control,
> Panic in the city, wicked weeping for their gold!'
> Everywhere this fiyah burning,
> Destroying and melting their gold,
> Destroying and waisting [sic] their souls.
> #RideNattyRide #JudgementTime #JabJab who said no carnival this year. Is real Mas outside here (ras_714, May 28, 2020)[1]

The black clothes and pig's head detailed in the photo are reminiscent of Grenada's 'Jab Jab' carnival tradition, wherein masqueraders paint themselves in black oil or paint and take to the road. David Lawrence explains that the word Jab 'was derived from the French word "Diable" meaning "devil", so a masquerader playing Jab Jab is playing the devil. Jab is a satirical representation of the evil inflicted by the white colonialist on the slaves.' As well as painting their skin, Jab Jab masqueraders are 'outfitted with goat horns, thick chains, and other artifacts to tell the story of the day'.[2] One of the most commonly used artefacts is the pig, in part because of long-standing folk traditions in Grenada.

The Jab Jab tradition is one that can be traced back to slavery. Its subversion of the word 'devil', given the racist ideologies that contributed to the justification for the enslavement of African people, suggests that the tradition is one rooted in resistance. Jab Jab masqueraders can be found across the world, including at Notting Hill Carnival. Contemporary engagement with this tradition serves as a reminder that all Caribbean

Figure 27.1 Sherween Gonzales, 'The Lajabless and the King Jab' (2021). © Sherween Gonzales Photographs.

carnivals are about celebration as much as they are about subversion and protest. ras_714's comment that through the Minnesota protests we were witnessing 'real mas' pays testament to the resistant spirit of carnival.

The first carnival in Notting Hill was held in 1966, although the first London Carnival celebration occurred some seven years earlier and was held as a direct response to building racial tensions following the mass migration of Caribbean immigrants to London and the ensuing Notting Hill race riots of 1958. Claudia Jones, a Trinidadian-born activist, journalist and founder of the *West Indian Gazette*, was leader of the committee responsible for organizing the first London Carnival. Held in St Pancras Town Hall on 30 January 1959, this first iteration of carnival included 'costume displays, the song and dance performances and the jump-up'.[3] This annual indoor celebration, held in 'a spirit of defiance against the kinds of division that had marked the riots in the Summer of 1958', continued to take place until Jones' death in 1964.[4] It wasn't until 1966 that Notting Hill Carnival began.

Despite Jones' indoor carnival being a community-run affair, for the first years of Notting Hill Carnival, there were a number of white English Notting Hill residents on the organizational team. Everton A. Pryce argues that, during these years, the carnival was little more than 'a caricature of Carnival in Trinidad, reflecting the organizers' perceptions of black culture in Britain, as that of a passive, fun-loving people'.[5] Such perceptions of Black British culture are reductive, and the suggestion that Black people in Britain were passive was particularly troubling, especially given the spirit of defiance in which the St Pancras Carnival celebrations were held. It did not take long for Black Londoners to demand a more active role in the organization of Notting Hill Carnival, and by the mid-1970s, the tone of the carnival had changed quite significantly. Pryce's article discusses the ways in which Britain's emerging 'Black Power' movement during the 1960s and 1970s helped to encourage young Black Britons to take more pride in their cultural and racial heritage. At the time of increased racial tension when, as John Solomos, Bob Findlay, Simon Jones and Paul Gilroy explain, 'there [had] been a consistent attempt to pin down the dangers posed by specific groups of the black population', the act of being hyper-visible and celebratory through participation in Notting Hill Carnival can be theorized as an act of resistance against racial hostility.[6]

The social and cultural context of the twenty-first century is, undoubtedly, very different to that of the 1960s and 1970s, and there have been several changes to the way that Notting Hill has been run since that time. Gavin Carver argues, 'Since 1976, the organizing body of the carnival has become increasingly and perhaps necessarily concerned with enterprise and cultural appeasement, but this has been achieved in the face of some opposition that has denounced the carnival for selling out West Indian heritage and identity.'[7] The official Notting Hill Carnival website describes the event as 'one of the globe's largest annual arts events' and the 'largest street event in Europe'.[8] Whilst the website does describe the carnival as being rooted in Caribbean culture, the tone and vagueness of its official marketing and the large numbers of attendees from a range of demographics suggest that Notting Hill Carnival is not solely a celebration of Caribbean culture. Rather, it is a multicultural affair, inclusive of all who wish to partake and emblematic of the hybrid city in which it is held. Because of this, Notting Hill Carnival can be thought of as a space of both community and resistance for multiple minoritized communities in Britain.

An integral part of the Notting Hill Carnival celebrations are the masquerade – or mas – bands and the road procession. Mas bands consist of a group of carnival attendees who wear the same or similar costumes, and march in the procession together, usually behind a big truck complete with large speakers. Mas bands have long been a staple of carnivals in the Caribbean. Ann Marie Simmonds writes that in Trinidad, historically, 'Carnival was a symbol of resistance, a means of giving voice to societal dissatisfaction, a way of masking/hiding and being invisible, yet completely visible'.[9] The act of masking, or masquerade, can be traced in Trinidad to the late eighteenth century, when white settlers would hold elaborate pre-Lenten masquerade balls. Enslaved people, unable to participate in these affairs, would observe the festivities and hold secret celebrations which included dancing, costumes, music and mockery.

Raedene Copeland and Nancy Hodges posit that post-emancipation Trinidad saw radical changes to the masquerade tradition, and that the costumes worn by formerly enslaved people 'were primarily designed to represent characters or communicate themes based on folklore and significant socio-political, economic and historical events'.[10] 'Pretty mas' – beautiful costumes often decorated with feathers, beads and gemstones – is now the most popular style at Caribbean carnivals across the world, but traditional masqueraders can still be found. Though the style is out of vogue, people like stylist Melissa Simon-Hartman and artist and community historian Fiona Compton can be found at Notting Hill Carnival in costumes directly inspired by Caribbean folklore. In addition, the J'ouvert tradition – the celebration that takes place before sunbreak on Carnival Sunday – offers an alternative to Pretty mas as it sees revellers partaking in 'Dirty mas', where steel pans offer the soundtrack as paints and powders are thrown on the crowds. Despite the changes in masking, it is still a practice that has been and continues to be subversive and political, both in Trinidad and Notting Hill. As well as acting as a reminder of the Caribbean roots of Notting Hill Carnival, masquerade provides, as Adela Ruth Tompsett articulates, 'the means for self-affirmation and personal expression'.[11] The ability to take the road as a masquerader, to be both seen and unseen, visible and invisible, can be regarded as an act of cultural and racial pride for people of Caribbean heritage.

Though Notting Hill Carnival takes place across two days of the August Bank Holiday weekend, it is a year-round affair, and the creation of costumes is a central component of the work that bands complete before the festivities. It is also a way in which carnival culture fosters both creativity and community. Typically, mas bands hold public launches for the year's costumes at least six months before carnival weekend, and costumes get created in what are called 'mas camps'. Numerous members of a band will come together to help with the creation of costumes, which can be a very labour-intensive process. In an interview given to the *Guardian*, costume designer Allyson Williams explains, '[if] you went to a mas camp you ended up working! Someone always put something in your hand that you had to do.'[12] But the function of mas camps is more than just costume creation. Mas camp is a community space; it is one where people can come and learn about the history of the band, laugh, eat, share ideas and share memories. It encourages a real sense of community and fosters an understanding that carnival is more than a weekend affair. Carnival can be family, it can be legacy, and it can be a greater appreciation for a culture that has so often been misunderstood and misappropriated within the UK.

Visibility can, in itself, be a form of protest, and I argue that, for minoritized communities, taking to the streets of Notting Hill in masquerade dress is an act of resistance. Prior to the Second World War, Notting Hill was an affluent area, but the Blitz saw a large number of town houses destroyed and subsequently rebuilt as houses for multiple occupancy (HMOs). Following the 1948 Nationality Act, which gave Commonwealth citizens the legal right to live and work in the UK, a high number of Afro-Caribbean immigrants settled in the Notting Hill area, largely because of the availability of cheap housing. Caryl Phillips describes how landlords like the infamous and controversial Peter Rachman 'would purchase once grand but now shabby townhouses and turn a fast profit by subdividing them into multiple units that he'd rent out as "furnished" dwellings to those who found it otherwise difficult to obtain affordable lodging in London'.[13] From the 1990s, Notting Hill began to regain popularity with the middle class, and a wave of gentrification saw the displacement of a community that had called the area home since the mid-twentieth century.

In her 2009 novel *The Wonder*, Diana Evans reflects on the changing face of the area:

> If there was a place in London in 1962 that was in need of this kind of social enterprise, Ladbroke Grove was one such place. Outside Oscar's walls were slum digs, rubbish heaps, frontiers [...] This was not the kind of place you would come to buy a psychedelic toaster or a leather watering can. This is not where you would stop for aubergine tea [...] Rats and mice stalked the streets, feasting amid the demolition scrap piles left by cranes in '58, when large patches of the grove had been bulldozed to make way for boxy council housing, creating apocalyptic scenes that, to any local, to Toreth walking by with her shopping for instance, were not unlike those seen during the Second World War.[14]

The narrator's description of Notting Hill highlights the massive changes to the area, both in terms of architecture and demographics, across three generations of one family. And in this passage, the narrator highlights the ways in which a single place can have multiple histories, and be remembered differently by different people and generations. The references to psychedelic toasters and leather watering cans, as signifiers of Notting Hill's gentrified present, are particularly cutting and give a sense that the processes of gentrification have contributed to a loss of authenticity in the area. Against this backdrop, with its multiple histories, Notting Hill Carnival takes place. Across London, gentrification has negatively affected hosts of minoritized communities, and that carnival provides an opportunity to celebrate culture in the very area that has undergone gentrification is significant and quite a powerful demonstration of cultural and community resilience.

In June 2017, Grenfell Tower, a twenty-four-storey block of residential flats in North Kensington, London, caught fire, killing seventy-two people and displacing the surviving occupants, the majority of whom were ethnic minority, working-class Londoners. The tragedy was felt keenly by the London community, not least because of the difficulty in holding anybody accountable for the events. Due to its proximity to Latimer Road and Ladbroke Grove, Grenfell Tower can be seen from Notting Hill Carnival's procession route. Since August 2018, in collaboration with the Grenfell United Organisation, Notting Hill Carnival has observed a seventy-two-second silence on both days at 3 pm in remembrance of the lives lost during the fire. The carnival website explains, 'we took our lead from local organisation Grenfell United, who expressed that the local community and all those affected by the Grenfell Tower fire would appreciate our support in creating "brief moments of reflection and respect in the midst of the two days of revelry"'.[15] Despite its status as a festival and an opportunity to celebrate, Notting Hill Carnival remains, at its core, an organization that is committed to supporting and uplifting local communities. The commitment to offer moments of silence, remembrance and reflection (which was also honoured during 2020's online carnival celebration) is a reminder of the spirit of carnival that persists, despite the way in which the celebration has evolved.

Despite the changing social context from carnival's genesis in the 1960s to the present day, Black Britain is still victim to various institutional threats and attacks. Only in the last few years we have witnessed the 'Windrush Scandal' unfold, which revealed that hundreds of Commonwealth citizens were detained and/or deported unlawfully, thus highlighting the problems with the Home Office and Britain's hostile immigration environment. In March 2021, the *Commission on Race and Ethnic Disparities: The Report* was released. Shockingly, the report concluded that Britain was no longer institutionally racist. Part of the report focused on educational resources, and said of Britain's involvement in transatlantic slavery: 'There is a new story about the Caribbean experience which speaks to the slave period not only being about profit and suffering but how culturally African people transformed themselves into a re-modelled African/Britain.'[16] The rebranding of slavery as an 'experience' that was not solely horrific is violent in that it seeks to rewrite a part of British history that, whilst horrific, is integral to understanding the UK as well as the Caribbean. Given all of this, the ability to take to the streets of London for two days a year, in celebration of yourself, your history and your culture, is a defiant act, and one of the many beautiful elements of Notting Hill Carnival.

Adela Ruth Tompsett argues that the 'claiming of public space is at the heart of NHC [...] Carnival performance says "I am here".'[17] Notting Hill Carnival, across its almost sixty-year history, has changed immeasurably. Though there have been concerns about its commercialization, the organizing body maintains that part of their mission is to 'Honour, Protect and Promote the heritage of Carnival.'[18] The carnival offers its participants an opportunity to reconnect with both self, history and community. London has always been an important site for Black British culture, and Notting Hill Carnival has long been a space to demonstrate resistance, visibility and pride. The carnival continues to be a celebration of local communities. Their response to tragedies like Grenfell and Covid-19 suggest that protest and social justice remain at the heart of the organization. And perhaps, most importantly, the ability to unapologetically claim space as a Black person, despite Britain's history of hostility towards marginalized communities, is a revolutionary act and one of the most powerful forms of protest.

Notes

1. ras_714 (@ras_714), 'Jab Jab inna Minnesota', Instagram, 28 May 2020.
2. David Lawrence, 'The Ascendance of Jab', *Caribbean Entertainment Hub*, https://caribbeanentertainmenthub.com/the-ascendance-of-jab.
3. Colin Prescod, 'Carnival', in *Claudia Jones: A Life in Exile*, ed. Marika Sherwood (London: Lawrence and Wishart, 1999), 158.
4. Ibid., 150.
5. Everton A. Pryce, 'The Notting Hill Gate Carnival – Black Politics, Resistance and Leadership 1976–1978', *Caribbean Quarterly* 31, no. 2 (1985): 35.
6. John Solomos, Bob Findlay, Simon Jones and Paul Gilroy, 'The Organic Crisis of British Capitalism and Race: The Experience of the Seventies', in *The Empire Strikes Back: Race and Racism in 1970s Britain* (Birmingham: Hutchinson & Co., 1982), 27.

7. Gavin Carver, 'The Effervescent Carnival: Performance, Context and Mediation at Notting Hill Carnival', *New Theatre Quarterly* 16, no. 1 (2000): 36.

8. 'Today's Notting Hill Carnival', *Notting Hill Carnival*, https://nhcarnival.org/nhcs-story.

9. Ann Marie Simmonds, 'The Complexities of Carnival Identities in Earl Lovelace's *The Dragon Can't Dance*', *Cankaya University Journal of Humanities and Social Sciences* 13, no. 1 (2019): 48.

10. Raedene Copeland and Nancy Hodges, 'Exploring Masquerade Dress at Trinidad Carnival: Bikinis, Beads and Feathers and the Emergence of the Popular Pretty Mas', *Clothing and Textiles Research Journal* 32, no. 3 (April 2014): 187.

11. Adela Ruth Tompsett, 'London is the Place for Me: Performance and Identity in Notting Hill Carnival', *Theatre History Studies* 25 (2005): 46.

12. Sirin Kale, '"I'm all feathered out": Why Mas is the Heart of Notting Hill Carnival', *Guardian*, 21 August 2019, https://www.theguardian.com/culture/costume-and-culture/2019/aug/21/mas-fashion-costume-makers-notting-hill-carnival.

13. Caryl Phillips, 'The Real Meaning of "Rachmanism"', *New York Review*, 23 December 2019, https://www.nybooks.com/daily/2019/12/23/the-real-meaning-of-rachmanism/?lp_txn_id=1266818.

14. Diana Evans, *The Wonder* (London: Vintage Books, 2009), 49.

15. 'Grenfell', *Notting Hill Carnival*, https://nhcarnival.org/grenfell.

16. 'The Report of the Commission on Race and Ethnic Disparities', https://www.gov.uk/government/publications/the-report-of-the-commission-on-race-and-ethnic-disparities.

17. Tompsett, 'London is the Place for Me', 46.

18. 'Our Mission', *Notting Hill Carnival,* https://nhcarnival.org/our-mission.

CHAPTER 28

'WHERE THE CITY DISSOLVES': SUBURBAN DIASPORAS, PSYCHOSIS AND REPARATIVE WRITING

Martin Dines

London's suburban development comprises a story – or, rather, a complex of stories – about infrastructure, mobility and migration. Those who have settled London's ever-advancing suburban frontier hail from everywhere: cramped city neighbourhoods, the English countryside and myriad other places across the globe. And, whether they are navigating the metropolis on a daily basis or negotiating newly emergent formations of culture and class, these suburbanites are always on the move. Because of their intersecting complexity, their expansiveness and their being in process, London's suburbs have presented writers with a challenge. To be sure, these places suffer from a certain inscrutability. Epitomizing the confounding confrontation between writer and suburb is a scene from Tim Lott's 1996 memoir *The Scent of Dried Roses*, in which the author revisits the place where he was raised, Southall. Lott dwells on the suburb's incoherence: it appears 'pastoral, urban, modern, postmodern, Victorian, an undifferentiated mess'; he is left wondering about what is made in a factory that 'pumps and boils anonymously', about the meanings of nearby signs and the identities of surrounding flora. Illegibility is its defining quality and yet what is remarkable to Lott is how Southall nevertheless sustains 'the art of the necessary', that is, everyday life.[1]

Lott's bewilderment is nothing new. Indeed, the suburb as an environment that fails to come fully into focus and which evades complete understanding – despite its apparent ordinariness – was an already-established trope in fiction and criticism by the end of the nineteenth century. For Lynne Hapgood, much late Victorian and Edwardian fiction was defined by its grappling with 'the enigma of a new kind of landscape which seemed single-mindedly intent on evading definition'.[2] This confrontation with barely comprehensible social and environmental transformations nevertheless precipitated narrative innovation. A new suburban geography was realized in fiction through a melding of the familiar genres of realism, utopianism and romance; this tendency to play with literary conventions and to work across generic boundaries helps explain why the emergent suburban mode of fiction was perceived to be casual and light-hearted.[3] Ged Pope insists that the suburb as a 'problematic object of knowledge' endures as a salient theme in British fiction; from Charles Dickens to Zadie Smith, suburban settings have foregrounded 'anxious epistemic dilemmas concerning what we can know of neighbours, visitors and strangers, about others' class, social status and origins [and, more recently,] around race and ethnicity'.[4] I contend that if contemporary writing about London's suburbs trades in 'epistemic dilemmas', these are as likely to be focused inwards as they are directed towards others. Indeed, this material is perhaps more preoccupied with questions of how suburbanity might define social identities and shared experiences. Where this experience is characterized by loss, violence and psychosis, this literature, predictably enough, resists the comic impulses of established modes that are evident in novels such as Hanif Kureishi's *The Buddha of Surburbia* (1990), which Ruvani Ranasinha discusses in this volume. And if such comedy is in large part a product of a traversing of generic boundaries, the seriousness of recent material stems from a refusal to engage with certain narrative modes, or a preparedness to undermine them. London's suburbs may have always been defined by migration and settlement; their literature, however, remains unsettled by its search for suitable forms and devices.

This chapter attends to two, formally very different if similarly serious, recent literary engagements with the suburb of Southall, once a municipal borough located in the former county of Middlesex and, since 1965, part of the outer London borough of Ealing. In *The Scent of Dried Roses*, Tim Lott identifies the suburb in which he grew up as being a product of 'the internal combustion engine and the arterial road' and defined by the cultural values and habits of a newly relocated white upper-working class. The secure sense of identity and purpose of his parents' and grandparents' generations has, however, since fallen away; Lott's own cultural formation is characterized by uncertainty and displacement, and 'with lives increasingly out of focus'.[5] To properly delineate both mid- and late twentieth-century Southall, Lott devises a narrative that simultaneously privileges clarity and ambiguity; *The Scent of Dried Roses* is a memoir that identifies the importance of telling believable, singular stories about people and places, but which also repeatedly undercuts its own truth claims. By contrast, in her experimental *Ban en Banlieue*, published in 2016, Bhanu Kapil largely repudiates autobiographical narrative. Nevertheless, like Lott she continually returns to Southall, the 'immigrant suburb' close to where she grew up in the 1970s; she focuses in particular on the self-sacrificing actions of 'a brown (black) girl' who lays herself down in the moments before a race riot.[6] Kapil's text asks what might come from 'reimagin[ing] the boundary' and becoming 'en banlieue, a part of the perimeter'. To study the place 'where the city dissolves' involves attending to hybrid, even monstrous, forms, and necessitates the delivery of text that is frangible. *Ban en Banlieue*'s peculiar form – 'notes for a novel never written' – is in part a response to the persistence of sexist and racist violence, both the most brutal kinds and those which are part of the background of everyday life, which shape lives yet render them inconceivable.[7] Neither Lott nor Kapil, then, try to make sense out of the senseless, to find meaning in the inexplicable; rather, they seek to develop modes of writing that are consonant with the determining conditions of suburbanity, with forces and elements that do not cohere but which nevertheless define ways of being. This willingness to attend to historical and material processes coupled with a refusal to offer either systematic analysis or definitive (auto)biographical narrative provides, I suggest, the basis for a reparative mode of writing, one which assembles resources for engaging with the causes and effects of social and mental breakdown.[8]

If Kapil's designation of Southall as an 'immigrant suburb' jars, it is because the term is – purposefully – exonymic: *Ban en Banlieue* was written while its author was living and working in the US and, as its title suggests, Kapil's articulation of suburbanity is informed by geographies external to the UK. These adventitious frames and perspectives are appropriate, however, given that Southall has been entirely transformed by international migration. Significant settlement from overseas began in the 1950s, with Indian men – mainly from the Punjab region – attracted by work available in factories owned by British industrialists, some with military and colonial ties to the Indian subcontinent. Continued immigration throughout the following decades, mainly from India, Pakistan and East Africa, led to Southall becoming one of largest and most important South Asian population centres in Britain. In the 1970s and 1980s, Southall's streets witnessed both racist violence and anti-racist resistance. In 1976, eighteen-year-old student Gurdip Singh Chaggar was stabbed to death by white youths; his brutal killing and the failure of the legal establishment to recognize the crime's racial motivation prompted large numbers of young Asians not only to come out into the streets in protest, but also to organize. The Southall Youth Movement, whose purpose was to defend the Asian community, was established immediately after Chaggar's murder.[9] In 1979 – on St George's Day – a provocative rally held outside Southall Town Hall by the white supremacist party the National Front led to the killing of anti-racist activist Blair Peach by a member of the Special Patrol Group, a specialist unit within the Metropolitan Police. Public protests in response to Peach's death were immediate, but responsibility was only admitted by the Met in 2010. In recent decades, Southall's demographics have changed further following the arrival of immigrants from Somalia, Afghanistan and elsewhere, and with the departure of many Indians to wealthier suburbs, though Sikhism remains the largest faith group. Notably, Southall has, according to the 2011 census, the least white population in all Britain: over 91 per cent of its residents are Black, Asian and Minority Ethnic.

In his memoir, Tim Lott gives a similarly perfunctory account of these developments. His disinterest is perhaps merely realistic: he reports that, in the 1970s, Southall's white and Asian communities were equally insular and indifferent to one another. On the other hand, for the teenaged Lott, Southall's Asian population at least gave the place 'some identity'. But not enough: he and his brothers bolted from their suburb at the first opportunity, not, Lott hastens to add, because they disliked Asians, but because 'Southall was a dump, because it was nowhere'. Manifestly, Lott's interest lies with another diaspora altogether: the white, 'respectable' working classes who made Southall their home during the interwar years. These settlers included his grandparents, hard-working men and women who came from places like Gipsy Hill and Shepherd's Bush. The relocation of thousands of families from inner and outer London neighbourhoods, where everything was 'interlinked, communal, close-weaved', to the 'new suburbs that were rising on the clay at the city's edges' did not, according to Lott, precipitate immediate, wholesale cultural change, nor was it experienced by individuals as especially disturbing. For sure, buying a house in the suburbs was understood by many inner-city Londoners to be 'the modern thing'; once relocated, moreover, they constituted 'an entirely new class':

'the suburban, home-owning working class'. Yet, patterns of life endured. Indeed, for Lott, the most important defining quality of the English upper working classes in the mid-twentieth century was precisely their certainty about how their lives would unfold. Observing a photograph of Art Lott, his paternal grandfather, Lott comments that the fact that his ancestor 'knows who he was' marks the 'first great dividing line between him and me'. Art's self-assurance stemmed from his secure sense of his position within the English class system, his masculinity and his whiteness, as well as his being both metropolitan – a Londoner – and firmly rooted in a particular neighbourhood. The family photos that Lott peruses over several chapters move him so profoundly because there is no telling in them of the impending desolation of an entire class. Technological and cultural change in the post-war years – television and automobility in particular – erodes 'collective, communal' life and yields 'a loss of place' that is so devastating Lott likens it to 'murderous, invisible fall-out'.[10] The nowhere that is subtopian England is Lott's mother country;[11] his 'tribe', he comes to understand while moving in liberal circles at university, is 'a shameful one: white, male, not "properly" working class' and therefore unclaimable.[12] He therefore cannot map his life onto a greater whole, or connect it to a legitimate, broader story.

Lott's motivation for diagnosing his class's loss of direction and crisis of confidence stems partly from his experience of severe depression in his late twenties. Much of his memoir, though, is given over to grappling with his apparently contented mother Jean's inexplicable suicide in 1986. One line in her departing note appears to offer a clue to answering Lott's father Jack's despairing question '*why, my Jeannie, why?*': 'I hate Southall, I can see only decay'. For, according to Lott, his mother loved the 'ordinary, suburban England suspended in her imagination'. Later he contemplates Durkheimian rationalizations for depression: 'A sort of collective unhinging took place as societies became more complex [...] atomized and less integrated. Suicides kill themselves because their accustomed world has been destroyed or lost and they cannot make sense of what replaces it.' However, after oscillating between physiological, psychological and sociological explanations for depression, Lott rejects singular aetiologies; cause and effect, he argues, are impossible to establish, since 'so many explanations fit the facts, so many meanings are sustainable'. His refusal – his inability – to determine the root causes of his and his mother's malaise is fitting; the defining characteristic of his class, of subtopian England, is, after all, uncertainty. Indeed, suburbanity itself becomes a fitting metaphor for this state of being: 'here, in this mind-suburb, this ribbon-built self, everything changes as you look at it'.[13]

But if he longs for his 'father's ballast', his parents' sense of their lives fitting into a larger, 'common story', Lott knows that these narratives are lies, albeit helpful – because comprehensible – ones. The narrative-making in *The Scent of Dried Roses* is thus driven by a twofold moral impulse. On the one hand, Lott feels duty-bound to articulate his parents' 'quiet certainty', their keen sense of the shape of their own lives, through the careful crafting and arranging of 'true' vignettes that he nonetheless recognizes read like works of fiction. On the other hand, the memoir's privileging of uncertainty avoids 'fix[ing] in place what is unfixable, what is always moving, twisting and changing as we watch, finally uncomprehending'; Lott notes some of history's grossest atrocities have been facilitated by a holding fast to a story and a refusal of 'the awesome responsibility that accepting uncertainty and insignificance entails'. Lott practices what he preaches. Several of the memoir's chapters begin with statements that unpick previous assertions or which express doubt about his narrative's sustainability; elsewhere he belittles his own attempts to theorize cultural change as lazy intellectualizations, as 'the reflex distancing of a full-grown parvenu'. Yet his conclusions following a *dérive* through Southall – 'Jean's England has gone now, even as an idea, a dream. There is nothing we have thought of to put in its place. There is, in fact, no place to put it; the cohering forces themselves have collapsed' – ought to be read less as a jeremiad than as an exhortation. The 'ribbon-built selves' raised in this void must learn – and, Lott demonstrates, have learned – to engage with and narrate this absence of cohering forces in ways which are both respectful and reparative. 'In finding a solution to identity, you begin to find a solution to depression,' Lott declares at the end of his memoir.[14] *The Scent of Dried Roses* suggests that the 'solution to identity' entails giving up on the project of sustaining a coherent personal story while remaining attentive to those constructed by others; in so doing, it develops a postmodern narrative mode which might sensibly be described as 'subtopian realist'.

Whereas Lott elaborates on the formation of 'mind-suburbs', Bhanu Kapil writes of a suburban existence constituted of bitumen and dog shit. Like *The Scent of Dried Roses*, *Ban en Banlieue* focuses on suburban psychoses, but, much more than Lott's memoir, it attends to the materiality of the urban periphery. Further, for Kapil, the suburbs' blurring of boundaries is not disorientating; rather, it is an observable phenomenon with clear material consequences. In contrast to Lott's bafflement by the inscrutable factory in the 'undifferentiated mess' that is Southall, Kapil states, more evenly: 'These suburbs are, in places, leafy and industrial; the Nestle factory spools a milky, lilac effluent into the Grand Union canal that runs between Hayes and Southall.' In *Ban en Banlieue*, the discharge, circulation and dissipation of materials are key thematic and formal preoccupations. Indeed, both Kapil's protagonist – a girl called Ban who, like the book's author, grew up in the suburbs around Southall in the 1970s – and her book are composites of residual materials. Ban and the suburbs in which she is raised are merely the city's exhaust, 'a warp of smoke looping around the orbital road surrounding London'; Ban is soot, charcoal: the indistinct residue of violent processes.[15]

The deprecation of the book's protagonist and setting – neither of which ever come fully into view – is purposeful. *Ban en Banlieue* takes as its base the effects of low-level racism, the 'bad snow' that is a kind of corrosive background static and a principal contributory factor to higher rates of schizophrenia amongst immigrant populations, particularly women. This continual barrage is more damaging even than the trauma of migration, but it cannot be shaped into a narrative. Neither can it be conceived of as an event, as historic, as might, for instance, a race riot. It is not an object that stands analysis: its effects are precisely dissociative. Thus Kapil rejects storytelling; she does not 'have the kind of life that support[s ...] narrative forms'. The few autobiographical stories not excised from the book are, noticeably, typically aborted by violence. Indeed, one – which describes a close encounter with horses at the city's green, mist-shrouded periphery –

takes its concluding instance of domestic violence as the moment that Kapil herself 'became Ban', a figure who 'fails portraiture' just as she 'fails life'.[16]

In the place of stories are copious notes, the materials of the literary project that has fallen away. These fragments, Kapil contends, might be more easily dispersed, might 'circulate then ebb, just as immigrant memory is fragile, replaced by the next incoming wave of life'. They might also be more readily immolated and returned to the earth, the 'charnel ground' of the immigrant suburb with its layered lost histories. Much more than historical fiction – which Kapil complains induces a vertiginous 'weightlessness', a sense of the distance between 'unlived time' and the present – the notes promise greater proximity and fidelity to the material conditions of both immigrant experience in the past and the author's current circumstances. Indeed, Kapil acknowledges that the notes' production involves writing 'the middle of the body to its end', an 'excruciating' drawn-out process akin to disembowelment that takes place 'in the absence of social services'. These notes, then, perhaps best realize Kapil's ambition to create 'a literature that is not made of literature', to 'write a book that was like lying down'.[17]

The latter motif, which recurs throughout the book, suggests several things about Kapil's project. First, it indicates that *Ban en Banlieue* is written out of sympathy for, and memorializes the fallen bodies of, victims of sexist and racist violence. These include the anti-racist activist Blair Peach, to whom Kapil's book is dedicated, and Jyoti Singh – who became known as Nirbhaya, 'the fearless one' – the murdered twenty-three-year-old Indian woman who in 2012 was beaten, raped and disembowelled with a tire iron by her killers, five men and one boy, who left her lying in the dirt by the side of the road to Delhi Airport. Second, the repeated invocations of lying down throughout the book – most frequently realized as Ban's collapsing to the ground in the moments before a race riot in Southall – suggest not only a traumatized response to a violent event, but also a refusal to narrate it. What seems merely a consequence of psychosis might then – in part because it pre-empts the event – be understood as a defiant, albeit sacrificial, intervention. And, third, as Amy De'Ath argues, lying down signals 'a desire to be close to the world, or get to know it, both in the material sense of land and landscape – the solid earth and its historicity – and in terms of the real abstractions of global capital that emerge from and determine this physical landscape'.[18] Kapil's commitment to lying down thus serves to counter the dissociative effects of everyday racism; to be *en banlieue* promises, if not an alternative mode of analysis, then at least opportunities for engagement with material and social formations at the urban periphery.

Yet, even if her book succeeds in 'lying down', in all these senses, Kapil insists that it is still a failure. She sympathizes with any reader who manages to get through the notes, which are, out of necessity, 'stupid' and 'bland'; she further acknowledges that her project has no power to modulate the resurgence of anti-immigrant sentiment. Such pessimism is tempered, however, by the book's figurations of suburbanity. Southall and neighbouring areas are presented as banlieues because of the racial composition of their populations and because of their architectural character: 'Tower blocks dominate the place I am from. Imagine a Parisian suburb.'[19] While apposite in these ways, 'banlieue' is also – and more so than the English term 'suburb' – freighted with numerous productive associations to which Kapil closely attends. Beyond the felicitous connection between banlieue and Kapil's figure of Ban, the French term invokes expulsion: to ban is to outlaw – as in to banish or abandon – that is, to condemn someone to leave a country or city. Such exclusion is, for Kapil, a defining condition of the immigrant suburb. But her book also circles around Giorgio Agamben's discussion, in his essay 'The Ban and the Wolf', of the Roman legal institution of *homo sacer*: the man who is set apart, who is banished from society, whose laws no longer protect him, even while he remains under the protection of the gods. Kapil finds the ambivalence of *homo sacer* – a figure who is, in Agamben's words, 'at once excluded and included, removed and at the same time captured' – to be consonant with a racialized suburbanity. The connection is especially potent following the medieval association between *homo sacer* and the wolf-man, which is, according to Agamben, 'a monstrous hybrid of human and animal, divided between the forest and the city'.[20] Kapil repeatedly invokes the nearby Park Wood in Ruislip, into which she would frequently escape as a child, and which once served to contain populations of wild boar for royal hunts. Boar, wolves and other wild animals stalk Kapil's text; they sometimes threaten to devour and ravage, but they are also penned and butchered. Kapil repeatedly refers to her notes as livestock or meat; she even organizes and stores them in cages attached to a repurposed butcher's block, and learns how sentences and punctuation might serve as her 'butcher's shop'.[21] But if these figurations render Kapil's writing as appropriately monstrous, and as a brutal process – which obviously also invokes the brutalized bodies of Nirbhaya and others – being-with or becoming animal is also rendered much more positively. Kapil declares that her obsession with 'feral events' is due to their capacity to cut across public histories; like lying down, they indicate a different way of attending to suburban places and lives.[22]

Finally, in an associative chain labelled 'inversions', Kapil muses that if to ban is to sentence, then 'to abandon is [. . .] to write prose'. And from banlieue Kapil also derives 'leucine', an essential amino acid – found in most animal proteins – which contributes to the growth and repair of muscle and bone tissue and wound healing. To be *en banlieue*, therefore, need not inhibit literary production, and might even facilitate the writing of 'a book for recovery from an illness. A book that repeats a sentence until that sentence recuperates its power to attract, or touch other sentences.'[23] Despite the manifest differences between Lott's and Kapil's projects, in terms of form and focus, their writing has in common this reparative aim. These contemporary works grapple with migration and suburbanity less out of a need to make sense of it all, but rather in order to produce materials that might help make a difference to the lives that have emerged from these processes and places.

Notes

1. Tim Lott, *The Scent of Dried Roses* (London: Penguin, 1997 [1996]), 30–1.
2. Lynne Hapgood, *Margins of Desire: The Suburbs in Fiction and Culture, 1880–1925* (Manchester: Manchester University Press, 2005), 3.

3. Ibid., 6.

4. Ged Pope, *Reading London's Suburbs: From Charles Dickens to Zadie Smith* (Basingstoke: Palgrave Macmillan, 2015), 5.

5. Lott, *The Scent of Dried Roses*, 128.

6. Bhanu Kapil, *Ban en Banlieue* (New York: Nightboat, 2015), 14, 20. The parentheses are Kapil's and designate political blackness; as she subsequently explains, she grew up in 'an era when, in solidarity, Caribbean and Asian Brits self-defined as black'. Ibid., 30.

7. Ibid., 41, 44.

8. My use of the term reparative writing draws on Eve Kosofsky Sedgwick's distinction between paranoid and reparative reading practices. Whereas the former – which has come to dominate critical theory – perpetually seeks 'an unmystified view of systemic oppressions', the desire of a reparative impulse is 'additive and accretive'; 'it wants to assemble and confer plenitude on an object that will then have the resources to offer to an inchoate self'. Eve Kosofsky Sedgwick, *Touching Feeling: Affect, Pedagogy, Performativity* (Durham, NC: Duke University Press, 2003), 127, 149.

9. For a detailed account of the SYM and other Asian youth movements in Britain, see Anandi Ramamurthy, *Black Star: Britain's Asian Youth Movements* (London: Pluto, 2013).

10. Lott, *The Scent of Dried Roses*, 29, 38–43, 53–5.

11. Lott adopts the term 'subtopia' from a 1955 essay by architectural critic Ian Nairn, who excoriates post-war planning in the UK for producing uniformly banal environments. Ian Nairn, 'Outrage', *Architectural Review*, 1 June 1955.

12. Lott, *The Scent of Dried Roses*, 232.

13. Ibid., 14, 28, 73, 196, 255.

14. Ibid., 37, 122, 132, 265–9.

15. Kapil, *Ban en Banlieue*, 30–1, 50.

16. Ibid., 24, 55.

17. Ibid., 13, 19–20, 22, 32, 42, 44, 77.

18. Amy De'Ath, 'L(a)ying Down in the Banlieue', *Mute*, 21 September 2016, https://www.metamute.org/editorial/articles/laying-down-banlieue.

19. Kapil, *Ban en Banlieue*, 24, 77, 84.

20. Cited in Kapil, *Ban en Banlieue*, 12, 41.

21. Kapil, *Ban en Banlieue*, 89.

22. Ibid., 69, 89.

23. Ibid., 31, 41, 63.

INFRASTRUCTURE: TRANSPORT II

A BUS FOR EVERYONE: THE ROLE OF THE LONDON OMNIBUS IN ENABLING ACCESS TO THE CITY

Joe Kerr

On a bright morning early in December 2005, a large crowd had gathered outside a surprising location, namely Brixton bus garage, deep in South London. They generally seemed in good spirits, if a little melancholy, although there was one small group who were chanting defiantly and waving placards in evident opposition to the prevailing mood. All were clearly awaiting an imminent arrival, but exactly who or what would not have been immediately apparent to a casual observer.

I was there that morning, and the thought persisted in my mind that this jostling, expectant throng was probably not so different to the London mobs that had once turned out to cheer on the last journey of some poor unfortunate on their way to the gallows. And the comparison was merited, for this crowd was indeed there to witness the final journey of one condemned. But there any similarities ended, for as an expectant buzz and a steady press forwards signalled that the wait was over, what hove into view was not a tumbril, but an old-fashioned double-decker London bus.

For this was the last ever Routemaster bus to run in service on the streets of London, the bus that Londoners had taken to their hearts, *The Bus We Loved* as a then recently published book had christened it.[1] It was the passing of an era, not only marking the end of half a century of faithful service by this remarkable vehicle, but also signifying the demise of the bus conductor, a quintessential London figure for 175 years, but now extinct forever. But for the purposes of this chapter, it was not so much that iconic bus as the men who crewed it on that final journey who merit our attention.

For the honour of operating that last Routemaster fell to two veterans of Brixton garage, chosen specifically as the longest serving crew there: driver Winston Briscoe who had come to London from Jamaica in 1962, and his conductor Lloyd Licorish who had arrived from Barbados in 1965.[2] It is entirely possible that it wasn't simply a matter of seniority that bestowed such a singular privilege on these two, but a deliberate gesture of recognition for the inextricable link that had been forged between the pioneers of the Windrush generation and London's transport systems, especially its buses, which had provided employment for so many newly-arrived men and women.

Indeed, it's hard to think of any other institution in London that is more closely associated with the growth of the city's extraordinary diversity than its distinctive double-decker red buses. It could be argued that the story of London's buses is a microcosm of the wider narratives of migration, arrival and assimilation that are so central to the recent history of the metropolis. But this chapter proposes a more ambitious claim for the London bus, that over nearly two centuries of service it has consistently paralleled a greater history of struggle for access to the city by all of its citizens, especially those who had traditionally been restricted and excluded from the totality of urban life, whether by class, gender, race, age or disability. It argues that the humble London bus has been instrumental not only in moving the mass of its population across the city, which after all is its primary purpose, but also in enabling the movement of people to the city from elsewhere. Thus, London's bus services have played their part in the process of democratizing the city, providing a measure of equality to its many millions of users and also to the formidable ranks of its workforce. They deserve to be recognized as more than just a familiar visual symbol of London, but as fitting representatives of the higher values and ideals that have helped to shape the 'mighty heart' of the metropolis.[3]

To explore this proposition further, we need to make our own journey, travelling back to the very first bus journeys made in London, and to the extraordinary ambition and idealism that was embodied in the very idea of a bus. London owes its first buses to one man, George Shillibeer, who began operating a service on 4 July 1829, modelled on a new innovation that he'd witnessed on the streets of Paris. Crucially, he also imported the French name for this new kind of public transport, with *Omnibus* emblazoned on the side of his horse-drawn carriages – an appropriated Latin word that simply means 'for all'. The name was almost immediately adopted as the universal term for this new form of transport, and it was then contracted within a couple of years to the more familiar form of *bus*.

The ambition that buses would be a mode of transport for everyone, regardless of economic status or any other previous impediment to travel, is explicit in its very name. However, the London omnibus most certainly didn't operate for all in its early years, as the fares were at best only affordable to middle-class commuters. When horse-drawn trams appeared on the streets of London from the 1860s onwards, their lower operating costs meant cheaper fares, to the point where exclusive suburbs such as Kensington and Hampstead actively opposed trams operating there in favour of buses in order to prevent the working classes from accessing their exclusive enclaves.[4] Indeed, it has taken most of the following 200 years for the bus to literally live up to its name.

It is also worth noting that the omnibus has played a significant role in the increasing migration of people to the city, and also of the outward expansion of the metropolis. Further, the transformative effects of migration on the metropolis should not only be understood in terms of people arriving from elsewhere, but also in terms of the movement of citizens within London: invisible barriers of class and gender have always operated within the city, but equally have been progressively challenged and undermined by London's transport networks. These micro-migrations are less widely acknowledged, but have proved of fundamental importance in shaping the modern demographics of London.

A case in point is the role that buses played in opening up the city to women. Perhaps surprisingly, women made use of buses from the very earliest years, as an early guide to omnibus etiquette published by *The Times*, suggests: 'Behave respectfully to females, and put not an unprotected lass to the blush because she cannot escape from your brutality.'[5]

Victorian art and literature show that both working-class and middle-class women were regular users of the omnibus, although modesty dictated that they sat crammed

Figure 29.1 Sidney Starr, *The City Atlas* (*c*. 1888–9). Gift of the Massey Collection of English Painting, 1946. National Gallery of Canada, Ottawa. Photo: NGC.

inside on the new 'knife-board' double-decker buses that appeared from mid-century, and were potentially subject to harassment from male passengers.[6] However, when garden seat buses and spiral access stairs were introduced in the 1880s, it became socially acceptable for women to climb up to the top deck.[7] Sidney Starr's 1888 painting *The City Atlas* shows a well-dressed young woman seated confidently alone on the front seat, and perched high above the surrounding city, suggestive of a new-found freedom for a modern woman to navigate the city (see Figure 29.1). This idea is most famously explored by Virginia Woolf in her 1925 novel *Mrs Dalloway*, when Elizabeth travels unaccompanied by bus through London, behaving in a manner that clearly defies the conventional codes of behaviour for a privileged young woman:

> Buses swooped, settled, were off – garish caravans, glistening with red and yellow varnish. But which should she get on to? She had no preferences [...] Suddenly Elizabeth stepped forward and most competently boarded the omnibus, in front of everybody. She took a seat on top. The impetuous creature – a pirate – started forward, sprang away; she had to hold on the rail to steady herself, for a pirate it was, reckless, unscrupulous, bearing down ruthlessly, circumventing dangerously,

boldly snatching a passenger, or ignoring a passenger, squeezing eel-like and arrogant in between, and then rushing insolently all sails spread up Whitehall [...] The fresh air was so delicious.[8]

But whatever freedoms the omnibus might offer to upper-class women as passengers, the truly liberating experience fell to working-class women during the First World War, as they were enlisted to work on the buses. By 1915, opportunities were opening for women to work in a range of public transport roles, but it was as bus conductors, or 'hurry along girls' as they became known, that women were able to experience an unprecedented degree of freedom and power, symbolized by the newly-designed uniforms they were issued: as Emmanuelle Dirix argues, 'its most appealing aspect resided with the authority and visibility this official uniform afforded women for the first time in their lives and the manner in which it commanded respect from civilians'.[9] Thus, despite the rather lurid, sexualized images of these young women that appeared on contemporary postcards, they enjoyed freedoms previously denied them in their positions as domestic servants or clerical workers, and carried real authority on the streets of London.

Unfortunately, those new freedoms were removed as suddenly as they had first appeared once war was ended, with the active connivance of the male-dominated trade unions, although not before women transport workers had mounted the first ever successful strike for equal pay. A generation later, women were once again required to serve during the Second World War, and as far as politicians and unions were concerned, they would once again be dismissed when that conflict ended. But in the event, post-war labour shortages dictated that women remained in employment as bus conductors, or 'clippies' as they were now known.[10] There was, however, one last battle for gender equality, and it took another generation before Jill Viner became the first female bus driver in London in 1974.

Thus, over a century and a half of the London omnibus, women had firstly colonized the lower deck, then the upper deck, followed by the rear platform, and finally the driver's cab, becoming both users and providers of the bus service on an absolute par with men. But equally they had used the bus to migrate from the home to the public realm, from the suburbs to the city centre, and they had crossed what Victorians had dubbed 'the great divide' between East and West. The role that the bus has played in gaining women what Henri Lefebvre described as the 'Right to the City', and all that entails, deserves greater recognition than it has generally received.

It was those same post-war labour shortages that had dictated the retention of female staff on the buses, which also lay behind the most familiar and significant narrative of migration associated with the omnibus, namely the role that it played in enabling mass migration to London from the Commonwealth, particularly from the Caribbean. But this particular narrative of migration has a surprisingly early antecedent, one that deserves to be better known. For, nearly half a century prior to the active recruitment of bus staff from the West Indies, Jamaican-born Joe Clough became London's – and probably Britain's – first Black bus driver when he joined the London General Omnibus Company in 1910. Having followed his employer to London from Jamaica, he learned to drive cars as his chauffeur, before becoming one of the first generation to train as a motor

Figure 29.2 'Joseph Clough in front of a London General Omnibus Company Bus' (1908). © TfL from the London Transport Museum collection.

bus driver; a photograph survives of him in charge of a B-Type, London's first purpose-built, mass-produced motor bus (see Figure 29.2).

But it's the Windrush generation who are irrevocably associated with London's public transport.[11] What makes this association particularly unusual in comparison with other comparable industries is that men and women were actively recruited in their home countries to come and work for London Transport, whereas Black workers faced epic struggles against discrimination and an informal colour bar to gain employment in comparable skilled roles on London's railways, as recent commemorations have highlighted.[12] In the immediate post-war years, London Transport recruited staff from the rest of Britain and from Ireland, but continuing shortages led them to open a recruitment office in Barbados in 1956, the first major employer to do so. The Barbadian government lent the fare money, which recruits would then pay back over two years. This scheme, which was later extended to Jamaica and Trinidad, continued until 1970 and successfully recruited over 4,000 men and women, although numbers declined in later years as UK government legislation placed stringent restrictions on Caribbean immigration.[13]

The challenges of matching workers from small Caribbean islands to the demands of a great city were gently parodied in Sam Selvon's short story 'Working the Transport'. This was included in his 1957 collection *Ways of Sunlight*, which Peter Maber and Karishma Patel discuss in this volume:

'Can you Drive?' they ask Change.

'Me? Drive?' Change smile and make his face look like he driving a bus ever since he born. 'I was born behind a wheel.'

'Have you got a licence?'

'Yes, but not right here. I could go back home for it, though, if you want [...]'

Of course, when the ship reach England it wasn't long before they find Change don't know anything about driving. In the garage a test tell him to move a bus, and Change get in as cool as anything, sit down, start the engine, and throw in a reverse gear by mistake and back the bus up against the wall and give it a big dent right where it had an advertisement for binoculars, besides breaking up the glass in the back window where does have the names of the places where the bus going to.

[...] Jackfish say 'You better try conducting old man.'[14]

In fact, the opposite situation was more likely to be true, where skilled and educated recruits were forced to take lower-status jobs as a way of joining the organization, with the hope of promotion later, although opportunities were severely limited by hostile trade unions and deep-seated racist attitudes. In particular, many women found themselves working as cleaners and canteen staff, although London Transport was keen to promote the increasing numbers of young Black women who were employed as conductors. Many of those recruits had only intended to stay for a few years, a perception shared by their employers, which contributed to their limited employment opportunities, but ultimately remained for their working lives, and today's bus workforce includes many children and grandchildren of those first Commonwealth recruits.[15]

Full-time employment was of course no safeguard against the wider societal problems facing Black and minority ethnic staff in London, particularly that of poor and overcrowded housing, and tensions remained palpable within the workforce itself for decades. When I started work in the mid-1970s, my garage canteen operated an unofficial system of segregation, in which white crews predominantly sat on the tables on one side, and Black crews on the tables on the other side, although it was far from universally adhered to. But at least the benign paternalism of London Transport, with its networks of sports and social clubs, offered opportunities for friendship and community beyond work, and famously the Central Road Services cricket team, representing the best players from garage teams, consistently won the national cup for bus workers for three decades from the 1960s.

In the last fifty years, London's public transport authorities have taken a range of further progressive measures that have ensured the omnibus fully lives up to its name, particularly the introduction of free travel for senior citizens in 1973. Initially their concessionary passes were only permitted for travel in off-peak hours, thus leading to a famous piece of bus slang: as the elderly congregated at bus stops prior to the time at which the pass could be used, they would call out 'Is it too early?' and were thus christened 'Twirlies'! In 2005, free travel was introduced for all under-sixteens, not a universally popular policy amongst passengers or drivers, but it was based on the reasonable principle that it encourages greater bus usage and thus contributes to a move away from private cars, and offers greater safety and security to children on London's streets.

But there was one final barrier to universal inclusivity, one previously thought to be extremely difficult to overcome, until it was easily enacted. Remembering that very last Routemaster journey with which this chapter commenced, there was one group of protesters there to applaud the demise of that emblematic bus. They were campaigners for the disabled, flourishing placards that read 'Routemaster Good Riddance'. They had been actively protesting against inaccessible buses for over a decade, memorably blocking Westminster Bridge in February 1995, and singing 'They call us wheelchair warriors, we're kicking up some fuss, And we will keep on marching, 'til you let us on the bus.'[16] London's first low-floor double-decker was finally introduced in 1998, and now all buses are accessible to wheelchairs, ending the last practical barrier to universal bus travel.

As we approach the bicentenary of the London bus, significant cuts in service are being proposed and implemented. However, our buses still carry over 2 billion people per year, roughly twice as many as the tube, and so continue as an omnibus for all, and remain a good and decent standard bearer for diversity and inclusion within the city that they have served so well for so long.

Notes

1. Travis Elborough, *The Bus We Loved: London's Affair with the Routemaster* (London: Granta Books, 2005).

2. Matthew Wharmby, *Last Years of the London Routemaster* (Barnsley: Pen & Sword Transport, 2023), 115.

3. Wordsworth's famous metaphor for London, in 'Composed Upon Westminster Bridge, September 3, 1802', used as the title of a 1962 British Transport Film about London's transport, and featuring the Windrush generation at work.

4. For the class prejudice against trams, see Robert J. Harley, *LCC Electric Trameways,* (Crowthorne: Capital Transport, 2002); Gavin Weightman and Steve Humphries, *The Making of Modern London: A People's History of the Capital From 1815 to the Present Day* (London: Ebury Press, 2007), 13, 62–3.

5. 'Omnibus Law', *Times*, 30 January 1836, quoted in Ivan Sparkes, *Stagecoaches & Carriages* (Bourne End: Spurbooks, 1975), 145–6.

6. As shown in the popular and widely reproduced painting *Down Piccadilly: Returning from Covent Garden Market One June Morning* of 1882 by Maria Brooks.

7. Knife-board buses featured a single row of back-to-back seats running the length of the top deck, and despite modesty boards along the outside edge, were seen as unsuitable for women to climb the vertiginous stairs and sit facing the street. Garden seat buses had forward-facing pairs of seats with gentler staircases.

8. Virginia Woolf, *Mrs Dalloway* (London: Penguin, 2000), 148–9.

9. Emmanuelle Dirix, 'The Lure of the Omnibus: Hurry Along Girls and World War I', in *Bus Fare: Writings on London's Most Loved Means of Transport*, ed. Travis Elborough and Joe Kerr (Basingstoke: AA Publishing, 2018), 100–6.

10. For the history of women's wartime work on London's transport, see Anna Rotondaro, *Women at Work on London's Transport 1905–1978* (Cheltenham: History Press, 2004).

11. This could be for the better or for the worse. When I signed up with London Transport in the mid-1970s, it was a commonplace to hear the racist trope that you actually had to belong to an ethnic minority to get a job there; at least that was the attitude outside London. I was commonly told, and only partly in jest, that I would have to learn 'Pakistani' or similar.

12. See, for instance, the case of Xavier Asquith, whose fight to become the first Black guard at Euston Station in 1966 led to a strengthening of the 1968 Race Relations Act, and of Wilston Samuel Jackson, who faced down a potential boycott from his fellow workers to become Britain's first Black steam engine driver at King's Cross in 1962. There are now plaques to both men at their respective stations. Outside of London, the Bristol Omnibus Company famously refused to employ Black and Asian workers, leading to the Bristol Bus boycott of 1963, partly inspired by the Montgomery boycott of 1955–6.

13. In 1965 a much smaller scheme recruited a small number of drivers from Malta, the rationale being that they were already familiar with driving on the left.

14. Sam Selvon, 'Working the Transport', in *Ways of Sunlight* (London: MacGibbon & Kee, 1957), 132–4.

15. Current Mayor of London Sadiq Khan, and the politicians Sajid Javid and Baroness Sayeeda Warsi are all the children of bus drivers from Pakistan.

16. Damon Rose, 'The Wheelchair Warriors: Their Rebellious Protests to Change the Law', BBC News, https://www.bbc.co.uk/news/extra/8rvpt6bclh/wheelchair-warriors-disability-discrimination-act.

NORTH

CHAPTER 30
MOORGATE, ENFIELD, EDMONTON AND HAMPSTEAD: THE CROSS-CITY MIGRATIONS OF JOHN KEATS
Flora Lisica

There is something strange about glimpsing lines from Keats's 'To Autumn' (1819) on the London tube, where its last stanza is displayed by Poems on the Underground: amidst the busy rush hour rattle of the Bakerloo line, the passing seasons which are the subject of Keats's poem feel rather remote. This seems appropriate, too, however, given that, despite repeatedly being drawn to natural subjects in his poetry, Keats was born in London and spent most of his life in the city and its surroundings.

It may therefore seem counterintuitive to think of Keats in the context of migration. John Gibson Lockhart infamously branded Keats a 'Cockney' poet precisely because he felt that Keats could never shake off his London background, not even when writing about nature.[1] But when read in the context of Keats's migrations between London and its surrounding countryside, and in light of the broader currents of migration which were pulling many Londoners to and from the city at the start of the nineteenth century, Keats's insistent flights from the urban to the natural in his poems gain additional significance.

Born in Moorgate, Keats spent a substantial portion of his childhood and teens in Edmonton and Enfield; now firmly understood as part of Greater London, they were still very much outside of the city in Keats's time, and his move to Southwark in his late teens to pursue his medical studies signified a shift back from a rural to an urban environment. This was a common experience: up to 10,000 people were moving to London from other parts of Britain annually in the period, typically to find work, and Keats therefore resembled many other migrants upon his return to the city centre.[2]

At once, the capital's expansion was pushing the countryside further and further away as the city was, figuratively speaking, migrating into the countryside and contributing to the increased cultural significance of nature in the city. By Keats's time, London was becoming large and well connected enough for people to cross fairly substantial distances to relocate from one area of the city to another. Now an ubiquitous part of the texture of the city, migrations of this kind began to be an increasingly significant part of Londoners' lives by the start of the nineteenth century, when the city was at once becoming expansive enough to require such travel, and was developing the infrastructure to facilitate it. The insistent desire of Keats's poems to imaginatively transport readers to natural settings can be read as reflective of these shifts, while considering Keats's poems in this context in turn also helps us understand the varied experiences of migration.

In 'O Solitude' (*c.* 1815–16), which was the first of Keats's poems to be published, and written while he was living in Southwark, Keats makes his preference for a rural environment to the realities of the city apparent:

O Solitude! if I must with thee dwell,
Let it not be among the jumbled heap
Of murky buildings; climb with me the steep, –
Nature's observatory – whence the dell,
Its flowery slopes, its river's crystal swell,
May seem a span[3]

Keats's description of 'the jumbled heap / Of murky buildings' brings to mind the Georgian terraces which had by the early 1800s taken over the south side of the river; they appear stiflingly dense in the Rhinebeck Panorama of London (*c.* 1806–7), the geometric pattern of the sharp roofs stretching into infinity.[4] In Keats's poem, the city and the countryside emerge as binary opposites, and the dark urban claustrophobia is evidently deemed inferior to the elevated vantage point of 'Nature's observatory'.

Keats's preference for the rural, like that of many of his contemporaries, can be read as a result of London's exponential growth in the period. In the early nineteenth century, London was the largest city in Europe: the 1801 census counted 866,000 inhabitants in inner London, and 1.1 million in what we would now term Greater London, and by 1850, its population would double.[5] The result was a construction boom; in 1776, the writer and politician Horace Walpole remarked how 'rows of houses shoot out every way like a polypus; and so great is the range of building everywhere, that if I stay here [at his country residence] a fortnight, without going to town, I look about to see if no new house is built since I went last'.[6]

London was spilling into, and submerging, the countryside around it, and the transition was not necessarily smooth or always welcome. This is suggested by George Cruikshank's etching *London going out of Town – or – The March of Bricks and Mortar!* (1829; see Figure 30.1), where Cruikshank satirizes the sprawl of London's urbanization as a military charge against the surrounding countryside. Foreshadowing more recent discussions about gentrification in London resulting in population 'shifts and ultimately displacement', in Alberto Duman's words, Cruikshank depicts the rural population emblematized as trees and hay bales, fleeing, with their livestock, from the showers of catapulted brick and the advancing army of anthropomorphized chimneys and building tools.[7] It is not difficult to see where one's sympathies are meant to lie.

Keats's own experiences of different parts of London reflect this transition. Having lived in Moorgate for the first seven years of his life, he spent the next decade outside the city. He was at school in Enfield from 1803 until 1810, spending his school holidays with his grandmother near Edmonton, where he was then apprenticed to the local surgeon until 1814.[8] The Enfield and Edmonton of Keats's childhood were small towns, still village-like, each with less than 6,000 inhabitants.[9] The walk from Clarke's Academy to Keats's grandmother's end-of-terrace house led across meadows and country lanes; both

Figure 30.1 George Cruikshank, *London going out of Town – or – The March of Bricks and Mortar!* (1829). © Chronicle/Alamy Stock Photo.

buildings backed on to fields, and there were brooks and ponds nearby to paddle and swim in.[10] In a letter to his sister Fanny, Keats recalls 'how fond [he] used to be of Goldfinches, Tomtits, Minnows, Mice, Ticklebacks, Dace, Cock salmons and all the whole tribe of the Bushes and the Brooks', and his repeated returns to natural subjects in his poetry can be traced to his joy at his natural surroundings as a child.[11]

London was twelve miles away: close enough for Keats's friend and teacher Charles Cowden Clarke to recall walking there and back to attend plays in the West End, but the approximately three-and-a-half hour walk from Enfield to the city centre was distinctly rural, taking one along 'the "Green Lanes", as they were called, between Holloway and Enfield – through picturesque Hornsey, rural Wood Green, and hedge-rowed Winchmore Hill'.[12] By the mid-nineteenth century, Enfield and Edmonton's populations would double; advancements in transport technology were turning towns surrounding London into suburbs.[13] The construction of canals enabled goods to be brought into London more cheaply, while the improvement of road management and the gradual introduction of macadam meant that some coach journey times, particularly those linking towns to London, halved in the last decades of the eighteenth century. This resulted in ribbon developments along the main travel routes, which were binding towns and villages to the city centre, and also increasing their dependence on London.[14] Had Keats's life not been cut short prematurely he would have seen the railway reach Enfield in 1849. The train station was initially housed in Keats's old school building, pre-empting the countryside of his youth being subsumed into the urban sprawl of London which Enfield and

Edmonton are part of today, with the Overground firmly tying them to central London.[15] Keats would then have seen train carriages stopping on the ground where he had, along with fellow students of Clarke's Academy, enacted a living solar system in the playground, and where they had tended their garden plots and watered their strawberries.[16]

The longing for the nature of his childhood is evident in Keats's sonnet 'To One Who Has Been Long in City Pent' (1816). Written in the summer of 1816, when Keats was living in Southwark and making frequent excursions to Hampstead, it describes the city-dweller delighting in a rural day trip: 'To one who has been long in city pent, / 'Tis very sweet to look into the fair / And open face of heaven' (ll. 1–3). The poem's first line echoes Coleridge's 'Frost at Midnight', whose speaker describes their own childhood in 'the great city', where they were 'pent 'mid cloisters dim' (l. 52), which are in Coleridge's poem contrasted with the sublime expansiveness of nature.[17] For Coleridge's speaker, nature offers us glimpses of divine order: 'The lovely shapes and sounds intelligible / Of that eternal language, which thy God / Utters' (ll. 59–60).[18] But the city is man-made, and as such emits no such eternal truth. In spite of evident urbanistic attempts at order, which the regularity of London's terrace developments and squares of the eighteenth century suggest, these attempts are, for Coleridge and implicitly also for Keats, ultimately in vain: London is a 'jumbled heap', to recall Keats's terms from 'O Solitude!', exposing humankind's failure at keeping chaos at bay.

Keats reiterates Coleridge's dichotomy, and its religious connotations, in 'To One Who Has Been Long in City Pent'. The speaker delights in the 'pleasant lair / Of wavy grass' (ll. 6–7), from where they can perceive a wide, expansive 'open face of heaven' – the sky implicitly liberated from the confining frame of city buildings – 'to breathe a prayer / Full in the smile of the blue firmament' (ll. 3–4), before returning to their city home in the evening. But with the phrase 'city pent', both Keats and Coleridge are also recalling Milton's wording in *Paradise Lost* (1667), where he describes Satan emerging from Hell, and advancing towards Eden in order to corrupt Eve:

> As one who long in populous City pent,
> Where houses thick and sewers annoy the air,
> Forth issuing on a summer's morn to breathe
> Among the pleasant villages and farms
> Adjoined, from each thing met conceives delight,
> The smell of grain, or tedded grass, or kine,
> Or dairy, each rural sight, each rural sound (IX, ll. 445–52)[19]

To think of London as hellish is not uncommon among Keats's contemporaries: Shelley quips that 'Hell is a city much like London', and Byron scathingly describes it as the 'Devil's drawing room'.[20] But Milton's simile seems to go further: by comparing Satan with a Londoner taking a trip to a nearby rural tourist spot, the similarity of the latter to the former is also implied. If Satan's delight to be free from Hell is like the day tripper's delight in their respite from the city, the latter might also be understood to share, if inadvertently, some of Satan's insidiously corruptive influence. As Satan is about to irrevocably disturb the happy tranquillity of Eve in Eden, the Londoner's arrival in the countryside seems to threaten the nature which they have come to find, and this subtext remains present, if latently, in Keats's allusion. Cruikshank's etching makes a similar suggestion with its title, which draws parallels between London's expansion and Londoners' 'going out of Town' to the countryside for rural amusements: as London goes 'out of Town', it seems to take the town along with it. The quiet rural simplicity and undisturbed nature which Londoners hoped to find in the city's rural environs is precisely what is eroded as a consequence of their arrival.

In 1757, Robert Lloyd had satirized this in his poem 'The Cit's Country-Box': the construction of a small-scale landscape garden complete with a Chinese temple, a ha-ha and a series of statues of classical deities to accompany a Londoner's rural residence leaves nothing natural in sight.[21] By the early decades of the 1800s, a compromise between nature and culture became accessible to the city's middle classes as well; London's surroundings were turning into suburbs as they provided country retreats for merchants and tradesmen.[22] Hampstead was one area on such a trajectory. In 1837, Mary Shelley, writing to Leigh Hunt, a mutual friend of hers and Keats's, and a fellow Hampstead resident, lamented '[h]ow altered' she found Hampstead: 'how bepainted & becocnified are its little Cottages – & all the old washerwomen's cots turned into villinas & a Villa', in contrast to the Hampstead of her youth.[23]

Keats, Hunt and others who had come to settle there in the early 1800s marked the beginning of this process, however; what is now Keats House, then called Wentworth Place, was built in the late 1810s, and was a brand new development in Keats's time.[24] Then, Hampstead was where the overflowing city still met the countryside, offering a desirable marriage between nature and culture for the middle classes.[25] By the mid-nineteenth century, two-thirds of London's suburbs' inhabitants had, like Keats in the 1810s, moved there from London's rural surroundings, and Anne Bermingham goes as far as reading the suburb as 'a refuge from the disappointing realities of both urban and rural life'.[26] Indeed, Lockhart's characterization of Keats as a Cockney nature poet reflects this; the term 'Cockney' in the period becomes increasingly associated with the suburbs as places where distinctions between different classes, and between the city and the country, became blurred.[27]

This desire for a marriage between nature and culture also reveals itself in Keats's poems, and is at the heart of Keats's vision of literature. In 'To One Who has Been Long in City Pent', the city-dweller's pleasure in their natural setting is exacerbated by their reading a 'tale of love and languishment' (l. 8) in the grass. Elsewhere, nature and poetry are evoked figuratively to describe one another. In 'On the Grasshopper and Cricket' (1816), Keats writes of 'The poetry of earth' (l. 1) to describe the sounds of the countryside; in 'On Sitting Down to Read *King Lear* Once Again' (1818), he compares the experience of reading Shakespeare's play with walking through an 'old oak forest' (l. 11). Similarly, in an echo of Wordsworth's vision of poetry in his preface to *Lyrical Ballads* (1800), in an 1818 letter, Keats writes that 'if Poetry comes not as naturally as the Leaves to a tree it had better not come at all'.[28]

Keats's 'Ode to a Nightingale' (1819) has been taken as testament to the notion of Keats's fulfilment of his maxim: supposedly, Keats composed the poem in one sitting, under a plum tree in his Hampstead garden, in response to the song of a nightingale who had made its nest there in the spring of 1819.[29] Lucasta Miller writes of the way that Keats 'crushes images together' in the poem, imparting a 'sense of instability and boundary breaking'; further, the two images crushed together most intensely throughout are those of the nightingale's song and the speaker's poem, of nature and of poetry.[30] The 'immortal Bird' (l. 61) shapes the 'wings of Poesy' (l. 33), while the nightingale is a 'light-winged Dryad' (l. 7), and its song cannot be heard without the echoes of a series of literary associations. If in 'To One Who Has Been Long in City Pent' the natural and the urban seem at a distance from one another, as Hampstead was from Southwark, in the Nightingale ode, composed in liminal, suburban, semi-urban Hampstead, nature and culture cannot but conglomerate.

Keats's figurative intertwining of the nightingale's song and the poet's suggests the difficulty of viewing nature outside of the prism of the cultural frame. Similarly, when in 'O Solitude!', Keats is wishing to escape the 'jumbled heap / Of murky buildings' and immerse himself in nature, images of urban architecture intrude upon images of nature, suggesting the difficulty of experiencing one set apart from the other. 'Let me thy [nature's] vigils keep / 'Mongst boughs pavillion'd' (ll. 6–7), Keats writes – but the notion of 'pavillion'd' boughs suggests their resemblance to buildings, and Keats's adjective encases the speaker's desire for the genuine natural experience in a man-made, urban context.

Lockhart criticized Keats's depictions of nature precisely in those terms, as 'descriptions of flowers seen in window-pots, or cascades heard at Vauxhall', suggesting that Keats's poetry is continually revealing nature's limitations rather than exalting its sublime expansiveness.[31] The latter is a reference to the renowned artificial waterfall at Vauxhall Pleasure Gardens, where a system of tin sheets set in motion by mechanical means, accompanied by light and sound effects, imparted the illusion of flowing water. A representation of nature, the waterfall at Vauxhall for Lockhart suggests that nature encountered in London is ultimately fake: nature recreated in the image of the cultural idea of what nature is or should be.

But Keats's experiences of urban nature were shared by many Londoners, for whom it was physically contained by plant pots, fences, or buildings, and who encountered nature as a mingling of experience and representation; this is the case for many more Londoners now. And the artificial could be a helpful reminder of the real thing for many of Keats's contemporaries, who shared his experience of migrating to London from its surroundings. An extract from 'To Autumn', glimpsed in an underground carriage where it sits squished between brashly-coloured adverts, reminds us to look out for the seasons when we emerge from the seasonless underground. The clouds, the gnats, the lambs, the redbreast and the cricket become part of the urban landscape as they keep the commuter company on their journey across – and beneath – the city.

Notes

1. Z [John Gibson Lockhart], *Blackwood's Edinburgh Magazine*, August 1818, 521.

2. James K. Chandler and Kevin Gilmartin, 'Introduction: Engaging the Eidometropolis', in *Romantic Metropolis: The Urban Scene of British Culture, 1780–1840*, ed. James K. Chandler and Kevin Gilmartin (Cambridge: Cambridge University Press, 2005), 2.

3. John Keats, *The Poems of John Keats*, ed. Jack Stillinger (Cambridge, MA: Harvard University Press, 1978), ll. 1–6.

4. John Summerson, *Georgian London*, ed. Howard Colvin (New Haven, CT: Yale University Press, 2003), 330.

5. Jerry White, *London in the Eighteenth Century: A Great and Monstrous Thing* (London: Bodley Head, 2012), 79–80; Chandler and Gilmartin, 'Introduction', 2.

6. Quoted in White, *London in the Eighteenth Century*, 76.

7. Alberto Duman, 'Dispatches from "the Frontline of Gentrification"', *City* 16, no. 6 (2012): 676.

8. Nicholas Roe, *John Keats: A New Life* (New Haven, CT: Yale University Press, 2012), 19, 44, 57.

9. A. P. Baggs, Diane K. Bolton, Eileen P. Scarff and G. C. Tyack, *A History of the County of Middlesex: Hendon, Kingsbury, Great Stanmore, Little Stanmore, Edmonton Enfield, Monken Hadley, South Mimms, Tottenham*, ed. T. F. T. Baker, 13 vols (London: Institute of Historical Research, 1976), V, 137–42, 212–18; William Page (ed.), *A History of the County of Middlesex: General; Ashford, East Bedfont With Hatton, Feltham, Hampton With Hampton Wick, Hanworth, Laleham, Littleton*, 13 vols (London: Institute of Historical Research, 1911), II, 112–20.

10. Roe, *John Keats*, 19–20, 33.

11. John Keats, *The Letters of John Keats 1814–1821*, ed. Hyder Edward Rollins, 2 vols (Cambridge, MA: Harvard University Press, 1958), II, 46.

12. Charles Cowden Clarke and Mary Cowden Clarke, *Recollections of Writers* (London: Sampson Low, Marston, Searle, & Rivington, 1878), 14.

13. Baggs et al., *A History of the County of Middlesex*, 137–42, 212–18.

14. White, *London in the Eighteenth Century*, 75–6; Summerson, *Georgian London*, 326–5; Ruth Livesey, *Writing the Stagecoach Nation* (Oxford: Oxford University Press, 2016), 15, 18–19.

15. Andrew Motion, *Keats* (London: Faber and Faber, 1997), 297.

16. Roe, *John Keats,* 20, 22–3, 29–30, 33.

17. Fiona Stafford, *Local Attachments: The Province of Poetry* (Oxford: Oxford University Press, 2010), 230.

18. Samuel Taylor Coleridge, 'Frost at Midnight', in *The Complete Poems*, ed. William Keach (London: Penguin, 1997), 231–2.

19. John Milton, *Paradise Lost*, ed. Stephen Orgel and Jonathan Goldberg (Oxford: Oxford University Press, 2004); Keats, *The Poems of John Keats*, 421; Harry Buxon Forman, *The Poetical Works and Other Writings of John Keats*, 4 vols (London: Reeves & Turner, 1883), I, 75, n. 1.

20. George Gordon, Lord Byron, *The Complete Poetical Works*, ed. Jerome J. McGann, 7 vols (Oxford: Clarendon Press, 1988–93), V, 461; Percy Bysshe Shelley, *The Poems of Shelley*, ed. Michael Rossington, Jack Donovan and Kelvin Everest, 4 vols (Harlow: Longman, 1989–2014), III, 103.

21. Robert Lloyd, 'The Cit's Country-Box', in *Eighteenth-Century Poetry: An Annotated Anthology*, ed. David Fairer and Christine Gerrard (Oxford: Blackwell, 2015), 478–82.

22. White, *London in the Eighteenth Century*, 78–9.

23. Mary Wollstonecraft Shelley, *The Letters of Mary Wollstonecraft Shelley*, ed. Betty T. Bennett, 2 vols (Baltimore, MD: Johns Hopkins University Press, 1983), II, 286–7.

24. Kenneth Page, 'Wentworth Place: "A Small Cottage, Pleasantly Situate"', in *Keats's Places*, ed. Richard Marggraf Turley (London: Palgrave Macmillan, 2018), 246–7, 255.

25. Summerson, *Georgian London*, 317–18; Elizabeth Jones, 'Keats in the Suburbs', *Keats–Shelley Journal* 45 (1996): 43.

26. Ann Bermingham, *Landscape and Ideology: The English Rustic Tradition, 1740–1860* (Berkeley: University of California Press, 1986), 168; Gregory Dart, *Metropolitan Art and Literature, 1810–1840: Cockney Adventures* (Cambridge: Cambridge University Press, 2012), 12.

27. Dart, *Metropolitan Art and Literature*, 8, 28, 31.

28. Keats, *Letters*, I, 238–9.

29. Lucasta Miller, *Keats: A Brief Life in Nine Poems and One Epitaph* (London: Jonathan Cape, 2021), 224.

30. Ibid., *Keats*, 220, 222.

31. Z [Lockhart], 521.

CHAPTER 31
THE BATTLE FOR AN AFRICAN SPACE IN LONDON: WASU HOSTEL AND AGGREY HOUSE

William Whitworth

Few figures embody the opportunities and limitations of the Black student politics of 1930s London quite like Ladipo Solanke, founder and long-term head of the West African Students Union Association (WASU). In a career of activism spanning three decades, Solanke met and worked alongside countless celebrities, activists and politicians, both Black and white, helping to fundamentally reshape the geography of Black London through his activities. WASU's hostel, originally based on Camden Road in North London, was Solanke's most enduring legacy. The hostel developed into an important focal point for West African networks in the city and later became a battleground, as Solanke and WASU combated plans by the British government to form their own hostel for Black (predominantly West African) students, Aggrey House, in Bloomsbury.

In 1922, Solanke, a Yoruba from western Nigeria, moved to London to study law at University College. The young student was shocked by the lack of interest that his West African peers displayed towards their heritage whilst living in England. He began to teach the Yoruba language and perform Yoruba poetry and in 1924 gave the first radio address in Yoruba on the BBC.[1] Still, Solanke felt that a greater effort was needed and in 1925 the ambitious student founded WASU, with the intention of not only organizing the cultural and political life of West African students in London, but their social life too. In 1926 the organization began to publish its own journal, also named *Wasu*, with the majority of the articles written by Solanke himself. Solanke's plan was now to create a hostel which would offer Black students in London a place to stay for both short- and long-term visits, whilst also serving as the headquarters of his new organization.

The focus on investing in a hostel must be placed in the context of the rampant housing discrimination Black people experienced in interwar London, with comfortable and affordable lodgings difficult to find and landlords unwilling to let to 'coloured people'.[2] Unfortunately, buying a property in London was also a very expensive venture, and financial issues dogged the impoverished Solanke and WASU throughout the organization's existence. To raise money, in 1929 Solanke embarked on a three-year tour of West Africa, sponsored by *West Africa* magazine.[3] Solanke's tour was extensively reported by the West African press, and he became something of a minor celebrity in many of the places he visited. He spoke excitedly of his vision: a centre for Black learning in the *very heart* of London, commanding the respect and attention of the imperial government, all possible with only a small donation.

Numerous West Africans signed on to the project, enough that Solanke secured the money needed to lease a property to use as a hostel. In March 1933, 'Africa House' opened on 62 Camden Road. Solanke took on the direct responsibility of running the new hostel as 'Warden'. Rather than being located next to the corridors of power as Solanke had claimed his hostel would be, Camden was over an hour's walk from Parliament. On top of this, the rent was exorbitant, but the hostel provided Solanke with a much-needed base from which to launch his activities. It also supported his ongoing attempts to repair WASU which was undergoing the first of many splits between members from Nigeria and those from the Gold Coast, who felt that they had inadequate representation or access to leadership positions.[4] The new hostel was almost immediately popular, attracting not only students but also general visitors from West Africa.

The British Colonial Office feared that WASU was using the hostel to promote anti-imperial attitudes. In 1934, the British government founded its own hostel, Aggrey House, on 47 Doughty Street in Bloomsbury, with the intention of providing a space for Africans to stay whilst encouraging visitors to adopt pro-imperial beliefs. From the very beginning, Black Londoners played an important role in the conceptualization and administration of Aggrey House, most notably Harold Moody, a Jamaican-born doctor and leader of the League of Coloured Peoples, an organization set up to support Black people in the United Kingdom.[5] Gold Coast members of WASU – still smarting over Nigerian influence at Africa House – flocked to the new hostel, helping to fuel a mutual feeling of dislike between the two centres of African student life in London.[6] WASU organized a boycott of Aggrey House and released a pamphlet covering 'the truth of Aggrey House [and the] government plan to control African students'. The pamphlet decried Aggrey House as a government ploy and even drew direct parallels between attempts of the British government to control African bodies in London with the ongoing violence of British rule in the colonies.[7] Trinidadian intellectual George Padmore, affiliated with Africa House, went so far as to describe Aggrey House as a 'little Jim Crow hostel'.[8]

Open opposition to Aggrey House from WASU continued until financial difficulties in 1935 led to the two hostels participating in 'peace talks', after which an uneasy concord developed between them, punctuated only by the occasional barb thrown by one side or the other.[9] A number of events were held to celebrate the new period of cooperation, including joint Christmas dinners and dances.[10] With its future now secured by Colonial Office funding, Africa House continued to attract an eclectic mix of visiting celebrities, from actor and activist Paul Robeson to Alake (King) Ladapo Ademola II of Abeokuta and Nnamdi 'Zik' Azikiwe, the future President of Nigeria. All of the visitors met with Solanke, with Zik spending an evening dancing in Soho nightclubs and eating at Amy Ashwood Garvey's 'International Afro Restaurant'. Visitors were well supported at the hostel by the all-female support staff, headed by 'Matron' Olu Solanke, whom Ladipo had married following his trip to Africa. As the *Comet* newspaper of Nigeria observed:

[The Hostel] has played a most worthy part in providing residence for all persons irrespective of race, colour or creed. An Englishman, an Indian, an African, or a

West Indian, each and every one at one time or another has found the hostel quite comfortable during his stay in it.[11]

Rather than being overshadowed by the success of the WASU hostel, Aggrey House also began to flourish. By 1937, membership at the house had more than quadrupled, reaching 236 residents, Caribbean students and African Americans visiting alongside their African peers.[12] Long-term Black London residents, such as the future President of Kenya Jomo Kenyatta, also visited the government's hostel with their network of friends.[13] Despite this popularity, the Colonial Office's plans to use the hostel to inspire pro-imperial attitudes were, however, failing. By creating a Black space, the British government had indirectly made Aggrey House a site where a shared Black identity could be fostered between people with disparate national origins. This process was accelerated by the debating clubs and study groups which were formed at the hostel and in which current affairs in the colonies were discussed. Talks were also given at the hostel by a number of radical thinkers, possibly including George Padmore, although this matter is disputed.[14]

WASU, and by extension Solanke, reached the height of its influence in the early years of the Second World War following a financially motivated move to South Villas, also in Camden.[15] During the Blitz, as clubs across London closed their doors, WASU remained open and would often be crowded with visitors – both Black and white. As the organization's journal declared, 'Despite the Nazi air blitzkrieg in London during the first four months of the year, the holding of the fortnightly social and dance at the hostel went on with as little interruption as possible [...] WASU has almost acquired a new meaning in this country signifying a spot in London where dullness is unknown or a place of unending cheerfulness.'[16]

On the political front, Solanke greeted ever-more important officials, culminating with the visit of Clement Attlee, Deputy Prime Minister of the UK, in August 1941. The Colonial Office, noting that WASU was not going anywhere and was playing an important role in rallying Black London behind the war effort, began increasing the money they were putting into the Africa House project. As they did so, however, they noted in their reports a number of concerns regarding the way Solanke ran things. For one, he drew a greater salary as Warden than was the norm for this position, whilst massively underpaying his wife, who not only did most of the cleaning in the building but all of the cooking as well.[17] In addition, Solanke had also ensured that the vast majority of the leadership positions in the 'West African' hostel had gone to Nigerians – and of those the majority were fellow Yoruba.

Meanwhile at Aggrey House, growing differences between the increasingly radical student guests and the more conservative board came to a head in 1940, when the board temporarily closed the institution. The reason for this decision was stated to be the 'immoral conduct' of a certain Mr Wilkins, a Caribbean student who had supposedly brought the house 'into disrepute'. Under the surface, however, conservative members of the board, spearheaded by Moody, used the incident as an excuse to permanently ban suspected communists (as well as the unfortunate Wilkins) from Aggrey House. The hostel was then cautiously reopened; the famous African American reporter Ollie Stewart visited in 1942. Nonetheless, by 1943 it had closed permanently. As a replacement, a new 'Colonial Centre' was opened nearby on 18 Russell Square in 1943, but, despite an initial wave of enthusiasm, this site never saw the levels of political activity that Aggrey House did.[18] Times had changed – stories from the Colonial Centre mention Christmas parties, services for African American GIs and meetings with local children as opposed to talks on independence. In 1944, members of the Colonial Centre *almost* demonstrated in anger following the famous barring of cricketer Learie Constantine from the Imperial Hotel, also located on Russell Square.[19] The relative peace and quiet of the Colonial Centre meant that Moody had achieved his vision of an apolitical Black space; however, this occurred just as his own politics began to take a more radical turn. In a twist of fate, the doctor spent his final years (unsuccessfully) campaigning for a Colonial Cultural Centre in London free from the influence of the British government.[20]

Due to his overbearing control of WASU, it came as a relief to many in the organization when Solanke departed in 1944 to go to Africa on another funding trip. During his absence, the organization increasingly came under the sway of a non-Nigerian, left-wing group centred on Kwame Nkrumah. Citing his opposition to communism as a motivating factor, Solanke stepped down as secretary-general of WASU upon his return in 1949. Unable to wrest WASU away from the organization's left wing, in 1953 Solanke left the union entirely following its decision to close Africa House, running it himself independently, despite his declining health. Solanke died from lung cancer in 1958, aged seventy-two. Although his career ended in controversy, the fact that Solanke was able to keep a hostel functional until the very end speaks to the level of care which he had devoted to his project.[21]

Solanke may have never built the hostel that he proposed in central London, but he did something even more extraordinary – he created a new African hub in Camden, an area of London which had seen only a brief African presence before his arrival. His hostel, Africa House, represented one vision for an African space in London. Aggrey House provided another: it was more centrally located than Africa House, but at the cost of sacrificing some independence to the British government. Whilst Aggrey House never achieved the international reputation of Africa House, for a brief period between 1935 and 1937 the hostel appeared to be in a much healthier state than its more famous counterpart, boasting a higher membership and a firmer financial footing. The fact that figures such as Jomo Kenyatta chose to visit and speak at Aggrey House speaks to the pull of the institution in the networks of Black London at the time. That the Black members of the hostel's board were not radicals does not detract from its importance; rather, Aggrey House offered a glimpse of an alternative vision for Black London, in which the colour bar would be dissolved while imperial loyalties would remain intact. Both it and the WASU hostel represent competing, yet important, examples of African spaces in London years before mass immigration from Africa began.

Notes

1. Daniel Stephen, *The Empire of Progress: West Africans, Indians, and Britons at the British Empire Exhibition 1924–25* (New York: Palgrave Macmillan, 2013), 70.

2. Gemma Romain, *Race, Sexuality and Identity in Britain and Jamaica: The Biography of Patrick Nelson, 1916–1963* (London: Bloomsbury Academic, 2017), 78–9. For the 1940s, see also 'Colour Discrimination in the UK: General Policy of the Colonial Office', CO 859/80/7, The National Archives of the United Kingdom, Kew Gardens (henceforth: TNA).

3. 'Report on WASU Hostel, Submitted by Dr. R. B. Wellesley Cole, from Data Supplied by Mr. Ladipo Solanke', June 1942, CO 876/56, TNA.

4. Hakim Adi, 'West African Students in Britain, 1900–60: The Politics of Exile', in *Africans in Britain*, ed. David Killingray (Ilford: Francis & Taylor, 1994), 127.

5. For more information on Moody's beliefs and his role in the project, see Barbara Bush, *Imperialism, Race and Resistance: Africa and Britain, 1919–1945* (New York: Routledge, 1999), 220.

6. Marc Matera, *Black London: The Imperial Metropolis and Decolonization in the Twentieth Century* (Oakland: University of California Press, 2015), 59.

7. Daniel Whittall, 'Creating Black Places in Imperial London: The League of Coloured Peoples and Aggrey House, 1931–1943', *London Journal* 36, no. 3 (2011): 225–46.

8. Quoted in Matera, *Black London*, 58.

9. 'Report on WASU Hostel, Submitted by Dr. R. B. Wellesley Cole, from Data Supplied by Mr. Ladipo Solanke', June 1942, CO 876/56, TNA.

10. 'WASU Christmas Arrangements', December 1936, CO 847/7/2, TNA.

11. 'West African Students' Union, African Hostel', 29 February 1936, CO 847/7/2, TNA.

12. Whittall, 'Creating Black Places in Imperial London', 237.

13. Matera, *Black London*, 269.

14. Whittall, 'Creating Black Places in Imperial London', 246.

15. For the financial difficulties behind the decision, see 'Report on WASU Hostel, Submitted by Dr. R.B. Wellesley Cole, from Data Supplied by Mr. Ladipo Solanke', June 1942, CO 876/56, TNA.

16. *Wasu* 9, no. 1 (1942).

17. Anonymous Colonial Office report on WASU, June 1943, CO 876/57, TNA.

18. For the rationale for, and debates surrounding, the founding of the Colonial Centre, see CO 876/63, TNA.

19. Sonya O. Rose, *Which People's War? National Identity and Citizenship in Wartime Britain 1939–1945* (Oxford: Oxford University Press, 2003), 250–1.

20. Colin Holmes, *John Bull's Island: Immigration and British Society, 1871–1971* (Houndsmill: Macmillan Press, 1988), Chapter 4.

21. For information on Solanke's later years, see Hakim Adi and Marika Sherwood, *Pan-African History: Political Figures from Africa and the Diaspora since 1787* (London: Routledge, 2003), 176.

CHAPTER 32
NORTHVIEW: A SNAPSHOT OF MULTIRACIAL LONDON DURING THE SECOND WORLD WAR
Oliver Ayers

As Europe lurched towards war through the crises of 1938, workers in North London were finishing yet another building as the city's interwar construction boom neared its conclusion. Northview, a low-rise development of flats on the corner of the Tufnell Park and Holloway roads in Islington, reflected the desire among constructors and residents to find more spacious and modern accommodation away from the built-up city centre and overcrowded East End. Mock-Tudor semi-detached houses came to dominate much of the city's periphery, but flats and apartments were less commonplace but important ways for interwar planners to appeal to younger aspirational Londoners. With two brick-built blocks placed around a central grassed lawn, the design attempted to bring a flavour of the country into harmony with the town, echoing principles expressed in the turn-of-the-century garden city movement. Northview's understated Art Deco touches, including curved bay windows, chrome pipework and Egyptian-influenced balustrades, bore further testament to its 1930s pedigree.

Yet almost as soon as this forward-looking development was completed, Northview and its residents were plunged into war. When hostilities began, the government quickly conducted a mini-census to survey the population. The picture of life the 1939 National Register produced in Northview was revealing: seventy-seven people lived in its forty-one flats, with an average age of just over thirty. Young married couples were common, such as the Nichols at number 24 – a laundry manager and a bookkeeper who lived with a young child. Many did skilled manual work or had lower-end professional occupations: there were milliners, fur finishers, stationers, watch repairers and post-office clerks.[1]

Yet as much as the Register produced a portrait of Northview – and indeed Britain at large – coloured by class, it told a less familiar but important story about race. At number 21 lived Nigerian-born 'Dance Hall Pianist' Fela Sowande, his wife Mildred (who carried out 'unpaid domestic duties') and their two young children. At number 33 lived Clara Deniz – a mixed-race Briton originally from Cardiff – and her fellow-musician husband Frank, whose father hailed from the Cape Verde Isles.[2] This chapter examines how the Sowandes and Denizes came to Northview and what happened to them in the war and its aftermath. The result is a snapshot of an often-overlooked multiracial dimension to wartime London that focuses on a suburban enclave and the wider city, but reveals in the process the connection of these local worlds to international cross-currents of empire, migration and war.

* * *

Imperialism was an unsurprising but crucial force that carried Sowande from Lagos in Nigeria to Northview. His father, Emmanuel, was a musician in the Nigerian church, an institution bound up with the development of colonial rule in the nineteenth century. Yet although the imposition of music in the European classical tradition on the Nigerian Christian church was a symbol and tool of British rule, African 'subject peoples' found some ways of retaining or incorporating their own musical traditions. Fela Sowande was a case in point. He grew up receiving both formal training in European classical and church music as well as acquiring a deep-rooted knowledge of traditional Yoruban styles.[3]

Sowande's virtuoso musical ability was obvious during his adolescent years in 1920s Lagos, but by the 1930s it became clear that London – the imperial metropole – was the best place to receive the level of training his talent deserved. Born into a comparative Nigerian elite, Sowande also had ability in the sciences: he taught at the Lagos Grammar School before joining the Lagos Survey Department to study mathematics. When he arrived in London in 1934, it was originally to study civil engineering, but music soon took over.[4] He became part of a burgeoning black student community from West Africa centred around the university district in Bloomsbury. He was acquainted with Ladipo Solanke, the founder and president of the West African Students Union (WASU), whose hostels in Camden were another hub of student-intellectual black life, as William Whitworth discusses in this volume. Within six months, Sowande abandoned his engineering course at Regent Street Polytechnic to pursue his career in music. This choice created both objections from some family members, as well as the real-world problem of how to fund his studies.[5]

The answer lay in the musical form that dominates views of interwar black culture and that of the age more broadly: jazz. As Sowande later recalled, the move to playing in London's growing number of musical clubs and theatres was both an outlet of expression and a way of making ends meet to fund formal musical training. He solicited help from white jazz musician Jerry Moore, while capitalizing on his church music expertise to become well known on the London stage as a jazz organ player and pianist.[6] Upon joining the *Blackbirds* revue in 1936 – the most successful American jazz import on the interwar London stage – one reviewer reported that Sowande 'really shines in accompanying blues singers and hoofers [. . .] he has loads of technique and loads of swing'.[7]

Sowande's success was down to talent and background. Mixing and adapting national musical styles was part of his upbringing. Colonial Nigeria was part of a wider Atlantic world and American jazz reached a young Sowande who listened to famous Harlem band-leader Duke Ellington on a small crystal radio set.[8] Years later, Sowande found it easy – and expedient – to adopt an American identity as his London career took off, as did many West Indian musicians with whom he often played. Jazz allowed connections to form between American, Caribbean and African musicians, but American-inspired identities predominated.[9] Sowande's American connection also had a further personal dimension: in 1936 he married fellow revue member Mildred Bernice Marshall, who hailed from Texas and New York in the USA. The African-American press carried news of their wedding, picturing them smiling outside the church alongside Lew Leslie, the white producer of the famous *Blackbirds* revue.[10]

*   *   *

Yet while it might not have been obvious to the white audiences flocking to see 'American' jazz, black London was tremendously diverse. The Denizes's journey to Northview demonstrated this clearly. Clara Wason (later Deniz) was born in 1911 in Grangetown, Cardiff. Her father was a sailor from Barbados who died when she was eighteen months old. Her mother, a white woman called Louise Bryant from Somerset, subsequently moved with Clara into the home of a Mrs Knight, herself a mixed-race Briton originally from Bristol. The community they were part of in Cardiff was one of several growing multiracial communities in Britain's port cities. Like Sowande, Wason's talent grew from an early age as she learnt piano and played her late father's guitar.[11] Despite their different upbringings in Lagos and Cardiff, music also offered Wason a creative outlet and the hope of material advancement.

In 1936, Wason joined other Cardiff musicians who decided sensibly that London's – or more precisely, Soho's – jazz scene offered better prospects for a successful career. Francisco (known as Frank) Deniz soon had the same idea. The Deniz family, which included musician brothers Joe and Laurie, hailed from the other side of Cardiff Bay in Butetown. Their father, Antonio, was a merchant seaman originally from the Cape Verde Isles – a Portuguese colony that was a key staging post for the transatlantic slave trade – while their mother Gertrude was reportedly of Anglo-Afro American descent. Frank was taught violin by his father and played Portuguese-inspired music before following his path into the merchant navy. He travelled the world, visiting China, India, Australia and the Soviet Union where his father, on the same ship, died in 1931. During these journeys, Frank experienced adventure and freedom but also racial discrimination in various forms, including visiting the southern port of Jacksonville, Florida, during the heyday of 'Jim Crow' segregation.[12]

Clara first moved to London to play with Joe Deniz, but soon returned to Cardiff to marry Frank.[13] When the couple returned to the capital, they began playing in Soho's notorious 'bottle parties', places that served alcohol without licenses and stayed open until the small hours. Clara was the first to get a more official gig, playing piano for Ken 'Snakehips' Johnson's popular West Indian band. Soon after, Frank established himself as a guitar player at the same place: the Old Florida Club – an establishment in Bruton Mews in Mayfair owned by African-American singer Adelaide Hall and her Trinidadian husband Bertram Hicks.[14] The pianist at the Florida, meanwhile, was Fela Sowande, beginning an acquaintance between them all that lasted over a decade. The *Melody Maker* took notice, reporting that the band wore 'white suits with black shirts, white ties and shoes, and red carnations in their button holes', often playing until five in the morning. The Old Florida Club's success reached the USA too, with the 'What's Going on in London' column in the *Chicago Defender* reporting that the 'Race swing combo' was 'all set for big business'.[15]

We do not know who moved in first or if they were both tipped off about the opportunity together, but it was clearly no coincidence that the Sowandes and Denizes

Figure 32.1 'Adelaide Hall and Fela Sowande at the Florida Club' (1940). © The Stephen Bourne Collection/Mary Evans Picture Library.

ended up as neighbours. Shared historical forces, musical interests and abilities, and financial incentives brought them together, despite their diverse backgrounds from the British and Portuguese empires. These connections were forged not just on the London stage, but in a more domestic setting just a short journey up the Northern Line to a symbol of middle-class advancement at Northview.

* * *

The blocks' residents experienced a mixture of high drama and humdrum semi-normality when war came. The Nichols at number 24 took up posts as Air Raid Precaution (ARP) wardens, responsible for ensuring the blackout was maintained. Yet during the 'Phony War' that lasted until the spring of 1940, life would have continued comparatively normally, save for the privations of rationing. The handful of children in the flats were mostly infants, meaning evacuation also made little impact.

Things soon changed. As the Blitz began, central Holloway was bombed several times. North London was not hit as hard as the East End docks, but its proximity to central London and the fact that many munitions factories were dotted around the nearby North

Circular Road made it a target. The closest Northview came to destruction was when a bomb hit the Gaumont Theatre – itself only constructed in 1938 – on the opposite corner of the junction. The auditorium was badly damaged, though most of the architecturally imposing façade survived.[16] The raid would have been a common talking point for local residents: it certainly would have disrupted the lives of Marian Christie who lived at number 6 and Marie Stevens at number 16, both in their early twenties and who worked as a cinema attendant and usherette.[17]

Life on the wartime London stage also found a way to continue despite the blackout, rationing and occasional bombardment. The 1940 Pathetone film *Behind the Blackout* captured this 'carry on' spirit, including a selection of music hall and variety acts to show how life was enduring. In an upbeat scene from the Florida, Sowande accompanied Adelaide Hall in a lively rendition of "Tain't what you do it's the way that you do it', providing a rare but revealing cinematic glimpse into the burgeoning black presence in London's theatres and clubs.[18] Yet the reality of war was close by. That same club was destroyed by a bomb just a few months later, though a new Florida Club was established nearby which became popular with American service personnel and was subsequently visited by Bob Hope and Fred Astaire. For some performers, however, the war brought a cruel end. Ken 'Snakehips' Johnson, well known to both Sowande and the Denizes and famous on the London scene, was one of several killed when a bomb hit the Cafe de Paris on Piccadilly Circus in March 1941. The venue had previously been advertised as 'London's safest restaurant'.[19]

Fela Sowande escaped this brutal fate, but experienced personal problems of his own. A month after war broke out, his African-American wife, Mildred, left for New York City and took their two young daughters with her, fearful of the impending bombardment of the capital.[20] Soon after, Sowande found himself in trouble with the law, accused of assaulting white actress Laura Hudson and called before Marylebone police court to answer the charge. Sowande's counter-claim was that Hudson had put a curse on him that was responsible for his unemployment, while Hudson argued that he had stormed into her Regent's Park apartment and threatened to 'break every bone in her body' if she contacted his wife in the USA. The court, however, found Hudson's story 'exaggerated' and, rather than convicting Sowande, placed both parties under a year-long peace bond. The story was high-profile (and perhaps salacious) enough to receive coverage from the Associated Negro Press (ANP) and was picked up by the *Chicago Defender*.[21]

One is left to guess what lay behind this turbulent period in Sowande's life, as well as whether this episode reached Mildred in America, but the war soon offered new professional opportunities. He was awarded his degree by the University of London and was elected a fellow of the Royal College of Organists.[22] As his reputation grew, Sowande began working for the government as a composer for the Colonial Film Unit (CFU), a group set up in 1939 under the control of the Ministry of Information based at Senate House in Bloomsbury. The CFU's wartime remit was to produce films to promote loyalty among African people during the war – a patronizing enterprise that also offered a back-handed compliment that the African continent was an important theatre of battle and, with Indian independence becoming more likely, central to Britain's post-war imperial vision. Sowande's job was to compose background music; his hybrid compositional styles, which were also used by the BBC's Africa Service, made his work a perfect fit for propaganda that aimed to appeal to African sensibilities while retaining notions of British superiority.[23]

The irony was, of course, that Sowande was involved with groups like WASU that were fiercely critical of British imperial policies before, during and after the war. In this sense, Sowande experienced his own version of an insider-outsider 'double life' experienced by other black Londoners during wartime. Jamaican poet, playwright and journalist Una Marson was another example, whose creative work addressed the problems of racism and empire but who also spent the war working for the BBC presenting the programme *Calling the West Indies*. Moreover, creative black Londoners like Sowande and Marson found the war offered new opportunities and a greater degree of acceptance into 'mainstream' British culture, at the very same time as the arrival of a segregated US Army meant racial discrimination became a newly visible problem on London's streets.[24]

The turbulence of war, meanwhile, was shaking the British imperial edifice in ways that officials in London could scarcely comprehend. Frank Deniz saw this reality first-hand when he was recalled into the merchant navy to work in the engine rooms of ships alongside his brother Joe, typical of the 'below decks' roles to which non-white sailors were relegated. Visiting the Americas offered him a global perspective on the war, as well as opportunities to reacquaint himself with the Latin American music that had been part of his life since childhood. In North America, meanwhile, he met Louis Armstrong while his ship was docked in San Francisco. Closer to home, Deniz played for wounded troops in France as part of a service jazz quartet and survived a bombing attack while onboard his ship.[25]

When he returned, with the musical ability and worldwide experience to traverse multiple cultural worlds, Deniz's music took a Latin turn. Three Denizes – Clara, Frank and Joe – formed the Hermanos Deniz Cuban Rhythm Orchestra and were featured by the BBC in a radio broadcast that reached an audience of five million. The Denizes' musical abilities and possession of a racial 'exoticism' meant they easily appeared as an authentic Latin act to white audiences.[26] This shift toward South American music, meanwhile, can be read as an attempt to move beyond the more limited roles and negative connotations associated with American-style jazz.[27] Therefore, not only was there a multiracial black presence in the heart of the wartime city, but it was a presence within which racial identities were complex, overlapping and ever-evolving.

* * *

The racial remapping of London, and of notions of the Londoner, became an ever-more important feature of life in the post-war city. But the Sowandes' and Denizes' wartime experiences provide an important reminder that the arrival of the SS *Windrush* in 1948 was far from 'year zero' in this history. In the period that followed, they remained part of a growing number of black musicians and performers who began to carve out a more regular space in British public life. In 1953, set against a backdrop of the upcoming coronation and amidst large-scale immigration from the Caribbean, these musical neighbours were reunited on the BBC radio programme *Club Ebony*. Listeners were invited to join the 'coloured guests in their club of the air', as Clara sang, Frank played guitar and Fela Sowande led the musical direction.[28]

The programme exemplified the slow, often grudging, progress black people made towards acceptance in 'mainstream' culture in post-war Britain. It was no coincidence that some of those who made even greater headway subsequently, like Shirley Bassey, had comparable backstories to earlier pioneers like Clara Deniz. Yet the Second World War's legacies went far beyond London, or even Britain. The conflict helped foment the end of empire in sub-Saharan Africa, an event Sowande witnessed first-hand. After leaving London in the mid-1950s, he was appointed head of music at the Nigerian Broadcasting Corporation before moving into academia at the University of Ibadan.[29] Reflecting some enduring connections to Britain, Sowande was commissioned by the BBC to compose a *Folk Symphony* to mark independence in 1960. Sowande's academic career subsequently took him to the USA, where he arrived during the heyday of the Civil Rights and Black Power movements and was uniquely well positioned to address an upsurge in interest in black culture in all its international guises.[30]

Northview's wartime story may have offered just a small snapshot of these bigger historical forces. It is worth dwelling on the fact, however, that these same forces were integral to the conflict and its aftermath: that the war's front line was on Britain's bomb-damaged and ration-hit streets as well as the battlefields of Europe and the Pacific; that Britain's empire was a source of vital support but whose subjects would not accept a return to the pre-war status quo; and that race was becoming a category alongside class that shaped both the social reality and cultural perception of life on London's streets. Like these long-range trends, Northview itself endures into the twenty-first century as a rare but important example of a pre-war multi-storey residential building. Its residents' stories remind us that London's multiracial experience was not the sole preserve of the post-war period but, instead, was part of a longer history. The bigger history revealed by this snapshot, moreover, was decided by an interplay of the profoundly local – including the bricks and mortar of Art Deco buildings and the intersections of road and rail routes – and the truly global forces of empire, immigration and war.

Notes

1. 1939 National Register, RG101/0260D/006/31. Among the more colourful residents was Sidney Solomon Daniels, a Jewish East-Ender who achieved a degree of fame as a 'radio magician' and adopted a comedic act in which he wore a fez – anticipating a device deployed successfully years later by Tommy Cooper.
2. Ibid.

3. Bode Omojola, 'Style in Modern Nigerian Art Music: The Pioneering Works of Fela Sowande', *Africa: Journal of the International African Institute* 68, no. 4 (1998): 455–6.

4. Val Wilmer, 'Sowande, Charles Emanuel Olufela Obafunmilayo (Fela) (1905–1987)', *Oxford Dictionary of National Biography* (Oxford: Oxford University Press, 2020), https://doi-org. ezproxy.neu.edu/10.1093/odnb/9780198614128.013.94664.

5. Ibid.

6. Eileen Southern and Fela Sowande, 'Conversation with Fela Sowande, High Priest of Music', *Black Perspective in Music* 4, no. 1 (1976): 95.

7. Wilmer, 'Sowande'.

8. Southern and Sowande, 'Conversation with Fela Sowande', 96.

9. Bode Omojola, 'Black Diasporic Encounters: A Study of the Music of Fela Sowande', *Black Music Research Journal* 27, no. 2 (2007): 148.

10. 'African, American Married', *Pittsburgh Courier*, 17 October 1936, 7.

11. Wilmer, 'Sowande'.

12. Val Wilmer, 'Frank Deniz', *Guardian*, 30 July 2005, https://www.theguardian.com/news/2005/jul/30/guardianobituaries.artsobituaries; 'The Deniz Dynasty', https://gypsyjazzuk.wordpress.com/36-2/the-deniz-dynasty/.

13. 'Trailblazer for Bassey Dies Aged 91', *Wales on Sunday*, 5 January 2003, 13.

14. Stephen Bourne, *Mother Country: Britain's Black Community on the Home Front, 1939–45* (Cheltenham: History Press, 2010), 89; David Dabydeen, John Gilmore and Cecily Jones, *The Oxford Companion to Black British History* (Oxford: Oxford University Press, 2007), 522.

15. Andy Gray, 'What's Going on in London', *Chicago Defender*, 14 January 1939, 19; A. Simons, 'Black British Swing', *IAJRC Journal* 41, no. 4 (2008): 65.

16. 'Odeon Cinema', https://britishlistedbuildings.co.uk/101384986-odeon-cinema-st-georges-ward#.YJwlr7VKhPY.

17. 1939 Register.

18. *Behind the Blackout* (UK: British Pathé, 1940).

19. Bourne, *Mother Country*, 76, 89; Dabydeen et al., *Oxford Companion*, 522; Constantine FitzGibbon, *The Blitz* (London: Wingate, 1957), 245–6.

20. 'Passage of St John from Southampton to New York City, 16 October 1939', Passenger Lists Leaving UK 1890–1960, https://www.findmypast.co.uk.

21. 'Tells Actress Put Curse on Him', *Chicago Defender*, 13 April 1940, 21.

22. Omojola, 'Style in Modern Nigerian Art Music', 456.

23. Ibid., 457. 'Colonial Film Unit', http://www.colonialfilm.org.uk/production-company/colonial-film-unit.

24. Oliver Ayers, 'Jim Crow and John Bull in London: Transatlantic Encounters with Race and Nation in the Second World War', *Studies in Ethnicity and Nationalism* 20, no. 3 (2020): 244–66.

25. Val Wilmer, 'Deniz, Francisco Antonio [Frank] (1912–2005), Guitarist and Bandleader', *Oxford Dictionary of National Biography* (Oxford: Oxford University Press, 2020), https://doi-org.ezproxy.neu.edu/10.1093/ref:odnb/95285.

26. Simons, 'Black British Swing', 63.

27. Wilmer, 'Frank Deniz'.

28. 'Club Ebony', *Radio Times*, 3 April 1953, 24. Cy Grant, who was also part of the show, was another good example of a black Briton who both served in the war and later became a recognizable figure on post-war radio and television.

29. Omojola, 'Style in Modern Nigerian Art Music', 457.

30. Omojola, 'Black Diasporic Encounters', 150.

CHAPTER 33

EXILES OF NW3: THE 'FREE GERMAN LEAGUE OF CULTURE' IN UPPER PARK ROAD

David Anderson

The wanderer through London finds only occasional traces of German presences that have shaped the city. One example is the battered plaque attached to the railway bridge serving Cannon Street station, marking the former site of a complex known in the Middle Ages, for reasons that are unclear, as the 'Steelyard'. An outpost of the federation of city-states known as the Hanseatic League, this was a hub of German culture long before the federal republic now known as Germany came into existence. The plaque was unveiled in 2005. A citation from Schiller's *Wilhelm Tell* (1804) sits beneath an inscription celebrating 'sixty years of peace between the peoples of Britain and Germany':

> *Das Alte stürzt, es ändert sich die Zeit,*
> *Und neues Leben blüht aus den Ruinen.*

> [The times are changing, what is old must fall,
> And new life bursts in blossom from the ruins.][1]

As mighty as the Steelyard may once have been, and however grand the ceremony of the plaque's unveiling (presided over by the Duke of Kent and the then German Ambassador to the UK, Thomas Matussek), there's a note of sadness to the location. A decade before the British people voted to leave the European Union, the strain in a never fully *seamless* relationship can be detected. The plaque is sited in what is, today, an inauspicious spot. A short stretch of the riverbank here is called 'Hanseatic Walk', but the almost complete lack of public awareness of the Steelyard – which was, after all, a significant institution located on this site for six centuries – attests to the strange mixture of uneasiness and indifference on the British side of the post-1945 'peace'.

When it comes to commemorative prompts in the urban landscape, the spirit of the age in Britain is surely more acutely represented by Arthur 'Bomber' Harris's statue outside the Royal Air Force church on the Strand, a mile or so to the west, unveiled on the anniversary of Harris's birthday on 31 May 1992. The event is captured in Patrick Keiller's documentary-fiction film *London* (1994): the brass avatar of the 'Butcher of Dresden', cloaked in a Union Jack, is presented to watching crowds with full state circumstance (the Queen Mother was present at the occasion). The scene is of a piece with Keiller's depiction of London's public spaces in the 1990s as 'either void, or the stage sets for spectacles of nineteenth-century reaction, endlessly re-enacted for television', as well as a sense of Britain having failed to reinvent its national self-image after the loss of empire, depending instead upon 'heavily filtered and idealised portraits of anti-Nazi war', as Paul Gilroy put it in 2008.[2] 'The times are changing, what is old must fall', in Schiller's words, but in what form 'new life bursts in blossoms from the ruins' is another question entirely.

One example of a different mnemonic angle on the period of 1939–45 is presented by an address around the corner from Belsize Park station in Hampstead: 36 Upper Park Road, NW3. This was the clubhouse of the *Freier Deutscher Kulturbund in Großbritannien* or 'Free German League of Culture in Great Britain'. Part of 'a significant, but largely forgotten chapter in the history of the refugees from Hitler in Britain', the League gathered together many prominent figures – its honorary presidents included Alfred Kerr, Berthold Viertel, Oskar Kokoschka and Stefan Zweig; among its members were John Heartfield and Ernst Hermann Meyer – yet, particularly among the non-German-speaking community, it is little known today.[3] The house that was its base lacks even a blue plaque to commemorate what took place there.

The League was founded after a sharp increase in the number of German-speaking refugees from Europe following the *Anschluss* of Germany and Austria in March 1938, the *Reichskristallnacht* ('Night of Broken Glass') in November of the same year, and the seizure of Prague, where many political dissidents had hitherto found safe harbour, in March 1939. As Charmian Brinson and Richard Dove remark in their meticulous 2010 history of the League, *Politics by Other Means*, there are 'differing and even contradictory accounts' of who exactly founded it or precisely when.[4] It is agreed, however, that the idea became reality during a meeting held at 47 Downshire Hill, home of Fred and Diana Uhlman – the former a German-Jewish painter originally from Stuttgart, the latter a dissident descendant of the aristocratic Croft dynasty and daughter of nationalist Tory MP Henry Page Croft. Also present at the meeting were Hans Flesch, Jürgen Kuczynski and John Heartfield, whose four-year stay at this address *is* now commemorated with a blue plaque.

It was through Kuczynski's connections and the generosity of the Church of England, which owned the building, that the League secured its permanent premises at 36 Upper Park Road in December 1939, initially in the lower levels before occupying the entire house by the end of 1940. Though shunted up against the comparatively benighted neighbourhood of west Kentish Town (just a stone's throw away, on Malden Road, a huge spray-painted mural reads 'WHAT IF THE IGNORED UNITE?'), these streets now radiate warmth and wealth. Yet the early days of the League's tenancy were austere: Gerhard Hinze, one of its secretaries, 'remembered that the first meeting of the executive committee in the new house was held by candlelight, in icy-cold temperatures'. Only later were there creature comforts, including a restaurant, café and library. Brinson and Dove note that appeals were made to fund these additions as well as, 'above all, a piano' – their phrasing playing up the sense of culture as vital for survival.[5]

The League was separate from the 'Austrian Centre', headquartered in Paddington, even though key figures like Kokoschka and Zweig were actually Austrian (Kokoschka, in fact, was by the time of his emigration to England in October 1938 a Czech citizen, sparing him from internment as an 'enemy alien' after September 1939). It published a monthly newsletter, *Freie Deutsche Kultur* ('Free German Culture'), and hosted all manner of events including lectures, art classes and exhibitions, theatrical performances and other social gatherings, to which anti-Nazis of all nationalities were welcomed. Its five 'Sections' comprised Writers, Actors, Artists, Musicians and Scientists. Although the last of these might seem an odd fit, it is explained by the wider valency of the German concept of *Wissenschaft* and is perhaps better translated as 'Academic Section'. Its plans for a Free German University in exile bore fruit in the 'Free German Institute', which marked the League's focus on the role to be played by returning exiles in the reconstruction – cultural, political and practical – of a possible post-war Germany. Soon springing the nest of Upper Park Road, the Institute gained some degree of eminence: Einstein became its honorary president in 1943.

The League provided a solid base in a city experienced by refugees not only as a strange and foreign culture, but also as a bewildering array of associations, organizations, fronts and clubs, each with its own acronym, representing frequently overlapping cadres of refugees and anti-fascists. The profusion is indeed sometimes reminiscent of the joke about the 'People's Front of Judea' in *Monty Python's Life of Brian* (1979), yet the reality was hardly so light-hearted. In 1944, Kokoschka wrote a letter to Heinz Wolfgang Litten, director of the League's Kleine Bühne ('Little Theatre'), praising him as 'a water diviner in a parched desert' for his production of Heinrich von Kleist's *Amphitryon* (1808). Kokoschka's description of 'the feeling of rapture' produced by the play and his wish to send praise before this was 'sullied' by 'the journey home in the tube, past the advertisements for the theatrical offerings in this most unintellectual of cities' conveys something of the bitterness of exile even in a 'safe' place, where cultural and political activities were interrupted by internment and war work (including, for some of the League's actors, broadcasting on the BBC's German Service), and often went largely unrecognized outside of the milieu of the League itself.[6] Kokoschka's comment may have been prompted by his difficulties gaining the kind of recognition to which he was accustomed, yet his frustration wasn't simply vanity: as Cordula Frowein has observed, it's worth remembering that one of Herbert Read's chief anxieties when co-curating the *Twentieth Century German Art* exhibition, held at the New Burlington Galleries in 1938 as a counterweight to the Nazis' 'degenerate art' exhibition of the previous year, had been that an aesthetically conservative British public might actually be shocked into *agreeing* with the Nazis' taste.[7]

In this context of sometimes strained cultural exchange, it's notable that the Actors' Section of the League worked in both English and German, apparently managing with great skill the daunting task of staging dual-language performances aimed at mixed emigré and British audiences. Its 'Little Stage' in the largest room at 36 Upper Park Road measured just seven by ten feet, with eighty seats crammed into the space, but the section also broke out with works like *Mr Gulliver Goes to School*, premiered in July 1942, which made a small provincial tour. The production of politicized, topical ensemble revues like this one was, like the socially critical timbre of work made by the Artists' Section, without analogue in Britain. It broke new cultural ground, fusing elements of the English literary tradition into unfamiliar settings. At the same time, it ensured that an ember of the Berlin cabaret of the 1920s was kept glowing.

Figure 33.1 Front cover of the pamphlet for the *Allies Inside Germany* exhibition (1942). Printed courtesy of The Haldane Papers, UCL Library Services, Special Collections.

Max Zimmering estimated that the League organized an average of between three and four events per week across its lifespan. The sheer number created potential for comic occurrences like Johannes Fladung's double-booking to speak at the turn of midnight on New Year's Eve 1944 at celebrations held by the League and the affiliated 'Free German Youth' nearby. Adjustment of the clocks at each venue, one put forward five minutes, the other back, meant Fladung was able to see in the new year of 1945 in both places at once.[8] The incident reads like something from a comedy by J. B. Priestley, who was in fact a supporter of the League and spoke at some of its events. It speaks volumes in adding a touch of lightness to a period surrounded by gloom, sometimes on both sides. (Fladung, who had been tortured by the Nazis in the 1930s, was also prosecuted in the 1960s for supposed 'sedition' after returning to Düsseldorf, in a trial eventually called off due to his ill health). It also produces a strong image of the rich exilic texture of this chunk of north-west London, where a truly cosmopolitan cultural hubbub might make the review pages of local papers like the *Hampstead and Highgate Express* but was unlikely to register in the national press.

As in the case of *Mr Gulliver Goes to School*, there were exceptions to this rule. One was the revelatory *Allies Inside Germany* exhibition, a collaborative effort between all the League's various sections, which opened at 149 Regent Street in July 1942. A pamphlet advertising it promised to 'present documentary and other proof of the opposition to Hitler' among the German people:

> It will show the conditions under which the anti-Nazi opposition inside Germany is carrying on the heroic struggle against the Hitlerite force, who the people are, what methods they use and with what sacrifices and difficulties they are working to oppose Hitler's tyranny.[9]

The exhibition attracted 30,000 visitors to Regent Street before a year's tour to other cities, including Manchester, Oxford, Glasgow and Bristol. It represented a high point in the League's ability to transmit its political message to a British audience. As time wore on, however, its link to a possible future Germany became ever more strained. A 1943 pamphlet entitled *10 Jahre Kulturbarbarei im Dritten Reich, 10 Jahre freie deutsche Kultur im Exil* ('10 Years Cultural Barbarism in the Third Reich, 10 Years Free German Culture in Exile') bears the unmistakable symptoms of this disquiet. Its foreword speaks of the 'destruction, counterfeiting and perversion of culture' in the decade since the *Bücherverbrennung* ('book burning') in Germany.[10] Jürgen Kuczynski's contribution, taken from a debate on the theme of 'forms of life', opens with the bleak observation that 'what we are really talking about [...] is forms of death: of the death of culture in Germany; of the death of that which we call human; of that from which we derive the terms "humane" and "humanity"'.[11]

This note of pessimism and agonized uncertainty rings through the reflections of 1943 like the leaden wail of an air-raid siren. In fact, the work of League members during the Blitz, like the League's earlier advocacy against internment, had helped it win credibility among an exile constituency largely out of step with its pronounced left-wing alignment. As Keith Holz has remarked in a recent essay on German and Austrian exile artist groups, one of the League's distinguishing features was 'a leadership increasingly controlled by communists', and members who did return to Germany after 1945 mostly went to the Soviet Zone, staying in the GDR.[12] Even Kokoschka, sometimes regarded as a usefully 'unpartisan fig leaf' in his role as honorary president, had strong pro-Soviet leanings, painting the portrait of Soviet ambassador Ivan Maisky in 1942–3 to raise funds for a Stalingrad hospital.[13] Other key figures like Jürgen Kuczynski were later revealed to be Soviet spies. Brinson and Dove play down the 'undue communist influence' within the League, but this clearly ran deep. Yet, as they point out, most wartime emigrants were '"racial" refugees: Jewish, middle class and politically uncommitted'. Many non-partisan artists consistently viewed the League with suspicion. Kurt Schwitters, for example, kept his distance: for him, the League's concept of 'free culture' as committedly anti-fascist, unproblematic as that might seem, was nevertheless culture in the service of politics and not quite 'free' enough.[14]

The benefits of a good restaurant in bridging such differences of political opinion could not be underestimated. In a 1986 essay, refugee dramatist and scholar Martin Esslin reflected that 'the reputation of a decent *Lokal*, in which there was a palatable goulash or apple strudel to be had, could tempt even those at ideological loggerheads together'.[15] In this respect, the League's own 'continental kitchen' competed with others like the Austrian Centre's 'Laterndl' in nearby Swiss Cottage. Another key social hub was the stylish 'Isobar' in the basement of the Lawn Road Flats, a striking modernist development which opened in 1934 barely 200 metres away from the League's headquarters, and which is now familiarly known as the 'Isokon building' after the firm that built it.

With their innovative concrete construction (thought to be bomb-proof), clean modernist lines and efficient living spaces, the Lawn Road Flats are a more obvious relic of Anglo-German cultural fusion in this area. In fact, the maverick boss of Isokon, Jack Pritchard, who had been inspired by the German Bauhaus school and had visited its home in Dessau in 1931, later made sure that his building became home to refugee Bauhaus pioneers Walter Gropius, Marcel Breuer (who co-designed the Isobar) and László Moholy-Nagy during their brief time in London.[16] Other residents included Jürgen Kuczynski and his family, as well as the recruiter of the so-called 'Cambridge Spies' Arnold Deutsch, attesting to the heady mix of aesthetic and political avant-gardes on this site.

Although intended as a prototype for future social housing, the Lawn Road Flats were always themselves meant for 'middle-class people of moderate means' and struck some, like the International Brigades veteran Alexander Foote, who was recruited to Soviet intelligence there by Brigitte Kuczynski (sister of Jürgen) in 1938, as existing in glorious seclusion from anything resembling a workers' struggle.[17] Aesthetically out of step with their immediate surroundings, they're of a piece with the pioneering social housing developments which pepper this part of London, as well as other modernist icons like Berthold Lubetkin's Penguin Pool at London Zoo, which opened the same year. Unmissable as they are, they are part of a cultural legacy that has begun to be valued: in 2003 the site, which had been sold to Camden Council in 1972 and ultimately fallen derelict, was wholly purchased, renovated and remarketed as an outstanding example of modernist heritage. The unassuming brickwork of the Free League of German Culture's base at 36 Upper Park Road does not stand out in quite the same way, but its story attests to the rich cultural histories gathered up in this locality; to the ways that 'new life' can, after all, 'burst in blossom from the ruins', even in the direst of circumstances.

Notes

1. Friedrich Schiller, *William Tell*, trans. Francis Lamport (London: Libris, 2005), 4.2.

2. Patrick Keiller, *London* (London: FUEL, 2020), 54; Paul Gilroy, 'A Land of Tea-drinking, Hokey Cokey and Rivers of Blood', *Guardian*, 18 April 2008, https://www.theguardian.com/commentisfree/2008/apr/18/britishidentity.race.

3. Anthony Grenville, 'The Free German League of Culture', *AJR Journal* 10, no. 9 (2010): 1–2.

4. Charmian Brinson and Richard Dove, *Politics by Other Means: The Free German League of Culture in Great Britain* (London: Valentine Mitchell, 2010), 13.

5. Ibid., 28.

6. Ibid., 86.

7. Cordula Frowein, 'Ausstellungsaktivitäten der Exilkünstler', in *Kunst im Exil in Grossbritannien, 1933–1945*, ed. Hartmut Krug and Michael Nungesser (Berlin: Frölich & Kaufmann/Neue Gesellschaft für Bildende Kunst, 1986), 36–7.

8. Brinson and Dove, *Politics by Other Means*, 175–6.

9. Freier Deutscher Kulturbund in Großbritannien, *Allies Inside Germany* (London: FDKB, 1942), 4.

10. Freier Deutscher Kulturbund in Großbritannien, *10 Jahre Kulturbarbarei im Dritten Reich, 10 Jahre freie deutsche Kultur im Exil* (London: FDKB, 1943), 1. My translation.

11. Ibid., 59. My translation.

12. Keith Holz, 'Not Only Biographies: A Brief Institutional History of German and Austrian Exiled Artists in Britain', in *Insiders/Outsiders: Refugees from Nazi Europe and their Contribution to British Visual Culture*, ed. Monica Bohm-Duchen (London: Lund Humphries, 2019), 219.

13. Diether Schmidt, 'Partisan Oskar Kokoschka', in *Kunst im Exil in Grossbritannien, 1933–1945*, ed. Hartmut Krug and Michael Nungesser (Berlin: Frölich & Kaufmann/Neue Gesellschaft für Bildende Kunst, 1986), 192. My translation. See also Rüdiger Görner, *Kokoschka: The Untimely Modernist* (London: Haus, 2020), 179–84.

14. Brinson and Dove, *Politics by Other Means*, 15–17, 63–4.

15. Martin Esslin, 'Deutsche Intellektuelle im Englischen Exil', in *Kunst im Exil in Grossbritannien, 1933–1945*, ed. Hartmut Krug and Michael Nungesser (Berlin: Frölich & Kaufmann/Neue Gesellschaft für Bildende Kunst, 1986), 222. My translation.

16. See also Leyla Daybelge, 'The Lawn Road Flats', in *Insiders/Outsiders: Refugees from Nazi Europe and their Contribution to British Visual Culture*, ed. Monica Bohm-Duchen (London: Lund Humphries, 2019), 165–71.

17. David Burke, *The Lawn Road Flats: Spies, Writers and Artists* (Woodbridge: Boydell Press, 2014), 38, 112.

BIBLIOGRAPHY

Literature, film and music

al-Shaykh, Hanan. *Only in London*. London: Bloomsbury, 2002.

Anon., 'London, thou art of townes A per se'. In *London: A History in Verse*, edited by Mark Ford, 56–8. London: Belknap Press, 2012.

Bowen, Elizabeth. *The Death of the Heart*. Harmondsworth: Penguin, 1989.

Bowen, Elizabeth. *The Heat of the Day*. London: Vintage, 1998.

Bowen, Elizabeth. *Collected Stories*. London: Vintage, 1999.

Bowen, Elizabeth. 'Regent's Park and St John's Wood'. In *People, Places and Things: Essays by Elizabeth Bowen*, edited by Allan Hepburn, 100–5. Edinburgh: Edinburgh University Press, 2008.

Brathwaite, E. R. *To Sir, With Love*. London: Vintage, 2005.

Breaking Point: The Sus Law and Black Youth. Directed by Menelik Shabazz. ATV, 1978.

Dostoevsky, Fyodor. *Winter Notes on Summer Impressions* (1863). Translated and introduced by Kyril FitzLyon. Richmond: Alma Books, 2016.

Dread, Beat and Blood. Directed by Franco Rosso. BBC, 1979.

Hazlitt, William. *The Collected Works of William Hazlitt*. Edited by P. P. Howe. 21 vols. London and Toronto: J. M. Dent, 1930–4.

Johnson, Linton Kwesi. *Selected Poems*. London: Penguin, 2006.

Kapil, Bhanu. *Ban en Banlieue*. New York: Nightboat, 2015.

Keats, John. *The Poems of John Keats*. Edited by Jack Stillinger. Cambridge, MA: Harvard University Press, 1978.

Kureishi, Hanif. *The Buddha of Suburbia*. London: Faber, 1990.

Kureishi, Hanif. *The Black Album*. New York: Simon & Schuster, 1996.

Kureishi, Hanif. *My Beautiful Laundrette and Other Writings*. London: Faber, 1996.

Lord Kitchener. 'The Underground Train'. Shellac 10". Parlophone, 1950.

Lord Kitchener. 'London is the Place for Me'. Shellac 10". Melodisc, 1952.

Rodker, John. *Poems & Adolphe 1920*. Edited by Andrew Crozier. Manchester: Carcanet, 1996.

Sancho, Ignatius. *Minuets, Cotillons & Country Dances for the Violin, Mandolin, German Flute, & Harpsichord Composed by an African Most Humbly Inscribed to his Grace Henry Duke of Buccleugh*. London: Printed for the Author, [c. 1767].

Selvon, Sam. *Ways of Sunlight*. Harlow: Longman, 1981.

Selvon, Sam. *The Lonely Londoners*. London: Penguin, 2006.

St. Erkenwald. In *A Book of Middle English*, 3rd edn, edited by John Burrow and Thorlac Turville-Petre, 233–46. Oxford: Blackwell, 2005.

Woolf, Virginia. *Mrs Dalloway*. London: Penguin, 2000.

Interviews, letters and diaries

Keats, John. *The Letters of John Keats 1814–1821*. Edited by Hyder Edward Rollins. 2 vols. Cambridge, MA: Harvard University Press, 1958.

Bibliography

McCabe, Colin. 'Interview: Hanif Kureishi on London'. *Critical Quarterly* 41, no. 3 (1999): 37–56.

Sancho, Ignatius. *Letters of the late Ignatius Sancho, an African. In two volumes. To which are prefixed, memoirs of his life*. London: printed by J. Nichols, 1782.

Schlote, Christiane. 'An Interview with Hanan al-Shaykh'. *Literary London: Interdisciplinary Studies in the Representation of London* 1, no. 2 (2003).

Southern, Eileen and Fela Sowande. 'Conversation with Fela Sowande, High Priest of Music'. *The Black Perspective in Music* 4, no. 1 (1976): 90–104.

Van Gogh, Vincent. *The Complete Letters of Vincent Van Gogh*. 3 vols. London: Thames and Hudson, 1978.

Von la Roche, Sophie. *Sophie in London 1786, being the Diary of Sophie v. la Roche*. Translated by Clare Williams. London: Jonathan Cape, 1933.

Biographies and autobiographies

Blake Hannah, Barbara. *Growing Out: A Biography*. London: Hansib, 2010.

Glendinning, Victoria. *Elizabeth Bowen*. New York: Alfred A. Knopf, 1978.

Lott, Tim. *The Scent of Dried Roses*. London: Penguin, 1996/1997.

Markino, Yoshio. *A Japanese Artist in London*. London: Chatto & Windus, 1910.

Prescod, Colin. 'Carnival'. In *Claudia Jones: A Life in Exile*, edited by Marika Sherwood, 150–62. London: Lawrence and Wishart, 1999.

Rodker (née Cohen), Sonia. *The End Has Various Places*. Privately published, 2018.

Roe, Nicholas. *John Keats: A New Life*. New Haven, CT: Yale University Press, 2012.

Journalism and surveys

Anon., *The Practice of the Mendicity Society. By 'One who knows it well.'*. London: n.p., 1847.

Gilroy, Paul. 'A Land of Tea-drinking, Hokey Cokey and Rivers of Blood'. *Guardian*, 18 April 2008.

Judah, Ben. *This is London: Life and Death in the World City*. London: Pan Macmillan, 2016.

Mayhew, Henry. *London Labour and the London Poor*. 4 vols. London: Griffin, Bohn, and Company, 1861.

Nairn, Ian. 'Outrage'. *Architectural Review*, 1 June 1955.

Smith, John Thomas. *Vagabondiana: Or, Anecdotes of Mendicant Wanderers Through the Streets of London, with Portraits of the Most Remarkable Drawn from the Life*. London: n.p., 1817.

Stow, John. *A Survey of London by John Stow*. Edited by Charles Lethbridge Kingsford. Oxford: Clarendon Press, 1908.

Tristan, Flora. *Flora Tristan's London Journal 1840: A Survey of London Life in the 1830s*. Translated by Dennis Palmer and Giselle Pincetl. London: George Prior Publishers, 1980.

Ward, Ned. *The London Spy Compleat, in Eighteen Parts*. 4th edn. London: n.p., 1709.

Histories

Ackroyd, Peter. *London: A Biography*. London: Chatto & Windus, 2000.

Ackroyd, Peter. *Queer City: Gay London from the Romans to the Present Day*. New York: Abrams Press, 2018.

Adi, Hakim. 'West African Students in Britain, 1900–60: The Politics of Exile'. In *Africans in Britain*, edited by David Killingray, 107–28. Ilford: Francis & Taylor, 1994.

Adi, Hakim and Marika Sherwood. *Pan-African History: Political Figures from Africa and the Diaspora since 1787*. London: Routledge, 2003.

Akala. *Natives: Race & Class in the Ruins of Empire*. London: John Murray, 2019.

Ayers, Oliver. 'Jim Crow and John Bull in London: Transatlantic Encounters with Race and Nation in the Second World War'. *Studies in Ethnicity and Nationalism* 20, no. 3 (2020): 244–66.

Black, Eugene C. *The Social Politics of Anglo-Jewry, 1880–1920*. Oxford: Basil Blackwell, 1988.

Bourne, Stephen. *Mother Country: Britain's Black Community on the Home Front, 1939–45*. Cheltenham: History Press, 2010.

Brinson, Charmian and Richard Dove. *Politics by Other Means: The Free German League of Culture in Great Britain*. London: Valentine Mitchell, 2010.

Bucholz, Robert O. and Joseph P. Ward. *London: A Social and Cultural History, 1550–1750*. Cambridge: Cambridge University Press, 2012.

Bush, Barbara. *Imperialism, Race and Resistance: Africa and Britain, 1919–1945*. New York: Routledge, 1999.

Chater, Kathleen. *Untold Histories: Black People in England and Wales During the Period of the British Slave Trade, 1660–1807*. Manchester: Manchester University Press, 2009.

Cottrett, Bernard. *The Huguenots in England: Immigration and Settlement c.1550–1700*. Cambridge: Cambridge University Press, 1991.

Cox Jensen, Oskar. *The Ballad-Singer in Georgian and Victorian London*. Cambridge: Cambridge University Press, 2021.

Dabydeen, David, John Gilmore and Cecily Jones. *The Oxford Companion to Black British History*. Oxford: Oxford University Press, 2007.

Dennis, Ferdinand. *Behind the Frontlines: A Journey into Afro-Britain*. London: Gollancz, 1988.

Dodson, Danielle K. 'Minding the Gap: Uncovering the Underground's Role in the Formation of Modern London, 1855–1945'. Doctoral thesis, University of Kentucky, 2016.

Duffy, Eamon. *Royal Books and Holy Bones: Essays in Medieval Christianity*. London: Bloomsbury, 2018.

Elborough, Travis and Joe Kerr, eds. *Bus Fare: Writings on London's Most Loved Means of Transport*. Basingstoke: AA Publishing, 2018.

Feldman, David. *Englishmen and Jews: Social Relations and Political Culture, 1840–1914*. New Haven, CT, and London: Yale University Press, 1994.

Fryer, Peter. *Staying Power: The History of Black People in Britain*. London: Pluto Press, 1984.

Gartner, Lloyd. *The Jewish Immigrant in England, 1870–1914*. 2nd edn. London: Simon Publications, 1973.

Gerzina, Gretchen. *Black London: Life before Emancipation*. New Brunswick, NJ: Rutgers University Press, 1995.

Goose, Nigel and Lien Luu. *Immigrants in Tudor and Early Stuart England*. Brighton: Sussex Academic Press, 2005.

Grenville, Anthony. 'The Free German League of Culture'. *AJR Journal* 10, no. 9 (2010): 1–2.

Griffin, Sean. *The Liturgical Past in Byzantium and Early Rus*. Cambridge: Cambridge University Press, 2019.

Gwynn, Robin. *Huguenot Heritage: The History and Contribution of the Huguenots in Britain*. Brighton: Sussex Academic Press, 2001.

Hall, Stuart. 'The Local and the Global: Globalization and Ethnicity'. In *Culture, Globalization and the Third World System: Contemporary Conditions for the Representation of Identity*, edited by A. D. King, 19–40. Basingstoke: Macmillan, 1991.

Hall, Stuart. 'Frontlines and Backyards: The Terms of Change'. In *Black British Culture and Society: A Text Reader*, edited by Kwesi Owusu, 127–30. London: Routledge, 2000.

Bibliography

Hall, Stuart, Chas Critcher, Tony Jefferson, John Clarke and Brian Roberts. *Policing the Crisis: Mugging, The State, and Law and Order*. London: Macmillan, 1978.

Halliday, Stephen. *The Great Stink of London: Sir Joseph Bazalgette and the Cleansing of the Victorian Metropolis*. Stroud: Sutton Publishing, 1999.

Hingley, Richard. *Londinium: A Biography: Roman London from its Origins to the Fifth Century*. London: Bloomsbury, 2018.

Hitchcock, David. *Vagrancy in English Culture and Society, 1650–1750*. London: Bloomsbury Academic, 2016.

Hitchcock, Tim. *Down and Out in Eighteenth-Century London*. London: Continuum, 2004.

Hitchcock, Tim and Robert Shoemaker. *London Lives: Poverty, Crime and the Making of a Modern City, 1690–1800*. Cambridge: Cambridge University Press, 2015.

Holmes, Colin. *John Bull's Island: Immigration and British Society, 1871–1971*. Houndsmill: Macmillan Press, 1988.

Jackson, Lee. *Dirty Old London: The Victorian Fight Against Filth*. New Haven, CT: Yale University Press, 2014.

Keene, Derek, Arthur Burns and Andrew Saint, eds. *Saint Paul's: The Cathedral Church of London 604–2004*. New Haven, CT: Yale University Press, 2004.

Kerr, Joe and Andrew Gibson, eds. *London: From Punk to Blair*. London: Reaktion, 2003.

Koole, Simeon. 'How We Came to Mind the Gap: Time, Tactility, and the Tube'. *Twentieth Century British History* 27, no. 4 (2016): 524–54.

Lamont, Peter and Crispin Bates. 'Conjuring Images of India in Nineteenth-Century Britain'. *Social History* 32, no. 3 (2007): 308–24.

Lapshyna, Iryna. 'Do Diasporas Matter? The Growing Role of the Ukrainian Diaspora in the UK and Poland in the Development of the Homeland in Times of War'. *Central and Eastern European Migration Review* 8, no. 1 (2019): 51–73.

Matera, Marc. *Black London: The Imperial Metropolis and Decolonization in the Twentieth Century*. Oakland: University of California Press, 2015.

Olusoga, David. *Black and British: A Forgotten History*. London: Pan Books, 2017.

Ormrod, W. Mark, Bart Lambert and Jonathan Mackman. *Immigrant England, 1300–1550*. Manchester: Manchester University Press, 2019.

Ormrod, W. Mark, Joanna Story and Elizabeth M. Tyler, eds. *Migrants in Medieval England, c. 500–c. 1500*. Oxford: Oxford University Press, 2000.

Panayi, Panikos. *Migrant City: A New History of London*. New Haven, CT: Yale University Press, 2022.

Porter, Roy. *London: A Social History*. 1994 repr. London: Penguin, 2000.

Ramamurthy, Anandi. *Black Star: Britain's Asian Youth Movements*. London: Pluto, 2013.

Solomos, John, Bob Findlay, Simon Jones and Paul Gilroy. 'The Organic Crisis of British Capitalism and Race: The Experience of the Seventies'. In *The Empire Strikes Back: Race and Racism in 1970s Britain*, 9–46. Birmingham: Hutchinson & Co., 1982.

Stedman Jones, Gareth. *Outcast London: A Study in the Relationship Between Classes in Victorian Society*. 2nd rev. edn. London: Verso, 2013.

Summerson, John. *Georgian London*. Edited by Howard Colvin. New Haven, CT: Yale University Press, 2003.

Taylor, Michael. *The Interest: How the British Establishment Resisted the Abolition of Slavery*. London: Bodley Head, 2020.

Velten, Hannah. *Beastly London: A History of Animals in the City*. London: Reaktion, 2013.

White, Jerry. *London in the Nineteenth Century: A Human Awful Wonder of God*. London: Vintage, 2008.

White, Jerry. *London in the Twentieth Century: A City and Its People*. London: Vintage, 2008.

White, Jerry. *London in the Eighteenth Century: A Great and Monstrous Thing*. London: Bodley Head, 2012.

Whittall, Daniel. 'Creating Black Places in Imperial London: The League of Coloured Peoples and Aggrey House, 1931–1943'. *The London Journal* 36, no. 3 (2011): 225–46.

Winder, Robert. *Bloody Foreigners: The Story of Immigration to Britain.* 2nd edn. London: Abacus 2013.

Wise, Sarah. *The Italian Boy: Murder and Grave-Robbery in 1830s London.* London: Pimlico, 2005.

Literary, cultural and art criticism

Bohm-Duchen, Monica, ed. *Insiders/Outsiders: Refugees from Nazi Europe and their Contribution to British Visual Culture.* London: Lund Humphries, 2019.

Carey, Brycchan. '"The Extraordinary Negro": Ignatius Sancho, Joseph Jekyll, and the Problem of Biography'. *British Journal for Eighteenth-Century Studies* 26, no. 1 (2003): 1–13.

Carver, Gavin. 'The Effervescent Carnival: Performance, Context and Mediation at Notting Hill Carnival'. *New Theatre Quarterly* 16, no. 1 (2000): 34–49.

Cederwell, William. *Reading London in Wartime: Blitz, The People, and Propaganda in 1940s Literature.* Abingdon: Routledge, 2019.

Copeland, Raedene and Nancy Hodges. 'Exploring Masquerade Dress at Trinidad Carnival: Bikinis, Beads and Feathers and the Emergence of the Popular Pretty Mas'. *Clothing and Textiles Research Journal* 32, no. 3 (April 2014): 186–201.

Dadswell, Sarah. 'Jugglers, Fakirs, and *Jaduwallahs*: Indian Magicians and the British Stage'. *New Theatre Quarterly* 23, no. 1 (2007): 3–24.

Dart, Gregory. *Metropolitan Art and Literature, 1810–1840: Cockney Adventures.* Cambridge: Cambridge University Press, 2012.

Fanon, Frantz. *Black Skin, White Masks.* London: Pluto Press, 2008.

Grafen, Alex. 'The Whitechapel Renaissance and Its Legacies: Rosenberg to Rodker'. Doctoral thesis, UCL, 2020.

Hapgood, Lynne. *Margins of Desire: The Suburbs in Fiction and Culture, 1880–1925.* Manchester: Manchester University Press, 2005.

Heinz, Evi. 'John Rodker (1894–1955) and Modernist Material Culture: Theatre, Translation, Publishing'. Doctoral thesis, Birkbeck, 2018.

Krug, Hartmut and Michael Nungesser, eds. *Kunst im Exil in Grossbritannien, 1933–1945.* Berlin: Frölich & Kaufmann/Neue Gesellschaft für Bildende Kunst, 1986.

Landon, Philip. 'Great Exhibitions: Representations of the Crystal Palace in Mayhew, Dickens, and Dostoevsky'. *Nineteenth-Century Contexts* 20, no. 1 (1997): 27–59.

MacDougall, Sarah. 'Whitechapel Girl: Clare Winsten and Isaac Rosenberg'. In *Whitechapel at War: Isaac Rosenberg and His Circle*, edited by Rachel Dickson and Sarah MacDougall, 99–114. London: Ben Uri Gallery, 2008.

MacDougall, Sarah. '"Something Is Happening There": Early British Modernism, the Great War and the "Whitechapel Boys"'. In *London, Modernism, and 1914*, edited by Michael J. K. Walsh, 122–47. Cambridge: Cambridge University Press, 2010.

Makdisi, Saree. *Making England Western: Occidentalism, Race, and Imperial Culture.* Chicago: University of Chicago Press, 2014.

Mazower, David. 'Lazar Berson and the Origins of the Ben Uri Art Society'. In *The Ben Uri Story from Art Society to Museum and the Influence of Anglo-Jewish Artists on the Modern British Movement*, 37–58. London: Ben Uri Gallery, 2001.

Murdoch, Tessa. *Europe Divided: Huguenot Refugee Art and Culture.* London: V&A Publishing, 2021.

Natarajan, Uttara. 'The Veil of Familiarity: Romantic Philosophy and the Familiar Essay'. *Studies in Romanticism* 42, no. 1 (2003): 27–44.

Bibliography

Omojola, Bode. 'Style in Modern Nigerian Art Music: The Pioneering Works of Fela Sowande'. *Africa: Journal of the International African Institute* 68, no. 4 (1998): 455–83.

Omojola, Bode. 'Black Diasporic Encounters: A Study of the Music of Fela Sowande'. *Black Music Research Journal* 27, no. 2 (2007): 141–70.

Proctor, James. *Dwelling Places: Postwar Black British Writing.* Manchester: Manchester University Press, 2003.

Pryce, Everton A. 'The Notting Hill Gate Carnival – Black Politics, Resistance and Leadership 1976–1978'. *Caribbean Quarterly* 31, no. 2 (1985): 35–52.

Ranasinha, Ruvani. *South Asian Writers in Twentieth-Century Britain: Culture in Translation.* Oxford: Oxford University Press, 2007.

Rosenfeld, Sybil. *The Theatre of the London Fairs in the Eighteenth Century.* Cambridge: Cambridge University Press, 1960.

Sandhu, Sukhdev. *London Calling: How Black and Asian Writers Imagine a City.* London: HarperPerennial, 2004.

Scriven, Tom. 'The Jim Crow Craze in London's Press and Streets, 1836–39'. *Journal of Victorian Culture* 19, no. 1 (2014): 93–109.

Tompsett, Adela Ruth. 'London is the Place for Me: Performance and Identity in Notting Hill Carnival'. *Theatre History Studies* 25 (2005): 43–60.

Whale, John. 'Indian Jugglers: Hazlitt, Romantic Orientalism, and the Difference of View'. In *Romanticism and Colonialism: Writing and Empire, 1780–1830,* edited by Tim Fulford and Peter J. Kitson, 206–20. Cambridge: Cambridge University Press, 1998.

Wohlcke, Anne. *The 'Perpetual Fair': Gender, Disorder, and Urban Amusement in Eighteenth-Century London.* Manchester: Manchester University Press, 2014.

Young, Sarah J. *Russian Literature, History and Culture,* www.sarahjyoung.com.

INDEX

The letter *f* following an entry indicates a page with a figure.

10 Jahre Kulturbarbarei im Dritten Reich, 10 Jahre freie deutsche Kultur im Exil ('10 Years Cultural Barbarism in the Third Reich, 10 Years Free German Culture in Exile') pamphlet 283
19 Princelet Street, Spitalfields 95, 96–7, 98–9, 100–1
21 Princelet Street, Spitalfields 100
36 Upper Park Road, NW3 280, 281, 284
87 Hackford Road, Stockwell 145, 146*f*, 147
1851; Or, the Adventures of Mr. and Mrs. Sandboys and Family who came up to London to 'enjoy themselves,' and to see the Great Exhibition (Mayhew, Henry) 140

Aboulela, Leila
    Minaret 221, 222
Abraham, Mahomet 61
abstraction theory 44
accessibility 251
Adam Bede (Eliot, George) 149
Addison, Joseph 131, 184
Admonitions of the Instructress to the Court Ladies scroll (Gu Kaizhi) 6, 63*f*–7
Africa 273–4
Africa House 264–5, 266
African people 11, 273–4, 269, 270 *see also* West African people
    Lane, William Henry 132–3
    Sancho, Ignatius 27–33
    Solanke, Ladipo 263–4, 265, 266, 270
    Solanke, Olu 264, 265
    Sons of Africa 37
    Sowande, Fela 269, 270, 271, 272*f*, 273–4, 275
Agamben, Giorgio
    'Ban and the Wolf, The' 241
Aggrey House 264, 265–6
agriculture 127, 128
Alexander II (tsar of Russia) 138–9, 143
All the Tiny Moments Blazing: A Literary Guide to Suburban London (Femi, Caleb) 3
Allies Inside Germany exhibition 282*f*, i283
Allingham, Esther 35–6
Allinson, Adrian 110–12
American identities 270

Amphitryon (Kleist, Heinrich von) 281
Anansi (Akan character) 208–9
Anglo-Swedish Society 194, 195
animals 174–5, 177, 241
Anne (queen of Great Britain) 177, 183–4
Anthony, John 103
Applicants for Admission to a Casual Ward (Fildes, Luke) 150
Arab literature 221–2
Arab people 217, 218–22
Arabian Nights 218–19
archaeology 2, 19, 89–90, 127
architecture 203
art 8–9, 10, 13*f*–14 *see also* craft *and* Gogh, Vincent van
    Admonitions of the Instructress to the Court Ladies scroll (Gu Kaizhi) 63*f*–7
    avant-garde 110–12
    British 191, 192, 194, 195
    Chinese 65–6, 67
    colophons 64–5
    dealers 146
    English 149
    German 281
    Hayman, Francis 132
    illustration 149–50
    Jewish 110–11
    realist 224
    Swedish 191, 194–5
Arthurian legend 212
As You Like It (Shakespeare, William) 132
Ashmole, Elias 130
Ashmolean Museum, Oxford 130
Asian people 8, 11–12, 103–5, 156, 237, 240
Asquith, Xavier 252 n. 12
assimilation 158, 211
Austin Friars Priory 90
Austrian Centre 280
avant-garde, the 110–12
Azikiwe, Nnamdi 'Zik' 264

Baker, John 38
'Ban and the Wolf, The' (Agamben, Giorgio) 241
Ban en Banlieue (Kapil, Bhanu) 12, 236, 237, 239–41

Index

banlieues 240–1
Baptista, John 35
Barbauld, Anna
    Eighteen Hundred and Eleven 182, 188
Barbon, Nicholas 57
Bartholomew Fair 173, 175, 176
Bartholomew Fair: An Heroi-Comical Poem 176
'Basement Lullaby' (Selvon, Sam) 205
Bassano family 91
Bayswater 200, 205, 211
Bede 19–20, 22
    Ecclesiastical History of the English People 5, 19
Beer in the Snooker Club (Ghali, Waguih) 221
Beggar's Opera, The (Gay, John) 54
begging 49–50, 51, 53, 54 *see also* Mendicity Society
Behind the Blackout film 273
Bell journal 138
belonging 166–7, 169
Bezer, John James 58–9, 61
Bhabha, Homi
    Location of Culture, The 159
Bickham, George 186–7
    Three Cherokees, Came Over from the Head of
        the River Savanna to London, The 187f
Billy Liar (Waterhouse, Keith) 158
Binyon, Laurence 65–6
    Painting in the Far East 65
Black Album, The (Kureishi, Hanif) 160
Black and British: A Forgotten History (Olusoga,
    David) 37
Black Lives Matter movement 1, 2
Black people 6–7, 11–12, 35, 60, 211–12 *see also*
    race/racism *and* slavery
    Abraham, Mahomet 61
    Allingham, Esther 35–6
    belonging 166–7, 169
    Blake Hannah, Barbara 165–6
    celebration of 13f
    community 37–8
    culture 229
    double life 274
    employment 176, 209, 249, 250
    as entertainment 175
    Fanon, Frantz 164–5
    hostels 263–6
    hostility 13
    Johnson, Joseph 52
    Johnson, Linton Kwesi 167, 168
    Lane, William Henry 132–3
    lived experience 164
    location 38–9
    McGee, Charles 49–53
    'mugging crisis' 167–8
    Narayan, Rudy 168
    in Notting Hill 163–4
    as performers 27, 32–3, 38

policing 167–8, 169
    Samee, Ramo 41–2f, 43, 45–6
    Sancho, Ignatius 27–33
    Selvon, Sam 166–7, 205–7
    sex industry 35, 38
    Smith, John Thomas 52
    Solanke, Ladipo 263–4, 265, 266, 270
    Solanke, Olu 264, 265
    Sons of Africa 37
    St Giles 'Black-Birds' 35–9
    style 164
    transport 164–7
    WASU 263
Black Skins, White Masks (Fanon, Frantz) 164,
    211–12
Blake Hannah, Barbara 165–6
Blanchard, Jerrold
    London, a Pilgrimage 150
Blitz, the 11, 265, 272–3
Bloch, Martin 11
    'Bomb Damage, City of London' 11f
Bloomsbury 270
boar 241
'Bomb Damage, City of London' (Bloch,
    Martin) 11f
Bomberg, David 107, 110, 111
Book of Snobs, The (Thackery, W. M.) 41
Booth, Charles
    'Poverty Map' 99
botany 130, 208
Bourdon, Peter 98
Bowen, Elizabeth 11, 69–74
    'Coming to London' 69
    Death of the Heart. The 71–2
    'Forgotten Art of Living, The' 72
    'Happy Autumn Fields, The' 73
    Heat of the Day, The 72–3, 74
    House in Paris, The 70–1
    'I Hear You Say So' 74
    'Mysterious Kôr' 11
    'Oh, Madam . . .' 73
    Pictures and Conversations 69
    'Regent's Park and St John's Wood' 70
Brathwaite, E. R. 165
    To Sir, With Love 165
Brave New World (Huxley, Aldous) 142
Bréauté, Falkes de 128
Brick Lane Mosque 222
Bridge Street, Blackfriars 50f–1
Bridgerton TV show 39
Brighter Sun, A (Selvon, Sam) 206, 207
Brighton Exhibition of Swedish Art (1911) 194
Brinson, Charmian and Dove, Richard 283
    Politics by Other Means 280
Briscoe, Winston 245
British Empire 6

British Museum 6, 63, 65–6
Brixton 167, 168–9, 245
Bromley 157
Bronze Age structures 127
Bronze Woman (Barbat, Aleix) 13*f*
Brutus of Troy 5, 22, 23
Buddha of Suburbia, The (Kureishi, Hanif) 12, 156–9, 236
Bunyan, John
    Pilgrim's Progress, A 149
Burbage, James 91, 92
Burbage, Richard 92
burial grounds 103, 105
Burman, Chila Kumari Singh
    Remembering a Brave New World 14
Burne-Jones, Edward 193, 194
Burton, Richard 218
Bus We Loved, The (Elborough, Travis) 245
buses 165–6, 168, 211, 245–51

Cafe de Paris 273
Calling the West Indies radio programme 274
calypso 168, 207, 209–10, 212
'Calypso in London' (Selvon, Sam) 207, 209–10
Camden 264, 266
Cameron, Alan 69, 72, 73
Canboulay 209
Cardiff 271
Caribbean, the 209
    carnivals 227–30
Caribbean (West Indian) people 11, 163–7, 207–15, 248 *see also* Windrush generation
    McGee, Charles 49–53
    Selvon, Sam 166–7, 205–7
Caribbean literature 207, 208–9
Caribbean Voices radio programme 207
carnival/s 176, 209, 227–30, 231–2
    Notting Hill Carnival 13, 134, 210, 228–30, 231, 232
Carter, J. 177
Cathay (Pound, Ezra) 66
Cavanagh, John 45
cesspools 119
CFU (Colonial Film Unit) 273–4
Chadwick, Edwin 118–19
Chagger, Gurdip Singh 237
charity 53, 54, 99, 105, 184 *see also* Mendicity Society
Charles McGee (Smith, John Thomas) 52*f*
Chaste Maid in Cheapside, A (Middleton, Thomas) 79–81, 82–4
Chernyshevsky, Nikolai 138–9, 140, 143
    What is to be Done? 139–40, 142, 143
Cherokee people 184–5, 186–8
Chevras Nidvath Chen Synagogue 99
Chill October (Millais, John Everett) 149

China Cantos (Pound, Ezra) 67
Chinese and Japanese Painting AD 500–1900 exhibition (1910) 6, 65–6
Chinese art 65–6, 67 see also *Admonitions of the Instructress to the Court Ladies* scroll
Chinese people 8 *see also* Lascar people
Chinese poetry 66–7
Christianity 19, 20–4
    Nigeria 270
    Rus people 223–4, 225
Chronicle of Nestor 224
'Cit's Country-Box, The' (Lloyd, Robert) 259
City Atlas, The (Starr, Sidney) 247*f*
city comedies 80
City Gardener, The (Fairchild, Thomas) 97
Clarence Terrace 69–70, 72, 73–4
Clausen, George 193, 194
Cloud, The (Eugen [prince of Sweden]) 194
Clough, Joe 248–9*f*
Club Ebony radio programme 275
Cockney 259
Cohen, Sonia 107, 108, 109*f*–10, 111–12
    Way to Beauty: A Complete Guide to Personal Loveliness, The 108
coinage 121–2, 174*f*–5
Coleridge, Samuel Taylor
    'Frost at Midnight' 258
Colonial Centre 265–6
Colonial Film Unit (CFU) 273–4
colonizing imagination 44
colophons 64–5
colour-blind casting 39
Colthurst, Edmund 81–2
Colvin, Sidney 65
'Coming to London' (Bowen, Elizabeth) 69
commemorations 279
Commission on Race and Ethnic Disparities: The Report 232
communal living 140
communication 187–8
communism 283
community 23, 36–8, 59–60, 230, 231, 232
Complete and Humorous Account of the Remarkable Clubs and Societies in the Cities of London and Westminster (Ward, Ned) 177
Connolly, Cyril 70
Constable, John
    Valley Farm 149
Contemporary journal 137, 138
Cook, James 6
Coper, Hans 199, 200, 201, 202, 203
Coper, Hans and Rie, Lucie 201
    'Sgraffito Bowl, Manganese Glaze' 201*f*
corruption 258
cosmopolitanism 12
costume 230

Index

Counterflows to Colonialism (Fisher, Michael) 105
Covid-19 pandemic 227
Cowper, William
    'On Mrs Montagu's Feather Hangings' 185–6
craft 199–203
Crane, Walter 194, 218
Crime and Punishment (Dostoevsky, Fyodor)
    141–2
Cruikshank, George
    London going out of Town – or – The March of
    Bricks and Mortar! 256, 257*f*, 259
Crystal Palace 137–8, 139*f*, 140–1, 142, 143
crystal palaces 137, 139–40
cultural appropriation 218
culture 181, 182, 184, 275, 281
    Black 229
    German 10, 280–4
    global 60, 137, 175–6, 182, 185, 186
    nature and 259, 260
    salon 185–6
    street 59–60, 61
Cumberland, George 29

dance 132–3
de Waal, Edmund
    Library of Exile 13–14
Death of the Heart, The (Bowen, Elizabeth)
    71–2
Demons, The (Dostoevsky, Fyodor) 143
Deniz, Antonio 271
Deniz, Clara (née Watson) 269, 271, 274, 275
Deniz, Frank 269, 271, 274, 275
Deniz, Joe 271, 274
depression 238, 239
deprivation 8, 36 *see also* Mendicity Society *and*
    poverty
    Lascar people 103–5
    begging 49–50, 51, 53, 54
Deserted – A Foundling (Holl, Frank) 150
Dickens, Charles 132–3, 151
    Great Expectations 158
    Mystery of Edwin Drood, The 150
    Sketches by Boz 133
    'Vauxhall Gardens by Day' 133
Digswell 202, 203
diplomacy 183–4, 186
Dirty mas 230
discrimination 13, 30, 249, 263
disorder 176
dissidence 138
diversity 39
division 211–12
docklands 8
Doré, Gustav 150
    London, a Pilgrimage 150
    Newgate Prison Exercise Yard 151

Dostoevsky, Fyodor 140–2
    Crime and Punishment 141–2
    Demons, The 143
    Notes from Underground 142
    Winter Notes on Summer Impressions 141
Dubois (Duboc), Esther 96
Duckworth, George H. 99
Duke, Richard 27
Dunton, John
    He-Strumpets, The 177
Dutch people 90 *see also* Gogh, Vincent van

Earl's Court Station (Markino, Yoshio) 9*f*
East End, the 107–12
East India Company (EIC) 103, 105
Ecclesiastical History of the English People
    (Bede) 5, 19
economy 8
Edgware Road 217, 219, 221–2
Edmonton 255, 256–8
EIC (East India Company) 103, 105
Eighteen Hundred and Eleven (Barbauld, Anna)
    182, 188
elephants 174–5, 177
Eliot, George
    Adam Bede 149
employment 8, 59, 176, 209
    buses 248, 249, 250
    sex industry 35, 38, 176, 219, 220
    women 248, 250
Empty Chair, The (Fildes, Luke) 151
Enfield 255, 256–8
entertainment 32–3, 38 *see also* music
    Africa House 264
    Aggrey House 265
    animals 174–5, 177
    Black people as 175
    calypso 168, 207, 209
    Canboulay 209
    carnival/s 176, 209, 227–30, 231–2
    colour-blind casting 39
    dance 132–3
    ethnicity 175
    fairs 173–6, 177–8
    juggling 41–6
    literary gatherings 70
    Lord Mayor's inauguration 82
    masquerade 229–30
    Notting Hill Carnival 13, 134, 210, 228–30,
        231, 232
    pleasure gardens 130–4, 260
    theatre 32–3, 91–2, 273, 281
    water 81, 82
equality 248, 251
Erkenwald, Saint (bishop) 19–24
Essay on Shakespeare (Montagu, Elizabeth) 188

Esslin, Martin 284
ethnicity 175
Eugen (prince of Sweden) 191, 192*f*, 193–4, 195
    Cloud, The 194
Evans, Diana
    Wonder, The 231
Evil May Day 12
expansion 7–8

Fairchild, Thomas 96
    City Gardener, The 97
fairs 173–6, 177–8
'Famous Voyage, The' (Jonson, Ben) 81
'Fan-Piece for Her Imperial Lord' (Pound, Ezra) 66
Fanon, Frantz 164–5
    Black Skins, White Masks 164, 211–12
Fathers and Sons (Turgenev, Ivan) 139
feather wall 185
Femi, Caleb
    All the Tiny Moments Blazing: A Literary Guide
        to Suburban London 3
ferries 131
Fielding, Henry
    Tom Jones 158
Fildes, Luke 150
    Applicants for Admission to a Casual
        Ward 150
    Empty Chair, The 151
    'Houseless and Hungry' 150
First World War 248
Fisher, Michael
    Counterflows to Colonialism 105
Fladung, Johannes 282–3
Fleet River 80, 81, 82
Folk Symphony (Sowande, Fela) 275
foreigners 91
'Forgotten Art of Living, The' (Bowen, Elizabeth)
    72
found objects 121–2
Fournier Street, Spitalfields 96, 99–100
France 186
Frears, Stephen 155
Free German League of Culture in Great Britain
    (*Freier Deutscher Kulturbund in*
        Großbritannien) 10, 280–4
French people. *See* Huguenot people
'Frost at Midnight' (Coleridge, Samuel
    Taylor) 258
Fryer, Peter
    Staying Power 36

Garcia, Humberto 103
gardens 96–7, 259 *see also* horticulture
    Vauxhall Gardens 130–4, 260
Gaugin's Chair (Gogh, Vincent van) 151
Gaumont Theatre 273

gentrification 13, 231
Geoffrey of Monmouth 5, 22
    History of the Kings of Britain 22
geography 3
German people 7, 12, 175, 176, 279 *see also* Free
    German League of Culture in Great Britain
Germany 279 *see also* Free German League of
    Culture in Great Britain
Gertler, Mark 110, 111
Ghali, Waguih
    Beer in the Snooker Club 221
Giles, Herbert
    History of Chinese Literature, A 66
global culture 60, 137, 1756, 182
    Montagu, Elizabeth 185, 186
glottaling 213
Goldsmith's Row 80
Gole, Abraham 103–4
Gole, Abraham, Junior 103–4
Gogh, Vincent van 9, 145–9, 150–2
    Gaugin's Chair 151
    Potato Eaters, The 150
    Van Gogh's Chair 151
Gordon Riots 12
Graphic newspaper 149, 150, 151
Great Exhibition (1851) 137–8, 140
Great Expectations (Dickens, Charles) 158
Green, James
    Indian Jugglers, The 42*f*
Grenada 227
Grenfell Tower 231
Grupil & Co. 146, 147
Gu Kaizhi 63, 66
    Admonitions of the Instructress to the Court
        Ladies scroll 6, 63*f*–7
Guinea 174–5
guineas 174*f*–5
Guo Xi 67
Gustaf VI Adolf (king of Sweden) 195

Hackford Road, Stockwell 145, 146*f*, 147
Hackney, That Rose-Red Empire (Sinclair, Iain) 3
Hall, Adelaide 271, 272*f*, 273
Hall, Stuart
    Policing the Crisis 168
Hampstead 246, 259, 260, 280
Handel, George Frederic 131–2
    Music for the Royal Fireworks 132
Hanseatic League 279
'Happy Autumn Fields, The' (Bowen, Elizabeth)
    73
Harlots TV show 38, 39
Harriot (sex worker) 38
Harris, Arthur 'Bomber' 279
Harris's List of Covent Garden Ladies 38
Hatfield House 128

Index

Hayman, Francis 132
Hazlitt, William 41, 45
    abstraction theory 44
    epistemology 44–5
    'Indian Jugglers, The' 41, 42–6
He-Strumpets, The (Dunton, John) 177
Heartfield, John 280
Heat of the Day, The (Bowen, Elizabeth) 72–3, 74
Heidegger, John James 131
Herzen, Alexander 9, 138, 141, 142, 143
hiatus 213–14
History of Chinese Literature, A (Giles, Herbert) 66
History of the Kings of Britain (Geoffrey of Monmouth) 22
Hoffmann, Josef 200
Holl, Frank 150
    Deserted – A Foundling 150
Holland Park 217, 223
Hollar, Wenceslaus
    Monument to Saint Erkenwald in Old St Paul's Cathedral 21f
Hollywell Priory 89–90, 91
Holmes, (Isabella M.) Basil 104, 105
homo sacer 241
horticulture 128–30, 208 *see also* gardens
hostels 263–6
hostility 12–13, 24, 90, 211, 232 *see also* race/racism
    Notting Hill riots 13, 134, 228
House in Paris, The (Bowen, Elizabeth) 70–1
household goods 97–8, 101
'Houseless and Hungry' (Fildes, Luke) 150
housing 230–1, 256
    19 Princelet Street, Spitalfields 95, 96–7, 98–9, 100–1
    hostels 263–6
    overcrowding 100
Hudson, Laura 273
Huguenot people 7, 92, 96, 97–8
Huidi (emperor of Jin) 64
Hunt, Leigh 259
Huxley, Aldous
    Brave New World 142
hybridity 159
Hyde Park 214

'I Hear You Say So' (Bowen, Elizabeth) 74
identity 239
Illustrated London News newspaper 149, 150
illustrated newspapers 149–50
illustration 149–50
Imagistes, Des (Pound, Ezra) 66
Imperial Tomb, The (Roth, Joseph) 200
imperialism 6, 12, 156, 181, 182, 186
    Aggrey House 264, 265
    fairs 174–5

Nigeria 270
    Selvon, Sam 206
    trade 31
in-betweenness 205, 207–8, 210, 213, 214, 215
In the Eye of the Sun (Soueif, Ahdaf) 220
Indian Jugglers, The (Green, James) 42f
'Indian Jugglers, The' (Hazlitt, William) 41, 42–6
'Indian Jugglers, The' (*Satirist, or Monthly Meteor, The*) 41–2
Indian people 8, 11, 156, 237, 240 *see also* Lascar people
    Samee, Ramo 41–2f, 43, 45–6
infrastructure 2, 7 *see also* transport
    waste 80–3, 97, 117–22
    water 79–84
'Inglan is a Bitch' (Johnson, Linton Kwesi) 167
Ingram, Herbert 149–50
inhabitants 23
'Insiders Outsiders' festival 14
interiors 98, 107–8, 185, 200, 217, 218
interpretation 187–8
Irish people 7, 8, 12, 60
    Bowen, Elizabeth 11, 69–74
    Cavanagh, John 45
    fairs 175, 176
    Second World War 73
Iroquois people 183–4
Islam 221–2
Isokon building 284
Ivan III (prince of Muscovy) 224–5

Jab, etymology 227
Jab Jab tradition 227
Jackson, Wilston Samuel 252 n. 12
Jazer Terrace, Stockwell 147
jazz 270–1, 273, 274
Jekyll, Joseph 27, 31–3
'Jewel Stairs Grievance' (Pound, Ezra) 66–6
Jewish people 7, 9–10, 12
    in the East End 108–11
    expulsion 12, 24
    Rie, Lucie 10, 199, 200–1, 202f–3
    Russian migrants 9, 108
    in Spitalfields 99, 100–1
Jia Nanfeng (empress consort of Jin) 64
Johnson, Clarence 65
Johnson, Joseph 52
Johnson, Linton Kwesi 167, 168
    'Inglan is a Bitch' 167
    'Sonny's Lettah' 168
'Johnson and the Cascadura' (Selvon, Sam) 207
Jones, Claudia 134, 228
Jones, Harry 103, 104, 105

Jonson, Ben
  'Famous Voyage, The' 81
J'ouvert tradition 230
Juba 132–3
juggling 41–6

Kapil, Bhanu
  Ban en Banlieue 12, 236, 237, 239–41
Keats, John 255–60
  'O Solitude' 256, 258, 260
  'Ode to a Nightingale' 259–60
  'On Sitting Down to Read *King Lear* Once
    Again' 259
  'On the Grasshopper and Cricket' 259
  'To Autumn' 149, 255, 260
  'To One Who Has Been Long in City Pent' 258,
    259, 260
Keiller, Patrick
  London 279
Kensington 191, 193, 231, 246
Kerby-Fulton, Kathryn 22
Kindertransport – The Arrival (Meisler, Frank) 10*f*
Kitchener, Lord
  'London Is the Place for Me' 168
  'Underground Train, The' 166, 167
Kleist, Heinrich von
  Amphitryon 281
Kokoschka, Oskar 280, 281, 283
Konody, P. G. 194
Koole, Simeon 166
Kuczynski, Jürgen 280, 283, 284
Kureishi, Hanif 155, 160
  Black Album, The 160
  Buddha of Suburbia, The 12, 156–9, 236
  My Beautiful Laundrette 155
  Sammy and Rosie Get Laid 155
  'That Was Then' 159–60
Kyiv 223–5

la Roche, Sophie von 6, 38
Ladbroke Grove 207, 231
Lambeth 127–9, 130–4
  etymology 127
Lane, William Henry 132–3
language 187–8, 193, 212–14, 220, 281
Lanier, Emilia 91
Lascar people 8, 103–5
Latin American music 274
Lawn Road Flats 284
Leftwich, Joseph 110
legends 4–5
Leighton, Frederic 194, 217–18
Leighton House 217–18
Leith-Ross, Prudence 130
Letters of Ignatius Sancho, an African, The (Sancho,
  Ignatius) 29–30, 31

Letters of the Late Rev. Mr. Laurence Sterne
  (Medalle, Lydia de) 29
Lewis, Wyndham 108
Library of Exile (de Waal, Edmund) 13–14
Licorish, Lloyd 245
Life and Opinions of Tristram Shandy Gentleman,
  The (Sterne, Laurence) 28, 29
literary gatherings 70, 185–6
literature 12, 43–4, 219
  Arab 221–2
  Caribbean 207, 208–9
  city comedies 80
  locality 69, 92
  poetry 66–7, 92, 127, 255, 259
  reparative writing 236, 239, 241
  Sancho, Ignatius 28–30
  suburbs, the 235–41
  trickster tales 207, 208–10, 212
Litten, Heinz Wolfgang 281
Lloyd, Robert
  'Cit's Country-Box, The' 259
Location of Culture, The (Bhabha, Homi) 159
Lockhart, John Gibson 255, 259, 260
London (Keiller, Patrick) 279
London, a Pilgrimage (Jerrold, Blanchard and Doré,
  Gustav) 150
London: A Social History (Porter, Roy) 3
London Can Take It! (Jennings, Humphrey and
  Watt, Harry) 11
London going out of Town – or – The March of
  Bricks and Mortar! (Cruikshank, George)
  256, 257*f*, 259
'London is the Place for Me' (Kitchener, Lord)
  168
London Labour and the London Poor (Mayhew,
  Henry) 60, 117, 118, 119, 120
London Spy, The (Ward, Ned) 173, 174, 175, 176
London Transport 249, 250
Lonely Londoners, The (Selvon, Sam) 12, 166, 167,
  205, 210–15
Lost Kingdom (Plokhy, Serhii) 224
Lott, Art 238
Lott, Jack 238
Lott, Jean 238
Lott, Tim
  Scent of Dried Roses, The 12, 235, 236, 237–9
Loyer, Eugenie 147, 148, 152
Loyer, (Sarah) Ursula 147, 148
Ludgate Hill 50, 51
Lundgren, Egron 191
Lyrical Ballads (Wordsworth William) 259

McGee, Charles 49–53
'Man on Westbourne Park Tube Station' (Phillips,
  Charlie) 163*f*, 164, 169
'Mango Tree, The' (Selvon, Sam) 208

Index

Mansions of Misery: A Biography of the Marshalsea Debtor's Prison (White, Jerry) 3
manure 119
Markino, Yoshio 8
    Earl's Court Station 9f
Marshall, Mildred Bernice. *See* Sowande, Mildred Bernice
Marson, Una 274
mas bands 229, 230
mas camps 230
masquerade 229–30
May Fair 173, 174–5, 176, 177–8
Mayhew, Henry 117, 119, 120–2
    1851; Or, the Adventures of Mr. and Mrs. Sandboys and Family who came up to London to 'enjoy themselves,' and to see the Great Exhibition 140
    London Labour and the London Poor 60, 117, 118, 119, 120
Mean Streets (Scorsese, Martin) 160
Medalle, Lydia de
    Letters of the Late Rev. Mr. Laurence Sterne 29
Meisler, Frank 10
    Kindertransport – The Arrival 10f
Mendicity Society 8, 57–61
mental illness 236, 238, 239, 240
Merchant of Venice, The (Shakespeare, William) 92
miasmatic theory 119
Michell, Simon 95
Middleton, Thomas 79, 82
    Chaste Maid in Cheapside, A 79–81, 82–4
    Triumphs of Truth, The 82
Midsummer Night's Dream, A (Shakespeare, William) 92
migration narratives 2
Millais, John Everett 193
    Chill October 149
Millennium Dome, the 143
Milton, John
    Paradise Lost 258–9
Minaret (Aboulela, Leila) 221, 222
minimalism 202
Mithras 4
    relief sculpture of 4, 5f
Modern Life and Modern Subjects (Tickner, Lisa) 110–11
modernism 66, 200, 201, 284
Mol, Leo 224
    'Statue of Saint Volodymyr' 223f, 224, 225
mollies 177
Monroe, Harold
    'Overheard on a Salt Marsh' 108
Montagu, Elizabeth 184–6, 187–8
    Essay on Shakespeare 188
Montagu family 27, 29, 31, 32
Montagu House 185–6

Monty Python's Life of Brian (Jones, Terry) 281
Monument to Saint Erkenwald in Old St Paul's Cathedral (Hollar, Wenceslaus) 21f
Moody, Harold 264, 265, 266
morality 176–7
Mr Gulliver Goes to School (Fischer, Heinrich; Larsen, Egon; Gray, Allan) 281, 283
Mrs Dalloway (Woolf, Virginia) 247–8
'mugging crisis' 167–8
multiculturalism 159
Musaeum Tradescantianum 129, 130 *see also* 'Tradescant's Ark'
music 27–8, 60, 132
    calypso 168, 207, 209, 212
    CFU 273–4
    Deniz, Clara 269, 271, 274, 275
    Deniz, Frank 269, 271, 274, 275
    Deniz, Joe 271, 274
    jazz 270–1, 273, 274
    Latin American 274
    Sowande, Fela 269, 270, 271, 272f, 273–4, 275
Music for the Royal Fireworks (Handel, George Frederic) 132
My Beautiful Laundrette (Kureishi, Hanif) 155
Myddleton, Hugh 5–6, 82, 83–4
Myddleton, Richard 84
Myddleton, Robert 84
Myddleton, Thomas 82, 83–4
'Mysterious Kôr' (Bowen, Elizabeth) 11
Mystery of Edwin Drood, The (Dickens, Charles) 150

names 211
Narayan, Rudy 168
Nash, Geoffrey 220
National Front 159
Native American people 183f–5, 186–8
nature 255, 257, 258, 259–60
Nazism 10, 224, 281
Netherlands 90 *see also* Dutch people
Nevinson, C. R. W. 111
New Court barracks 104f, 105
New River 82
Newgate Prison Exercise Yard (Doré, Gustav) 151
Nichols family 269, 272
Nigeria 270
Nigerian people 269, 270
    Solanke, Ladipo 263–4, 265, 266, 270
    Sowande, Fela 269, 270, 271, 272f, 273–4, 275
nightmen 119–20
Nirbhaya case 240 241
Nocturnal Revels; Or, the History of King's-Place and Other Modern Nunneries
Northview development 12, 269, 272–3, 275
Notes from Underground (Dostoevsky, Fyodor) 142
Notting Hill 159–60, 163–4, 168–9, 205, 230–1

Notting Hill riots 13, 134, 228
Notting Hill Carnival 13, 134, 210, 228–30, 231, 232

'O Solitude' (Keats, John) 256, 258, 260
obeah 207–8
'Obeah in the Grove' (Selvon, Sam) 207, 209, 212
'Ode to a Nightingale' (Keats, John) 259–60
Ogier, Esther (née Dubois [Duboc]) 96
Ogier, Jeanne 96
Ogier, Peter (Pierre) Abraham 95–6, 97, 98
'Oh, Madam . . .' (Bowen, Elizabeth) 73
Old Florida Club 271, 272f, 273
Olusoga, David 38
    Black and British: A Forgotten History 37
'On Mrs Montagu's Feather Hangings' (Cowper, William) 185–6
'On Sitting Down to Read King Lear Once Again' (Keats, John) 259
'On the Grasshopper and Cricket' (Keats, John) 259
'On the Historical Unity of Russians and Ukrainians' (Putin, Vladimir) 225
'On Westminster Bridge' (Wordsworth William) 127
One Thousand and One Nights 218–19
Only in London (al-Shaykh, Hanan) 12, 217, 218, 219–20, 221, 222
Orientalism 45, 220
Orientalism (Said, Edward) 218
Osborne, Anne 30, 31, 37
Othello, the Moor of Fleet Street (Mathews, Charles) 53–4
othering 43–5, 175–6
overcrowding 100
'Overheard on a Salt Marsh' (Monroe, Harold) 108

paganism 4–5, 20–2
paint 98
Painting in the Far East (Binyon, Laurence) 65
Pakistani people 12, 237
Pamela (Richardson, Samuel) 132
Panayi, Panikos 12
Paolo and Francesca (Watts, G. F.) 194
Paradise Lost (Milton, John) 258–9
Park Wood, Ruislip 241
patriarchy, the 212
Peach, Blair 237, 240
Penge 159
People's Paper 61
personal space 166
Petty France 90
Phillips, Charlie 163, 169
    'Man on Westbourne Park Tube Station' 163f, 164, 169

Pictures and Conversations (Bowen, Elizabeth) 69
Piers Plowman (Langland, William) 23
Pilgrim's Progress, A (Bunyan, John) 149
Pinkethman, William 174–5
'Plan of the Cities of London and Westminster, and Borough of Southwark, with the Contiguous buildings, A' (Roque, John) 127
plane trees 208
'Plantarum in Horto Iohannem Tradescanti' (Tradescant, John, the Elder) 130
pleasure gardens 130–4, 260
Plokhy, Serhii
    Lost Kingdom 224
poetry 66–7, 92, 127, 255, 259
Policing the Crisis (Hall, Stuart) 168
political persecution 9–10
politics 2
    foreign policy 183–4, 186
    language 187–8
    'mugging crisis' 167–8
    radicals 138, 139
    Russia 138
    Sancho, Ignatius 30–1
    suffrage 30–1, 110
    welfare 53
Politics by Other Means (Brinson, Charmian and Dove, Richard) 280
Pope, Alexander 182–3
    Windsor Forest 181–2
population 7, 11–12, 60, 256
Porter, Roy
    London: A Social History 3
Portman Square 184, 185
Portuguese people 134
Potato Eaters, The (Gogh, Vincent van) 150
pottery 199, 200–3
Pound, Ezra 66–7
    Cathay 66
    China Cantos 67
    'Fan-Piece for Her Imperial Lord' 66
    Imagistes, Des 66
    'Jewel Stairs Grievance' 66–6
poverty 49–54, 99, 117, 157, 160 see also deprivation and Mendicity Society
    begging 49–50, 51, 53, 54
    illustrations 150
'Poverty Map' (Booth, Charles) 99–100
Powell, Enoch 157, 159
prehistoric structures 127
prejudice 24 see also discrimination
    religious 7, 9–10, 12, 24, 91, 96, 109
Pretty mas 230
Princelet Street, Spitalfields 95, 96–7, 98–9, 100–1
Princes Street Synagogue 99, 100–1

Index

privatization 82, 84
promiscuity 176–7, 214
protest 228, 230, 232
Pryce, Everton A. 229
Putin, Vladimir 224
    'On the Historical Unity of Russians and
        Ukrainians' 225

Qianlong (emperor of the Qing Dynasty) 64–5

race/racism 6–7, 11–12, 13, 157–60, 211, 227, 232
    see also Black people *and* slavery
    Blake Hannah, Barbara 165–6
    Brathwaite, E. R. 165
    Commission on Race and Ethnic Disparities: The
        Report 232
    discrimination 30, 249, 263
    employment 249, 250
    hostility 12–13, 24, 90, 211, 232
    housing 263
    Lascar people 103, 105
    legislation 159
    low-level 239
    Mendicity Society 61
    National Front 159
    policing 167–8, 169, 237
    Powell, Enoch 159
    Sancho, Ignatius 30
    segregation 250, 274
    Southall 237
    spaces 164–6, 167–8, 169
    St Giles 35–9
    Sterne, Laurence 29
    topography of 164, 166, 167
    transport 164–6
    violence 13, 105, 134, 159, 228, 237, 240
racialization 164, 166, 167, 168, 169
radicals 138, 139
radio 274, 275
Raleigh, Walter 90
Ramasamy. *See* Samee, Ramo
ras_714, Instagram user 227, 228
Read, Herbert 281
realism 149, 224
Reasons for Suppressing the Yearly-Fair in
    Brook-field, Westminster 176, 177
Red-Lion Square 57, 58
Redvers, Margaret de 128
refugee, etymology 92, 96
Regent's Park 69–74
'Regent's Park and St John's Wood' (Bowen,
    Elizabeth) 70
Regent's Park Mosque 221, 222
religion 43, 90, 221–2 *see also* Christianity
religious persecution 7, 9–10, 12, 24, 91, 96, 109
Remarks on London (Stow, William) 177

Remembering a Brave New World (Burman, Chila
    Kumari Singh) 14
removal campaigns 53, 61, 108
    expulsions 12, 24
reparative writing 236, 239, 241
restaurants 284
Rhinebeck Panorama of London 256
Richardson, Samuel
    Pamela 132
Richmond 193
Rie, Lucie 10, 199, 200–1, 202*f*–3
Rie, Lucie and Coper, Hans 201
    'Sgraffito Bowl, Manganese Glaze' 201*f*
Ritchie, Charles 72
Road from Damascus, The (Yassin-Kassab, Robin)
    221–2
Roberts, William 111
Rodinsky, David 101
Rodker, John 107, 108, 110, 112
Romans, the 2, 4–5, 89, 241
Romany people 7
Romeo and Juliet (Shakespeare, William) 92
rookeries 36
Roque, John
    'Plan of the Cities of London and Westminster,
        and Borough of Southwark, with the
        Contiguous buildings, A' 127
Rose, Elizabeth Langley 6
Roth, Joseph
    Imperial Tomb, The 200
Ruislip 241
rural environment 256–7, 258–9
Rus people 223–5
Rushdie, Salman 159
    Satanic Verses, The 159
Russia 2, 137–9, 140, 141, 143, 223–5 *see also* Soviet
    Union
Russian people 9, 108, 223–5
    Chernyshevsky, Nikolai 138–9, 140, 143
    Dostoevsky, Fyodor 140–2
    Herzen, Alexander 9, 138, 141, 142, 143

Said, Edward
    Orientalism 218
Salih, Tayeb
    Season of Migration to the North 221
salon culture 185–6
Samee, Ramo 41–2*f*, 43, 45–6
Sammy and Rosie Get Laid (Kureishi, Hanif) 155
Sancho, Anne (née Osborne) 30, 31, 37
Sancho, Ignatius 27–33, 37
    Letters of Ignatius Sancho, an African, The 29–30
    'Sancho's Best Trinidado' trade card 31, 32*f*
    'Sancho's Best Trinidado' trade card (Sancho,
        Ignatius) 31, 32*f*
sanitation 118–20

Satanic Verses, The (Rushdie, Salman) 159
Saxons, the 4, 22, 23
    Erkenwald, Saint 19–24
Scent of Dried Roses, The (Lott, Tim) 12, 235, 236,
    237–9
Schiller, Friedrich
    William Tell 279, 280
Season of Migration to the North (Salih, Tayeb) 221
seasons, the 214–15
Second World War 10–1, 73–4, 248, 265, 269,
    272–4, 275
    commemorations 279
    Free German League of Culture in Great Britain
        280–4
segregation 250, 274
Selvon, Sam 166–7, 205–7
    'Basement Lullaby' 205
    Brighter Sun, A 206, 207
    calypso 209
    'Calypso in London' 207, 209–10
    'Johnson and the Cascadura' 207
    language 212–14
    Lonely Londoners, The 12, 166, 167, 205, 210–15
    'Mango Tree, The' 208
    'Obeah in the Grove' 207, 209, 212
    Turn Again Tiger 205
    Ways of Sunlight 12, 207–10, 249–50
    'Working the Transport' 249–50
Sentimental Journey, A (Sterne, Laurence) 36
Sermons of Mr Yorick, The (Sterne, Laurence) 28
sewer-hunters 117–18*f*, 120–2
sewerage system 117, 119, 120–2
sex industry 35, 38, 176, 219, 220
sexual promiscuity 176–7, 214
sexual violence 240
Shadwell 103–5
Shakespeare, William 5, 91–2
    As You Like It 132
    Merchant of Venice, The 92
    Midsummer Night's Dream, A 92
    Romeo and Juliet 92
    Timon of Athens 108
al-Shaykh, Hanan 219, 220
    Only in London 12, 217, 218, 219–20, 221, 222
Shelley, Mary 259
Shillibeer, George 246
shipping 8, 103, 105
Shoreditch 89–92
Sinclair, Iain
    Hackney, That Rose-Red Empire 3
Singh, Jyoti 240, 241
Sir Gawain and the Green Knight 22
Sketches by Boz (Dickens, Charles) 133
slavery 2, 6, 52–3, 175, 181
    Sancho, Ignatius 28–9, 30, 31, 32
    Jab Jab tradition 227

Commission on Race and Ethnic Disparities: The
    Report 232
    rebranding 232
    Mendicity Society 61
    masquerades 229–30
    abolition 31, 37
    Sons of Africa 37
    trickster tales 208–9
    Sterne, Laurence 28–9
Sloan, Hans 6
Slot-Meter, the 107–8, 110, 111, 112
Smith, Horace 128
Smith, James 128
Smith, John Thomas 51–3
    Charles McGee 52*f*
    Vagabondiana 50
social class 13, 23, 71–2, 100, 112
    buses 248
    suburbs, the 158–9, 237–8, 259
Soho 271
Solanke, Ladipo 263–4, 265, 266, 270
Solanke, Olu 264, 265
'Sonny's Lettah' (Johnson, Linton Kwesi) 168
Sons of Africa 37
Sophia (queen of Sweden) 192–3
Soueif, Ahdaf
    In the Eye of the Sun 220
South Ethical Society 109–10
Southall 235, 236, 237, 238, 239, 240
Soviet Union 143, 224, 283 *see also* Russia
Sowande, Fela 269, 270, 271, 272*f*, 273–4, 275
    Folk Symphony 275
Sowande, Mildred Bernice (née Marshall) 269,
    270–1, 273
spaces
    craft 202*f*, 203
    race and 164–6, 167–8, 169, 232
Spitalfields 7, 89, 95–101
Spitalfields Historic Buildings Trust 101
Spring Gardens 131
St Erkenwald 4, 19–24
St George's Fields 127–8
St Giles 35, 36, 38–9
St Giles 'Black-Birds' 35–9
St Paul's Cathedral 4, 19–20, 22, 23, 50
Starr, Sidney
    City Atlas, The 247*f*
'Statue of Saint Volodymyr' (Mol, Leo) 223*f*, 224, 225
status 23 *see also* social class
Staying Power (Fryer, Peter) 36
Steelyard, the 279
Sterne, Laurence 28–9
    *Life and Opinions of Tristram Shandy
        Gentleman, The* 28, 29
    Sentimental Journey, A 36
    Sermons of Mr Yorick, The 28

Stockholm Exhibition (1897) 191, 192, 194, 195
Stockwell 145, 146*f*, 147–8
Stone Age structures 127
Stow, John 89
    Survey of London 81, 89
Stow, William
    Remarks on London 177
strangers 90, 91
Stratton House 90
street culture 59–60, 61
student hostels 263–6
suburbs, the 156, 157–8, 159, 235–41, 257, 259
    Gogh, Vincent van 147
    transport 246
suffrage 30–1
    women 110
Survey of London (Stow, John) 81, 89
Sweden 192–3, 194
Swedish Art Exhibition (1924) 194
Swedish Industrial Arts and Crafts exposition (1931) 194–5
Swedish people 191, 192–5

' 'Tain't what you do it's the way that you do it' (Oliver, Melvin 'Sy' and Young, James 'Trummy' 273
Tale of Bygone Years, The 224
Tatlin, Vladimir 143
Taxi Driver (Scorsese, Martin) 160
Temple of Mithras 4
textiles 90, 96, 97–8
Thackery, W. M.
    Book of Snobs, The 41
Thames River 127, 131, 181, 182
'That Was Then' (Kureishi, Hanif) 159–60
theatre 32–3, 91–2, 273, 281
    etymology 91
Theatre 91–2
Thomas, William Luson 150
Three Cherokees, Came Over from the Head of the River Savanna to London, The (Bickham, George) 187*f*
Tickner, Lisa
    Modern Life and Modern Subjects 110–11
Timon of Athens (Shakespeare, William) 108
'To Autumn' (Keats, John) 149, 255, 260
'To One Who Has Been Long in City Pent' (Keats, John) 258, 259, 260
To Sir, With Love (Brathwaite, E. R.) 165
tobacco 31
tolerance 138
Tom Jones (Fielding, Henry) 158
trade 5–6, 8, 206 *see also* slavery
    cloth 90, 96, 97–8
    refuse 121

Sancho, Ignatius 31
shipping 8, 103, 105
Tradescant, Hester 130
Tradescant, John, the Elder 128–9, 130
    'Plantarum in Horto Iohannem Tradescanti' 130
Tradescant, John, the Younger 128, 129, 130
'Tradescant's Ark' 128, 129–30
trains 164, 257–8
transport 7, 163–9, 257
    accessible 251
    buses 165–6, 168, 211, 245–51
    London Transport 249, 250
    shipping 8, 103, 105
    subsidized 250
    trains 164, 257–8
    tube, the 163*f*, 165–6, 167, 168, 255
transvestism 176–7
trees 208
trickster tales 207, 208–10, 212
Trinidad 209, 229–30
    language 213
'Trip to the Devil's Summer-house, A' 174
Tristan, Flora 8
Triumphs of Truth, The (Middleton, Thomas) 82
tube, the 163*f*, 165–6, 167, 168, 255
Turgenev, Ivan
    Fathers and Sons 139
Turn Again Tiger (Selvon, Sam) 205
Turret House, South Lambeth 129*f*
Twentieth Century German Art exhibition 281
Tyers, Johnathan 131–2, 134

Uhlman, Diana 280
Uhlman, Fred 280
Ukraine 223–5
Ukrainian people 2, 225
uncertainty 238–9
'Underground Train, The' (Kitchener, Lord) 166–7
Upper Park Road, NW3 280, 281, 284
urbanization 255–6, 257, 258, 259, 260
Utrecht, Treaty of 181

Vagabondiana (Smith, John Thomas) 50
Valley Farm (Constable, John) 149
van Gogh, Vincent. *See* Gogh, Vincent van
Van Gogh's Chair (Gogh, Vincent van) 151
Vauxhall 128, 134
    etymology 128
Vauxhall Gardens 130–4, 260
'Vauxhall Gardens by Day' (Dickens, Charles) 133
Victoria (queen of the United Kingdom of Great Britain and Ireland) 191
Vienna 199, 203

violence 12–13, 90, 105, 134, 155, 159, 228, 237, 240
visibility 49
Volodymyr the Great (prince of Kiev) 223–5

Walloons, the 90
war 248 *see also* Second World War
    refugees 10–11
Ward, Ned 173
    *Complete and Humorous Account of the
        Remarkable Clubs and Societies in the Cities
        of London and Westminster* 177
    London Spy, The 173, 174, 175, 176
Wason, Clara. *See* Deniz, Clara
waste 80–3, 97, 117–22
    as fertilizer 119
WASU (West African Students Union Association)
    263, 264, 265, 266
Wasu journal 263
water 79–84, 91
Waterhouse, Keith
    Billy Liar 158
Watts, G. F. 193, 194
    Paolo and Francesca 194
*Way to Beauty: A Complete Guide to Personal
    Loveliness, The* (Cohen, Sonia) 108
Ways of Sunlight (Selvon, Sam) 12, 207–10, 249–50
wealth 98, 100, 118, 122
weaving 90, 96, 97–8
welfare 53 *see also* Mendicity Society
Welsh people 84
Wernher, Harold 195
West African people 263–4
West African Students Union Association (WASU)
    263, 264, 265, 266
West Indian (Caribbean) people 11, 163–7, 207–15,
    248 *see also* Windrush generation
    McGee, Charles 49–53
    Selvon, Sam 166–7, 205–7
Westbourne Park underground station 163*f*
Westminster Bridge 127
Whale, John 43

What is to be Done? (Chernyshevsky, Nikolai)
    139–40, 142, 143
White, Jerry 38
    *Mansions of Misery: A Biography of the
        Marshalsea Debtor's Prison* 3
Whitechapel Art Gallery exhibition (1914) 110–11
'Whitechapel Boys' 110
Wilkinson, John 109
William Tell (Schiller, Friedrich) 279, 280
Windrush generation 163, 167, 168, 205, 209
    buses 245, 249
    scandal 2, 232
Windsor Forest (Pope, Alexander) 181–2
Winter Notes on Summer Impressions (Dostoevsky,
    Fyodor) 141
wolves 241
women 199–200, 212
    Arab 219–20
    buses 246–8, 250
    employment 248, 250
    suffrage 110
Wonder, The (Evans, Diana) 231
Wood, Charles 95
Woolf, Virginia
    Mrs Dalloway 247–8
Wordsworth William 127
    Lyrical Ballads 259
    'On Westminster Bridge' 127
'Working the Transport' (Selvon, Sam) 249–50
World Fair (1862) 141
Worrall, Samuel 95

Yassin-Kassab, Robin
    Road from Damascus, The 221–2
You Wang (emperor of the Zhou dynasty) 67
Young Socialist League 110

Zhang Hua 64
Zorn, Anders 191, 194
Zweig, Stefan 280